T0396989

Spatial Demography and Population Governance

This series aims to strengthen the development of spatial demography in Asia, accelerate the application of new spatial analysis and spatial econometric methods in population research, and promote modern population governance in numerous developing countries. To achieve these goals, the series focuses on different important demographic phenomena, including internal migration and talent flows, urbanization, fertility change, population aging, labor force change, population-environment interactions, and regional population projections. By applying different methodologies from different perspectives, the relationship between demographic change, population policy, and economic development is further explored, thus providing policymakers with theoretical support for modern population governance.

Tiyan Shen · Xin Lao · Hengyu Gu

Migration Patterns and Intentions of Floating Population in Transitional China

The Road for Urban Dream Chasers

 Springer

Tiyan Shen
School of Government
Peking University
Beijing, China

Xin Lao
School of Economics and Management
China University of Geosciences
Beijing, China

Hengyu Gu
Department of Geography and Resource
Management
The Chinese University of Hong Kong
Hong Kong, China

Spatial Demography and Population Governance
ISBN 978-981-19-3374-5   ISBN 978-981-19-3375-2 (eBook)
https://doi.org/10.1007/978-981-19-3375-2

This Springer imprint is published by the registered company Springer Nature Singapore Pte Ltd.
The registered company address is: 152 Beach Road, #21-01/04 Gateway East, Singapore 189721,
Singapore

Preface

Since the 1990s, accompanying the rapid urbanization, an important feature of China's social transition is its large-scale interregional migration, originating from not only the huge economic disparity between the coastal region and the inland region but also the gradual loosening of migration and household registration (*hukou*) policies. China's floating population, referring to migrants (mainly migrating from rural areas to urban areas) without local *hukou* status, accounts for a large proportion of the mobile population globally and becomes an important issue influencing China's economic and social development. These migrants come to work in the destination cities to pursue a better life, while they have difficulty in integrating into the urban society and sharing the same benefits with urban residents limited by the *hukou* system, on the road to realize their urban dreams. The urban dreams of floating population are not just about seeking happiness for migrants themselves but about realizing the dreams of better urban governance and even the Chinese dream of great rejuvenation. Based on China's national population census data, China Migrants Dynamic Survey data and other data sources, this book comprehensively employs statistical analysis, spatial analysis, social network analysis, econometric and spatial econometric methods to analyze the spatial pattern and influencing mechanism of migration and migration intentions of floating population from different levels and different perspectives. It aims at better revealing the road to chase urban dreams and its obstructive factors, from both the geographical and individual angles, thus providing scientific evidence for China's people-oriented new-type urbanization development. The main discoveries are shown below: the main direction of migration is still from the western and central regions to the eastern coastal region, affected by the social and economic factors of origin and destination regions and the interregional distance, while the return migration trend occurs in recent years; there exist spatial differences in terms of the *hukou* transfer intentions, settlement intentions and return intentions of floating population, mainly determined by individual-level factors and city-level factors with spatially-varying effects. The research results of this book have significant policy implications for the urban governance on the floating population and the further acceleration of *hukou* system reform.

This book is composed of three parts: Chaps. 1–2 analyze the spatial pattern and influencing factors of the internal migration pattern in China mainly based on the national population census data; Chaps. 3–6 investigate the spatial pattern and influencing factors of migration intentions of floating population in China mainly based on the data of the China Migrants Dynamic Survey(CMDS); based on the above results, Chaps. 7–6 discuss the urban governance on floating population.

Beijing, China   Tiyan Shen
Beijing, China   Xin Lao
Hong Kong, China   Hengyu Gu

Contents

Part I
Internal Migration Patterns

Chapter 1
Interprovincial Migration

1.1 Spatial Patterns of Interprovincial Population Migration in China

1.1.1 Introduction

China is a typical and ideal study area for analysing the spatial distribution of population migration and its spatial concentration patterns. In China, interprovincial migration is a long-standing socioeconomic phenomenon that fuels the spatial redistribution of population [53, 86]. Data from previous population censuses and population sample surveys suggest that, since the relaxation of migration restrictions in the 1980s, population migration has been constantly increasing, making it an even more important macroscopic index [52]. Meanwhile, migration flows have changed over the years, with an increasing spatial concentration. The migrant population tends to migrate to destinations with more employment opportunities, higher income, better social security systems and more developed transportation networks [23]. Collectively, as research into multiple periods has suggested, provinces in middle and western China such as Sichuan, Hunan, Hubei and Anhui are the major origins of population migration, and those flows go towards more developed eastern coastal areas such as Beijing, Shanghai and Guangdong, which hold a great number of immigrants [18, 84, 91, 94, 95]. Most of the migration flows are concentrated between these major origins and destinations, which can be quantitatively addressed [6]. Insights on the spatial concentration pattern of population migration in China can not only influence policymaking in China, but also provide enlightenment and social implications to other countries or regions, as there are similarities among countries. In addition, it can benefit cross-national comparative research in the field of population migration.

The pattern of spatial concentration (also known as spatial focusing) of population migration flows has been a long-studied subject, since it contains information about

T. Shen et al., *Migration Patterns and Intentions of Floating Population in Transitional China*, Spatial Demography and Population Governance, https://doi.org/10.1007/978-981-19-3375-2_1

the non-uniform spatial distribution of migration [85]. Building a well-off society in an all-round way by 2020 is a top priority, in which population migration will play an important role. Population migration produces element flows of human resources and social capital [54], and it impacts economic coordination, people's lives and cultural building profoundly. Recently, in light of the increasingly imbalanced population migration and hence population distribution, scholars have thoroughly discussed how spatial redistribution of population relates to socioeconomic issues, including: (a) How does population migration affect urbanization in different regions [90]? (b) Is migration reducing or creating regional imbalance [19]? (c) Should the rural population be urbanized locally or directed to large cities to exploit economies of scale [56, 57]? Nevertheless, such discussions cannot be made quantitative unless migration flows can be correctly inferred from collected data, which are often incomplete. Therefore, a reliable inference framework should further promote such discussion as well as providing references for policy-making and execution.

To measure the spatial concentration of population migration, there are five popular methods: Coefficient of Variation (CV), Index of Migration Dissimilarity (IMD), Gini Index (GI), Theil's Entropy Index (TEI) [78] and Atkinson's Index [2, 4, 6, 20, 33, 70, 85]. Plane and Mulligan [66] commented that GI is the natural choice for measuring regional imbalance (including spatial concentration of population migration), as the other indexes are often artificial (even random), hard to interpret, and/or less suitable. In contrast, GI has the following advantages [20, 66]: (a) all migration flows are standardized to the same scale, so that comparison between flows is meaningful with a clear interpretation, (b) GI is better at capturing the spatial variations of the studied distribution; (c) GI can be computed for regions of different sizes; and (d) most migration data today are in the form of migration matrices, from which GI can be readily computed. Hence, we used GI as the major source of statistics.

GI was first proposed by Gini [27], an Italian economist, in the 1920s for measuring income inequality. The index system then underwent further adaptation and generalization, and it found its application in multiple subjects at different scales. On one hand, GI has been adapted to different scenarios in the study of income distribution, including improvement of computational efficiency [47, 92], extended application of grouped data [59] and decomposition of effects (Lau et al. 2017). On the other hand, GI has been applied into industrial agglomeration and population migration. Krugman [44] proposed using location GI to study the concentration of industrial space, classifying it into absolute GI and relative GI. White [85] introduced a GI system to demographic research, aiming to measure the concentrations of population migration flows. More recently, Janská et al. [43] applied GI to track how migration changes and migrants settled over time in Czechia. To sum up, since its application in measuring income inequality, GI has been constantly adapted and increasingly applied in different fields, whether a quantity of interest is concentrated or spread over the studied spatial coordinates.

In terms of drawbacks, GIs is sensitive to missing data in censuses or surveys, which leads to deviations in the inferred spatial–temporal trends. Therefore, in this study, we specifically address the accurate inference of the spatial concentration of population migration from incomplete data by proposing a GI system that is corrected at origin, at destination and from a global perspective. This study entails: (a) taking missing data into consideration in population migration and proposing the GIc system, and (b) applying the GIc to analyse spatial–temporal features of population migration in multiple periods. The most significant contribution of this study is that we re-standardize the GI in topological structure, through which we recognize that the concentrations of population migration may be underestimated. We hope that this proposed GI correction will broaden and deepen the study of the spatial concentration of population migration and population migration in general.

1.1.2 Research Methodology and Data Source

1.1.2.1 Research Methodology

(1) Raw GI and its correction

GI is a well-known and widely applied statistics for measuring the spatial concentration of population migration, offering direct comparisons between flows (M_{ij} and M_{kl}, see below). After corrections and extensions, Bell et al. [6] proposed a standardized GI system that can be used to compare population migration in different regions, and which includes three components: global GI, origin GI and destination GI. These indexes have been widely applied since then [5, 7]. The formal definitions of raw GIs read:

Global GI:

$$GG = \frac{\sum_i \sum_{j \neq i} \sum_k \sum_{l \neq k} \left| M_{ij} - M_{kl} \right|}{2[n(n-1)-1] \sum_i \sum_{j \neq i} M_{ij}} \tag{1.1}$$

Origin GI:

$$OG_i = \frac{\sum_{j \neq i} \sum_{l \neq i, j} \left| M_{ij} - M_{il} \right|}{2(n-2) \sum_{j \neq i} M_{ij}} \tag{1.2}$$

Destination GI:

$$DG_j = \frac{\sum_{i \neq j} \sum_{k \neq j, i} \left| M_{ij} - M_{kj} \right|}{2(n-2) \sum_{i \neq j} M_{ij}} \tag{1.3}$$

where n denotes the number of regions, i, j denote different origins and k, l denote different destinations. M_{ij}(kl) denotes migration flows from i to j (or k to l). In addition, GG, OG_i, $DG_j \in [0, 1]$. A value of 1 indicates a complete concentration in which all the migration concentrates in a single flow. If the index is 0, it implies a complete balance in which the migration population is evenly distributed among the flows.

However, these defined GIs ignore missing data (null). In this situation, the numerator and denominator, especially the counts of flows, are affected. Therefore, GI cannot reach 1 even in the case of complete concentration, violating the original interpretation of the formula. Under this circumstance, we try to standardize GI better, focusing particularly on the denominator. Accordingly, we propose GIc as below:

Global GIc:

$$GG^* = \frac{\sum_i \sum_{j \neq i} \sum_k \sum_{l \neq k} |M_{ij} - M_{kl}|}{2[n(n-1) - 1 - p] \sum_i \sum_{j \neq i} M_{ij}} \tag{1.4}$$

Origin GIc:

$$OG_i^* = \frac{\sum_{j \neq i} \sum_{l \neq i,j} |M_{ij} - M_{il}|}{2(n - 2 - p_i) \sum_{j \neq i} M_{ij}} \tag{1.5}$$

Destination GIc:

$$DG_j^* = \frac{\sum_{i \neq j} \sum_{k \neq j,i} |M_{ij} - M_{kj}|}{2(n - 2 - p_j) \sum_{i \neq j} M_{ij}} \tag{1.6}$$

Here n, i, j, k, l and M_{ij}(kl) are the same as they are in Eqs. 1.1–1.3. p denotes the number of flows missing from the migration data, p_i denotes the number of migration flows missing from origin i and p_j is the count of migration flows missing from destination j.

To illustrate the effect of this correction, consider a randomly generated 5×5 migration data matrix M (see Table 1.1).

In this matrix, the rows and columns correspond to five demographic regions A-E, between which there are 20 pairwise migration flows (excluding the internal migration, expressed by diagonal elements). A randomly chosen population migration flow is set to population m (as A_{41} in the matrix) and five randomly chosen migration flows are set to missing (null), whereas all other off-diagonal elements are set to 0. According to the definition of complete concentration [6, 7], when migrant

Table 1.1 A 5×5 random migration data matrix

	A	B	C	D	E
A		0	0	null	0
B	0		0	0	0
C	0	null		null	0
D	m	0	0		null
E	null	0	0	0	

populations concentrate into one flow, the index is 1. In this situation, overall GI = emigration GI of region D = immigration GI of region A = 1.

After calculations, $OG_D = 0.667$, $DG_A = 0.667$, $GG = 0.737$, and $OG_D^* = DG_A^* = GG^* = 1$. Note that GI is supposed to equal 1, since all the migration flow is carried by population migration from region D to region A, which is not the case in the raw GI due to the missing value here. In contrast, the GIc is indeed equal to 1, and it represents the concentration of the migration flow well, as it is more standardized.

(2) **Chord diagram**

Since population migration flows are essentially directed edges between population nodes in mathematical terms, a Chord Diagram (CD) is particularly useful in its visualization due to its topological structure [38]. The main elements of a CD are nodes and arc lengths corresponding to nodes and chords among nodes, which can reveal the origin, destination, flow direction and tie intensity (volume). In the diagram, arc length indicates the total tie intensity of nodes, migration direction is presented based on the colouring of origins, and arrows make this clearer. Nodes are connected by chords; chord width indicates tie intensity among nodes; width and tie intensity are directly proportional [1]. Moreover, with colouring, a CD is clearer, brighter and more distinct than a traditional diagram.

The first application of a CD was in visualizing how expressions of genes on the topologically continuous genome are correlated [93]. Thereafter, CDs were extensively applied to visualize weighted connections between entities with topological constraints, including highway passenger flows (Chen et al. 2017) and population migrations [69], with great success. CDs are complementary to traditional spatial heatmaps, and a combination of both is particularly powerful in revealing patterns hidden in the interactions between the nodes of study.

1.1.2.2 Data Sources

To see the proposed GI system in action, we applied it to analyse the concentration of interprovincial population migration in China from 1985 to 2015.

The interprovincial migration data in China came from (a) the 4th to 6th population censuses from 1985 to 2015 and (b) nationwide 1% population sample surveys in 1995, 2005 and 2015. We aggregated migration data in five-year periods, to capture the long-term features of migration, as opposed to the short-term features of population flow. The data cover 31 provinces, municipalities and autonomous regions in China (excluding Hong Kong, Macao and Taiwan). Except for the data from the 5th and 6th population censuses, the data of other years are incomplete to different extents: there are 30, 44, 15 and 4 missing migration flows in the 4th population censuses and 1% population sample surveys in 1995, 2005 and 2015, respectively. Most of the missing values are related to Tibet, while some other missing flows are related to Ningxia and Qinghai. In addition, considering the conversion ratio of data and the non-negative integer nature of the migrant population, the migration data are restored by years based on the sampling ratio and rounded off. Of note, the census data is referred to by the period during which it is collected e.g., "data from 2005 to 2010" refers to the 6th population census, when the migrant population was recorded.

1.1.3   *Analysis of Results*

With MATLAB, we calculated the raw GIs and GIcs, and they compared the results. The calculated values reflect the concentration of interprovincial population migration from the global perspective, the origin perspective and the destination perspective, collectively depicting a spatially imbalanced migration.

1.1.3.1   **Comparison of Raw GI and GIc**

According to the results (Fig. 1.1), the raw GI underestimates migration concentration, and the GIc better reveals the spatial imbalance of population migration. The raw GI has a smaller value when migration data are incomplete for a particular period, hence underestimating the migration concentration. Whereas GI deviation is positively correlated with the number of population migration flows missing, global GI and local coefficient are impacted differently. From the global perspective, the missing 4–44 migration flows (a missing rate of around 0.4–5%) gives a GI absolute deviation of 0.004–0.051. From the local perspective, based on origins and destinations, we calculated the missing rate ranking stratified by the period, which also suggests a positive correlation with the corresponding GI deviation. Hence, we conclude that raw GI suffers from underestimation when there is missing data, regardless of the perspective of GI, be it global or local.

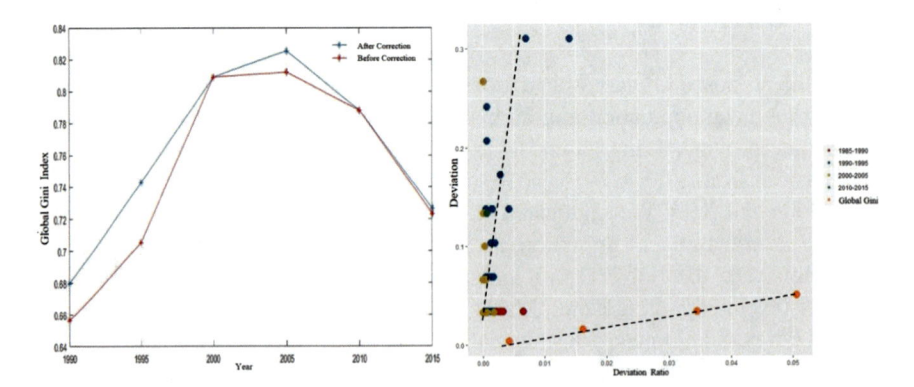

Fig. 1.1 Effect of GI correction

1.1.3.2 Spatial Concentration of Population Migration Based on the Global Perspective

Figure 1.1 shows that a reduction occurred after the increase of the interprovincial migration concentration in China in 2005. In other words, it shows an inverse U-shaped trend. The rate at which the spatial concentration of population migration increases gradually reduced in the concentration phase, whereas the rate of reduction slightly increased during the decline stage.

Based on our analysis, Stage I refers to the developing stage of reform and opening up, when Guangdong and the Yangtze River Delta (especially Guangdong), the door of the economic opening up, attracted a great number of migrants looking for better jobs and higher incomes. Meanwhile, there was also population migration from well-populated regions with less developed economies to more developed regions. In Stage II (after 2005), some origins (except some traditional provinces of emigration) of migration flow received a backflow from the developed regions, as previous migrants moved back to their hometowns or nearby. From the destination perspective, some undeveloped regions underwent improvements that promoted investment and infrastructure as a result of policy inclination, and they reached a higher level of urbanization. Therefore, many regions other than the traditional destinations like the Pearl River Delta, the Yangtze River Delta and the Beijing-Tianjin region are increasingly attractive to the migration population, resulting in a diversification of population migration destinations. As a result of changes at both origins and destinations, population migration is becoming less concentrated.

1.1.3.3 Strong Linkages Between Origins and Destinations with High Spatial Concentration

Origins and destinations are correlated, and they need to be viewed collectively. Here, we point out two definitions: (a) if an origin is highly concentrated, the emigrants from such an origin will often choose certain destinations, and the population flow will become larger; (b) similarly, for a destination with high concentration, immigrants often share certain origins.

CDs were plotted to visualize these observations topologically. For each period, the top three origins and destinations in terms of the originated or received population migration flows were highlighted, and the three strongest population migrations were plotted for each of the highlighted region (Fig. 1.2). In the Figure, black arrows indicate migration direction; purple areas indicate the top three origins of this period; green areas indicate the top three destinations; and grey areas indicate other regions that are strongly related to the top three origin or destination regions.

The results suggest that the origins and destinations of the highest GIs are often strongly related by population migration flows. These strong linkages lead to imbalanced spatial distributions of population migration in China. Temporally speaking, such population migration flows weakened from 1985 to 1995 but they strengthened

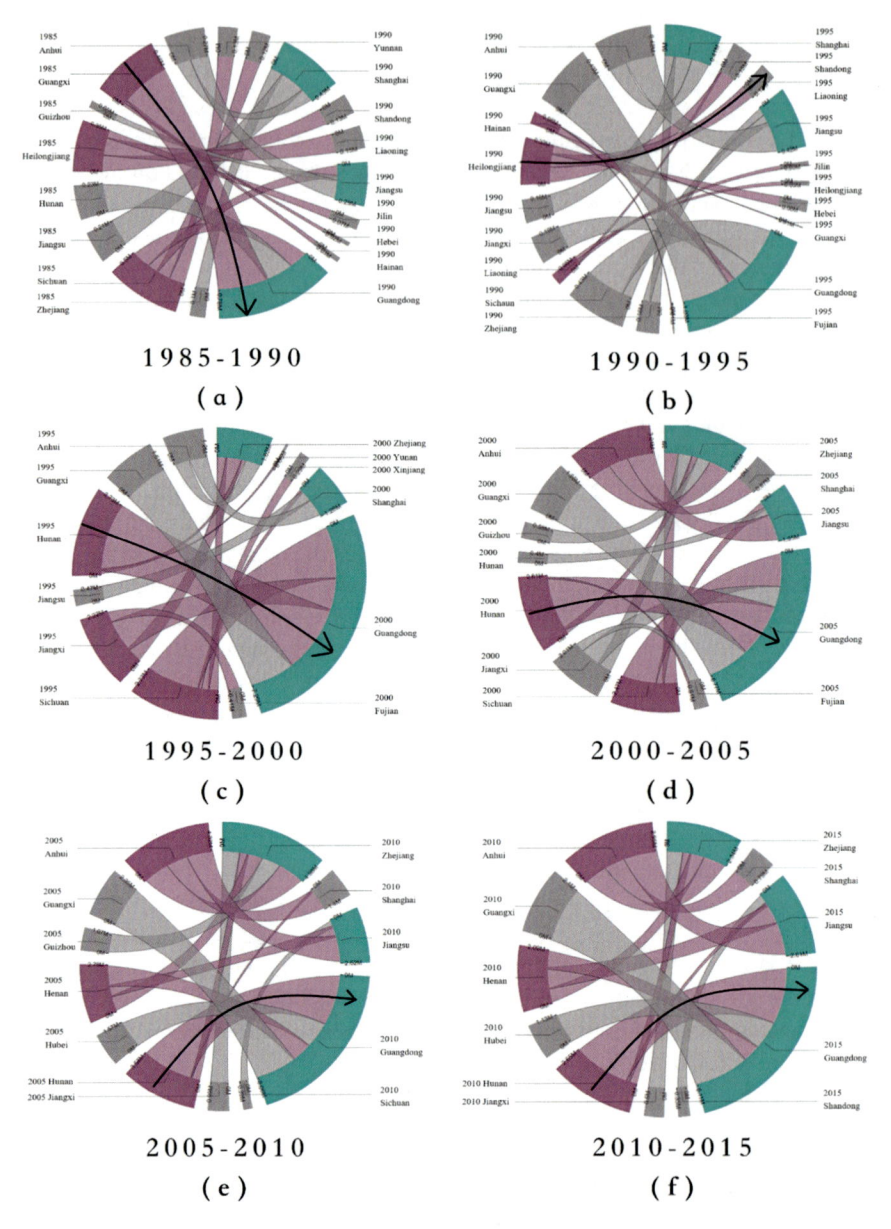

Fig. 1.2 Correspondent migration linkages between origins and destinations with high concentration (1985–2015)

afterwards, and they contributed a large fraction of the overall migration flow of the origin or destination.

Most of the origins in 1990 were traditional emigration provinces, except Hainan Province, and the top four destinations, Guangdong, Jiangsu, Zhejiang and Shanghai are constantly receiving large immigrant populations, indicating an active ongoing population migration. In the regions with high destination GIcs, large numbers of immigrants are coming from provinces with high origin GIcs. On zoning, origins with high population migration concentrations are often located in the middle and west of China; destinations with high population migration concentrations are often in the east of China and near the coast. Of note, the observed population migration is also reminiscent of the long-term flow from the middle or west to the east of China since the 1980s [84], reflecting the highly spatially directed nature of the migration flow.

1.1.3.4 Spatial Concentration Pattern of Out-Migration

Generally, from the perspective of origins (namely, based on the origin GIc), the spatial structure of migration tends to be stable: emigration from the middle and some regions of the west of China is concentrated.

A high emigration concentration means that the emigrants from a region often move to certain areas, whereas a low concentration means the emigrants are scattered extensively across different destinations, which is calculated according to Eq. 1.5. Based on the overall spatial distribution, a pattern of high migration in middle China and some western regions has gradually taken shape since 1995.

Temporally speaking, the emigration flows from the northeast were mostly concentrated in nearby provinces. Later, as socio-economic development slowed down, the migrating population was attracted to the eastern coastal regions with better job opportunities and transportation, reducing the population migration concentration.

Population migration originating from the middle regions is highly concentrated, showing a steady increase due to the dependency of population migration on its destination. Emigrants from the middle often move to eastern coastal regions. For a given origin, the emigrant population will concentrate around a certain destination [67]. For instance, from 2005 to 2010, 3.7 million emigrants moved from Hunan to Guangdong, Fujian, Shanghai and Zhejiang, accounting for 80.76% of the total population migration from Hunan. Note that these four destinations are in close demographic contact. Generally, emigrants from middle China tend to concentrate in eastern coastal regions.

As for population migration from the west, two different scenarios are observed. The southern provinces including Sichuan, Chongqing, Guangxi and Guizhou are in contact with the aforementioned middle provinces, and they exhibit a similarly large and highly concentrated emigrant population. In ethnic minority regions like Tibet, Xinjiang, Gansu and Ningxia, however, the emigration concentration has been low for a long time, with small fluctuations occurring in some of the regions.

1.1.3.5 Spatial Concentration Pattern of In-Migration

A destination with a high population migration concentration often receives immigrants from certain origins, and vice versa. The degree of concentration is calculated using Eq. 1.6. Generally, immigration is highly concentrated in the eastern coastal regions, with a decreasing concentration in Xinjiang.

Unlike other areas, the Pearl River Delta and the Yangtze River Delta have experienced concentrated immigration in all the observed periods. Specifically, Guangdong received the most concentrated immigration in all periods, and two out of Zhejiang, Jiangsu and Shanghai came second and third depending on the period. In these regions, a large immigrant population forms the basis of a highly concentrated population, which is shared between several origin provinces. These regions are typically: (a) highly developed, with more job opportunities and higher salaries; (b) coastal, hence offering more openness and freedom, as well as being more receptive and fairer to immigrants; (c) nationwide traffic hubs with convenient traffic and developed systems, hence they are within easy reach of immigrants.

On the other hand, immigrant population varies according to origins. For a specific destination, the immigrant population usually originates in a certain region and its neighbourhood; hence, it is spatially concentrated [12, 13]. From 1985 to 2015, these origins were usually Hunan, Hubei, Anhui, Jiangxi, Sichuan and Guizhou, most of which are neighbouring provinces, showing the route dependency of origins. More precisely, from 2005 to 2010, the immigrant population from Henan, Hunan and Hubei accounted for almost half of the total immigrants to Guangdong (49.34% of 6.84 million), compellingly suggesting that a strong migration flow tends to drive the population in its surroundings to move to the same destination (e.g., the population moved from Hunan and Hubei to Guangdong from 2010 to 2015). Notably, immigration concentration in Xinjiang reduced, owing to the policy support it received and the land resources available there attracting a great number of immigrants, mainly from Henan, Gansu and Sichuan [22, 73]. After that, the number of immigrants kept increasing, and the source provinces extended to include Shandong and Jiangsu. This diversification of origins translated to a reduced population migration concentration. Figure 1.3 maps the spacial concentration of on the origin GIc basis, and Fig. 1.4 maps it from the perspective of destination GIc.

In China, the spatial pattern of interprovincial population migration depends on topography and climate, and this pattern results in regional living conditions and differences in economic development. These relatively stable macro factors also contribute to the relative stability of population distribution and the pattern of internal population migration [83]. Since 1978, China has taken action to spur economic vitality, including reform and opening policies, a western development policy and a strategy for the rise of central China. These policies, however, have not changed the basic spatial pattern of regional development and economic growth; on the contrary, they have even aggravated regional imbalance, along with interprovincial migration. For instance, some regions like the Yangtze River Delta and the Pearl River Delta have stepped into a new era with high economic growth since 1978, having attracted many immigrants from less developed areas. Therefore, eastern coastal regions have

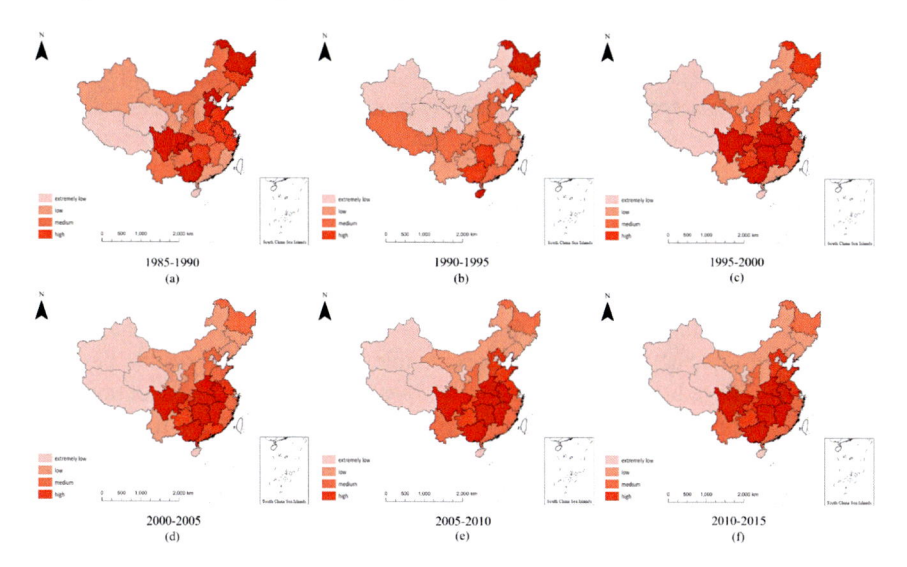

Fig. 1.3 Map of origin GIc (1985–2015)

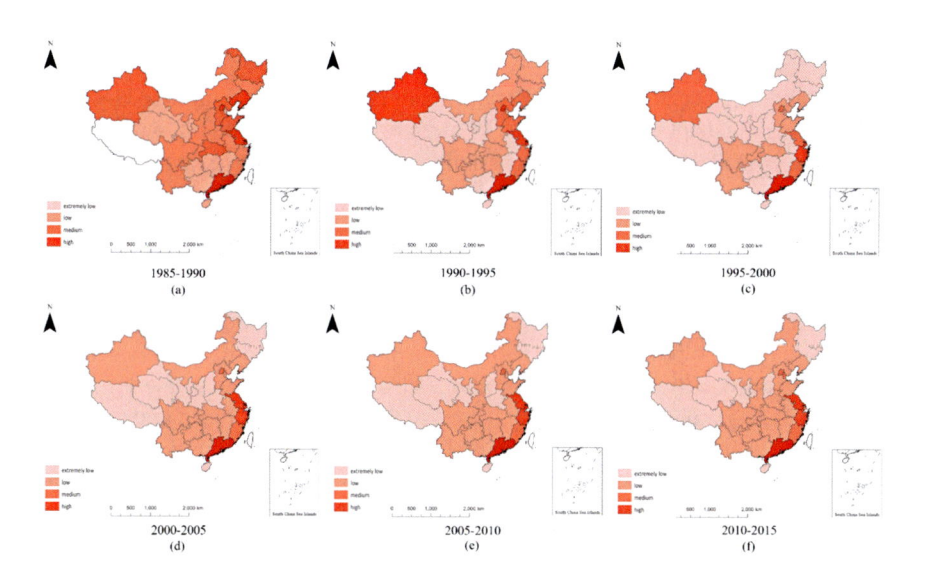

Fig. 1.4 Map of destination GIc (1985–2015)

had high spatial concentrations of immigration for a long period. From the beginning of the reform and opening-up policy to the late 1990s, interregional migration in China was mainly influenced by economic development, job opportunities and policy. However, in the twenty-first century, apart from the above factors, population migration is being more and more impacted by social networks and living conditions [39, 50, 54], and hence migration decision making is a comprehensive behaviour with multivariate factors. Moreover, strategies of regional development and the new urbanization planning (from 2014 to 2020) are promoting a dwindling trend of spatial concentration of population migration in China, with more and more migrants migrating to different regions, which are more attractive than before.

1.1.4 Conclusion and Discussion

Since population migration is an important social phenomenon in China, whose spatial pattern impacts multiple socioeconomic elements, it needs to be carefully studied. Based on the GIc system, we measured the spatial concentration of interprovincial population migration in China from 1985 to 2015 to uncover its imbalanced nature. The research reveals that:

First, the GIc system measures the spatial concentration of interprovincial population migration with less bias, whereas the traditional raw GI is biased, and it underestimates the spatial concentration of population migration. Specifically, this bias is positively correlated with the quantity of missing data, and it is more pronounced for global GI than for local GI. Use of the GIc should fuel more accurate analyses of spatially imbalanced population migration, and it should provide a better reference for policy making.

Second, from the perspective of global GIc, migration shows an inverse U-shaped trend, indicating that there is a dilution of migration after a concentration. However, global GIc exceeds 0.64 for all the six periods, showing that interprovincial migration in China from 1985 to 2015 was highly imbalanced, although there was a decline in GIc after 2005.

Third, origins and destinations with highly concentrated population migration are often connected by a strong migration flow that carries a large population. Given that the population migration flows studied involve a quite large population, a migration tie is more likely to be established between the top origins and destinations ranked by spatial concentration. These observations also indirectly confirm the long-term tendency of migrating from middle and west to the eastern developed areas.

Fourth, generally speaking, the emigration population concentration is high in middle China and some western regions (Chongqing, Sichuan and Guangxi). Moreover, the middle regions are associated with a constantly highly concentrated emigration density. The size of the emigrant population also evidently depends on the destination, and most migration is directed to the east and coastal regions, which are contiguous.

Fifth, destinations with highly concentrated immigration are in the Yangtze River Delta and the Pearl River Delta. The top three destinations are always Guangdong and two out of Zhejiang, Jiangsu and Shanghai. Such destinations have high concentrations of migrants and high immigrant populations, which means not only that the origins are shared, but also that relevant migration flows concentrate large populations. What is more, high concentration is also impacted by destination-related specifications. Based on a specific destination, the immigrants are sourced from a certain origin and its neighbourhood. Notably, with policy support and abundant resources, Xinjiang has gradually become a new source of growth. However, as the affected areas have extended, relevant emigration GI has gradually dropped.

One of the main findings of this study is that the global GIc of China's population migration shows an inverse U-shaped trend. After 1985, with the implementation of reform and the opening up policy, household registration in China was liberalized to some extent, and thus the binding of land to the labour force gradually declined, leading to the beginning of large-scale population migration. Due to the imbalanced regional economic development and the uneven supply of public services, the spatial concentration of population migration increased rapidly. The imbalanced supply of labour led to a further increase in the imbalance of regional economic and social development, thus forming a cyclic, cumulative causality effect. After entering the twenty-first century, the government realized this problem, and it began to implement a strategy of equalization of public services, encouraging labour to settle down into small and medium-sized cities, thus forming an orderly urbanization. Meanwhile, some strategies for balanced regional development were proposed and implemented, such as the development of the western regions, the rise of the central regions and the revitalization of the northeast regions. For provinces and regions that attract large numbers of migrants, a seller's market for labour has emerged, and a decline in wages and an increase in the cost of survival have also blocked further increases in immigration. The above reasons have led to a decline in the spatial concentration of population migration in recent years.

However, from the overall perspective, the GIc of China's inter-provincial population migration is still higher than 0.6, indicating that the population migration pattern is still highly imbalanced. According to our results, governors of destination provinces need to provide better urban space as well as improved environmental capacity for the highly concentrated immigration population. For instance, governments can supply high-quality and diversified public services, and they can enhance the urban built environment to provide citizens with comfortable urban lives. Also, owing to the significance of transportation in urban spaces, governments should develop public transportation networks to improve commuting convenience.

On the other hand, the central government needs to adhere further to the new-type urbanization strategy, to move further in relaxing the restrictions on the household registration system, and to encourage the floating population to settle down in small and medium-sized cities near their origins. In addition, economic resources need to be allocated properly to promote the rational distribution of labour; for example, shifting some labour-intensive industries to developing provinces to promote local employment rate and to attract migrant workers who have local *hukous* to return. Finally, the central government needs to implement the equalization strategy of public services, so that public service resources such as education and medical care can be dispersed to small and medium-sized cities to attract people to return by voting with their feet. Local governments in source provinces need to formulate relevant policies to encourage migrants to return to their hometowns and start businesses. Local governments in destination provinces need to control the size of the immigrant population by rationally arranging employment positions and resources.

Currently, population migration has two major impacts on economic and social development. On one hand, it drives element flow, resource allocation and information exchange among regions, while on the other, it promotes development imbalance among regions. When measuring the above effects, it is important to calculate and analyse the spatial concentration of population migration. Thus, GI is necessary. However, using traditional GI results in calculation bias, as it cannot solve the problem of missing data. One of the main contributions of this study is that we have proposed GIc, and hence we can analyse the concentration of migration in a more accurate way. Compared to the traditional GI, the main improvements of GIc are listed as below: first, through re-standardization, GIc is restricted to the range of [0,1] under the circumstance of missing data, so that the comparability of results across time and regions is enhanced. Second, the GI may underestimate the spatial concentration of migration, and GIc can solve this problem and give more accurate measurements. Thus, our new indexes can better reveal the imbalanced and concentrated spatial nature of population migration, and they can provide guidance for further study of its mechanism analysis and relevant policies research. In the future, the GI system should be extended to reflect the underlying population migration phenomena better, and it should be compared against other commonly used indexes in a more rigorous manner to develop an even more accurate indicator. In addition, the observed imbalanced nature of population migration should be studied with state-of-the-art quantitative models to reveal the major driving factors for mechanistic insights, which collectively provide this subject with a broad and deep meaning.

1.2 Influence Factors of Interprovincial Migration in China

1.2.1 Introduction

The issue of migration has long been the focus of scholars in the fields of demography and geography. It is of great significance to model the interregional migration flows and to study the driving forces behind it. Existing migration models fall into two types: macroscopic and microscopic models [68]. Based on census or other relevant statistics, macroscopic migration models mainly focus on the migration of the general population or specific groups in a certain region, analyse the push and pull factors in the migration process, simulate changes in the migration process, and predict the size of migration flow. Collecting individuals' information from censuses or social surveys, microscopic migration models concentrate on the migration behaviour of individuals or households, and they try to explain how potential migrants make their decisions to stay at their current residences or to move to other regions. Due to the difficulty in obtaining microscopic data, macro migration models are the mainstream of extant studies [68]. Among them, researchers have used the gravity model (GM) widely [75]. Initially, GM only includes three variables: population at origin, population at destination, and migration distance [53, 97]. Based on push–pull migration theory, expanded GMs consider a series of social economic indicators as driving factors to explain and predict interregional migration better [75].

In GM, variables should be independent of each other [39, 72]. Although this assumption of independence of interaction flows is necessary in spatial interaction modelling, there is always spatial autocorrelation (SA) in spatial data [12]. Without proper treatment, it leads to biased results [12, 15, 31]. SA takes Tobler's [81] First Law of Geography as its starting point. This means that attribute values of objects (or elements) have spatial relationships [10]. Currently, researchers most often use Moran's I coefficient (MC) to calculate SA [35, 79]. As for the migration origin–destination network, SA is a form of network autocorrelation (NA) based on topological structure. Eigenvector spatial filtering (ESF) is an advanced method to deal with NA, as it can capture and filter out NA by means of certain operators. ESF can reduce NA in residual error terms by separating spatial structure random components (i.e., spatial stochastic signal) in models [37]. This method is free from the limitations of specific regression models, and by adjusting the filter operator, researchers can reduce the NA effect of error terms more effectively [32].

The case in our study is the interprovincial migration network in China from 1995 to 2015. With the implementation of reform, the policy of opening up in the late 1970s, and the deregulation of migration in the 1980s, large-scale cross-regional migration caused a profound social change in China. Since the 1990s, with the deepening of economic reforms and rapid economic growth, inter-provincial migration has increased in China [38, 74]. From 1995 to 2000, 32.28 million people migrated to other provinces. From 2010 to 2015, the scale of interprovincial movement increased to 53.28 million, with a growth rate of more than 65%. The increasingly active large-scale population movement not only accelerates the process of urbanisation but also promotes the rapid development of China's social economy, and it poses a severe challenge to China's regional development planning, the Chinese government's social management, and public services. In this context, we tried to combine ESF with negative binomial GM (ESF NBGM), and we used panel data on interprovincial migration in China from 1995 to 2015 to explore the influencing mechanism of interprovincial migration, taking the effects of NA into consideration. We hope to provide references for the construction of new types of urbanisation and reform in the household registration system of China.

1.2.2 Literature Review

A large body of literature has focused on factors underlying population movements and migration. Neo-classical economists have claimed that labor mobility was driven by the regional disparity in incomes in agricultural, industrial and commercial sectors [49]. From the microeconomic perspective, economists believed that each worker has sufficient economic rationality, and that the motivation for migration comes from economic benefits [82]. When wage income is greater than migration cost, labor has sufficient motivation to move [82]. In the 1980s, the focus of migration economics theory shifted from the individual to the family [61]. Stark and Bloom [77] argued that labor migration is the result of household income diversification and risk minimization decisions. Labor migration occurs not only to maximize individual economic benefits, but also to achieve household economic income goals. In addition, some scholars explain migration from the perspective of job market and social network effects [61, 65], and push-pull migration theory states that both the pushing force of the origin region and the pulling force of the destination region affect migration [46].

GM is by far the commonest model that researchers use when they study the migration of aggregates to regional units using macrodata. Zipf [97] first proposed GM, and researchers have used it widely in simulating interregional migration flows. Scholars such as Wilson [87, 88] and Fotheringham [24, 25] expanded GM's form. Lowry [58] added social and economic variables to GM, extended it to a spatial interaction model, and analysed the interrelationships between regional differences in economic opportunity and the direction of migration flow. Rogers et al. [71] used a log-linear spatial interaction model to describe migration structure. Overall, GM and its expanded forms not only imply the ideas of push–pull theory by considering the combined effects of variables of origin and destination on interregional migration, but they also add various factors that draw on classic migration theories to demonstrate these theories.

Researchers on GM mainly focused on the following two aspects. First, some scholars focused on how to improve traditional GM to promote its model fitting and explanatory ability. They decomposed the effect of explanatory variables in GM through a series of measurement methods, and they analysed the error sources [45, 74, 75]. For example, Shen [74] used the multilevel Poisson migration model to analyse the factors influencing China's interprovincial migration from 1985 to 2000, along with deconstructing the increase of migration. The result showed that 62.28% of this increase was due to the change in explanatory variables, and 37.72% resulted from the changes in the model parameters. Second, in the use of GM, plenty of relevant studies drew on different specialised and categorised migration phenomena, such as comparisons of skill migration and gender migration [53]. Compared with previous studies, the main contribution of this study is the use of four-phase interprovincial migration panel data from 1995 to 2015 to construct a panel regression model for analysis.

In most cases, NA exists in migration origin–destination flows, violating the assumption of GM that variables are independent of each other [31]. This may lead to misspecified models and incorrect inferences [12]. Curry [15] first argued that NA and global distance decay intermingle in the estimation of GM specifications. Griffith and Jones [34] found that the number of out-migrants underwent influence from the tendency to migrate in local neighbourhoods, whereas the number of in-migrants to the same destination also underwent influence from the attractiveness of its neighbourhoods. The means of solving the above problems is to introduce a spatial weight matrix and to take spatial spillover effects into the regression model, from which we obtain a type of spatial autoregressive model [48]. The other method involves attempts to separate spatial effects from the variables' total effects, to filter NA in the data using a certain operator. This technique is called spatial filtering. The basic idea of spatial filtering is to deconstruct a spatial variable into the following three components: trend, spatially structured random component, and random noise [37]. Compared with spatial autoregressive specification, the most obvious improvement of spatial filtering specification is simplicity. Researchers can use the regression techniques of spatial filtering directly with georeferenced data using standard statistical software packages. This captures NA in a mean response term rather than in a variance term, thus, researchers can compute and interpret all the conventional diagnostic statistics for linear, logistic, and Poisson regression analyses without having to develop spatially adjusted counterparts [36, 37]. Furthermore, assumptions concerning spatial spillover effects in the spatial autoregressive model do not limit spatial filtering [37]. By adjusting the filtering operator, it is often possible to reduce NA in the error term significantly. Existing spatial filtering methods mainly include autoregressive linear operators, Getis's filtering approach, and ESF. Compared with the other two methods, ESF is less restrictive and more suitable for dealing with endogeneity in the model [28].

ESF has been combined with other regression methods (e.g., step-wise regressions [14]) and models (e.g., the geographically weighted regression ESF model [30], the zero-inflated ESF model [63], and the semiparametric ESF model [80]). In addition, researchers have applied ESF gradually in migration studies. For example, Chun [12] and Chun and Griffith [13] combined ESF with a Poisson model and a generalised linear model to capture the NA among interstate migration flows within the United States, and Chun found that the estimated regression parameters in the spatial filtering interaction model became more intuitively interpretable. Using an ESF Poisson GM, Shen [75] modelled the determinants of interprovincial migration in China from 2005 to 2010, and Shen employed an error analysis based on this model to see which factors of the migration process could make the model more accurate. Extending the ESF Poisson migration model to the ESF negative binomial migration model, Liu and Shen [53] examined the determinants of skilled and less skilled interprovincial migration in China, and they found that distance, unemployment rate, and foreign direct investment affected skilled worker migration moderately, but wages had a greater effect.

In China, scholars have done a lot of research on interprovincial migration. Their studies mainly focused on spatial patterns of migration and their evolution [52], the measurement of the concentration of migration [18], the influencing factors of migration [72, 74, 83], and the relationship between migration and regional economic development [22]. In the past 5 years, scholars have begun to pay attention to the influences of spatial spillover effects on migration flows. For example, on the basis of the related results in the new economic geography, Zhang, Liang and Yang [96] added factors such as market potential and expected income to the traditional GM, and they analysed the interprovincial migration factors using the spatial lag model and the spatial error model. They found that market potential and expected income played an important role in promoting the number of inflows in China, but they influenced the inflows in different ways. On the basis of the data from China's Sixth National Population Census in 2010, Pu et al. [68] analysed the factors of interprovincial migration in China with a spatial interaction model, and they captured the multilateral effect mechanisms of different variables in interprovincial migration, concluding that spatial spillover effects exist in variables such as distance and wage levels. However, there are still relatively few cases in which researchers have applied the ESF model in analysing China's interprovincial migration issues.

The contributions of this study are as follows: (a) In existing research on interprovincial migration, there is widespread use of spatial autoregressive models, whereas there are relatively few cases of SF. This study uses the ESF to reduce the NA in model's error term and to improve model fitting. (b) Traditional GMs based on ordinary least squares are still the mainstream, whereas models such as Poisson GM (PGM) and NBGM based on maximum likelihood estimation and better fitting migration data are less popular. In this study, we use the negative binomial model to make up for this deficiency. (c) Due to the limited census data in China, previous researchers have mostly conducted regression analyses based on cross-section data. This study uses four-phase panel data from 1995 to 2015 to construct a panel regression model for analysis.

1.2.3 Data and Methodology

1.2.3.1 Data and Variables

Interprovincial migration data came from population censuses and the 1% national population sample surveys in the period of 1995–2015. We excluded the migration flows of Hong Kong, Macau, and Taiwan. As there are 19 missing migration flows in the 1995 1% national population sample survey, we have 3,701 observations from 31 provincial administrative units. Considering the number of migrations, which is non-negative integer (count data), and the sampling ratio, we transformed the data by rounding for each statistical period.

Factors representing social network, economic, job, population character, education level, and distance influence migration flows. The basis for the economic factors is neoclassical migration economics theory and new economics of migration, which advocate that migrants make their migration decisions based on maximised expected profits and minimised costs [77, 82]. Dual labour market theory contributes to the selection of economics, labour, and education variables. This theory supports a viewpoint that both the socio-economic circumstances of the destination and the differences between the labour markets affect migrants' decisions [65]. Additionally, based on push–pull migration theory, both push and pull variables affect the migration. Therefore, pairs of factors were more likely to feature in our model. After the treatment of serious multicollinearity, we selected 14 variables that may affect interprovincial migration decision-making processes. The independent variables are in Table 1.2, including population size at origin and destination (POP_i and POP_j), sex ratio (SEX_i and SEX_j), average growth of regional gross domestic product (GDP) of the past 5 years ($GDPGROW_i$ and $GDPGROW_j$), average wages of urban workers per year

Table 1.2 Descriptions of independent variables in the models

Variable	Description
Economic and employment	
$GDPGROW_{i,j}$	Average growth rate of GDP in 1995–2000, 2000–2005,2005–2010, and 2010–2015
$WAGE_j$	Average wage of employed persons in urban area in 2000, 2005, 2010, and 2015
$POPDEN_{i,j}$	Population density in2000, 2005, 2010, and 2015
$UNEMPLOY_{i,j}$	Unemployment rate in urban areas in 2000, 2005, 2010, and 2015
Gravity variables	
$POP_{i,j}$	Population in 2000, 2005, 2010, and 2015
$DIST$	Distance between the capital of province i and that of province j
Education	
$CSTUDENT_{i,j}$	Number of college students in 2000, 2005, 2010, and 2015
Demography	
$SEX_{i,j}$	Sex ratio in 2000, 2005, 2010, and 2015

Data sources: 2000 Population Census of China, 2005 1% National Population Sample Surveys of China, 2010 Population Census of China, 2015 1% National Population Sample Surveys of China, China Statistical Yearbook(2000–2015).

calculated in yuan at the destination ($WAGE_j$), population density ($POPDEN_i$ and $POPDEN_j$), unemployment ($UNEMPLOY_i$ and $UNEMPLOY_j$), number of college students per 10,000 people ($CSTUDENT_i$ and $CSTUDENT_j$), and Euclidian spatial distance between the origin and the destination ($DIST_{ij}$). Table 1.3 summarises the statistic descriptions of these variables.

1.2.3.2 Gravity Model

(1) Poisson gravity model

Although scholars such as Diggle and Milne [17] and Matern [62] believed that there is no correlation between the Poisson and the negative binomial model specification of spatial data, researchers have implemented this combination, and PGM and NBGM have become representations of these models. PGM is a basic model of count data modelling, assuming that the dependent variable should be subject to a Poisson distribution. As migration data are a type of count data, researchers use Poisson regression widely in the field of migration studies [68, 76]. In regard to the dimension of time, our data support a panel model. Due to the fact that it is not possible to add time-invariant variables (e.g., distance and especially our selected eigenvectors) into a Poisson fixed effect model [89], we choose the Poisson random effect model for comparison. In such a model, the conditional distribution of migration from region i to j is

Table 1.3 Statistical descriptions of variables

Variable	Observation	M	SD	Min	Max
Migration	3,701	48,255.790	163,578.400	20.000	2,929,810.000
POP_i	3,701	4,235.251	2,692.440	258.000	10,849.000
POP_j	3,701	4,234.803	2,690.841	258.000	10,849.000
SEX_i	3,701	104.461	3.501	96.340	120.430
SEX_j	3,701	104.455	3.497	96.340	120.430
$GDPGROW_i$	3,701	0.111	0.019	0.075	0.174
$GDPGROW_j$	3,701	0.111	0.019	0.075	0.174
$WAGE_j$	3,701	32,115.910	23,181.280	6,917.999	113,073.000
$POPDEN_i$	3,701	1,838.876	1,484.864	2.100	6,031.000
$POPDEN_j$	3,701	1,839.291	1,487.343	2.100	6,031.000
$UNEMPLOY_i$	3,701	0.035	0.007	0.008	0.056
$UNEMPLOY_j$	3,701	0.035	0.007	0.008	0.056
$CSTUDENT_i$	3,701	167.058	111.572	21.200	619.600
$CSTUDENT_j$	3,701	167.209	111.741	21.200	619.600
$DIST_{ij}$	3,701	1,659.598	901.598	146.518	4,563.291

$$f(M_{ij1}, M_{ij2}, M_{ij3}, M_{ij4}|vij) = \prod_{t=1}^{4}(\frac{e^{-\mu_{ijt}}\mu_{ijt}^{M_{ijt}}}{M_{ijt}!}) \qquad (1.7)$$

where M_{ijt} denotes the migration from region i to region j in the period t, and v_{ij} has a Gamma distribution, which represents individual effects in the panel model. Here, we assume that M_{ijt} is i.i.d., on condition of some variables (see μ_{ijt} mentioned below) and v_{ij}. μ_{ijt} is a conditional mean, relating to a regression with independent variables:

$$\mu_{ijt} = \exp(\alpha_0 + \sum_{q=1}^{Q}\alpha_{1q}\ln X_{iqt} + \sum_{l=1}^{L}\alpha_{2l}\ln X_{jlt} + \alpha_3\ln D_{ij}) \qquad (1.8)$$

where X_{iqt} (or X_{jlt}) is the qth (or jth) independent variable of origin region i (or destination region l) in the period of t and D_{ij} refers to distance. α_{1q}, α_{2l} and α_3 refer to their corresponding estimated coefficients.

(2) **Negative binomial gravity model**

When using PGM to analyse interregional migration, there is overdispersion in the regression model, rejecting the equidispersion assumption. That is to say, the variance and condition mean should be equal in a Poisson model, which they are not. We thus choose a negative binomial model, which is suitable for overdispersion, by adding up a dispersion parameter. Considering that the time span of our data is from 1995 to 2015, we decided to use the negative binomial panel model. The Hausman test is useful for testing whether a random effect model or a fixed effect model is more appropriate. If the fixed model is more suitable, to attain robust estimation results, not only should we control time effects and individual effects, but also we will need to use bootstrap. In particular, the number of resamplings in bootstrap is 400 [11]. With bootstrap, we can get cluster-robust standard errors of the model, which may provide more convincing estimation results, especially on p values [8]. The migration flow M_{ijt} needs to meet a Poisson-Gamma mixture distribution:

$$\Pr(M_{ijt}|X_{iqt}, X_{jlt}, D_{ij}, T_t, \alpha) = \frac{\Gamma(M_{ijt}+\alpha^{-1})}{M_{ijt}!\Gamma(\alpha^{-1})}\left(\frac{\alpha^{-1}}{\alpha^{-1}+\mu_{ijt}}\right)^{\alpha^{-1}}\left(\frac{\mu_{ijt}}{\alpha^{-1}+\mu_{ijt}}\right)^{M_{ijt}}$$

(1.9)

and we can rewrite the joint probability function of each group as follows to manifest the type of fixed effect model better:

$$\Pr(M_{ij1}, M_{ij2}, \ldots, M_{ijT_{ij}^*}|X_{iqt}, X_{jlt}, D_{ij}, T_t, \sum_{t=1}^{T_{ij}^*} M_{ijt})$$

$$= \frac{\Gamma\left(\sum_{t=1}^{T_{ij}^*}\mu_{ijt}\right)\Gamma\left(\sum_{t=1}^{T_{ij}^*}M_{ijt}+1\right)}{\Gamma\left(\sum_{t=1}^{T_{ij}^*}\mu_{ijt}+\sum_{t=1}^{T_{ij}^*}M_{ijt}\right)}\Pi_{t=1}^{T_{ij}^*}\frac{\Gamma(\mu_{ijt}+M_{ijt})}{\Gamma(\mu_{ijt})\Gamma(M_{ijt}+1)}$$

(1.10)

where Γ is a standard Gamma distribution function, T_{ij}^* denotes the count of times of migration flows from i to j, and α is a dispersion parameter. X_{iqt}, X_{jlt}, and D_{ij} are the same as they are in Eq. (1.11). The conditional mean μ_{ijt} relates to an exogenous function:

$$\mu_{ijt} = \exp\left(\alpha_0 + \sum_{q=1}^{Q}\alpha_{1q}\ln X_{iqt} + \sum_{l=1}^{L}\alpha_{2l}\ln X_{jlt} + \alpha_3 \ln D_{ij} + \sum_{t=2}^{4}\gamma_t T_t\right)$$

(1.11)

where X_{iqt}, X_{jlt}, D_{ij}, α_{1q}, α_{2l}, and α_3 are the same as in Eq. (1.12), and T_t denotes the dummy variable of time (t = 2, 3, 4) in the period of t. γ_t refers to its corresponding estimated coefficient. When all the independent variables are set, the variance of M_{ijt} should be a function of the conditional mean μ_{ijt}, and we can write the dispersion parameter α as

$$Var(M_{ijt}|X_{iqt}, X_{jlt}, D_{ij}, T_t) = \mu_{ijt} + \alpha\mu_{ijt}^2$$

(1.12)

In a fixed effect model, we control both unobserved individual heterogeneity and time effect, aiming to reduce the influence of omitted variables.

To date, there are few studies of ESF using panel data, and most of them use random effect models. If we use a Poisson fixed effect model, we cannot estimate variables that do not change through time [8, 89]. That is to say, we cannot add ESF and distance variables into the GM. To fix this problem, we can only use a Poisson random effect model or change the settings of the model. However, if the results of statistical tests show that there are unobserved variables, using a Poisson random effect model will result in a biased estimation. Compared with the Poisson panel model, the negative binomial panel model has the advantage of estimating those time-invariant variables in the fixed effect model.

1.2.3.3   Eigenvector Spatial Filtering

ESF can reduce the estimation error due to NA. Compared with other spatial filtering methods, ESF has fewer restrictions, more flexibility, and better mathematical ability to capture NA [37]. The key points of ESF are as follows: Representing spatial structural information of the attribute variable, a transformed matrix will first decompose into a combination of eigenvectors and eigenvalues. Then, by some specific algorithms (e.g., stepwise), we can select eigenvectors that notably exhibit NA and add them into the model as proxy variables. The linear combination of those eigenvectors can represent the latent NA in migration data. As the selected eigenvectors can represent latent NA, we can filter out the impact of NA, which is due to spatial structure components. Furthermore, we can draw the values of eigenvectors into distinct and various mapping patterns of NA.

In our case, the steps of ESF are as follows: First, we develop an n-by-n binary spatial weight matrix S, which represents the connectivity of provinces in China (n denotes the number of geographical units). If provinces i and k are spatially linked, the related element in S is 1 (viz., $S_{ik} = 1$). When it comes to topological structure, we take both origin-related and destination-related specifications into consideration, developing network weight matrix SN. Based on recent research [12], three different types of network weight matrices can be defined:

$$S^N = S \otimes I \tag{1.13a}$$

$$S^N = I \otimes S \tag{1.13b}$$

$$S^N = S \oplus S \tag{1.13c}$$

where $\otimes$ and $\oplus$ denote the Kronecker product and Kronecker sum, respectively. Equation (13a) is interpreted as an origin-related specification that if network flows share a single origin and their destinations are spatially associated, the network flows are considered to be neighbours in the network. This specification reflects the competing destinations effects that spatial proximity of destinations has an impact on the destination choice of a migrant in one origin. The second specification (Eq. 13b) labelled a destination-related specification. For network flows that have a single destination, network flows whose origins are spatially associated are considered as network neighbours. This specification represents the effect of intervening opportunities [40]. Given a destination, if origins are located close to each other, migration flows between one of the origins and the destination tend to be affected by similar intervening opportunities. The third specification (Eq. 13c) combines these two effects together. In recent studies, more researchers used the third specification to define network weight matrix, and they showed the improvement of considering the competing destination effects and the intervening opportunities effects simultaneously into a network model (e.g., [3, 12, 39, 40, 53]). In this research, we defined a network weight matrix using the third specification. To meet our topic (interprovincial migration flow), it is necessary to delete the elements of the inner-provincial migration flow, and thus, S^N eventually turns into an $(n^2 - n)$-by-$(n^2 - n)$ matrix.

After the above preparations, we can develop a transformed matrix:, where I is an $(n^2 - n)$-by-$(n^2 - n)$ identity matrix, and 1 is an $(n^2 - n)$-by-1 vector of 1 s, and centres S^N. It follows that

$$\left(I - \frac{11'}{N}\right) S^N \left(I - \frac{11'}{N}\right) = E \Lambda E' \tag{1.14}$$

where E is the matrix of eigenvectors decomposed by the transformed matrix and Λ is a diagonal matrix with corresponding eigenvalues. Therefore, we can deconstruct the matrix, which represents spatial structure components, into a combination of eigenvalues and eigenvectors. Note that we can calculate an MC value of each eigenvector, with the network weight matrix S^N. With its eigenvector, every eigenvalue links to an MC value: The eigenvector with the largest eigenvalue, called E1, which corresponds to the largest MC value, can capture the highest SA [79]. The eigenvector with the second largest eigenvalue, called E2, corresponds to the second largest MC by any set that is uncorrelated with E1. This relation lasts to E_{n2-n}. The eigenvectors have two features: orthogonality and uncorrelation, which ensure the uncorrelated distinct map pattern of latent NA [28]. When a spatial matrix is set, no matter what the values of dependent variable are, the MC of attributes needs to be within range, of which the minimum and the maximum eigenvalues set the lower and upper limits [16]. Thus, after adding the selected eigenvectors into the regression model, we filtered out one possibility of latent NA. To capture the substantial NA, we set-up a threshold of 0.25 (MC/MC_{max}). After this step, we used stepwise criteria (forward) at the 1% significance level to select out the eigenvectors that were suitable for the model [32]. The linear combination of selected eigenvectors was capable of capturing latent NA in the model and reducing estimation error.

1.2.4 Empirical Analysis

On the basis of MATLAB, we deconstructed the transformed matrix in Eq. (1.15) into corresponding eigenvalues and eigenvectors. It is worth mentioning that, in our definition, Hainan province is a neighbour of Guangdong province. After selecting out eigenvectors with stepwise criteria, we built an ESF NBGM based on panel type. Its conditional mean was

$$\mu_{ijt} = \exp\left(\alpha_0 + \sum_{q=1}^{Q} \alpha_{1q} \ln X_{iqt} + \sum_{l=1}^{L} \alpha_{2l} \ln X_{jlt} \right.$$
$$\left. + \alpha_3 \ln D_{ij} + \sum_{k=1}^{k} \alpha_{4k} E_k + \sum_{t=2}^{4} \gamma_t T_t \right) \tag{1.15}$$

where α_0, α_{1q}, α_{2l}, α_3, γ_t, X_{iqt}, X_{jlt}, D_{ij}, and T_t are the same as in Eq. (1.15). E_k denotes the kth selected eigenvector, whereas α_{4k} is its corresponding estimator. To analyse the influencing mechanism of interprovincial migration in China from 1995 to 2015, we built four models based on panel type, namely, PGM, ESF PREPGM, NBGM, and ESF NBGM. Comparisons between Models 1 and 4 can shed light on how ESF affects estimations. Comparisons between Models 1 and 3 and Models 2 and 4 may show differences between Poisson regression and negative binomial regression, as well as the advantages of a two-way effect panel model. On the basis of the econometrics, we compare those models in the ensuing paragraphs.

1.2.4.1 Model Comparison

We calculated MC values of interprovincial networks in each period based on SN. The results showed that NA is significant and positive: For the four periods, the MC values were 0.305, 0.359, 0.383, and 0.380, respectively, indicating that there was a strong spatial dependence (or NA) in China's interprovincial migration networks from 1995 to 2015. To be specific, a steady ascent in MC value occurred from 1995 to 2010, followed by a slight decline. It was necessary to capture NA in the data to reduce estimation bias in our case, and ESF could identify it. Once we know the spatial structure of a certain region (or network weight matrix), different eigenvectors can exhibit a large range of possibilities of latent NA, regardless of attribute values [32]. From the perspective of ESF, there are the following improvements: Not only can Geographic Information Science (GIS) software map eigenvectors to exhibit distinct patterns and levels of NA, but also it is flexible, and it can reduce estimation bias due to NA in data.

To shed light on the differences in the ability of capturing NA, we scattered the rank based on eigenvalues and the ratio of MC/MC_{max}, as every eigenvector has an eigenvalue (hence, every eigenvector has a rank based on its eigenvalue) and an MC (hence, we can calculate the ratio). According to Table 1.3, the top 20% of eigenvectors can capture NA, whereas the top 1.4% of eigenvectors can exhibit spatial patterns with high NA. To summarise, a few eigenvectors with high rank can capture high NA in data, and those proxy variables will not burden the computing

Table 1.4 ESF's ability to capture network autocorrelation in the network weight matrix

Capturing ability of network autocorrelation	Range of	Number of eigenvectors	Proportion (%)
High	$MC/MC_{\max} \in (0.75, 0.1)$	13	1.398
Moderate	$MC/MC_{\max} \in (0.5, 0.75)$	44	4.732
Weak	$MC/MC_{\max} \in (0.25, 0.5)$	134	14.408
Slight	$\{E = MC/MC_{\max} | E \leq 0.25\}$	739	79.462

Abbreviations ESF, eigenvector spatial filtering; MC, Moran's I coefficient

process. Furthermore, if we adopt a threshold of selecting eigenvectors, the filtering effects can be controlled, which is better and more flexible.

The most important improvement of ESF is that, after filtering out NA in residuals, it can solve estimation bias. This provides more convincing results, as the Akaike information criterion (AIC) of regression models usually declines. After calculation, we found that whatever the model setting in the Poisson panel models or negative binomial panel models was, values of AIC had different reductions after integration. Without ESF, the AIC values were 14,514,031 and 52,776, respectively. However, if we add ESF into the models, the values declined to 14,513,273 and 52,520, respectively. Furthermore, Table 1.4 reveals that MCs of model residuals reduced if the model contained ESF. That is to say, our statistical results met our expectation that ESF can capture latent NA in data, improving model fitting.

We calculated the variance and the mean of the dependent variable. The variance was 555,400 times the mean, which rejected the equidispersion assumption with sufficient evidence. Thereafter, for a strict test, we built a statistic D (D = Pearson χ^2/degree of freedom). With a large sample, if D reaches 1.05, we can conclude that there is overdispersion [42]. After calculation, the statistics of the Poisson models (mixed regression and random effect model, respectively) were 93,562.512 and 27,634.409, which were much higher than the threshold, this proved overdispersion. That is to say, there was extreme overdispersion in our independent variable, and hence, the negative binomial model was much more suitable.

It is noteworthy that although the estimators of Poisson panel models seem notable, or even more significant than those of negative binomial panel models in some situations (but not in our circumstance, as there is no extreme difference in significance), the results come at a price: It is hard to meet the assumptions of the Poisson model. In contrast, if there is overdispersion in data, negative binomial models are more robust, and they can provide more convincing estimation results.

When it came to the selection of panel model, an likelihood ratio (LR) test rejected H0 at the 0.001 significance level, meaning that random effect panel model was better than a mixed regression. Then, we used the Hausman test to determine whether a random effect model or a fixed effect model was more suitable. The results preferred the latter, showing that there were time-invariant but individual-variant effects. Moreover, considering those time-variant but individual-invariant variables, we controlled the time fixed effect, and an F test of time trend variables supported our model setting. Therefore, we used the negative binomial two-way effect panel model along with ESF for further analysis (Table 1.5).

Table 1.5 Results of interprovincial migration in China, based on PGM, ESF PGM, NBGM, and ESF NBGM

Dependent variable	1 PGM migration	2 ESF PGM migration	3 NBGM migration	4 ESF NBGM migration
POP_i	−0.080 (0.074)	− 0.080 (0.074)	0.195*** (0.031)	0.098** (0.043)
POP_j	0.001 (0.518)	0.001 (0.518)	0.232*** (0.048)	0.273*** (0.067)
SEX_i	4.457*** (0.788)	4.457*** (0.788)	1.758*** (0.353)	1.996*** (0.364)
SEX_j	−0.893 (2.028)	−0.893 (2.028)	0.202 (0.209)	0.194 (0.352)
$GDPGROW_i$	−0.143 (0.095)	−0.143 (0.095)	−0.177*** (0.060)	−0.114* (0.059)
$GDPGROW_j$	0.222*** (0.074)	0.222*** (0.074)	0.174* (0.094)	0.144 (0.095)
$POPDEN_i$	−0.092*** (0.030)	−0.092*** (0.030)	−0.050*** (0.013)	−0.060*** (0.014)
$POPDEN_j$	0.080** (0.036)	0.080** (0.036)	−0.029* (0.017)	−0.024 (0.017)
$UNEMPLOY_i$	0.615*** (0.132)	0.615*** (0.132)	0.357*** (0.064)	0.431*** (0.077)
$UNEMPLOY_j$	−0.314** (0.129)	−0.314** (0.129)	−0.313*** (0.0630)	−0.333*** (0.083)
$CSTUDENT_i$	0.106 (0.087)	0.106 (0.087)	0.127*** (0.038)	0.079* (0.042)
$CSTUDENT_j$	−0.161 (0.117)	−0.161 (0.117)	−0.099** (0.049)	−0.086 (0.056)
$WAGE_j$	0.422*** (0.0730)	0.422*** (0.0730)	0.763*** (0.111)	0.822*** (0.123)
$DIST_{ij}$	−1.149*** (0.186)	−0.890*** (0.091)	−0.260*** (0.050)	−0.200*** (0.068)
time2			−0.310 (0.551)	−0.194 (0.559)
time3			−0.255 (0.595)	−0.153 (0.607)
time4			−0.487 (0.661)	−0.384 (0.675)
Intercept	0.149 (6.166)	−2.385 (6.53)	−15.772*** (2.464)	−16.945*** (3.067)
Eigenvectors	–	79	–	84
MCresidual	0.005**	−0.000	0.241***	0.230***
N	3,701	3,701	3,701	3,701
Log likelihood	−7,256,999	−7,256,542	−26,370	−26,211
Pseudo R^2	0.422	0.423	0.045	0.051
AIC	14,514,031	14,513,273	52,776	52,520

1.2.4.2 Analysis of Determinants

(1) Factors in initial GMs

According to our model, three basic variables in initial GM still exert significant impact on interprovincial migration. To be specific, population sizes at both origin (POP_i) and destination regions (POP_j) still act as driving factors of migration flows, with highly significant coefficients. With respect to distance ($DIST_{ij}$), however, its impact is weakening, and especially if we take NA into consideration, its influence is declining more. Without ESF, the model will overestimate the effect of distance, resulting in estimation bias.

The result showed that the estimators of POP_i and POP_j were both positive and significant, of which the estimator of POP_j was larger. If the population rises 1% in a province, the out-migration increases by $100 \times [|1.01^{0.098} - 1|] = 0.098\%$, whereas the in-migration increases by $100 \times [|1.01^{0.273} - 1|] = 0.272\%$. From the perspective of origins, with a much larger population stock, there is more possible and latent out-migration. As for the destination, with more population, there are effects of population concentration and economic agglomeration that may attract in-migration from other regions.

The distance variable $DIST_{ij}$ is another factor of GMs. The results indicated that when distance between origin and destination increased by 1%, interregional migration declined by $100 \times [|1.01^{-0.200} - 1|] = 0.199\%$. On the basis of the First Law of Geography, nearer geographic elements showed stronger relationships than elements at a distance; thus, distance should have a negative impact on migration. Our model result supported this with high significance. Noteworthy is that if we had not controlled the effect of NA, the model would have overestimated the impact of distance. In particular, the coefficient changed from -0.260 in Model 3 to -0.200 in Model 4. From our point of view, this happened because in modern China, rapid developments in the Internet, communication technologies, and transportation (e.g., high speed railways) lead to a compression of space and time, so the impact of spatial distance on migration reduces.

(2) Economic and employment factors

Economic and employment factors are of paramount importance, as migrants move mostly for jobs and better self-development [9, 21, 54]. Although most economic variables (e.g., $GDPGROW_i$, $UNEMPLOY_i$, $UNEMPLOY_j$, and $WAGE_j$) met our expectations and assumptions, some variables ($GDPGROW_j$ and $POPDEN_j$) did not.

The average growth rate of GDP represents a region's economic growth rate, and this variable is of great concern in existing studies [68, 72, 74, 76]. The result shows that if a province's GDP growth rate increases by 1%, there is a $100 \times [|1.01^{-0.114} - 1|] = 0.113\%$ reduction in its out-migrants. For out-migrants, if their hometowns are highly developed, they are more likely to settle down instead of leaving, because they can get better jobs with a lower cost of living. On the other hand, a destination's GDP growth rate does not significantly affect in-migrants. Although there is not enough evidence, this result may relate to the fact that for in-migrants, social factors matter a lot more than economic factors [55]. It follows that economics is not the only factor that migrants take into consideration. From the perspective of destinations, a region with a better environment and social security system may be more attractive to some extent.

In the aspect of population density (POPDEN$_{i,j}$), the coefficients of origin and destination showed different effects: The coefficient of POPDEN$_i$ was -0.060, which indicated a significantly negative pushing impact on outflows, whereas the pulling impact on inflows was not significant. In fact, population density represents a region's economic density and urban vitality. Residents can benefit from a more concentrated area to improve their well-being, find more suiTable jobs, share knowledge, and learn professional skills [26, 60]. Therefore, an agglomeration economy in a region should attract more in-migrants and exert a negative impact on the number of out-migrants. However, the model results were partly consistent with our expectation that once there is a reduction in population density, the number of out-migrants will increase, whereas population density is no longer a very important determinant of inflows. This is because in destination provinces, the excessive agglomeration may lead to intense competition among industries. Ultimately, less competitive industries will move away, leading to a reduction in the required labour force [26]. Furthermore, the results revealed a complicated decision-making process for in-migrants. When deciding whether to settle in destinations, potential migrants need to take many factors into consideration, in addition to POPDEN$_j$.

Unemployment rate (UNEMPLOY$_{i,j}$) was another vital factor in the labour market. In our model, the estimators of UNEMPLOY$_i$ and UNEMPLOY$_j$ were highly significant (at the 0.001 level). If the unemployment rate of a region increases by 1%, the outflows increase by $100 \times [|1.01^{0.431} - 1|] = 0.430\%$, whereas on the contrary, the inflows decrease by $100 \times [|1.01^{-0.333} - 1|] = 0.331\%$. To some extent, the unemployment rate represents the condition of the labour market, including job opportunity. Fewer people can get positions when UNEMPLOY$_i$ increases, and hence, people are more likely to migrate to new places for better jobs and a better employment environment. Similarly, the higher UNEMPLOY$_j$ is, the fewer migrants will move in. Our result satisfied our expectations and supported neoclassical migration economics theory [61].

Currently, searching for a better job with a good income is one of the major reasons for interprovincial migration [18], and therefore, wage level at destination (WAGE$_j$) is of great significance when considering determinants of internal migration. Our results also fitted this description, with the correspondent coefficient being significant at the 0.01 level. If WAGE$_j$ increases by 1%, $100 \times [|1.01^{0.822} - 1|] = 0.821\%$ more in-migration results. Also, from a cost-profit perspective, as income increases, migrants can gain more profit (utilities), and hence, their net profit will add up if their costs are fixed. Therefore, the possibility of migration will increase.

(3) **Demographic and education factors**

Demographic and educational factors not only influence people's migration choices but they also affect society on the macro level. We considered sex ratio (SEX) and educational level (CSTUDENT) as demographic and education variables in our models. Regional sex ratio contributed to a highly positive and significant influence on out-migration but not notably to in-migration. Note that the coefficient of SEX_i was the largest of the coefficients. Additionally, regional education level showed a negative impact on inflows, but it was not significant on outflows.

According to previous studies, sex ratio has a close relationship with the number of in-migrants and out-migrants [18, 41, 51]. In our model, the estimator of SEX_i took the first place (1.996). If the sex ratio of a province increases by 1%, the number of out-migrants increases by $100 \times [|1.01^{1.996} - 1|] = 2.006\%$. This relates to the sex difference in the labour market. In China, the main motivation for interprovincial migration is obtaining employment [18], and this means that male labour forces are more competitive in the labour market, especially in secondary industries [41]. Therefore, it is probably easier to move out of a province with a higher sex ratio. If men make up a large proportion of the local population, there are more surplus people in the labour market. Additionally, according to previous experience, a man is more likely to migrate to a new city for a higher income, leaving his wife or even children at home, especially in rural areas. However, as a pulling variable, SEX_j is not significant. This is because, intuitively, people do not consider the sex ratio immediately when considering moving into a region.

College students represent the level of education of a region, and they are necessary and excellent human capital resources. If there are more college students in an area, especially in proportion to the population, this will promote innovation. On the other hand, however, more college students means a more competitive local labour market, which requires a higher education level of labour forces. In our model, the estimator of $CSTUDENT_i$ was 0.079, showing a positive effect on out-migration. A 1% increase in the number of college students increases the expected number of migrants moving away from the origin by $100 \times [|1.01^{0.079} - 1|] = 0.079\%$, holding all other variables constant. Although this result did not meet our expectation, it was consistent with extent research on China's interprovincial migration [39]. The improvement of education level of a region may help to accelerate the number of labour forces (especially highly educated migrants) migrating among regions. However, from the perspective of a place of destination, $CSTUDENT_i$'s coefficient was not significant, meaning that the relationship between regional education level and in-migration was still uncertain. This is because, on one hand, a region with a higher educational level can appeal to migrants from other regions to find better jobs and settle down. On the other hand, as most migrants were less educated, at a highly educated destination, those less educated in-migrants working in labour-intensive sectors tended to suffer from unstable jobs, lower incomes, and less social security, and it was difficult for them to enter into capital-intensive sectors [61] and hence decreasing the in-migration.

1.2.5 Conclusions and Discussion

Interregional migration will be the major issue of population development in the coming decades. Previous studies have paid little attention to the effect of NA on migration flow data, and existing models have fallen short in their ability to handle count data. On the basis of this, we built an ESF NBGM based on a two-way effect panel type, with data from the population census and China's 2015 1% Population Sample Survey from 1995 to 2015 to analyse the determinants of interprovincial migration in China. The main results were as follows.

The spatial pattern of NA in our samples showed a space–time trend that NA increases first and then decreases. There was a notably positive NA in our data, and we needed to capture it to avoid estimation bias. Thus, we added selected eigenvectors into our models to solve it. We discovered that, with ESF, values of AIC declined at different degrees regardless of model settings and that the top 1.4% eigenvectors could capture high NA in the data. As a result, we concluded that model fit would increase if we add the selected eigenvectors into the model.

There is extreme overdispersion in the data, rejecting the equidispersion assumption of the Poisson models. This indicates that a negative binomial model is more suitable, as it can solve the overdispersion problem. From the panel data perspective, a Poisson fixed effect model cannot contain time-invariant variables, which a negative binomial fixed effect model can. In summary, in our case, NBGM with a two-way effect panel type was more suitable, and this is provable by log likelihood.

As for the initial variables of GMs, the population of both origin and destination greatly affected the interprovincial migration flows. We found that the pushing effect of population size was slightly greater than the pulling effect. However, with the development of communication and Internet technologies and the promotion of transportation (such as high-speed railways), the effect of distance is weakening. Without ESF, models will overestimate the effect of distance owing to the latent NA in migration data. Second, it seems that economy, employment, social security, and education variables still play significant roles in shaping the spatial structure of internal migration in China. If there is a 1% increase in regional unemployment and average income, the outflows and inflows increase by 0.331% and 0.821%, respectively. The improvement of regional education level can significantly promote the number of out-migrants, whereas the relationship between educational level and in-migrants is still unclear. Meanwhile, the coefficient of sex ratio at origin was 1.996. This relates to the migration motivations of migrants and the sex difference in the labour market in China.

Generally speaking, like the findings from previous studies using cross-sectional data [51, 54, 68, 72, 74, 76, 83], we found that the interprovincial migration in China from 1995 to 2015 was a complex process involving multiple factors. Under market conditions, economic development level, employment condition, social security system, and educational resources of a region are still the main causes for interregional migration flows, both inflows and outflows [83]. As the National New Urbanization Plan (2014–2020; [64]) pointed out, the government should ensure that migrants (especially agricultural migrant workers) can benefit from basic public services at their destinations, such as the rights to receive education and health services. Government should also improve the employment and entrepreneurship service system for migrants, expand social security for them, and improve basic medical and health conditions. On the other hand, although the impact of distance on interprovincial migration is declining, we cannot neglect the impact of social network factors on migration. It is necessary to formulate reasonable regional development strategies in line with local conditions and to pay attention to the impact of the social and cultural exchanges of various regions on migration to administer the flow direction and intensity of interprovincial migration appropriately and to balance regional development in China.

There is still room for improvement in future research. First, although ESF can handle NA in spatial data better than other theories, it has weaker explanatory power than spatial regression models, because it cannot estimate the spatial spillover effect. Second, due to the limited data, it is difficult to obtain variables such as the age, education level, and income of interprovincial migrants, which leads to bias due to missing variables to some extent. In view of this, we believe that the following improvements to this model are necessary in the future. First, further consider the factors that affect the inter-provincial migration and explore the reasons for the unexpected results in the extant findings. Second, expand empirical studies on interprovincial migration based on ESF. It is also necessary to deal with two types of space–time dependency (i.e., lagged and contemporaneous specifications) in panel models using methods such as eigenvector space–time filtering [29].

References

1. Abel GJ, Sander N (2014) Quantifying global international migration flows. Science 343(6178).1520–1522
2. Allison PD (1978) Measures of inequality. Am Sociol Rev 43:865–880
3. Almeida LM, Gonçalves MB (2001) A methodology to incorporate behavioral aspects in trip-distribution models with an application to estimate student flow. Environ Plann A 33(6):1125–1138
4. Atkinson AB (1970) On the measurement of inequality. J Econ Theory 2(3):244–263
5. Bell M, Muhidin S (2009) Cross-national comparison of internal migration. United Nations Development Programme, New York, NY
6. Bell M, Black M, Boyle P, Duke-Williams O, Rees P, Stillwell J, Hugo G (2002) Cross-national comparison of internal migration: Issues and measures. J Royal Stat Soc Ser A (Statistics in Society) 165(3):435–464
7. Bell M, Charles-Edwards E, Ueffing P, Stillwell J, Kupiszewski M, Kupiszewska D (2015) Internal migration and development: Comparing migration intensities around the world. Popul Develop Rev 41(1):33–58
8. Cameron AC, Trivedi PK (2010) Microeconometrics using stata (Vol. 2). Stata press, College Station, TX
9. Chan KW, Buckingham W (2008) Is China abolishing the Hukou system? China Quart 195:582–606
10. Chen J, Zhang Y, Yu Y (2011) Effect of MAUP in spatial autocorrelation. Acta Geogr Sin 66(12):1597–1606

11. Chen Q (2010) Advanced econometrics with stata eng. Higher Education Press, Beijing
12. Chun Y (2008) Modeling network autocorrelation within migration flows by eigenvector spatial filtering. J Geograph Syst 10(4):317–344
13. Chun Y, Griffith DA (2011) Modeling network autocorrelation in space-time migration flow data: An eigenvector spatial filtering approach. Annals Assoc Am Geograph 101(3):523–536
14. Chun Y, Griffith DA, Lee M, Sinha P (2016) Eigenvector selection with stepwise regression techniques to construct eigenvector spatial filters. J Geograph Syst 18(1):67–85
15. Curry L (1972) Spatial analysis of gravity flows. Reg Stud 6(2):131–147
16. De Jong P, Sprenger C, Van Veen F (1984) On extreme values of Moran's I and Geary's c. Geograph Anal 16(1):17–24
17. Diggle PJ, Milne RK (1983) Negative binomial quadrat counts and point processes. Scandinavian J Stat 257–267.
18. Ding J, Liu Z, Cheng D, Liu J, Zou J (2005) Areal differentiation of inter-provincial migration in China and characteristics of the flow field. Acta Geogr Sin 60(1):106–114 (in Chinese)
19. Duan P, Liu C (2012) Influence of China's inter-provincial migration on regional disparity. China Popul Resources Environ 22(11):60–67
20. Duncan OD, Duncan B (1955) A methodological analysis of segregation indexes. Am Sociol Rev 20(2):210–217
21. Fan CC (2002) The elite, the natives, and the outsiders: Migration and labor market segmentation in urban China. Ann Assoc Am Geograph 92(1):103–124
22. Fan CC (2005) Interprovincial migration, population redistribution, and regional development in China: 1990 and 2000 census comparisons. Prof Geograph 57(2):295–311
23. Fan CC (2005) Modeling interprovincial migration in China, 1985–2000. Eurasian Geogr Econ 46(3):165–184
24. Fotheringham AS (1983) A new set of spatial-interaction models: The theory of competing destinations. Environ Plann A: Econ Space 15(1):15–36
25. Fotheringham AS (1986) Modelling hierarchical destination choice. Environ Plann A 18(3)
26. Fujita M, Krugman PR, Venables AJ (2001) The spatial economy: Cities, regions, and international trade. MIT press, Cambridge
27. Gini C (1926) The contributions of Italy to modern statistical methods. J Royal Stat Soc 89(4):703–724
28. Getis A, Griffith DA (2002) Comparative spatial filtering in regression analysis. Geograph Anal 34(2):130–140
29. Griffith D (2012) Space, time, and space-time eigenvector filter specifications that account for autocorrelation. Estadística Española 54(177):7–34
30. Griffith DA (2008) Spatial-filtering-based contributions to a critique of geographically weighted regression (GWR). Environ Plann A 40(11):2751–2769
31. Griffith DA (2009) Modeling spatial autocorrelation in spatial interaction data: Empirical evidence from 2002 Germany journey-to-work flows. J geograph syst 11(2):117–140
32. Griffith DA (2013) Spatial autocorrelation and spatial filtering: Gaining understanding through theory and scientific visualization. Springer, New York
33. Griffith DA, Amrhein CG (1991) Statistical analysis for geographers. Prentice Hall, Englewood Cliffs, NJ
34. Griffith DA, Jones KG (1980) Explorations into the relationship between spatial structure and spatial interaction. Environ Plann A 12(2):187–201
35. Griffith DA, Paelinck JHP (2018) Morphisms for quantitative spatial analysis. Springer, Switzerland
36. Griffith DA, Fischer MM, LeSage J (2017) The spatial autocorrelation problem in spatial interaction modelling: A comparison of two common solutions. Lett Spatial Resource Sci 10(1):75–86
37. Griffith D, Chun Y (2014) Spatial autocorrelation and spatial filtering. In Handbook of regional science (pp. 1477–1507). Springer, Berlin, Heidelberg
38. Gu Z, Gu L, Eils R, Schlesner M, Brors B (2014) Circlize implements and enhances circular visualization in R. Bioinformatics 30(19):2811–2812

39. Gu H, Shen T, Liu Z, Meng X (2019) Driving mechanism of interprovincial population migration flows in China based on spatial filtering. Acta Geogr Sin 74(2):222–237
40. Guldmann JM (1999) Competing destinations and intervening opportunities interaction models of inter-city telecommunication flows. Papers Reg Sci 78(2):179–194
41. He C, Gober P (2003) Gendering interprovincial migration in China. Int Migration Rev 37(4):1220–1251
42. Hilbe J (2014) Modeling count data. Cambridge University Press, New York
43. Janská E, Čermák Z, Wright R (2014) New immigrant destinations in a new country of immigration: Settlement patterns of non-natives in the Czech Republic. Popul Space Place 20(8):680–693
44. Krugman PR (1991) Geography and trade. MIT Press
45. Kordi M, Fotheringham AS (2016) Spatially weighted interaction models (SWIM). Annals Am Assoc Geograph 106(5):990–1012. https://doi.org/10.1080/24694452.2016.1191990
46. Lee ES (1966) A theory of migration. Demography 3(1):47–57
47. Lerman RI, Yitzhaki S (1984) A note on the calculation and interpretation of the Gini index. Econ Lett 15(3–4):363–368
48. LeSage JP, Pace RK (2008) Spatial econometric modeling of origin- destination flows. J Reg Sci 48(5):941–967
49. Lewis WA (1954) Economic development with unlimited supplies of labour. Manchester School 22(2):139–191
50. Liang Z (2016) China's great migration and the prospects of a more integrated society. Annual Rev Sociol 42:451–471
51. Li S, Mei Z, Zhang R, Zhao S (2017) Analyze of spatial characteristics and its influencing factors of China's interprovincial migration. J South China Normal Univ (Natural Science Edition) 49(3):84–91
52. Li Y, Liu H, Tang Q (2015) Spatial-temporal patterns of China's interprovincial migration during 1985–2010. Geograph Res 34(6):1135–1148
53. Liu Y, Shen J (2017) Modelling skilled and less-skilled interregional migrations in China, 2000–2005. Popul Space Place 23(4):e2027
54. Liu Y, Xu W (2017) Destination choices of permanent and temporary migrants in China, 1985–2005. Popul Space Place 23(1):e1963
55. Liu Z, Wang Y, Chen S (2017) Does formal housing encourage settlement intention of rural migrants in Chinese cities? A structural equation model analysis. Urban Stud 54(8):1834–1850
56. Lu M, Gao H, Sato H (2012) On urban size and inclusive employment. Soc Sci China 10:47–66 (in Chinese)
57. Lu M, Ou H, Chen B (2014) Rationality or bubble? An empirical study on urbanization, migration and housing prices. J World Econ 37(1):30–54 (in Chinese)
58. Lowry I (1966) Migration and metropolitan growth: Two analytical reports. Chandler, San Francisco, CA
59. Lyon M, Cheung LC, Gastwirth JL (2016) The advantages of using group means in estimating the Lorenz curve and Gini index from grouped data. Am Statistician 70(1):25–32
60. Marshall A (1890) Principles of economics (8th ed.). Macmillan published in 1920, London
61. Massey DS, Arango J, Hugo G, Kouaouci A, Pellegrino A, Taylor JE (1993) Theories of international migration: A review and appraisal. Popul Develop Rev 19:431–466
62. Matérn B (1971) Doubly stochastic Poisson processes in the plane. Stat Ecol 1:195–213
63. Metulini R, Patuelli R, Griffith DA (2018) A spatial-filtering zero-inflated approach to the estimation of the gravity model of trade. Econometrics 6(1):9
64. National Development and Reform Commission (2016) National New Urbanization Plan (2014–2020)
65. Piore MJ (1979) Birds of passage: Migrant labor and industrial societies. Cambridge University Press, Cambridge
66. Plane DA, Mulligan GF (1997) Measuring spatial focusing in a migration system. Demography 34(2):251–262

67. Pu Y, Ge Y (2016) Multilateral mechanism analysis of interprovincial migration flows in China. Acta Geogr Sin 26(2):205–216 (in Chinese)
68. Pu Y, Han H, Ge Y, Kong F (2016) Multilateral mechanism analysis of interprovincial migration flows in China. Acta Geogr Sin 71(2):205–216
69. Qi W, Abel G, Muttarak R, Liu S (2017) Circular visualization of China's internal migration flows 2010–2015. Environ Plann A Econ Space 49(11):2432–2436
70. Rogers A, Raymer J (1998) The spatial focus of US interstate migration flows. Int J Popul Geogr 4(1):63–80
71. Rogers A, Willekens F, Little J, Raymer J (2002) Describing migration spatial structure. Papers Reg Sci 81(1):29–48
72. Shen J (2012) Changing patterns and determinants of interprovincial migration in China 1985–2000. Popul Space Place 18(3):384–402
73. Shen J (2013) Increasing internal migration in China from 1985 to 2005: Institutional versus economic drivers. Habitat Int 39:1–7
74. Shen J (2015) Explaining interregional migration changes in China, 1985–2000, using a decomposition approach. Reg Stud 49(7):1176–1192
75. Shen J (2016) Error analysis of regional migration modeling. Annals Am Assoc Geograph 106(6):1253–1267
76. Shen J (2017) Modelling interregional migration in China in 2005–2010: The roles of regional attributes and spatial interaction effects in modelling error. Popul Space Place 23(3):e2014
77. Stark O, Bloom DE (1985) The new economics of labor migration. Am Econ Rev 75(2):173–178
78. Theil H (1972) Statistical decomposition analysis; with applications in the social and administrative sciences (No. 04; HA33, T4.). North-Holland Pub. Co., CA
79. Tiefelsdorf M, Boots B (1995) The exact distribution of Moran's I. Environ Plann A 27:985–999
80. Tiefelsdorf M, Griffith DA (2007) Semiparametric filtering of spatial autocorrelation: The eigenvector approach. Environ Plann A 39(5):1193–1221
81. Tobler WR (1970) A computer movie simulating urban growth in the Detroit region. Econ Geogr 46(sup1):234–240
82. Todaro MP (1969) A model of labor migration and urban unemployment in less developed countries. Am Econ Rev 59(1):138–148
83. Wang GX, Pan ZH, Lu YQ (2012) China's inter-provincial migration patterns and influential factors: Evidence from year 2000 and 2010 population census of China. Chinese J Popul Sci 5:2–13
84. Wang G, Pan Z (2016) The robustness of China's migration and Heihe-Tengchong line. China Popul Today 4(8) (in Chinese).
85. White M (1986) Segregation and diversity measures in population distribution. Popul Index 52(2):198–221
86. Wu HX (1994) Rural to urban migration in the People's Republic of China. China Quart 139:669–698
87. Wilson AG (1967) A statistical theory of spatial distribution models. Transp Res 1(3):253–269
88. Wilson AG (1970) Entropy in urban and regional modelling. Pion, London
89. Wooldridge JM (2010) Econometric analysis of cross section and panel data. MIT press, Cambridge
90. Yang C, Ning Y (2015) Evolution of spatial pattern of inter-provincial migration and its impacts on urbanization in China. Geograph Res 34(8):1492–1506
91. Yang L, Hui L, Qing T (2015) Spatial-temporal patterns of China's interprovincial migration during 1985–2010. Geograph Res 34(6):1135–1148 (in Chinese)
92. Yitzhaki S (1983) On an extension of the Gini inequality index. Int Econ Rev 24(3):617
93. Zahn H, Steif A, Laks E, Eirew P, VanInsberghe M, Shah S et al (2017) Scalable whole-genome single-cell library preparation without preamplification. Nat Methods 14(2):167–173
94. Zang YZ, Zhou SL, Wu YY (2016) The volume changes and spatial pattern dynamics of China's interprovincial migration: A perspective of social network analysis. Human Geogr 4:16 (in Chinese)

95. Zeng M, Wu R, Zhang S (2013) Research on new situation of Chinese population redistribution and its socio-economic effects: Based on the analysis of Chinese sixth census data. Popul J 35(5):15–25 (in Chinese)
96. Zhang H, Liang Y, Yang W (2016) Market potential, expected wages and interprovincial migration—Based on spatial econometrics model. J Appl Stat Manage 35(5):868–880
97. Zipf GK (1946) The P 1 P 2/D hypothesis: On the intercity movement of persons. Am Sociol Rev 11(6):677–686

Chapter 2
Migration at the City Level

2.1 Spatial Patterns and Driving Factors of Migration at the City Level

2.1.1 Changes in the Spatial Patterns of In-Migration at the City Level

This study uses the 335 prefectural and higher level cities as its research subjects, selects the data of population inflows by county in the fifth and sixth census, and analyzes the spatial patterns of urban population flows at the prefectural and higher levels and their changes from the point of view of time and space. In this study, the in-migrants in prefectural and higher level cities refer to the floating population who leave their place of household registration and migrate to their current residence for "more than half a year," including the in-migrants from the same province (from another county/city or urban district to a given city in a given province) and other provinces (from another province to a given city), namely, intraprovincial population migration and interprovincial population migration. Only the in-migrants to prefectural cities are studied, without considering the out-migrants from prefectural cities. Moreover, migration size is indicated directly by the number of the in-migrants, and migration intensity is measured by the immigration rate, the ratio of the number of the in-migrants to the total population of a given city.

2.1.1.1 The Spatial Distribution Patterns of the Size of Population Flows at the Prefectural Level and Their Changes

According to the Report on China's Migrant Population Development in 2012, among China's cities that absorb migrant population, the top 50 cities concentrate more than 60% of China's migrant population. Municipalities, cities specifically designated in the state plan, provincial capital cities, prefectural and lower level cities' migrant population account for 13.2, 18.6, 22.3, 45.9% of China's total migrant population, respectively. Under this main population migration character, this study analyzes the detailed patterns of population migration changes between the two censuses, from the aspects of spatial distribution pattern and spatial focusing degree.

(1)   **The higher a city's level was, the more migrants it attracted; interprovincial floating population mainly concentrated in the three metropolitan areas with top increase rates in the list of cities; intraprovincial floating population were fragmentally distributed in provincial capital cities; centers of interprovincial and intraprovincial migration were both moving north**

Among China's prefectural and higher level cities, there are four municipalities, five cities specifically designated in the state plan, ten sub-provincial cities, seventeen regular provincial capital cities, and other regular prefectural cities. These divisions are mainly administratively oriented and the allocation of resources among these cities is highly influenced by their administrative level, which further influences the difference of population migration size among the cities with different levels. Table 1.1 shows that, except the intraprovincial migration in 2000, the general trend of intra- and interprovincial migration and the increase rates of population migration echo the hierarchical division of China's cities, namely, municipalities attract more migrants than cities specifically designated in the state plan and sub-provincial cities, cities specifically designated in the state plan and sub-provincial cities are more attractive than regular provincial capital cities, and provincial capital cities absorb more migrants than regular prefecture-level cities.

Analysis of China's prefecture and higher-level cities (335 prefectural administrative units) shows that there are increasing differences of population migration size among different prefecture-level cities. For instance, in 2000, Shenzhen had the largest scale of population migration (the sum of interprovincial migration and intraprovincial migration), with a total floating population of 5,848,539, while the Ali prefecture in Tibet had the smallest migration size, just 4,143 migrants, over 1,400 times smaller than the size of Shenzhen. In 2010, Shanghai had the largest scale of population migration, with a total floating population of 11,016,029, while the Ali prefecture was still the city that had the smallest migration size, with 6,988 migrants and more than 1,500 times smaller than Shanghai's migration size. In 2000, among the top 25 cities that attracted most floating population, there were four municipalities, four cities specifically designated in the state plan, nine provincial capital cities, and eight regular prefecture-level cities, all of which had more than 600,000 migrants, accounting for 52.5% of China's entire floating population. In 2010, among the top 25 cities that attracted most floating population, there were still four municipalities, four cities specifically designated in the state plan, ten provincial capital cities, and seven regular prefectural cities, all of which had more than 1,600,000 migrants, accounting for 53.7% of China's entire floating population. Moreover, interprovincial migrants in Dongguan, Shanghai, Beijing, Wenzhou, Quanzhou, Huizhou and Tianjin were both more than 70% in 2000 and 2010, which indicates that the change of time does not weaken these cities' strong attraction to interprovincial migrants (Table 2.1).

In general, interprovincial population flows at the prefectural level were 45,035,256 and 85,502,551 in 2000 and 2010, respectively. Interprovincial population migration at the prefecture level had the following characteristics in spatial distribution (see Fig. 2.1): (1) interprovincial migrants concentrated mostly in southeast coastal areas; cities that had largest floating population (more than one million) were located in the Yangtze River Delta, the Pearl River Delta and the Beijing-Tianjin-Hebei metropolitan areas; besides these three metropolitan areas, cities that had huge floating population (100,000–1 million) were scattered in central and western regions, including important provincial capital cities such as Chongqing, Chengdu, Urumqi, Kunming, Xi'an and Wuhan; other cities in central and western regions had relatively small scale of floating population. (2) The spatial distribution patterns of interprovincial population migration at the prefecture level between the two censuses remained unchanged, but the size of interprovincial floating population in the vast majority of prefecture-level cities increased (compared with 2000, there were more cities with high volume of floating population in 2010). The spatial pattern of the increased volume of interprovincial floating population was similar to the spatial pattern of interprovincial population migration; the larger a city's size of interprovincial population migration, the greater the increased volume of interprovincial population migration. (3) The center of interprovincial population migration between the two censuses moved toward the northeast; in 2000, the center of interprovincial population migration was (114.70 °E, 29.58 °N), located in east Xianning in Hubei province, while in 2010, the center of interprovincial population migration moved to (115.87 °E, 30.54 °N), located in east Huanggang, Hubei province.

In contrast, intraprovincial population flows at the prefecture level were 36,125,615 and 84,305,254 in 2000 and 2010, respectively. Intraprovincial population migration at the prefecture level had the following characteristics in spatial distribution (see Fig. 2.2): (1) the distribution of intraprovincial population migration was relatively fragmented, the largest hubs of intraprovincial population migration were several provincial capital cities, and Chengdu, Wuhan, Chongqing's size of intrapovincial population migration ranked in the top-ten list in both 2000 and 2010. (2) The spatial distribution patterns of intraprovincial population migration at the prefectural level between the two censuses remained unchanged, but the vast majority of prefecture-level cities' size of intraprovincial population migration increased (compared with 2000, the dark area expanded in 2010). The spatial pattern of the increased volume of intraprovincial population migration was similar to the spatial pattern of intraprovincial population migration; the larger a city's size of intraprovincial population migration, the larger the increased volume of intraprovincial population migration. (3) The center of intraprovincial population migration moved to the northwest direction; in 2000, the center of intraprovincial population migration was (114.14 °E, 31.34 °N), located in northeast Xiaogan in Hubei province, while in 2010, the center of intraprovincial population migration moved to (113.97 °E, 32.09 °N), located in west Xinyang, Henan province.

Table 2.1 Rank of population migration among prefectural cities with different levels

City types	Migration rank in 2000		Migration rank in 2010		Intraprovincial migration	Interprovincial migration
	Intra provincial	Inter provincial	Intra provincial	Inter provincial	Rank of increase	Rank of increase
Municipalities						
Beijing	59	4	6	2	2	2
Tianjin	164	10	27	7	14	4
Shanghai	2	3	5	1	13	1
Chongqing	9	20	7	20	4	19
Cities specifically designated in the state plan and sub-provincial cities						
Dalian	37	19	28	25	21	27
Ningbo	24	13	37	10	40	7
Qingdao	23	33	15	28	12	26
Xiamen	22	18	23	19	22	18
Shenzhen	1	2	2	3	17	5
Shenyang	30	31	12	34	9	35
Changchun	34	58	31	51	27	57
Harbin	18	61	24	60	25	63
Nanjing	16	22	9	22	8	21
Hangzhou	11	15	17	11	20	8
Jinan	42	66	21	46	15	40
Wuhan	6	29	4	30	3	32
Guangzhou	3	5	3	6	6	12
Chengdu	4	34	1	27	1	24
Xi'an	35	30	14	29	10	29
Regular provincial capital cities						
Shijiazhuang	28	37	34	58	32	114
Taiyuan	40	42	30	43	24	48
Hohhot	26	98	25	68	23	54
Hefei	27	131	11	59	7	41
Fuzhou	14	21	22	24	26	25
Nanchang	29	112	32	61	30	45
Zhengzhou	48	48	48	48	48	48
Changsha	13	74	16	48	16	44
Nanning	17	84	19	50	18	43
Haikou	66	40	44	41	38	46
Guiyang	15	36	26	44	28	60
Kunming	8	14	13	33	19	335

(continued)

Table 2.1 (continued)

City types	Migration rank in 2000		Migration rank in 2010		Intraprovincial migration	Interprovincial migration
	Intra provincial	Inter provincial	Intra provincial	Inter provincial	Rank of increase	Rank of increase
Lhasa	262	103	274	108	260	122
Lanzhou	41	59	40	56	34	61
Xi'ning	122	86	60	66	50	53
Yinchuan	96	55	53	45	48	47
Urumqi	38	24	36	26	33	30
The average rank						
Municipalities	59	9	11	8	8	7
Cities specifically designated in the state plan and sub provincial cities	20	35	14	32	12	32
Regular provincial capital cities	52	63	46	52	43	72

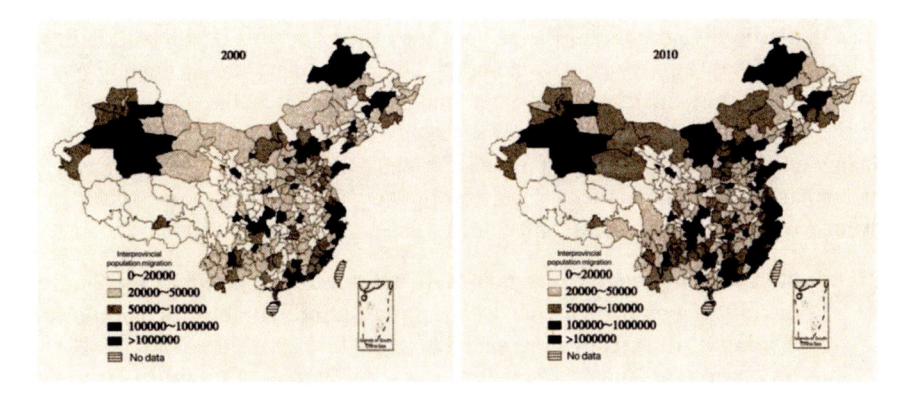

Fig. 2.1 Spatial pattern of the size of interprovincial population migration at the prefectural level in 2000 and 2010

At the same time, centers of both interprovincial population migration and intraprovincial population migration moved north, indicating that the attractiveness of cities in the Pearl River Delta as China's primary migration hub relatively weakened, and the attractiveness of the Yangtze River Delta and the Beijing-Tianjin-Hebei region was gradually rising.

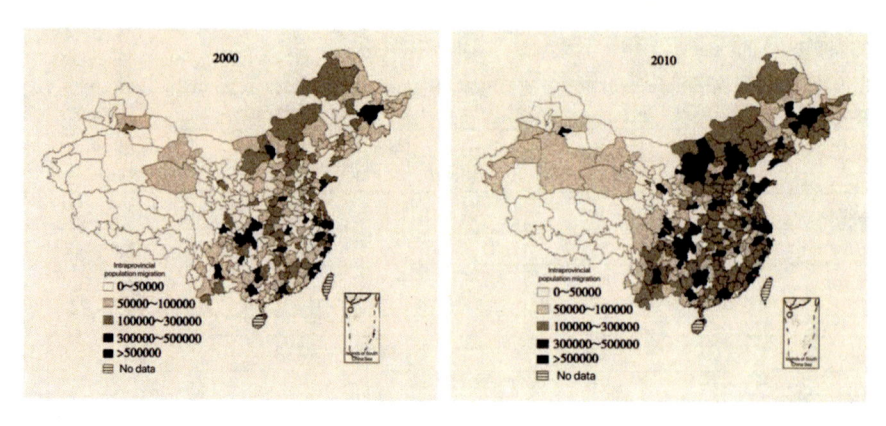

Fig. 2.2 Spatial pattern of the size of intraprovincial population migration at the prefectural level in 2000 and 2010

Table 2.2 shows that provincial capital cities in central and western regions' attractiveness to intraprovincial floating population was stronger than that of provincial capital cities in eastern coastal provinces; the former was basically the main destination for floating population within that given province and with strong attractiveness (its proportion was generally higher than 40% of the entire population migration of a given province), the latter's attractiveness to floating population was relatively weaker (its proportion was generally less than 40%). Other developed cities in eastern coastal provinces were not less attractive to floating population, compared to capital cities in these provinces. From the perspective of the direction of population flow, the capital city of a province was more attractive to intraprovincial floating population than interprovincial floating population; provincial capital cities accounted for the biggest proportion of the entire intraprovincial floating population (except Guangdong, Shandong, Jiangsu provinces), while the largest in-migrant group in interprovincial floating population were more likely economic developed cities in a given province (non-provincial capital cities), especially in eastern coastal provinces.

(2) **Spatial focusing degree of interprovincial floating population was higher than that of intraprovincial floating population; the hub of population migration moved from the Pearl River Delta area to the Yangtze River Delta area; the spatial focusing degree of intra- and interprovincial population migration remained unchanged**

From the analysis of the spatial distribution patterns of the size of population migration, we can see that the spatial distribution of population migration is uneven. Studying the unevenness of the spatial distribution of population migration will help to understand the spatial development trend of population flow, so as to explore how population change in a single city influences other cities' population change through population migration.

This study uses the coefficient of variation (CV) to analyze the degree of spatial focusing of population migration at prefecture-level cities [1]. In 2000, the CV value

Table 2.2 The top one city in intraprovincial floating population and interprovincial floating population in all provinces and its proportion of the entire floating population in a given province

Province	Intraprovincial migration		Interprovincial migration	
	2000	2010	2000	2010
Hebei	Shijiazhuang 24.97	Shijiazhuang 26.93	Shijiazhuang 18.16	Langfang 22.76
Shanxi	Taiyuan 27.94	Taiyuan 37.38	Datong 24.54	Taiyuan 30.46
Inner Mongolia	Hohhot 24.86	Hohhot 31.10	Hulunbuir 28.26	Ordos 28.39
Liaoning	Shenyang 22.31	Shenyang 34.62	Dalian 38.71	Dalian 43.87
Jilin	Changchun 39.86	Changchun 53.89	Changchun 34.60	Changchun 47.11
Helongjiang	Harbin 27.71	Harbin 41.72	Harbin 26.09	Harbin 38.46
Jiangsu	Suzhou 17.95	Nanjing 21.91	Suzhou 28.03	Suzhou 42.74
Zhejiang	Hangzhou 26.38	Hangzhou 31.97	Wenzhou 27.68	Wenzhou 23.04
Anhui	Hefei 31.47	Hefei 43.29	Hefei 16.99	Hefei 27.35
Fujian	Fuzhou 26.24	Fuzhou 27.03	Quanzhou 42.99	Quanzhou 39.22
Jiangxi	Nanchang 37.49	Nanchang 49.54	Jiujiang 19.20	Nanchang 32.39
Shandong	Qingdao 19.77	Qingdao 23.94	Qingdao 20.72	Qingdao 28.10
Henan	Zhengzhou 31.05	Zhengzhou 44.70	Zhengzhou 29.62	Zhengzhou 41.86
Hubei	Wuhan 46.43	Wuhan 60.69	Wuhan 43.17	Wuhan 54.95
Hunan	Changsha 30.91	Changsha 39.58	Changsha 22.97	Changsha 31.89
Guangdong	Shenzhen 29.94	Shenzhen 25.09	Dongguan 27.46	Shenzhen 26.96
Guangxi	Nanning 27.89	Nanning 36.39	Liuzhou 17.83	Nanning 26.29
Hainan	Haikou 84.60	Haikou 84.63	Haikou 79.02	Haikou 71.49
Sichuan	Chengdu 48.72	Chengdu 56.55	Chengdu 33.51	Chengdu 53.28
Guizhou	Guiyang 49.09	Guiyang 49.13	Guiyang 41.41	Guiyang 35.72
Yunnan	Kunming 41.14	Kunming 45.23	Kunming 49.70	Kunming 36.14
Tibet	Lhasa 61.81	Lhasa 50.99	Lhasa 47.41	Lhasa 48.07
Shaanxi	Xi'an 41.06	Xi'an 56.66	Xi'an 56.90	Xi'an 60.10
Gansu	Lanzhou 43.76	Lanzhou 48.28	Lanzhou 46.06	Lanzhou 47.63
Qinghai	Xining 44.03	Xining 62.31	Xining 54.18	Xining 57.88
Ningxia	Yinchuan 52.62	Yinchuan 66.48	Yinchuan 57.89	Yinchuan 71.79
Xinjiang	Urumqi 49.28	Urumqi 53.59	Urumqi 30.31	Urumqi 41.33

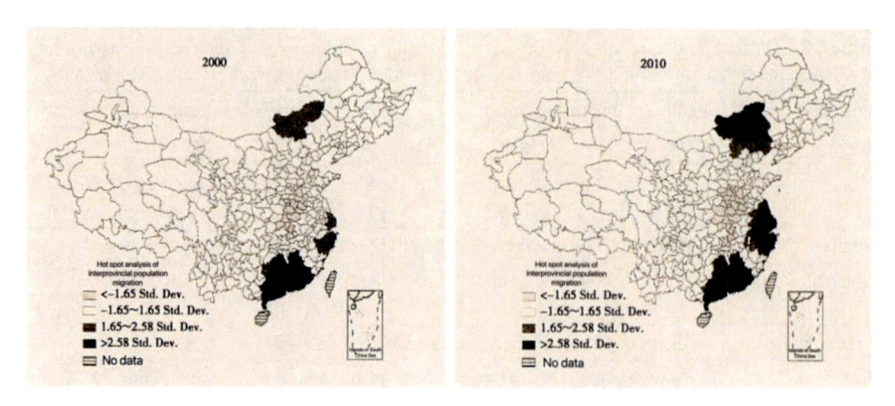

Fig. 2.3 Hot spot analysis of the size of interprovincial population migration at the prefectural level in 2000 and 2010

of prefecture-level cities' intraprovincial population migration was 1.648,while the CV value of interprovincial population migration was 3.360; in 2010, the CV value of intraprovincial population migration was 1.651, while the CV value of interprovincial population migration was 3.334. It shows that the degree of spatial focusing of interprovincial floating population was higher than intraprovincial floating population's, namely, interprovincial migrants were more likely to concentrate in several national cities, while intraprovincial migrants moved to various cities (mostly provincial capital cities) in a relatively even manner. Between the two censuses, the CV values of intra- and interprovincial population migration remained unchanged, indicating that floating population's distribution in each in-migration city was stable in general.

After measuring the degree of spatial focusing of prefecture-level cities' floating population size, hot spot analysis is further used to explore the major in- and out-migration fields' whereabouts. ArcGIS's Hot Spot Analysis tool (Getis-ord Gi*) can identify spatial clusters with statistically significant high value (hot spot) and low value (cold spot). Figure 2.3 shows that high value concentration areas of interprovincial population migration in 2000 were mostly distributed in the Pearl River Delta, while in 2010 the Yangtze River Delta area's high value concentration areas gradually expanded and the Pearl River Delta's concentration areas shrank relatively. It shows that cities in the Yangtze River Delta became more attractive to migrants, while cities in the Pearl River Delta became relatively less attractive to migrants, echoing the trend that the center of interprovincial population migration moved northward. Figure 2.4 shows, high value concentration areas of intraprovincial population migration in 2000 were also distributed in the Pearl River Delta, indicating the highly active intraprovincial population migration within that region. However, in 2010, intraprovincial population migration's concentration areas became less distinctive, and the Yangtze River Delta and the Pearl River Delta evenly absorbed intraprovincial migrants. In general, during the two censuses, the hot spots of population migration were mainly located in the Pearl River Delta and the Yangtze River Delta, and expanding northward from

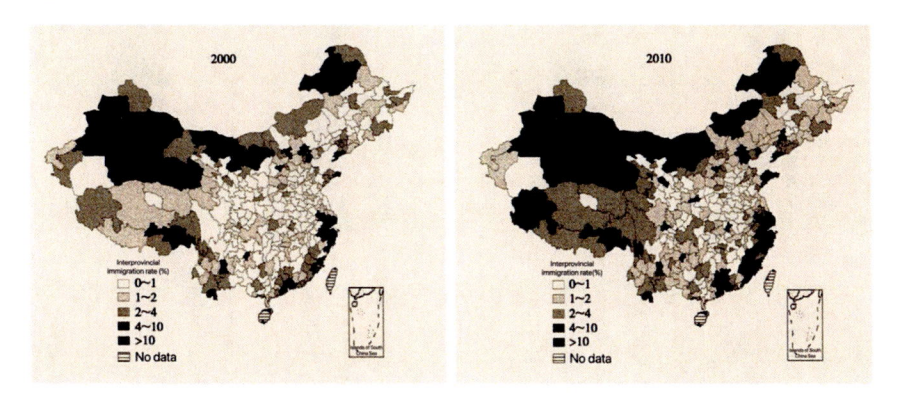

Fig. 2.4 Hot spot analysis of the size of intraprovincial population migration at the prefectural level in 2000 and 2010

the Pearl River Delta region to the Yangtze River Delta region. Low concentration areas were less statistically significant than high concentration areas, and they had relatively small sizes. The low value cluster of interprovincial population migration was located in the intersection of Henan, Hubei, and Anhui provinces, which was the main source of out-migration in China; the low concentration area of intraprovincial population migration lied on the border between Gansu and Qinghai provinces, which might be due to the fact that the region was vast and sparsely populated with a small population size, and therefore the size of intraprovincial floating population was small as well.

2.1.1.2 The Spatial Patterns of the Distribution of the Population Migration Intensity at the Prefectural Level and Their Changes

(1) **The intensity of interprovincial migration formed a pattern of "high in northwest—southeast and low in the middle;" the distribution pattern of intraprovincial migration intensity was similar to that of intraprovincial migration size, but the migration intensity in the northwest frontier region was relatively high; cities with high immigration rates also had higher increase in population inflows**

As to the spatial patterns of the intensity of interprovincial population migration (see Fig. 2.5), the cities with high rates of interprovincial migrants were mainly located in eastern coastal regions (especially cities in the Yangtze River Delta, the Pearl River Delta and the Beijing-Tianjin-Hebei metropolitan areas), in addition to a few cities in northwest China. The latter included Lhasa, Urumqi and its surrounding cities including Karamay, Bayingolin Mongol Autonomous prefecture, Nyingchi area, Alxa League and so on, indicating that major cities in the northwest region (especially Xinjiang) had high rates of interprovincial migrants. This was influenced

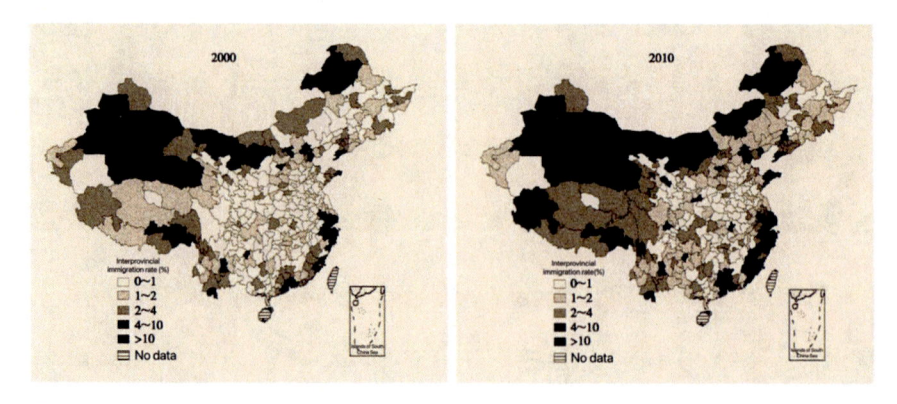

Fig. 2.5 Spatial pattern of the intensity of interprovincial population migration at the prefectural level in 2000 and 2010

by the strategy of developing the western region of China, resulting in intense population flows. In general, the northwest and southeast areas had high interprovincial immigration rates, while the central region's immigration rate was low, forming a "funnel"-shaped spatial distribution pattern with high value in the periphery and low value in the middle. Comparing the spatial distribution pattern of the intensity of interprovincial floating population with that of the size of interprovincial floating population, the size of migration was not big in northwestern cities, but the intensity of migration was very high. Major cities in central China had a large size of population migration, yet the intensity was not high. Cities in the eastern coastal region ranked in the top list both in migration size and migration intensity.

As to the spatial pattern of the intensity of intraprovincial population migration (see Fig. 2.6), the distribution of immigration rates was relatively fragmented. Cities with high immigration rates were mostly provincial capital cities. The distribution pattern of immigration rates was similar to that of inflow size; the only difference

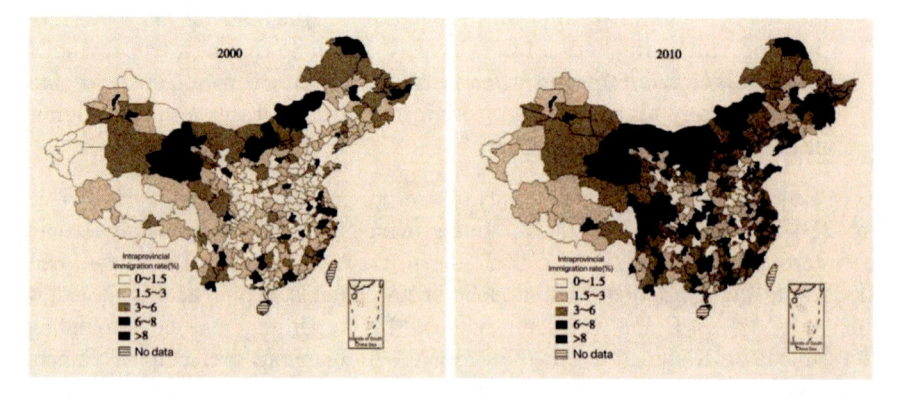

Fig. 2.6 Spatial pattern of the intensity of intraprovincial population migration at the prefectural level in 2000 and 2010

was in the northwest frontier region, the size of intraprovincial floating population was not big, but the immigration rate was very high.

Between the two censuses, the distribution patterns of the intensity of inter- and intraprovincial population migration at the prefectural level remained unchanged, with a certain degreed increase in the intensity of population migration in the vast majority of cities (compared with 2000, more cities had high immigration rates in 2010). The spatial pattern of the increased value of population migration intensity was similar to that of the intensity of population migration—the higher the intensity of population migration, the higher the increased value of population migration intensity. In other words, the migration intensity of most major in-migration places was "the high remain high, and the high get higher." That is, being affected by cumulative effect, the distribution of population migration became more concentrated. This was consistent with the evolving process of the aforementioned spatial distribution patterns of population migration size.

Table 2.3 shows the intensity of intra- and interprovincial population migration at the prefectural level in all provinces, with following characteristics: (1) compared with the top one city in migration size, the proportion of provincial capital cities being the top one in migration intensity dropped greatly. Provincial capital cities were more likely to be the top one city in intraprovincial immigration rate, rather than in interprovincial immigration rate, which was similar to that of the size of migration. Only in Henan, Hubei, Guizhou, Tibet, Shaanxi and Ningxia, the capital cities ranked first both in intraprovincial immigration rate and interprovincial immigration rate, and all of these provinces were net out-migration provinces. (2) The top one city in major in-migration provinces (Guangdong, Jiangsu, Zhejiang, Fujian) had high interprovincial immigration rate, while the top one city in major out-migration provinces (Henan, Sichuan, Anhui, Jiangxi, Hubei, Hunan, Guangxi) had low interprovincial immigration rate. This was in line with the actual situation. Among them, Guangdong was the province with the highest intraprovincial immigration rate and interprovincial immigration rate. In 2000 and 2010, Shenzhen's intraprovincial immigration rate was 25.58 and 23.96%, respectively; while Dongguan's interprovincial immigration rate was respectively as high as 64.17 and 64.87%, the most attractive city among all Chinese cities. (3) Except several major in-migration provinces (Guangdong, Jiangsu, Zhejiang, Fujian, Tibet, Xinjiang), the top one city's intraprovincial immigration rate was always higher than the city's interprovincial immigration rate in the rest provinces, indicating that the intensity of intraprovincial population migration was higher than the intensity of interprovincial population migration in most provinces. The intraprovincial population migration was dominant in population inflows in most prefecture-level cities. (4) Between the two censuses, in all provinces, the top one in-migration city's immigration rate was increasing, indicating that the top city became increasingly attractive to the in-migrant.

(2) **Population migration intensity's spatial focusing degree was lower than that of population migration size, and its distribution and evolution were more even; besides the two hot spots of Pearl River Delta area and the**

Table 2.3 The top one city in intraprovincial immigration rate and interprovincial immigration rate in all provinces and the immigration rates (%)

Province	Intraprovincial immigration rate		Interprovincial immigration rate	
	2000	2010	2000	2010
Hebei	Shijiazhuang 3.25	Zhangjiakou 7.41	Qinhuangdao 3.69	Langfang 7.33
Shanxi	Taiyuan 6.62	Taiyuan 19.48	Datong 5.46	Taiyuan 6.75
Inner Mogolia	Hohhot 12.73	Hohhot 32.48	Alxa League 10.34	Alxa League 25.20
Liaoning	Panjin 6.51	Shenyang 15.48	Dalian 6.86	Dalian 11.72
Jilin	Yanbian 4.48	Changchun 9.84	Yanbian Korean Autonomous prefecture 3.47	Yanbian Korean Autonomous prefecture 3.73
Heilongjiang	Da Hinggan Mountains prefecture 11.06	Qitaihe 12.59	Qitaihe 3.52	Da Hinggan Mountains prefecture 2.50
Jiangsu	Wuxi 7.32	Nanjing 17.25	Suzhou 10.47	Suzhou 30.15
Zhejiang	Hangzhou 6.66	Hangzhou 12.68	Wenzhou 13.51	Wenzhou 29.87
Anhui	Hefei 6.72	Hefei 22.44	Ma'anshan1.07	Wuhu 3.70
Fujian	Xiamen 16.21	Xiamen 27.31	Xiamen 20.22	Xiamen 28.99
Jiangxi	Nanchang 6.54	Nanchang 14.32	Jiujiang 1.10	Nanchang 3.85
Shandong	Dongying 7.67	Jinan 14.31	Weihai 5.41	Weihai 8.22
Henan	Zhengzhou 7.16	Zhengzhou 20.28	Zhengzhou 2.12	Zhengzhou 2.85
Hubei	Wuhan 8.84	Wuhan 22.89	Wuhan 3.01	Wuhan 5.38
Hunan	Changsha 7.16	Changsha 16.88	Zhuzhou 1.34	Changsha 3.28
Guangdong	Shenzhen 25.58	Shenzhen 23.96	Dongguan 64.17	Dongguan 64.87
Guangxi	Liuzhou 15.51	Nanning 15.93	Liuzhou 3.64	Beihai 3.78
Hainan	Haikou 15.33	Haikou 21.22	Haikou 19.47	Sanya 17.70
Sichuan	Chengdu 9.70	Chengdu 23.29	Suining 3.57	Chengdu 4.28
Guizhou	Guiyang 11.15	Guiyang 20.93	Guiyang 4.55	Guiyang 6.31
Yunan	Xishuangbanna Dai Autonomous prefecture10.54	Kunming 18.97	Kunming 10.01	Kunming 6.95
Tibet	Lhasa 5.80	Lhasa 8.66	Lhasa 10.86	Lhasa 14.21
Shaanxi	Xi'an 3.47	Xi'an 14.39	Xi'an 3.33	Xi'an 6.91
Gansu	Jiayuguan 10.19	Lanzhou 15.94	Jiayuguan 5.31	Jiuquan 6.93
Qinghai	Haixi Mongol and Tibetan Autonomous prefecture 16.74	Haixi Mongol and Tibetan Autonomous prefecture 19.48	Haixi Mongol and Tibetan Autonomous prefecture 9.37	Haixi Mongol and Tibetan Autonomous prefecture 15.16
Ningxia	Yinchuan 7.80	Yinchuan 16.34	Yinchuan 9.43	Yinchuan 12.63

(continued)

Table 2.3 (continued)

Province	Intraprovincial immigration rate		Interprovincial immigration rate	
	2000	2010	2000	2010
Xinjiang	Urumqi 10.95	Urumqi 19.91	Ili Kazak autonomous prefecture 18.66	Urumqi 22.05

Yangtze River Delta area, there were high-value concentration areas of population migration intensity in cities in the northwest region

Similar to the analysis of the spatial patterns of the size of population migration, we measure the CV values of the intensity of population migration at the prefectural level to gauge the spatial focusing degree. In 2000, the CV value of intraprovincial immigration rate was 1.086, while the CV value of interprovincial immigration rate was 2.110; in 2010, the CV value of intraprovincial immigration rate was 0.934, while the CV value of interprovincial immigration rate was 1.757. Similar to the size of population migration, the intensity of interprovincial population migration's spatial focusing degree was higher than the intensity of intraprovincial population migration. That is, the former's high inflow intensity was concentrated in certain major in-migration cities, while the latter's inflow intensity was relatively evenly distributed among several cities. Compared with the size of population migration, population migration intensity's spatial focusing degree was relatively lower. This might be due to the fact that population immigration rates were not directly influenced by the population base of a given city, thus immigration rates' spatial distribution was more even. Between the two censuses, the intensity of intra- and interprovincial population migration's spatial focusing degree both decreased, indicating that population migration intensity's distribution among cities had developed into a more even mode. Secondly, we still use hot spot analysis to investigate spatial focusing changes of prefectural level population migration. In terms of interprovincial immigration rate, the hot spot of interprovincial immigration rate was located in the Pearl River Delta in 2000; in 2010, the hot spot expanded northwards to the Yangtze River Delta, echoing the hot spot distribution pattern of the size of interprovincial population migration. At the same time, most areas surrounding Urumqi in Xinjiang Uygur autonomous region became the hot spots as well. Cold spot area was large and gradually expanded from north China to southwest China in Sichuan and Guizhou provinces, in line with major out-migration provinces in central China. In terms of intraprovincial immigration rate, the hot spot was mainly in the Pearl River Delta in 2000, and Inner Mongolia and Gansu provinces also had some hot spots; in 2010, hot spot areas mainly concentrated in Inner Mongolia (Hohhot, Baotou, Ulanchap, Ordos and Bayannur), and hot spot areas in the Yangtze River Delta and the Pearl River Delta areas became non-distinctive. In 2000, intraprovincial immigration rate's cold spot area covered the same area as interprovincial immigration rate did (provinces in north-central China), but the area was smaller; in 2010, cold spot area's range narrowed to Shaanxi and Henan provinces. Compared with population migration size's hot spot analysis results, in addition to the original hot spots—the Pearl River Delta and Yangtze River Delta, the northwest region (Xinjiang and Inner Mongolia) also had high value concentration in population migration intensity. This finding is consistent with Ding et al.'s [2, 3] research finding about China's interprovincial population migration: the net migration to Xinjiang, Tibet and Yunnan, the attractive "west-frontier" convergence area, was 1,350,100 from 1995 to 2000,in particular, the net migration to Xinjiang, totaled 950,100, ranking the fourth in China. In terms of intraprovincial population migration, Hohhot's intraprovincial immigration rate ranked the first among Chinese cities in 2010, reaching 32.48%. That was why it turned into a hot spot.

2.1.1.3 The Distribution of Out-Migratory Field for Major In-Migration Cities

In analyzing the spatial patterns of population migration, in addition to simple descriptions of the spatial characteristics of demographic index and applications of relevant spatial analysis methods, the migratory flow field distribution should also be explored. In this study, by sorting the size of interprovincial floating population, we select the top ten prefecture-level cities as major national in-migration cities and analyze the regional distribution pattern of their migratory fields (original provinces). The data we use here are from the 2000 and 2010 census data of the provinces to which these cities belong, specifically the long table of "residents' classified by current residence and their permanent residence in the preceding five-year period in a given province." Current residence in the census table is the prefecture-level city in a given province. There are 31 provinces in China. Let us suppose the floating population from a province i to a prefecture-level city j is M_{ij} and the proportion to the total number of immigration in the prefecture-level city j is SI_{ij}, then we can use SI_{ij} as the indicator of the out-migration province i's impact (the supply power) on the prefecture-level city j's inflow population. Let us set the threshold value as 5%. To a given city, the number of provinces whose SI_{ij} is greater than or equal to the set threshold is NI, which can be considered as "province i that impacts on a given city's inflow population, i.e., a given city's regional influence range (or influence circle)." We use NI as the ordinate and all provinces as the abscissa. According to the value of NI, we locate cities in the coordinate as major in-migration cities that have the most significant influence. Moreover, according to SI_{ij} and the set threshold, we connect the correspondent provinces on the abscissa with the selected major in-migration cities. In this way, we can expose the spatial patterns of interprovincial population migration's migratory field distribution at the prefectural level and their changes (see Fig. 2.7). The order of these major in-migration cities on the abscissa echoes that of their size of population migration, and SI_{ij} only lists two highest ranks—10–20% and above 20%. In addition, this study estimates the CV value of major in-migration cities' size of interprovincial population migration (see Fig. 2.7).

As showed in Fig. 2.7, main in-migration cities' distribution of out-migratory fields had the following characteristics.

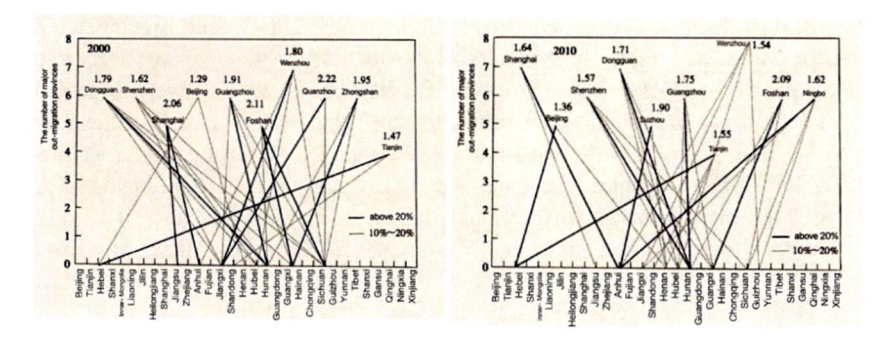

Fig. 2.7 Impact of the top ten in-migration cities on their main out-migration provinces

Firstly, in terms of major in-migration cities, the top ten in-migration cities contained Beijing, Shanghai, Guangzhou, several developed cities in Guangdong province, and several developed cities in eastern coastal provinces (Zhejiang, Jiangsu, Fujian). Among them, Guangdong province had the highest proportion and its influential areas to the in-migrants were also the broadest. In 2000, there were five Guangdong cities in the top ten list, while in 2010 the number dropped to four. In 2000, all cities in Guangdong ranked in the top spots, while in 2010, Beijing and Shanghai became more attractive, ranking the first and the second. This feature was consistent with the trend that the migration center moved northwards.

Secondly, in terms of mutual influential relationship between in-migration places and out-migration places, major out-migration provinces contained Anhui, Jiangxi, Henan, Hubei, Hunan, Guangxi, and Sichuan; except the two populous provinces Henan and Sichuan, the rest provinces' population migration were influenced by geographical proximity, and the in-migrants moved mainly to the neighboring provinces' prefecture-level cities. In this regard, the in-migration cities' influential provinces were distinctive: cities in Guangdong mainly attracted floating population from Hubei, Hunan, Guangxi, Sichuan and Jiangxi; Beijing and Tianjin mainly absorbed floating population from Hebei, Henan, and Shandong; eastern coastal cities (Wenzhou, Ningbo, Suzhou, Quanzhou) main influenced Anhui and Jiangxi; Shanghai mainly influenced Jiangsu and Anhui area. In terms of the number of inflow population, cities in Guangdong province ranked the top in both impact (SI) and influential range (NI).

Thirdly, in terms of the CV value of in-migranction cities, migrants' home provinces were more convergent in in-migration cities in the Yangtze River Delta and the Pearl River Delta areas than those in the Beijing-Tianjin-Hebei metropolitan area (the former had higher CV values). However, between the two censuses, the CV value of cities in the Yangtze River Delta and the Pearl River Delta region was on the decline, namely, in-migrant home provinces became more dispersed. In contrast, the CV value of Beijing and Tianjin increased, indicating that their in-migrant home provinces became more concentrated. The Beijing-Tianjin-Hebei region absorbed people from all parts of China. Although its impact on provinces was not big (with low SI), its influential range was broad (with high NI). Thus, its in-migrant spatial focusing degree was relatively low. Compared with cities in the Yangtze River Delta and the Pearl River Delta region, its in-migrant distribution was relatively dispersed. The distribution of migratory fields in cities in the Yangtze River Delta and the Pearl River Delta areas was mainly influenced by geographical proximity, so these cities' inflow fields were concentrated in their nearby provinces. Between these two newest censuses, in-migrant origin provinces in cities of the Beijing-Tianjin-Hebei region concentrated more and more in the neighboring area of Hebei and Henan provinces, while in-migrant origin provinces in cities of the Yangtze River Delta and the Pearl River Delta areas became increasingly diverse.

2.1.1.4 Conclusions and Discussion

This study uses spatial analysis techniques and data of two national censuses to make a comprehensively comparative study of the spatial patterns of China's population migration (including the spatial distribution pattern, spatial concentration intensity, and migratory field distribution), through different spatial units (the level of cities), different time dimensions (the fifth and sixth census), and different perspectives (migration direction—intraprovincial and interprovincial, migration size and intensity). Following are the research findings.

Firstly, the attractive centers of population migration were obvious. National migration hubs concentrated in three metropolitan areas of the Pearl River Delta, the Yangtze River Delta, and the Beijing-Tianjin-Hebei region, especially the Pearl River Delta area. Besides these three metropolitan areas, several cities in the northwestern border area (mostly Xinjiang) also had high intensity of population migration. The top ten in-migrant cities included Beijing, Shanghai, Guangzhou, other developed cities in Guangdong, and several developed cities in eastern coastal provinces (Zhejiang, Jiangsu, Fujian); among them, in-migrant origin provinces were less diverse in cities in the Pearl River Delta and the Yangtze River Delta areas, compared to cities in the Beijing-Tianjin-Hebei region. As major attractive hubs of intraprovincial population migration, central and western provincial capital cities' intraprovincial attractiveness was much stronger than that of eastern provincial capital cities. In major out-migration provinces (such as Henan, Hubei, and Guizhou), most in-migrants concentrated in the provincial capital cities, while in major in-migration provinces (such as Guangdong, Zhejiang, and Jiangsu), most in-migrants were scattered in various economic developed cities in these provinces.

Secondly, changes of the spatial distribution of population migration were obvious. Between the two censuses, the numbers of the in-migrant and the in-migration rates in the vast majority of prefectural cities have increased; the larger the size (intensity) of population migration, the larger the added volume of migrant population size (intensity). In the Yangtze and Pearl River Delta cities, in-migrant origin provinces became more diverse; while in the Beijing-Tianjin-Hebei region, in-migrant origin provinces became more concentrated. In terms of the size of population migration, between the two censuses, the spatial focusing degree of the size of intra- and interprovincial population migration remained unchanged in general; in terms of the intensity of population migration, between the two censuses, the spatial focusing degree of the intensity of intra- and interprovincial population migration both decreased, indicating that population migration intensity became more evenly distributed among cities; the attractive centers of national floating population moved from the Pearl River Delta to the Yangtze River Delta, and the center of floating population moved northwards as well; among the top ten in-migration cities, cities in the Pearl River Delta became less attractive, while cities in the Yangtze River Delta and the Beijing-Tianjin-Hebei region became more attractive.

Thirdly, the spatial distribution patterns of interprovincial population migration were different from those of intraprovincial population migration. Interprovincial floating population mostly moved to southeast coastal area; cities with the largest size of floating population concentrated in the three metropolitan circles of the Yangtze River Delta, the Pearl River Delta and the Beijing-Tianjin-Hebei region; the size of population migration in most cities in mid-west China was relatively small; the distribution of intraprovincial population migration was more scattered; cities with the largest sizes of floating population were mainly provincial capital cities; the spatial focusing degree of interprovincial population was higher than that of intraprovincial population migration, indicating that interprovincial floating population mostly moved to several national major cities in a relatively concentrated manner and intraprovincial floating population moved to each city (mostly provincial capital cities) in a more even way; provincial capital cities were more attractive to their provinces' intraprovincial floating population than interprovincial floating population; except several major in-migration provinces, the highest intraprovincial immigration rate in cities in the rest provinces was always higher than the highest interprovincial immigration rate.

Fourthly, the spatial distribution pattern of the size of population migration and that of the intensity of population migration were similar, with slight differences. The spatial distribution patterns of the size and the intensity of population migration were similar in general; the major differences were the following—cities in the northwest region had small migration size but high migration intensity, major cities in central China had big migration size but low migration intensity, and cities in eastern coastal region ranked the top both in migration size and migration intensity; population migration size was mostly influenced by the administrative level of a city, the higher the level of a city, the greater the number of in-migrants, while population migration intensity was relatively less influenced by the city's rank (compared with the top city in migration size in each province, the proportion of the provincial capital city being the top city in migration intensity dropped dramatically, namely, provincial cities that had a large migration size did not necessarily had high migration intensity).

In sum, changes of the spatial patterns of population migration at the prefecture and higher level Chinese cities from 2000 to 2010 were the following: cities in the east coastal areas (mainly the Yangtze River Delta, the Pearl River Delta and the Beijing-Tianjin-Hebei region) were still the attractive centers to population migration; between the two censuses, the significance of cities in the Pearl River Delta in attracting population migration relatively declined, while the significance of cities in the Yangtze River Delta and the Beijing-Tianjin-Hebei region rose; the center of population migration gradually moved northwards from the Pearl River Delta; between the two censuses, in the vast majority of prefecture-level cities, both the numbers of the in-migrants and the immigration rates increased, and the spatial distribution of the intensity of population migration developed into a more balanced way; the distribution of interprovincial population migration was more concentrated than the distribution of intraprovincial population migration—the former concentrated in several national major cities, while the latter sparsely distributed in each provincial capital city, and most prefecture-level cities mainly attracted intraprovincial migration; compared with population migration size, population migration intensity was less affected by city's level and it eliminated the influence of the population base of a given city, thus its spatial distribution was more even (its spatial focusing degree was lower than that of population migration size); in this regard, in the northwest frontier region (mainly in Xinjiang), cities' population migration size was not big but their migration intensity ranked the top among all Chinese cities.

This study's finding is consistent with similar studies' finding "the basic trend of population migration is still concentrating into coastal developed areas from inland China." Still, this study argues that "the distribution of size and intensity of interprovincial population migration at the prefecture level remain unchanged in general or have developed into a more balanced mode." However, Wang et al. [4] thought that interprovincial migration's trend of concentration becomes more obvious. This inconsistency may be due to various factors, such as difference of spatial units, difference of statistical data (interprovincial population migration refers to floating population whose current residence is different from the residence five years earlier), and different research methods (this study uses the coefficient of variation to measure population migration's spatial focusing degree, which can eliminate the dimension's influence). Secondly, about the distribution of migratory fields, through analyzing the mutually influential relationship between in-migration places and out-migration places, Wang et al. [4] pointed out that the Pearl River Delta is an important interprovincial in-migration polar that influences the out-migration of entire China, with a declining impact, however, the Yangtze River Delta and the Beijing-Tianjin-Hebei region are major in-migration places that only have regional influence, and the former has gradually developed into a national population migration destination, while the latter influences more regions, but the influence is relatively weak. Restricted by data availability, in this study, prefecture-level population migration is a one-way flow (only inflow data available), thus we can only analyze the impact of each out-migration province on major in-migration cities and unable to calculate the proportion of emigration from major in-migration cities to out-migration provinces. Yet, through calculating the coefficient of variation of each city, the conclusion that "in-migrant origin provinces are more dispersed in the cities in the Beijing-Tianjin-Hebei region, while in-migrant origin provinces are more concentrated in the cities in the Yangtze River Delta and Pearl River Delta" still has a certain reference value.

2.1.2 Spatial Pattern of Migration in a Certain Region

2.1.2.1 Introduction

The urban agglomeration in the middle reaches of the Yangtze River is an important part of the Yangtze River economic belt. As a new growth pole of China's economic development and a leading area of new-type urbanization in the central and western regions, it plays an important role in China's regional development strategy. The development plan of urban agglomeration in the middle reaches of the Yangtze River approved by the State Council defines its scope as 31 cities including Wuhan, Huangshi, Changsha, Zhuzhou, Nanchang and Jiujiang. It covers a land area of about 317,000 sq. km., and the regional GDP exceeded 6 trillion yuan and the total population was 127 million in 2014, accounting for 3.3, 9.7 and 9.3% of the country respectively. Influenced by national policies, urban agglomeration in the middle reaches of the Yangtze River has gradually become a research hot spot. In recent years, the studies on this urban agglomeration can be divided into the following three aspects: spatial interaction and competition and cooperation mechanism [5–7], industrial structure and economic ties [8, 9], regional development policies [10, 11]. In terms of population research, China's current research on population migration mainly includes the research on the number and attributes of population migration, the spatial pattern change of population migration, and the influencing factors of population migration. There are few studies on an important form of population migration-return migration [12, 13]. This study mainly analyzes the spatial pattern and evolution of population migration in the urban agglomeration in the middle reaches of the Yangtze River at the city level. At present, most studies on the spatial pattern of population migration in China analyze the regional differences in population migration from the provincial level [2, 3, 14, 15], the changes in the scale and intensity of migration population [16, 17], and identify population migration attraction centers and population outmigration centers [18–20], There are few studies focusing on the city level [21, 22]. The extant studies on the urban agglomeration in the middle reaches of the Yangtze River mainly focuses on the economic, industrial and regional development policies. As population is the core of urban development and the executor of policy practice and industrial development, it is urgent to make a breakthrough in population research on how to realize the rise of central China under the favorable national policies, especially the study of return migration.

Based on the analysis of the overall characteristics of population migration in the urban agglomeration in the middle reaches of the Yangtze River, it is found that the three provinces belong to the main net emigration provinces, with a net population outflow of more than 1 million people: from 2005 to 2010, Hubei Province had a net population outflow of 2.961 million people, ranking the fifth among the provinces with net emigration in China; Hunan Province had a net population outflow of 3.903 million people, ranking fourth; Jiangxi Province had a net population outflow of 2.785 million people, ranking sixth. The central region is the main net emigration area in

China, and the total emigration population of these three provinces accounts for 21.6% of the country. The large-scale population emigration has caused the collapse of the central region, forming the "empty nest" urban agglomeration with the largest emigration population in China. As this urban agglomeration is a cross-regional urban agglomeration with a wide area, the net population outflow is larger than that of the Central Plains urban agglomeration, Chengdu-Chongqing urban agglomeration and other urban agglomerations. Among the net emigration provinces, Jiangxi's net emigration accounted for 6.25% of its total population, ranking the second among the provinces in China, Hunan's net emigration accounted for 5.94% of its total population and Hubei's 5.17%, ranking the fourth and sixth in China respectively. The continuous large-scale population outflows have reduced the labor forces of the urban agglomeration in the middle reaches of the Yangtze River, accelerated the aging of the population, and posed great challenges to population, economic and social development.

Population represents regional competitiveness. At present, the declining demographic dividend in China [23–26] has driven a new round of competition for population among cities, which tends to be a zero sum game. The main direction of China's population flow is still from the central and western regions to the eastern coastal areas. The Yangtze River Delta, Pearl River Delta and Beijing-Tianjin-Hebei regions are the main attraction centers of interprovincial population flows. However, in recent years, the increasing returning flows have led to a slowdown in the growth of the permanent population in these three metropolitan areas. Urban diseases, such as rising cost of living, traffic congestion, environmental pollution and intensified competition, intensify in coastal metropolises where floating population are concentrated. With the transformation of China's economic development from export-oriented to internal-oriented, the development potential of second-tier and third-tier cities is also increasing. Since 2004, there emerges a "labor shortage" phenomenon in some economically developed areas. With the slowdown of population agglomeration in metropolitan areas, cities in central and western regions begin to have returning flows, which provides a sustainable driving force for local development. The purpose of local revitalization can be achieved by attracting returning flows. At present, there are few studies on return migration in China. The existing studies mainly rely on the questionnaire surveys conducted by respective scholars. Due to their different purposes, the definitions of return migration are also different [12]. The return migration in this study refers to the phenomenon that the population that migrated from the central and western areas to the eastern region return to their hometown. The net population outflow in the origin area is measured by the difference between the household registered population and the floating population, and the difference between the net outflows of this year and that of the previous year is the returning flows.

At present, the trend of return migration in the urban agglomeration in the middle reaches of the Yangtze River has emerged, which provides a good opportunity to promote the economic development of this urban agglomeration. Once the return migration has formed a large scale, it will have a far-reaching impact on the urban agglomeration in the middle reaches of the Yangtze River and even the regional economic pattern and urban system structure of China. Therefore, this study will analyze the characteristics of population migration (including the net outflows of population and the trend of return migration) and the consequences caused by the net outflows of population in the urban agglomeration in the middle reaches of the Yangtze River, put forward relevant policy suggestions to attract return migration, and make up for the insufficient research on the return migration and the lack of research on the population migration in the urban agglomeration in the middle reaches of the Yangtze River. It aims at not only providing targeted scientific basis for policy making, but also deepening the theoretical exploration of return migration by analyzing the population migration data at the city level. The population data employed in this study is from the 6th National Population Census (2010), the corresponding year's *China City Statistical Yearbook*, provincial statistical yearbooks and Municipal Statistical Bulletins.

2.1.2.2 The Characteristics of Population Migration at the Provincial Level

The three provinces of the urban agglomeration in the middle reaches of the Yangtze River are the main origin areas in China. According to the data of the sixth national population census, the population outflow from Hubei Province from 2005 to 2010 was 3.804 million people, among which 1.57 million moved to Guangdong (41.28%), 603,000 moved to Zhejiang (15.85%), and 7.09% moved to Jiangsu, 6.50% moved to Shanghai, showing a multipolar trend. The total emigration population of Hunan Province was 4.592 million, ranking first among these three provinces. The distribution of its emigration population was unipolar, highly concentrated in Guangdong Province (accounting for 63.80%). The total emigration population of Jiangxi Province was 3.483 million, among which 1.168 million migrated to Guangdong (33.54%), 991,000 to Zhejiang (28.45%), 13.74% to Fujian and 7.09% to Shanghai, presenting a multipolar distribution. Similar to Hubei and Hunan Provinces, the main destination areas of Jiangxi Province was Guangdong, but its proportion of population outflows to Guangdong was significantly lower than the other two provinces. Jiangxi's proportion of population outflows to Zhejiang Province was the highest among the three provinces, so it had the closest personnel exchanges with the Yangtze River Delta Region (Fig. 2.8).

In a word, there are two major destination areas for migrants from the three provinces of the urban agglomeration in the middle reaches of the Yangtze River: the first is Guangdong Province, and its main origin area is Hunan; the second is Zhejiang Province, and its main origin area is Jiangxi.

2.1.2.3 The Characteristics of Population Migration at the City Level

Except for the three central cities (Wuhan, Changsha and Nanchang), there exist net population outflows in most of cities in the urban agglomeration in the middle

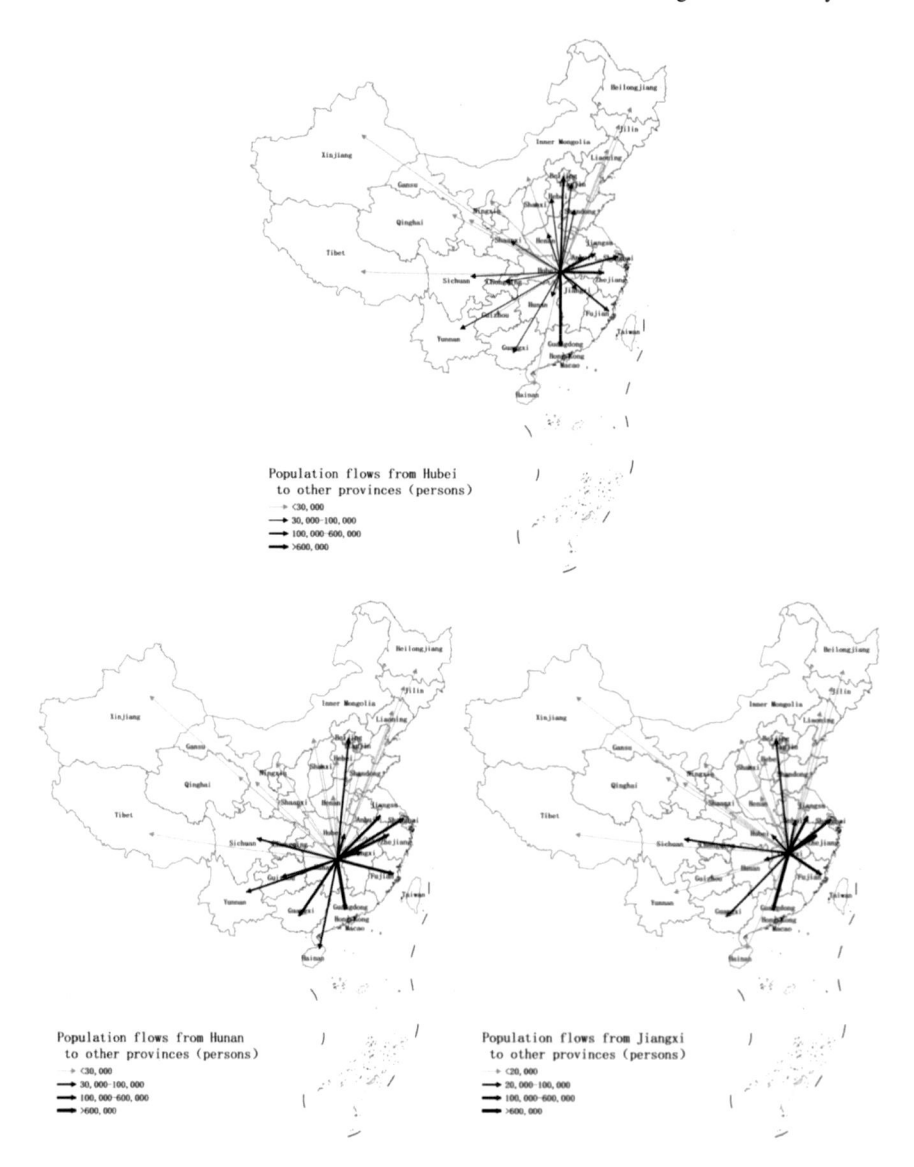

Fig. 2.8 Population outflows from the three provinces in the middle reaches of the Yangtze River (2005–2010)

reaches of the Yangtze River. The changes of population outflows of cities in the three provinces in recent years have been analyzed below (Fig. 2.9).

The net population inflow is measured by the difference between the permanent population and the household registered population. In Hubei Province, the net population inflows only occurred in Wuhan and Yichang (permanent population > household registered population) from 2005 to 2014. The population inflows of Wuhan had

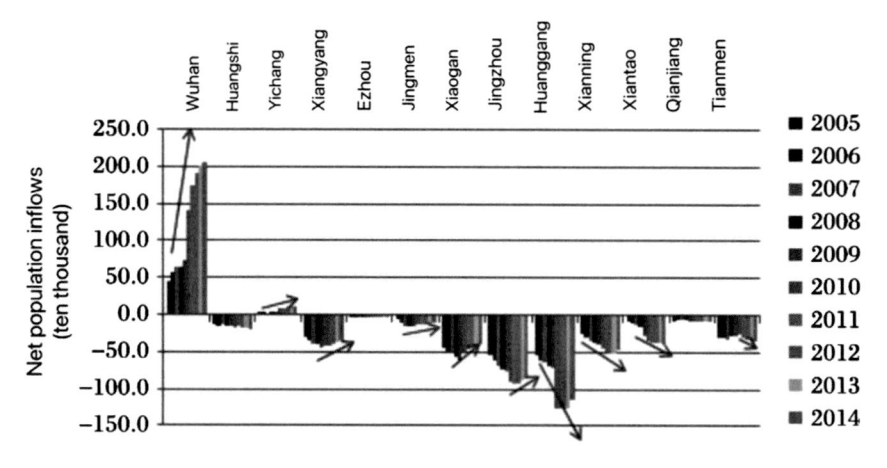

Fig. 2.9 Changes of net population inflows in Hubei Province from 2005 to 2014

increased rapidly, while the population inflows of Yichang were relatively small with a slow growth and basically stable (no more than 100,000). Xiangyang, Jingmen, Xiaogan and Jingzhou had experienced returning flows since 2010. The population outflows of Huanggang, Xianning, Xiantao and Tianmen increased gradually (Fig. 2.10).

In Hunan Province, the net population inflows only emerged in Changsha (permanent population > household registered population). Since 2010, Changsha's floating population had been growing rapidly. A trend of returning flows had happened in Zhuzhou, Xiangtan, Hengyang, Yueyang, Changde and Yiyang since 2010. Only the population outflows of Loudi were still gradually increasing.

In Jiangxi Province, the population migration trend in Nanchang had changed from net outflows to net inflows, and the floating population had increased slowly in recent years. The remaining cities all experienced net population outflows, and the population outflows continued to increase. The population loss is relatively serious

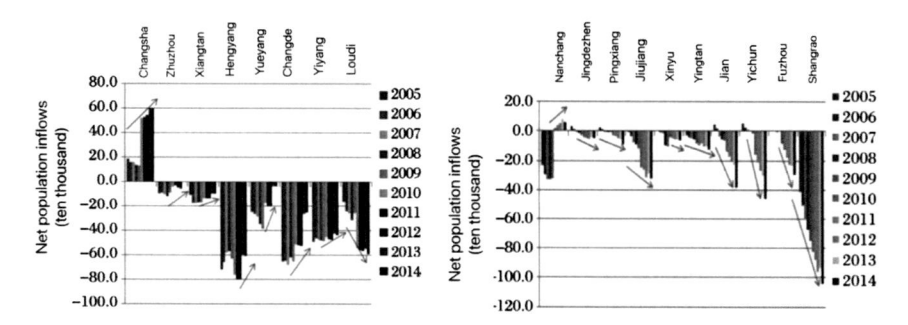

Fig. 2.10 Changes of net population inflows in Hunan Province and Jiangxi Province from 2005 to 2014

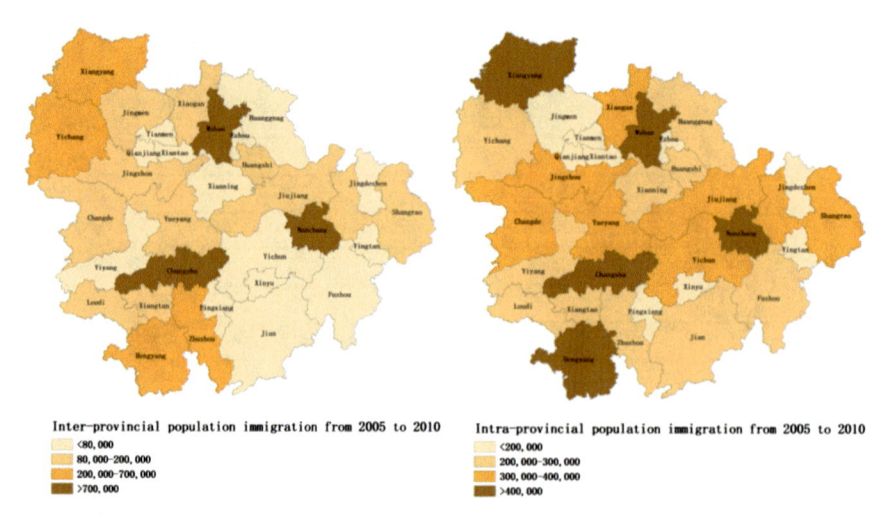

Fig. 2.11 Distribution of population immigration in the urban agglomeration in the middle reaches of the Yangtze River from 2005 to 2010

in Jiangxi Province, the only one province without return migration in the urban agglomeration in the middle reaches of the Yangtze River.

To sum up, in recent years, Wuhan and Changsha had a large number of population inflows with a significant growth, forming a dual-center structure of absorbing population in this region. Nanchang and Yichang had a small population inflows with a slow growth. The other cities in the urban agglomeration had net population outflows. Some cities in Hubei Province and Hunan Province had presented an obvious trend of returning flows. Based on the population immigration data of the Sixth National Census (Fig. 2.11), the intraprovincial population immigration is mainly concentrated in the three central cities (Wuhan, Changsha and Nanchang), Xiangyang in Hubei Province and Hengyang in Hunan Province. The interprovincial population immigration is mainly concentrated in the three central cities, Xiangyang and Yichang in western Hubei Province, and Hengyang and Zhuzhou in southern Hunan Province. Therefore, the population attraction centers of the urban agglomeration in the middle reaches of the Yangtze River can be divided into two levels: the main centers are the provincial capitals (Wuhan, Changsha and Nanchang), and the sub-centers include Xiangyang and Yichang in Hubei Province, Hengyang and Zhuzhou in Hunan Province. These cities have become the main attraction areas of returning flows.

2.1.2.4 Consequences of Net Population Outflows

One of the consequences caused by the net population outflows is that the growth of permanent population in most cities in the urban agglomeration was relatively slow, and even some cities had negative population growth (Jingzhou, Huanggang, Xianning, Xiantao, Tianmen, Loudi, etc.).

The second consequence of the net population outflows is that the labor force in the urban agglomeration in the middle reaches of the Yangtze River accounted for a low proportion of the total population and then its population aging accelerated (the proportion of people aged 65 or older increased from 6.7% in 2000 to 8.8% in 2010). Comparing the population age structure of this urban agglomeration with the other four urban agglomerations, it can be seen that the proportion of the labor forces (aged 15–64) of this urban agglomeration was 74.6%, lower than that of the urban agglomerations of Beijing-Tianjin-Hebei, Yangtze River Delta and Pearl River Delta, and its proportion of the elderly population and the underage population were relatively high (Fig. 2.12). The total dependency ratio of this urban agglomeration was 34.1%, higher than that of Beijing-Tianjin-Hebei, Yangtze River Delta and Pearl River Delta, raking only second to Chengdu-Chongqing Urban Agglomeration. Therefore, its demographic dividend was low, which could not create favorable demographic conditions for regional economic development. In general, the demographic dividend of this urban agglomeration was exported to the eastern coastal areas (the young and middle-aged labor forces continuously migrated to the Pearl River Delta and Yangtze River Delta). As a population outflow area, is difficult for this urban agglomeration to enjoy the benefits from the demographic dividend, which means not only the loss of the demographic dividend, but also the fact that it has to repay more population debts than developed areas after the demographic dividend disappears [27].

The third consequence of the net population outflows is that the average education attainment level of the population in the urban agglomeration in the middle reaches of the Yangtze River was not high. Comparing the educational structure of population of this urban agglomeration with that of the other four major urban agglomerations, it can be seen that its average years of education was not high (only 9.0 years), and its proportion of highly educated people was also very low (only 9.7%, far lower than the three major urban agglomerations), and only better than that of Chengdu-Chongqing Urban Agglomeration (Fig. 2.13). However, the average education years of Wuhan (11.1 years) was second only to Beijing (11.7 years) nationwide, which was inseparable from Wuhan's rich higher education resources (its number of universities ranks second in cities of China and its number of college students ranks first in China), However, its scientific and educational advantages were not enough to drive the improvement of the overall education level of this urban agglomeration.

As a whole, the imbalance of regional economic development has led to the flows of labor force from the urban agglomeration in the middle reaches of the Yangtze River to the areas with better employment opportunities and higher income levels. This urban agglomeration was experiencing serious population outflows, especially young and middle-aged labor forces and people with high education levels, resulting in the net output of the regional demographic dividend. It mainly includes the following three aspects of brain drain: a large number of skilled labors migrated to the neighboring Yangtze River Delta and Pearl River Delta regions, engaged in manufacturing and service industries; after graduation, local college students did not

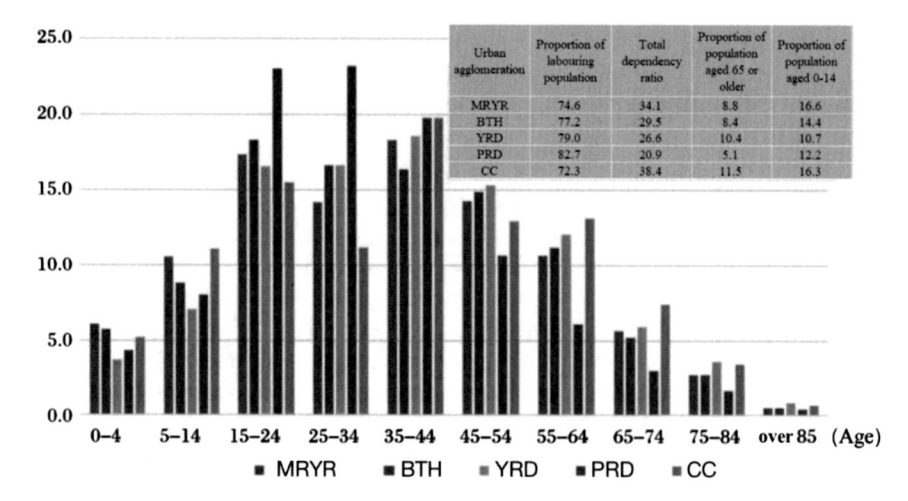

Fig. 2.12 Comparison of population age structures between the urban agglomeration in the middle reaches of the Yangtze River and other major urban agglomerations. *Notes:* The full names of the abbreviations in the Figure are shown as below: the urban agglomeration in the middle reaches of Yangtze River (MRYR), Beijing-Tianjin-Hebei Urban Agglomeration (BTH), Yangtze River Delta Urban Agglomeration (YRD), Pearl River Delta Urban Agglomeration (PRD), Chengdu-Chongqing Urban Agglomeration (CC)

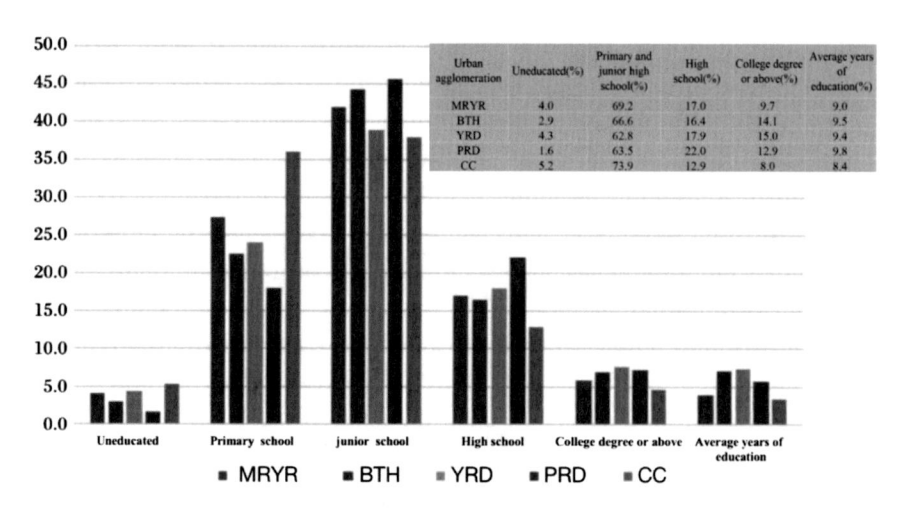

Fig. 2.13 Comparison of population education structures between the urban agglomeration in the middle reaches of the Yangtze River and other urban agglomerations

have enough jobs in this urban agglomeration and were attracted by higher levels of public services and better development opportunities in other developed regions; highly qualified talents also continued to flow out because there were no matching high-end jobs.

In the short term, the continuous population outflows will lead to the reduction of permanent population, labor forces and the average education level, as well as the gradual expansion of migrant workers, which will also cause a series of social problems, such as left-behind children and left-behind elderly. In the long run, it will lead to the decline of local economy, and affect the economic and social development of the whole region. Therefore, accelerating the attraction of return migration is very important for the future development of the urban agglomeration in the middle reaches of the Yangtze River. At present, this urban agglomeration is at the stage of rapid urbanization development. The national urbanization rate was 54.77% in 2014, and only 12 of the 31 cities in this urban agglomeration had reached the national average level, indicating a generally low urbanization level). Regional urbanization development will remain a key task in the future, so it is necessary to attract the returning flows to promote the high-speed urbanization development.

2.1.2.5 The Emergent Trend of Returning Flows

With the emergence of new urban agglomerations in the central and western regions (such as the urban agglomeration in the middle reaches of the Yangtze River), the overall pattern of China's population flows from the central and western regions to the eastern region will be affected. In fact, the trend of return migration has long appeared. From 2006 to 2010, as the first destination area of migrants from the urban agglomeration in the middle reaches of the Yangtze River, Guangdong Province had an annual increase of more than 2 million permanent population. However, this annual increase had decreased to less than 1 million since 2011. From 2010 to 2014, the number of floating population in Guangdong Province decreased from 19.194 million to 18.371 million, so the returning flow was 823,000 people. It is estimated that the returning flows to Hubei Province, Hunan Province and Jiangxi Province were 99,000, 183,000 and 68,000, respectively. In addition, as the second destination area of migrants from the urban agglomeration in the middle reaches of the Yangtze River, Zhejiang Province had experienced a slow growth in permanent population, and the average growth rate of recent years was only 1/4 of that in 2009. From 2010 to 2014, the number of floating population in Zhejiang Province decreased from 6.986 million to 6.488 million, so the returning flow was 498,000 people. It is estimated that the returning flows to Hubei Province, Hunan Province and Jiangxi Province were 39,000, 34,000 and 64,000, respectively.

The reasons for the above phenomena include the slowdown of China's population growth, and the transfer of many manufacturing industries from the eastern coastal areas to the central and western regions and Southeast Asia, resulting in the weakening of the attraction of eastern provinces and cities. The construction of national urban agglomerations in the central and western regions will lead to stronger attraction for the local population. The regional population competition tends to be a zero sum game, so the population flows to the eastern region will inevitably decline, and the population that migrated from the central and western regions to the eastern region will gradually return to their hometowns. In addition, in recent years, China's economic center began to move westward, which will further intensify the return migration. The proportion of the economy of the southeastern coastal area to the whole country began to decline after reaching the peak in 2006. For example, the proportions of Yangtze River Delta, Pearl River Delta and Beijing-Tianjin-Hebei regions decreased from 17.28, 9.21 and 10.75% in 2010 to 16.67, 9.06 and 10.46% in 2015, and will continue to decline in the future. The proportion of the economy of the central and western regions to the whole country had been rising since 2006. For example, the proportions of the urban agglomeration in the middle reaches of the Yangtze River and Chengdu-Chongqing Urban Agglomeration to the whole country increased from 8.59 and 5.67% in 2010, to 9.72 and 6.39% in 2014, and will continue to rise in the future.

Among the three provinces of the urban agglomeration in the middle reaches of the Yangtze River, the population flows to Hubei Province were mainly from Henan Province (115,000), followed by Guangdong (97,000), including a part of the returning flows. The third origin area was Hunan (74,000), indicating that Wuhan Metropolitan Area also had certain attraction for the population of Hunan Province. The population flows to Hunan Province mainly came from Guangdong Province (206,000 people mainly for return migration), followed by Hubei Province (81,000 people), indicating that there were also certain personnel exchanges between Wuhan Metropolitan Area and Changsha-Zhuzhou-Xiangtan Urban Agglomeration. Similarly, the population flows to Jiangxi Province mainly came from Guangdong Province (150,000 people), followed by Zhejiang Province (84,000 people) and Fujian Province (62,000 people). Hunan and Hubei Provinces in the urban agglomeration in the middle reaches of the Yangtze River, also had certain personnel contacts with Jiangxi Province. In recent years, the phenomenon of return migration had occurred in Hubei and Hunan Provinces: the net population outflows of Hubei Province in 2010 were 4.522 million, and the net population outflows in 2014 were 3.463 million, so the total returning flows were 1.06 million with an average annual returning flows of 265,000 people; Hunan Province had net outflows of 5.211 million people in 2010 and net outflows of 4.737 million people in 2014, so the total returning flows were 475,000, with an average annual returning flows of 119,000 people. The population of Jiangxi province continued to flow out, with net outflows of 2.336 million in 2010 and 3.811 million in 2014. From the perspective of the whole urban agglomeration, the net population outflows gradually increased from 2005 to 2009, peaked in 2009, and decreased from 7.289 million in 2009 to 6.454 million in 2014. In other words, there has appeared a trend of return migration since 2010, with returning flows of 835,000 people.

As for the return migration of each city, it can be seen from the above that although most cities in this urban agglomeration were still experiencing net population outflows, some cities had experienced returning flows. Figure 2.14 demonstrates that except Wuhan, Changsha, Nanchang and Yichang, the other cities still had net population outflows. Among the cities with net population outflows, some cities had returning flows: the cities with returning flows of more than 100,000 people from 2010 to 2014 included Changde, Hengyang and Yueyang in Hunan Province, Huanggang and Xiaogan in Hubei Province; those with returning flows

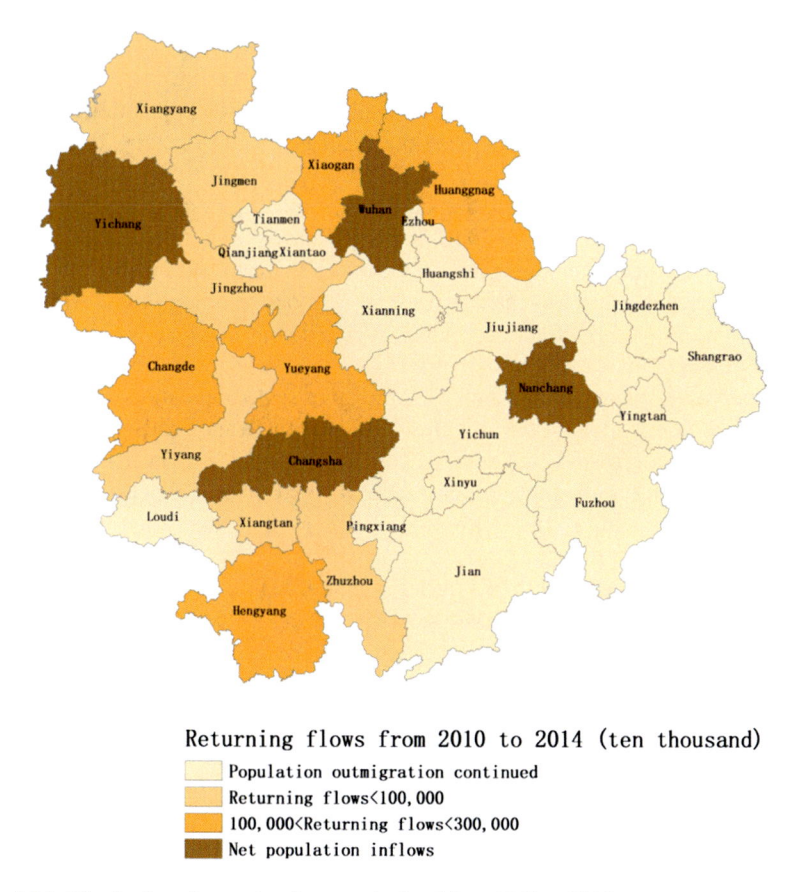

Returning flows from 2010 to 2014 (ten thousand)
- Population outmigration continued
- Returning flows<100,000
- 100,000<Returning flows<300,000
- Net population inflows

Fig. 2.14 Distribution of returning flows at city level from 2010 to 2014

of fewer than 100,000 people consisted of Xiangyang, Jingzhou and Jingmen in Hubei Province, Zhuzhou, Xiangtan and Yiyang in Hunan Province. The population of other cities continued to flow out, including Xianning, Huangshi and other cities in Hubei Province, Loudi in Hunan Province and all cities in Jiangxi Province except Nanchang. With the further economic and social development of the urban agglomeration in the middle reaches of the Yangtze River and the further westward movement of China's economic center, the floating population originating from the urban agglomeration in the middle reaches of the Yangtze River will continue to return.

2.1.2.6   Conclusions and Discussion

The characteristics of spatial pattern and evolution trend of population migration of the urban agglomeration in the middle reaches of the Yangtze River can be summarized as follows.

Firstly, there exists huge population outflows in this urban agglomeration, mainly to Guangdong and Zhejiang Provinces, forming China's largest "empty nest" urban agglomeration. Except for the three central cities (Wuhan, Changsha, Nanchang) and Yichang, other cities are characterized by net population outflows. Wuhan and Changsha are the main attraction centers of population mobility because of their large population inflows with a rapid growth.

Secondly, the consequences caused by the large-scale population outflows from the urban agglomeration in the middle reaches of the Yangtze River include the followings: a slow growth in the regional population (some cities even have negative population growth), a low proportion of labor forces to the total population, a high total dependency ratio, a limited average education level, and a net output of the regional demographic dividend.

Thirdly, the population outflows from the central region peaked in 2009, and the growth of floating population in the Yangtze River Delta and the Pearl River Delta also peaked at the same time. There emerged returning flows in the urban agglomeration in the middle reaches of the Yangtze River in 2010, ushering in a new opportunity for regional economic development: except for the continuous population outflows from Jiangxi Province, a considerable part of floating population in Guangdong Province have returned to Hubei and Hunan Provinces. The returning flows are concentrated in the three central cities, as well as Yichang, Xiaogan and Huanggang in Hubei Province, Hengyang, Changde and Yueyang in Hunan Province. The trend of return migration in the central region had long been heralded when the phenomenon of "labor shortage" appeared in the eastern coastal areas in 2004, but it did not really appear until 2010. The possible reason may be that in 2009, the executive meeting of the State Council discussed and approved the Plan on the Rise of Central China, which put forward the goal of comprehensively improving the economic development level, development vitality and sustainable development capacity of the central region. This national policy has played an important role in forming a turning point from the outmigration to the return migration in the central region.

In order to promote the returning flows and accelerate the economic development of the urban agglomeration in the middle reaches of the Yangtze River, we put forward the following policy suggestions:

(1)   It is necessary to promote regional integration and the construction of the urban agglomeration in the middle reaches of the Yangtze River: drawing on the development experience of from the urban agglomerations in the Yangtze River Delta, the Pearl River Delta and Beijing-Tianjin-Hebei, strengthening exchanges and cooperation among cities in the urban agglomeration of the middle reaches of the Yangtze River, gradually realizing the integration of

infrastructure, industries, public services and markets, and creating the fourth growth pole of China's economic development.

(2) It is important to increase the supply of public services and enhance regional attractiveness: relying on the rich resources of higher education and scientific research advantages of Wuhan and Changsha, strengthening the construction of municipal infrastructure and public service facilities (such as education and medical treatment), promoting the gradual distribution of these resources to the surrounding small and medium-sized cities and gradually realizing the equalization of public services in this region, thus increasing the attractiveness of this region; accelerating the full opening of urban public services to the return migrants, focusing on solving the core problems including children's education, medical insurance and housing for the return migrants, thus providing good social welfare for the return migrants.

(3) It is essential to reform the *hukou* (household registration) system to promote free population flows: accelerating the pace of *hukou* system reform and relaxing restrictions on obtaining local *hukou* in different levels of cities in this region step by step; introducing more talents for this region by eliminating the threshold of college graduates and introduced talents to obtain local *hukou*; promoting the free population flows among cities in the urban agglomeration by shortening the *hukou* differences between Wuhan and surrounding cities.

(4) It is of great importance to strengthen and expand the secondary and tertiary industries and attract the return migration of skilled labor forces: promoting the upgrading of industrial structure, providing sufficient jobs and a good employment environment for the return migrants, attracting the return migration of skilled labor forces, and enhancing population concentration through industrial agglomeration; developing labor-intensive manufacturing industries to attract labor forces from the Yangtze River Delta and the Pearl River Delta, by undertaking the gradient transfer of industries from the southeastern coastal region; making full use of the high-quality educational resources in Wuhan and Changsha, increasing investment in the education development, enhancing the competitiveness of migrant workers in the labor market by improving the training efficiency of migrant workers in this region.

(5) It is urgent to increase high-end employment opportunities, improve salary level and retain local talents: establishing a high-end industrial system based on the original industrial foundation, strengthening high-end service functions (including scientific and technological research and development, financial services, business management, information services and cultural creativity), relying on industrial parks and incubators of universities and research institutions to enhance the urban innovation capacity, so as to provide sufficient jobs for a large number of college graduates in this urban agglomeration and improve the welfare mechanism and the treatment of employees; realizing the integration of production, study and research, establishing a direct talent output chain between colleges and universities, encouraging enterprises to enter colleges and select the required talents in colleges in advance, and retain talents for local enterprises through joint training in both colleges and enterprises.

(6) It is necessary to create an urban agglomeration suitable for living and working, and introduce talents from other regions: enhancing urban livability by making full use of the ecological advantages of the Yangtze River Basin, optimizing the urban living environment, improving the quality of urban life, and creating a good employment and entrepreneurial environment to attract talents; improving the talent introduction policy by formulating more supporting policies and providing more attentive services for talents; establishing a complete social security system including social insurance, social relief and social welfare to effectively settle the troubles of introduced talents; creating a better investment environment with hometown affection to attract outstanding talents in other regions to return and start business.

(7) It is imperative to accelerate the development of the urban agglomeration around Poyang Lake and attract the returning flows: among the three provinces of the urban agglomeration in the middle reaches of the Yangtze River, only Jiangxi Province were experiencing a continuous net population outflows. It is necessary to further accelerate the economic development of the urban agglomeration around Poyang Lake and strengthen the function of Nanchang as a regional central city, so as to attract more returning flows. It is suggested that the Urban agglomeration around Poyang Lake should make full use of its role as a hub for the gradient transfer from coastal developed areas to inland areas, give full play to the R&D advantages of the aviation industry in Jiangxi Province, strengthen advantageous industries to create more jobs to absorb labor.

2.1.3 Intercity Mobility Patterns and Influencing Factors

2.1.3.1 Introduction

The massive interregional population mobility in China since the 1980s has played an essential role in reshaping the spatial distribution of population and the country's economic geography [28, 29]. As the world's most populous country with a vast territory accounting for largest proportion of the mobile population in the world, China's population mobility studies will provide references for related studies on the international and internal population mobility in other countries. In the past decades, China has witnessed huge inter regional population flows in different periods and regions, and their various spatial patterns have attracted considerable attention from scholars [30–35]. These spatial patterns of intercity mobility are impressive due to their complexity related to travel behaviours, travel purposes, regional attributes, and other city-level factors. The studies on population mobility in China can be divided into two main categories: the migration studies focus on the long-term behaviours of people changing their workplace and residence beyond a certain administrative region (county/city/province) and a certain period (over one month), based on the national population census and social survey data (annual or multi-annual), the transient population mobility studies focus on the daily travel behaviours of people moving from a city to another city for certain purposes through a certain transportation mode, based on daily location-based big data. Mobility has become a crucial geographic concept, and the transition from traditional data (census and survey data) to location-based big data provides a new avenue for mobility studies, as the realtime location-based big data can better reveal the intercity mobility pattern than the traditional data [36].

The internal migration in China has been studied by many scholars, focusing on its spatial pattern, evolution characteristics, and influencing factors. The spatial pattern of migration population sizes, migration intensity (migration rate), and migration flows are usually depicted by spatial visualization, spatial analysis, and network analysis methods [18, 30, 33, 37, 38]. Based on a series of migration theories, the influencing factors of internal migration in China include micro-level factors (personal attributes, migration features, household characteristics) and macro-level factors (characteristics of origin regions and destination regions), and many studies have combined the determinants on migration at both the individual level and the city level [39–42]. Due to the lack of intercity migration in census data, most migration studies focus on inter-provincial migration [43–45] instead of intercity migration, while online data (e.g., mobile positioning data) can address this lacuna by providing intercity mobility data [46–49].

The intercity mobility network is an essential type of city network, which is traditionally based on infrastructure (all kinds of transportation networks and communication networks) and economic networks (through all sorts of corporate organizations) [50]. The former branch of research on city network mainly employs passenger and cargo flows to construct the city network and then discuss its structural features [51–55], and the latter is usually measured in corporate organizations, concerning the ownership links between firms across space [56–59]. The complex network analysis method has become the primary tool for research on city networks. In recent years, the emergence of location-based big data has made it possible to conduct studies on the intercity mobility network. The intercity mobility network studies focus on revealing the network characteristics by using the survey data of long-distance travel and commuting [60–62] and analyzing the internal migration network features. The comparison between different intercity mobility networks is concentrated in networks of different travel modes [63–65] while neglecting the networks of different periods. The differences in travel modes, travel purposes, travel times, and regional attributes will result in the heterogeneity of travel behaviours at the individual level and travel patterns at the regional level [66].

With the rapid development of big data technology, the location-based big data collected from GPS and mobile phones have been extensively applied in population mobility studies, comprised of multi-source migration big travel data from Baidu, Tencent, Qihoo and Weibo [67]. Compared with traditional data, big data can better reveal the spatial pattern and intercity network of population movements due to its real-time dynamic monitoring of human mobility in different spatial scales and different periods with large data volume and high spatial–temporal resolution [68]. Large Internet companies in China, such as Baidu, Tencent, and Sina, provide location-based services. Compared with other big data, Tencent migration big data possesses advantages of larger sample size, multi-sourced data, higher accuracy, stronger analytical and predictive abilities, which can better delineate the population migration pattern in real-time and the population flow linkages between cities. As one of China's most influential Internet companies, Tencent is engaged in many business fields, including social contact, game, and communication. There are more than 55 billion daily location-based service calls of Tencent, occurring in apps like WeChat, QQ, JD, Mobike and Didi, and the monthly active users of WeChat (the most commonly used app of Tencent as well as the most popular instant communication app in China) have grown to over 1.1 billion in 2019. Therefore, the location-based services of Tencent nearly cover all smartphone users in China. Thus, Tencent's location-based big data is useful and representative in studies on internal migration and population mobility. During the Spring Festival holiday in 2015, Tencent released the travel heat data platform of the nationwide Spring Festival travel rush (hot.qq.com/qianxi), the website address of which has been changed to heat.qq.com/qianxi.php in 2016. The Tencent migration data demonstrated on this platform is massive location data obtained through numerous users' calls of location-based services while maintaining client confidentiality. With the of one-sided data from a single transportation mode, such as railway, highway, aviation, and water transport, thus leading to a synthetic judgment of intercity mobility.

As big data can record each day's population mobility throughout the year, scholars usually select typical periods or use the yearly aggregate and average value to conduct research. Except for weekdays and weekends, there are several holidays in China, including traditional holidays and non-traditional holidays. Traditional holidays are composed of Spring Festival, Tomb-sweeping Day, Dragon Boat Festival, and Mid-Autumn Festival. Non-traditional holidays consist of New Year's Day, May Day and National Day. As Spring Festival is the most important traditional holiday for a family reunion in China, migrants will come back to their hometowns from cities where they work and study; many scholars choose the data of this period to represent the annual (long-term) migration patterns [46, 48, 49, 68]. The Spring Festival travel rush is known as the largest periodic migration in the history of humanity. The Spring Festival is celebrated according to the Chinese lunar calendar, so the date of this holiday varies from January to February in the solar calendar. During the Spring Festival travel season of 2019, nearly 3 billion people travel through highways, railways and air transportation, twice the total population of China. Meanwhile, National Day is the most protracted non-traditional holiday in China, during which the population flows are mainly tourist flows. A fair amount of studies are conducted based on the National Day holiday data to reflect the intercity travel network during holidays [47, 69]. The existing studies on population mobility have mainly employed the Spring Festival holiday or National Day holiday data, and the conclusions obtained cannot reflect the situation of the entire year [29] and the differences among different periods.

Intercity mobility happening at different times will reflect various travel purposes, travel destinations, travel distances, and scales, thus presenting different travel behaviours and spatial patterns of intercity mobility, i.e., temporal heterogeneity of intercity mobility [70, 71]. Different holidays have different meanings for Chinese people, especially traditional holidays and non-traditional holidays at different times, thus causing temporal heterogeneity. Non-traditional holidays usually mean time to relax and refresh, while traditional holidays often have different special significances for Chinese people. Specifically, Spring Festival and Mid-Autumn Festival are both times for a family reunion. Spring Festival, as the beginning of a new year in the Chinese lunar calendar, derives from the ancient tradition of worshipping of the gods and praying for a good fortune in the agrarian society, and gradually develops into a series of conventions: enjoying family reunion dinner, staying up late or all night on New Year's Eve, posting couplets on doors, giving children money as a lunar New Year gift, paying New Year calls, going to the temple fair, etc. Mid-Autumn Festival, i.e. August 15th in the Chinese lunar calendar, derives from the ancient tradition of sacrificing the moon in Autumn and develops into various customs: family reunion, admiring the full moon, eating moon cakes, etc. Tomb-sweeping Day, i.e. April 5th in the solar calendar, originates from the ancient tradition of worshipping ancestors and rites of spring and becomes a time to sweep graves, honour the deceased relatives and satisfy the ancestors. Dragon Boat Festival, i.e. May 5th in the Chinese lunar calendar, originates from the ancient tradition of the sacrifice of the dragons and the commemoration of the patriotic poet Qu Yuan in the Warring States Period and evolves into diversified customs: eating traditional Chinese rice-pudding, racing dragon boats, hanging calamus and moxa, taking medicinal baths, etc. Under the context of globalization and the influence of western culture, though some Chinese people have gradually accepted the western Festivals (including Christmas, Valentine's Day and Halloween), Chinese traditional festivals, with their long history and widespread popularity, still play very important roles in contemporary society, which consist of enhancing family ties, spreading national culture, and promoting social harmony.

Nevertheless, only a few studies focus on time variation on mobility patterns, not to mention different population mobility patterns in different holidays. Thereinto, Liu and Shi [72] compared the urban hierarchical structure of human mobility and intercity population flow network among Spring Festival, Labor Day, weekdays and weekends, revealing different migration scales and coverage of intercity mobility systems in different periods. Li et al. [66] compared the intercity travel network's spatial structures between the National Day holiday and weekdays in China, discovering that the travel scale is more prominent in the National Day holiday, while the travel distance and network clustering degree are lower than those on weekdays. Cui et al. [70] compared the various spatial–temporal dynamics of daily intercity mobility among weekdays, weekends and national holidays (May Day) and unveiled the temporal heterogeneity of daily intercity mobility. Gao et al. [73] discovered that the effect of the high-speed rail connection on tourist flows is greater in the May Day holiday than in the National Day holiday.

Therefore, to rectify the deficiency of research on intercity mobility's temporal heterogeneity, this study employs the Tencent migration data of 2018 in China to examine the differences in spatial patterns of intercity mobility in different holidays and further analyze their influencing factors. This study will contribute to the growing literature on China's population mobility based on big data by providing a comprehensive view of the situation of a whole year, a new comparative perspective among different holidays, and a more in-depth insight into the potential causes (especially cultural elements).

2.1.3.2 Data, Methodology and Analytical Framework

The Tencent migration data has the following main characteristics: (a) it provides the top 10 records of inflows and outflows of each prefecture-level city; (b) it identifies the intercity mobility data of 3 transportation modes (railway, highway and aviation), respectively, and this study employs the synthetic data of these three transportation modes to reflect the intercity mobility pattern entirely; (c) it records the daily travel behaviours of users, which can cover the most travel behaviours of users (including long-distance travel and short-distance travel) and thus reduce the estimation bias. Though the Tencent platform only releases the records of each city's top 10 inflows and outflows, the other records can be supplemented by other cities' inflows and outflows records to depict the intercity mobility pattern at the national level. Therefore, this data has been widely applied in revealing the spatial patterns of intercity mobility [47, 66, 69, 74, 75]. We have collected the daily intercity mobility data of the entire year of 2018 in 362 cities (including 293 prefecture-level units, 4 municipalities directly under the central government and 65 county-level units).

To conduct comparative research, we select the following periods of population mobility data from Tencent migration data of 2018: Spring Festival departure period (February 1st to February 20th), Spring Festival return period (February 21st to March 12th), National Day departure period (September 30th to October 4th), National Day return period (October 5th to October 8th), New Year's Day (December 30th, 2017 to January 1st, 2018), Tomb-sweeping Day (April 5th to April 7th), May Day (April 29th to May 1st), Dragon Boat Festival (June 16th to June 18th), Mid-Autumn Festival (September 22nd to September 24th). Among these holidays, Spring Festival, Tomb-sweeping Day, Dragon Boat Festival and Mid-Autumn Festival belong to traditional holidays; New Year's Day, May Day and National Day belong to non-traditional holidays. Spring Festival and National Day are long holidays with 7 days off; the other holidays are short holidays with only 3 days off. As long holidays cover more than a week, the Spring Festival and National Holiday are usually divided into several parts to be investigated: departure period, journey period, return period [47], while some studies only consider the first half holiday as the departure period and the second-half holiday as the return period for convenience, corresponding to the trends of population outflows and inflows [49, 72, 73, 75]. Therefore, we divide the Spring Festival and National Day holidays into 2 time periods: departure and return periods. The annual Spring Festival travel season lasts for about 40 days surrounding Spring Festival each year, characterized by colossal population flows among regions and officially defined by National Development and Reform Commission to arrange nationwide transportation for the Ministry of Railways and Civil Aviation Administration. Considering that many people will usually ask for a day's leave before and

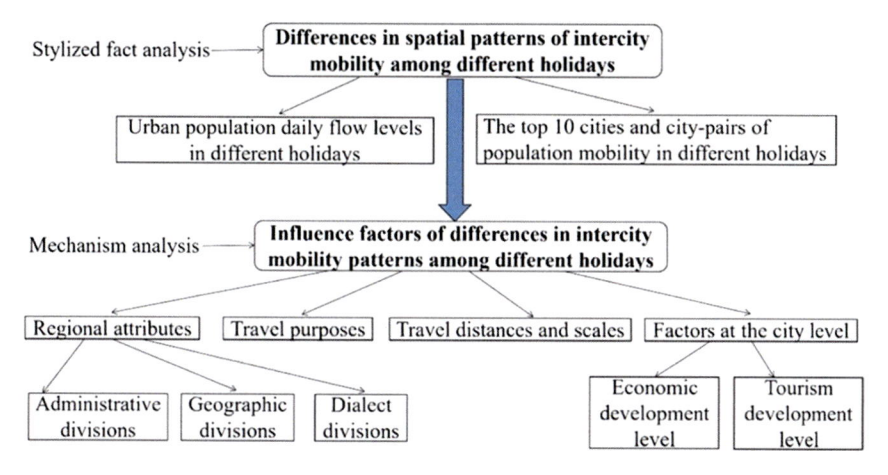

Fig. 2.15 The analytical framework of the study

after National Day to make the holiday long enough, we add 2 days to the National Day holiday period. As short holidays only cover 3 days, they are usually regarded as an entirety in extant studies [70, 72]. Since we conduct a comparative study among 7 different holidays, the long holidays are divided into 2 equal parts for convenience and clarity of comparison, and the short holidays are deemed a whole.

Following the analytical framework reported in Fig. 2.15, we calculate the daily average inflows and outflows of each city of the above periods, as well as the intercity flows (the flows between each city and its top 10 origin cities and destination cities as Tencent migration data reports), to measure the city hierarchical structures, spatial patterns of population mobility and the intercity mobility networks in different holidays. We further employ spatial and statistical analysis methods to explore the differences in intercity mobility patterns among different holidays and discuss the underlying reasons.

2.1.3.3 Differences in Spatial Patterns of Intercity Mobility in Different Holidays

The Spatial Patterns of Urban Population Daily Flow Levels

The spatial patterns of net population inflows in different holidays have been demonstrated in Fig. 2.16. To begin with, we compare the 7-day holidays-Spring Festival and National Day. The travel scale of the Spring Festival is much larger than that of the National Day. During the departure periods of Spring Festival and National Day, the main population flow direction is both from major metropolitan areas (central cities of the 3 biggest urban agglomerations and main provincial capital cities) to other cities; different from National Day, the destination cities in Spring Festival are more widely distributed. During the Spring Festival and National Day return

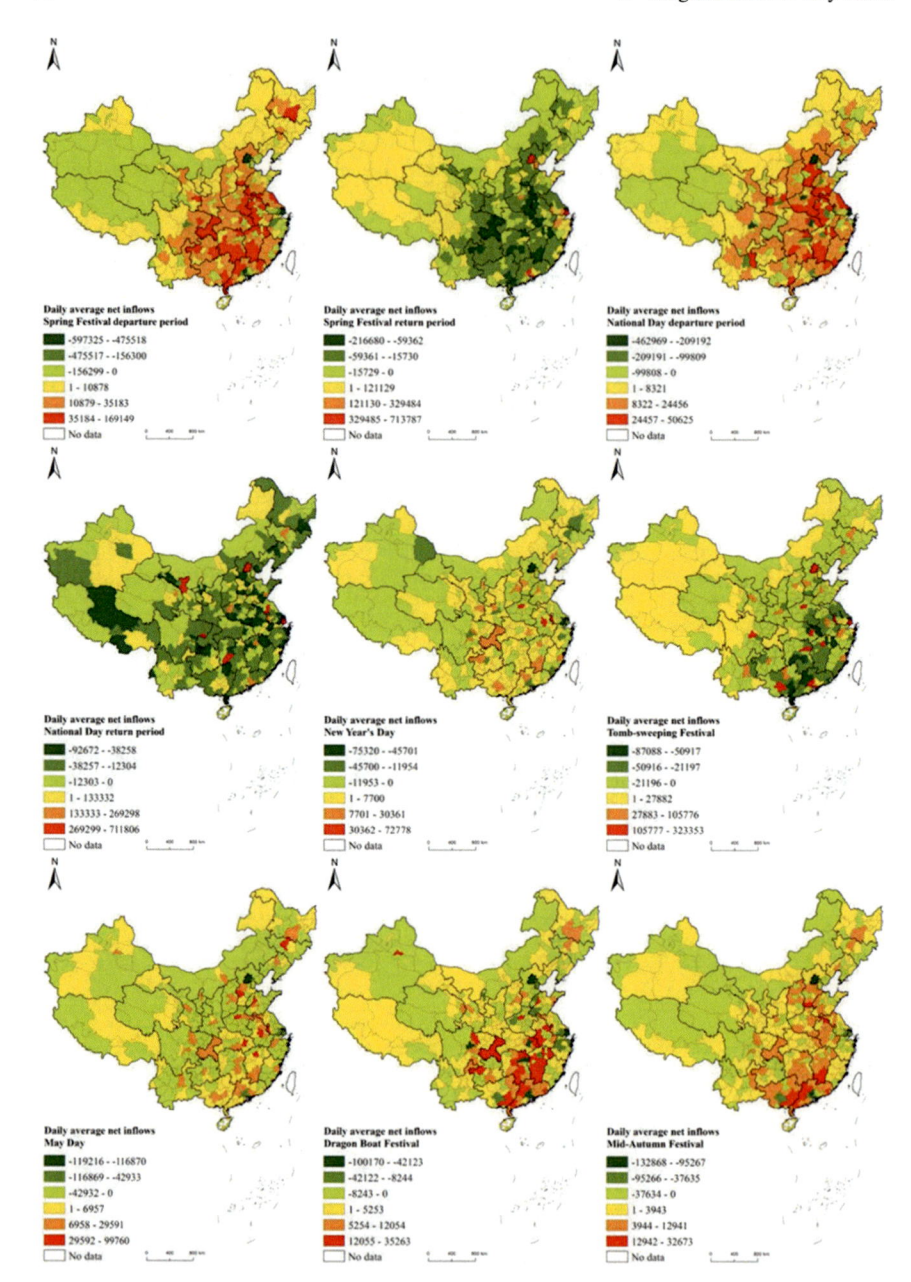

Fig. 2.16 Daily average net population inflows (persons) in different holidays in 2018

periods, people return from other cities to the major large cities where they work, thus presenting similar spatial patterns.

By comparing the 3-day holidays, we notice that people flow from major metropolitan areas to other cities. The destination cities of non-traditional holidays are mainly provincial capital cities and other tourism cities. Compared with non-traditional holidays, the destination cities of traditional holidays are more dispersed, indicating that people are inclined to return to their hometowns, and the people in the south are more likely to return home than those in the north, especially people in Guangdong, Guangxi, Hunan and Jiangxi Provinces. The fact that people in the south usually pay more attention to the family tradition is reflected in the ancestral temples everywhere in the south, while people in the north focus less on it due to various historical reasons (more frequent migration and more chaos caused by wars). As a traditional holiday, Tomb-sweeping Day is an exception, during which only a handful of cities (major large cities) present net population inflows, while most cities show net population outflows, probably due to the convention of returning to hometowns ahead of Tomb-sweeping Day, or the fact that many large cemeteries are located in large cities.

The Top 10 Cities and City-Pairs of Population Mobility in Different Holidays

As shown in Table 2.4, the top 10 cities in terms of daily average population mobility include central cities of the 3 biggest urban agglomerations (Beijing, Shanghai, Suzhou, Guangzhou, Shenzhen, Dongguan, Foshan), and other central cities in the central and western regions (Chengdu, Chongqing, Xi'an and Zhengzhou). The top 10 flow paths of the largest scale consist of the population flows between the top 10 cities with their surrounding cities, such as Guangzhou-Foshan, Shenzhen-Dongguan, Shanghai-Suzhou, Beijing-Langfang, Beijing-Baoding, Xi'an-Xianyang. Cities in Pearl River Delta Urban Agglomeration account for the largest proportion in the top 10 cities and city-pairs of intercity mobility, signifying the outstanding performance of Pearl River Delta Urban Agglomeration in attracting labour forces. It is worth noting that Xi'an also plays a significant role in the national population mobility system, with large population flows between Xi'an and its surrounding cities. On the one hand, Xi'an has made remarkable achievements in attracting population fueled by new policies of talent introduction since 2017; on the other hand, Xi'an has become a popular nationwide tourist destination in recent years, with its inherent advantage of traditional cultural tourism and increased tourism marketing activities since the Spring Festival of 2018.

Table 2.4 can reflect the important cities and city-pairs (levels of cities and intercity linkages) in the national population mobility system without revealing the differences in population mobility patterns among different holidays. Therefore, we list the top 10 cities of net inflows and net outflows in different holidays in Table 2.5. By comparing 3-day holidays, it is evident that the main destination cities are tourism cities or surrounding cities of large cities in non-traditional holidays (New Year's Day and May Day). In contrast, people mainly flow to cities in the south (Guangdong,

Table 2.4 The top 10 cities and city-pairs of intercity mobility

Periods	The top 10 cities of daily average population mobility (inflow + outflow)	The top 10 city-pairs of daily average intercity flows
Spring festival departure period	Beijing (1,944,804), Guangzhou (1,599,558), Chengdu (1,477,706), Shanghai (1,369,759), Shenzhen (1,364,984), Chongqing (1,146,009), Dongguan (775,940), Wuhan (761,202), Suzhou (735,796), Xi'an (733,584)	Guangzhou-Foshan (110,228), Foshan-Guangzhou (108,062), Dongguan-Shenzhen (105,260), Xianyang-Xi'an (96,317), Shenzhen-Dongguan (89,664), Suzhou-Shanghai (86,968), Xi'an-Xianyang (80,207), Shanghai-Suzhou (78,480), Langfang-Beijing (74,798), Ziyang-Chengdu (71,208)
Spring festival return period	Beijing (2,256,832), Guangzhou (1,868,975), Chengdu (1,631,905), Shenzhen (1,552,341), Shanghai (1,433,320), Chongqing (1,044,134), Dongguan (1,023,253), Zhengzhou (927,637), Xi'an (890,235), Wuhan (873,851)	Shenzhen-Dongguan (158,743), Guangzhou-Foshan (152,408), Foshan-Guangzhou (151,425), Dongguan-Shenzhen (143,814), Xi'an-Xianyang (111,743), Shanghai-Suzhou (101,873), Suzhou-Shanghai (96,944), Xianyang-Xi'an (93,386), Langfang-Beijing (87,387), Dongguan-Guangzhou (87,359)
National day departure period	Beijing (1,804,214), Guangzhou (1,613,951), Chengdu (1,534,617), Shenzhen (1,320,729), Shanghai (1,276,182), Zhengzhou (1,021,949), Wuhan (985,462), Xi'an (941,396), Dongguan (939,261), Suzhou (900,997)	Dongguan-Shenzhen (175,263), Shenzhen-Dongguan (166,276), Foshan-Guangzhou (166,198), Guangzhou-Foshan (153,621), Suzhou-Shanghai (129,673), Xianyang-Xi'an (120,871), Shanghai-Suzhou (106,793), Huizhou-Shenzhen (101,203), Xi'an-Xianyang (98,680), Baoding-Beijing (97,898)
National day return period	Beijing (1,965,219), Chengdu (1,404,149), Guangzhou (1,367,776), Shanghai (1,201,853), Shenzhen (1,114,718), Zhengzhou (1,001,403), Wuhan (940,465), Xi'an (865,479), Nanjing (803,061), Suzhou (726,005)	Guangzhou-Foshan (140,650), Foshan-Guangzhou (128,352), Shenzhen-Dongguan (127,946), Dongguan-Shenzhen (112,531), Xi'an Xianyang (111,886), Shanghai-Suzhou (99,063), Beijing-Baoding (91,461), Xianyang-Xi'an (89,541), Beijing-Langfang (81,917), Langfang-Beijing (79,453)

(continued)

Table 2.4 (continued)

Periods	The top 10 cities of daily average population mobility (inflow + outflow)	The top 10 city-pairs of daily average intercity flows
New Year's day	Guangzhou (2,088,309), Beijing (2,052,485), Shenzhen (1,927,794), Chengdu (1,777,171), Shanghai (1,577,278), Dongguan (1,354,708), Zhengzhou (1,218,906), Wuhan (1,079,818), Foshan (1,065,991), Suzhou (1,064,627)	Dongguan-Shenzhen (297,191), Shenzhen-Dongguan (292,471), Guangzhou-Foshan (250,558), Foshan-Guangzhou (241,925), Shanghai-Suzhou (162,760), Xianyang-Xi'an (161,583), Suzhou-Shanghai (161,020), Xi'an-Xianyang (152,236), Huizhou-Shenzhen (146,640), Shenzhen-Huizhou (143,570)
Tomb-sweeping day	Beijing (2,223,306), Guangzhou (2,028,099), Chengdu (1,828,393), Shenzhen (1,690,704), Shanghai (1,540,397), Wuhan (1,343,314), Zhengzhou (1,313,295), Xi'an (1,230,042), Nanjing (1,167,865), Dongguan (1,122,797)	Shenzhen-Dongguan (214,274), Dongguan-Shenzhen (211,591), Guangzhou-Foshan (189,956), Foshan-Guangzhou (174,226), Xi'an-Xianyang (159,516), Shanghai-Suzhou (146,346), Xianyang-Xi'an (144,555), Suzhou-Shanghai (137,336), Wuhan-Xiaogan (127,961), Wuhan-Huanggang (127,063)
May day	Beijing (2,761,733), Guangzhou (2,214,481), Chengdu (2,057,928), Shenzhen (1,951,178), Shanghai (1,766,650), Zhengzhou (1,566,236), Dongguan (1,395,665), Wuhan (1,380,915), Xi'an (1,356,091), Suzhou (1,241,427)	Dongguan-Shenzhen (285,401), Shenzhen-Dongguan (283,175), Guangzhou-Foshan (239,869), Foshan-Guangzhou (223,339), Xi'an-Xianyang (167,922), Shanghai-Suzhou (167,048), Xianyang-Xi'an (165,195), Suzhou-Shanghai (162,509), Huizhou-Shenzhen (152,608), Shenzhen-Huizhou (147,306)
Dragon boat festival	Beijing (2,177,397), Guangzhou (1,836,928), Chengdu (1,705,922), Shenzhen (1,683,011), Shanghai (1,420,634), Dongguan (1,264,793), Zhengzhou (1,088,269), Wuhan (984,344), Xi'an (968,991), Suzhou (952,837)	Dongguan-Shenzhen (268,611), Shenzhen-Dongguan (261,767), Guangzhou-Foshan (209,069), Guangzhou-Foshan (203,136), Xianyang-Xi'an (144,267), Xi'an-Xianyang (142,914), Shanghai-Suzhou (139,752), Suzhou-Shanghai (137,191), Huizhou-Shenzhen (136,819), Shenzhen-Huizhou (128,676)

(continued)

Table 2.4 (continued)

Periods	The top 10 cities of daily average population mobility (inflow + outflow)	The top 10 city-pairs of daily average intercity flows
Mid-autumn festival	Beijing (1,385,435), Guangzhou (1,306,824), Shenzhen (1,198,319), Chengdu (1,050,300), Shanghai (949,752), Dongguan (842,169), Zhengzhou (826,433), Foshan (720,164), Xi'an (688,343), Suzhou (670,602)	Dongguan-Shenzhen (183,867), Shenzhen-Dongguan (182,416), Foshan-Guangzhou (168,422), Guangzhou-Foshan (167,980), Xianyang-Xi'an (124,208), Xi'an-Xianyang (120,306), Suzhou-Shanghai (108,845), Shanghai-Suzhou (107,864), Langfang-Beijing (100,986), Beijing-Langfang (90,066)

Notes: The numbers of people (population flows) are shown in brackets

Guangxi, Jiangxi, Hubei and Hunan Provinces) on traditional holidays to return to their hometowns. The reverse trend to the Dragon Boat Festival and Mid-autumn Festival in Tomb-sweeping Day is probably due to the convention of sweeping tombs ahead of time in many areas.

We then compare the 7-day holidays-Spring Festival and National Day. The main destination and origin cities in the Spring Festival holiday are broadly in line with China's internal migration pattern. People return to their hometowns from cities where they work and study. During the departure period of Spring Festival, the main origin areas are cities of the 3 biggest urban agglomerations (Guangzhou, Shenzhen, Dongguan and Foshan of Pearl River Delta, Shanghai, Suzhou, Hangzhou and Nanjing of Yangtze River Delta, Beijing of Beijing-Tianjin-Hebei Urban Agglomeration), and the main destination areas are distributed in central and western regions; during the return period, the situation is opposite. The main origin areas in National Day holiday are the largest cities in China (Beijing, Shanghai, Guangzhou and Shenzhen) and other regional central cities (Zhengzhou, Wuhan, Chengdu, Nanjing, Hefei and Jinan), where residents have higher income and consumption levels and like travelling. The main destination areas in the National Day holiday are surrounding cities of the origin cities (Baoding-Beijing, Zhoukou-Nanyang-Zhengzhou, Anqing-Hefei, Huanggang-Wuhan, Nantong-Yancheng-Nanjing, Ganzhou-Ji'an-Guangzhou), for their proximity to these large cities makes it convenient for people to come and relax.

2.1.3.4 Influencing Factors of Intercity Mobility Patterns

Different holidays generally influence people's travel behaviours by affecting travel purposes, and the spatial patterns of intercity mobility are the aggregation of individual travel behaviours (scales and distances). There are both spatial disparity and temporal heterogeneity in intercity mobility, which relate to each other. Hence, the

Table 2.5 The top 10 destination cities and origin cities in different holidays

Periods	The top 10 cities of net inflows	The top 10 cities of net outflows
New Year's day	Zhengzhou, Nanjing, Hefei, Jinan, Nanchang, Shijiazhuang, Xianyang, Bijie, Fuzhou, Chongqing	Shenzhen, Beijing, Suzhou, Harbin, Dongguan, Guangzhou, Shanghai, Guiyang, Chengdu, Xi'an
Tomb-sweeping day	Guangzhou, Wuhan, Nanjing, Beijing, Shenzhen, Zhengzhou, Foshan, Changsha, Shanghai, Nanning	Zhaoqing, Zhanjiang, Qingyuan, Huanggang, Guigang, Jieyang, Yulin, Shangrao, Hengyang, Xiaogan
May day	Zhengzhou, Nanjing, Jinan, Changchun, Nanchang, Hefei, Shijiazhuang, Wuhan, Lanzhou, Xi'an	Shenzhen, Beijing, Suzhou, Shanghai, Guangzhou, Foshan, Dongguan, Zhongshan, Wuxi, Linyi
Dragon boat festival	Shangrao, Ganzhou, Jinan, Mianyang, Yueyang, Qinzhou, Bijie, Yichun, Zhaoqing, Yulin	Shenzhen, Guangzhou, Chengdu, Changsha, Beijing, Wuhan, Foshan, Dongguan, Shanghai, Suzhou
Mid-autumn festival	Zhaoqing, Jieyang, Qingyuan, Guigang, Ganzhou, Maoming, Yunfu, Yulin, Handan, Wuzhou	Guangzhou, Shenzhen, Beijing, Foshan, Dongguan, Shanghai, Nanning, Suzhou, Chengdu, Changsha
Spring festival	Chongqing, Hengyang, Ganzhou, Xinyang, Zhoukou, Guigang, Fuyang, Maoming, Shangrao, Shangqiu	Beijing, Guangzhou, Shenzhen, Shanghai, Dongguan, Suzhou, Hangzhou, Nanjing, Foshan, Zhengzhou
National day	Zhoukou, Baoding, Huanggang, Anqing, Nantong, Ganzhou, Handan, Yancheng, Nanyang, Ji'an	Beijing, Shanghai, Zhengzhou, Shenzhen, Wuhan, Guangzhou, Chengdu, Nanjing, Hefei, Jinan

regional attributes and city characteristics also affect intercity mobility's spatial patterns in different holidays. Therefore, this study divides the possible influencing factors into 4 categories: regional attributes, travel purposes, travel distances and scales, city characteristics [66, 70, 76]. The regional attributes can be further classified into administrative divisions, geographical divisions and dialect divisions.

Regional Attributes

(1) **Administrative divisions**

As illustrated in Fig. 2.17, only in Spring Festival holiday do intercity mobility patterns form a diamond-shaped structure, with Beijing, Shanghai, Guangzhou

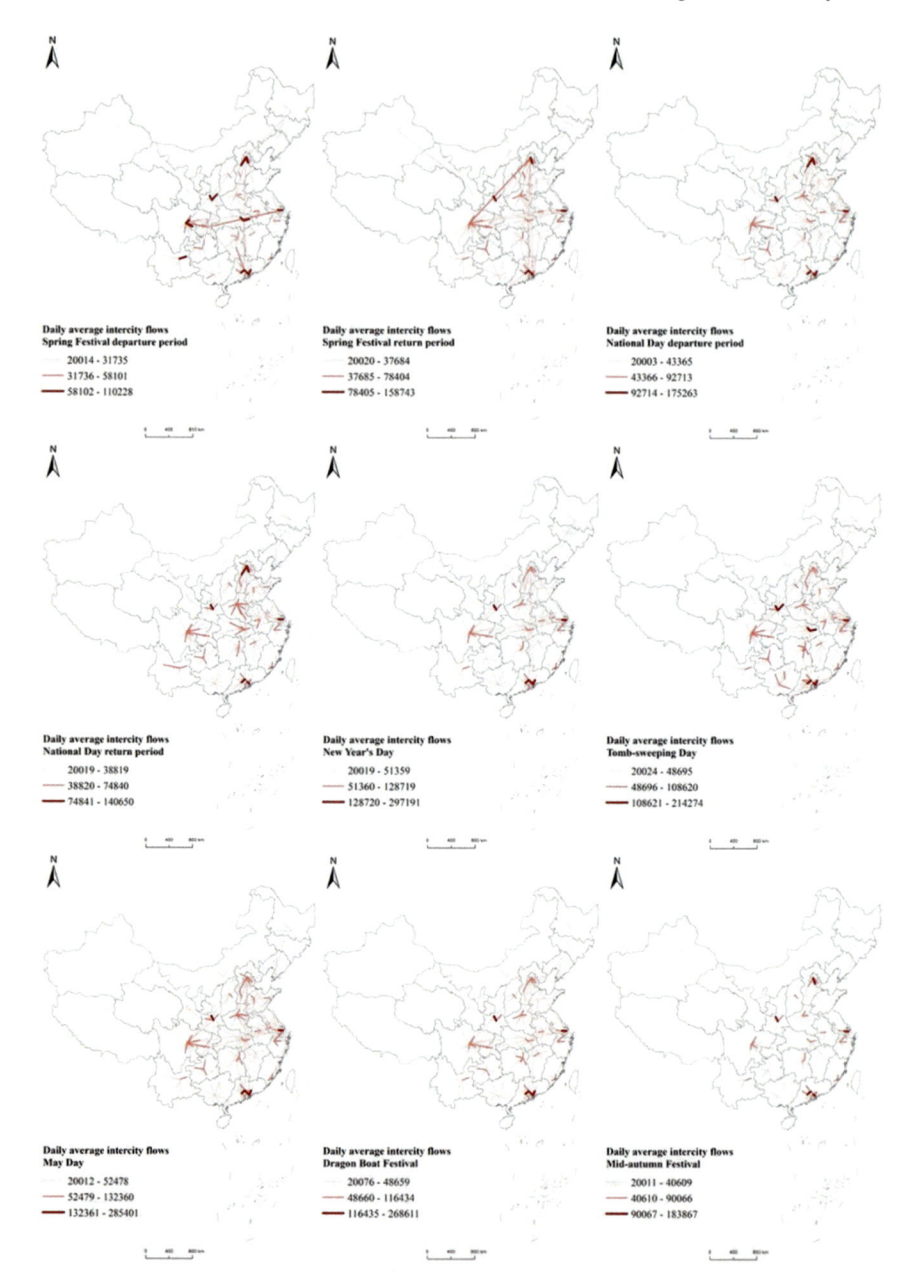

Fig. 2.17 Daily average intercity population flows in different holidays in 2018. *Notes:* We only show the intercity population flows larger than 20,000 (persons) in the maps to make the spatial patterns clear, with the administrative divisions of the provincial level

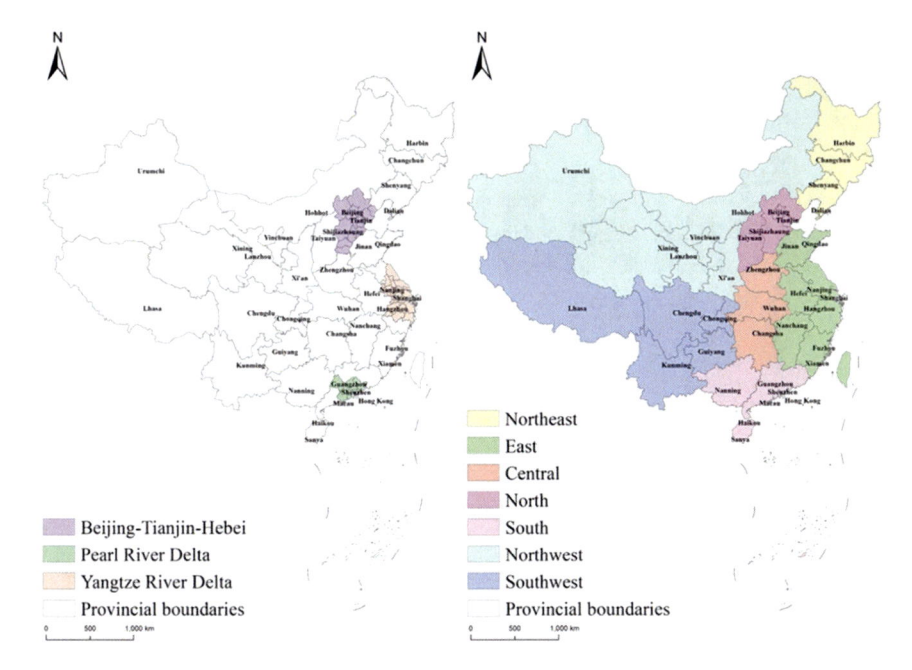

Fig. 2.18 Diagrammatic map of China's main urban agglomerations, main cities and 7 geographic divisions

(Shenzhen) and Chengdu (Chongqing) as vertexes, showing the features of long-distance travel. The population flows in other holidays are primarily medium or short distances, showing remarkable spatial proximity effects with the strongest connections between central cities (megacities and provincial cities) and surrounding secondary cities. Besides geographical proximity, the administrative divisions also matter, embodied in the fact that the largest population flows are mostly intra-provincial flows. In the same administrative division (province), cultural custom, management policies, resource allocation and factor mobility provide convenience for intercity linkages, making the intra-provincial connections much stronger than the inter-provincial connections. Provincial capital cities and major cities of a province function as the hub of both intra-provincial and inter-provincial linkages.

(2) **Geographical divisions**

To reveal the regional attributes, this study partitions China into 7 geographical divisions (Fig. 2.18): North China (Beijing, Tianjin, Hebei and Shanxi), Northeast China (Heilongjiang, Jilin and Liaoning), East China (Shanghai, Jiangsu, Zhejiang, Anhui, Jiangxi, Shandong, Fujian, Taiwan), Central China (Henan, Hubei, Hunan), South China (Guangdong, Guangxi, Hainan, HongKong, Macau), Southwest China (Chongqing, Sichuan, Guizhou, Yunnan, Tibet), Northwest China (Shaanxi, Gansu, Qinghai, Ningxia, Xinjiang, Inner Mongolia).

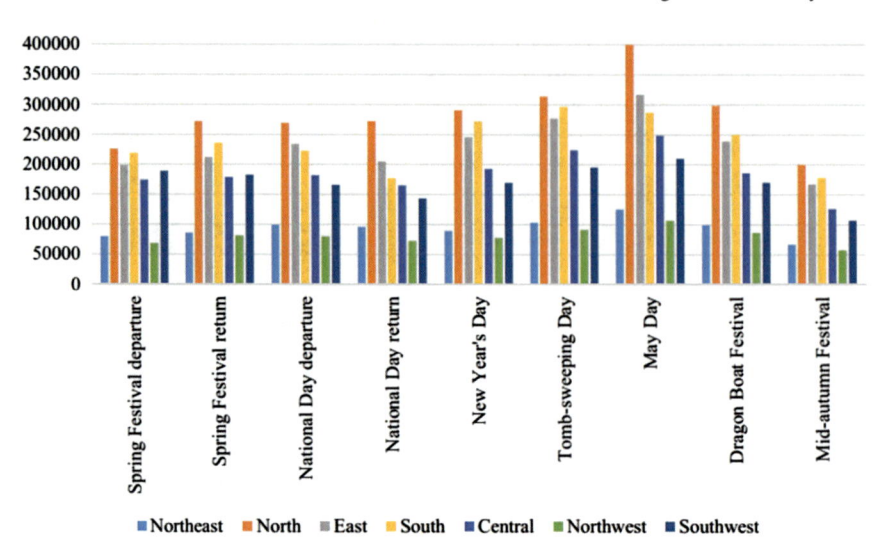

Fig. 2.19 Daily average population inflows + outflows (persons) of different regions in different holidays in 2018

On the whole, the daily average population mobility of North China is the largest, followed by East China and South China, the third level is Central China and Southwest China, and Northeast China and Northwest China come in last (Fig. 2.19).

Among the 3-day holidays, the population mobility is the strongest in the May Day holiday, followed by Tomb-sweeping Day, New Year's Day and Dragon Boat Festival, and Mid-autumn Festival have the relatively weakest population mobility. It displays that people are more likely to travel in the May Day holiday, while the population mobility of the Mid-autumn Festival is largely influenced by the National Day holiday that follows it immediately. Among these 7 geographical divisions, only South China has the largest population mobility during the Tomb-sweeping Day holiday, while the strongest population mobility characterizes other regions during the May Day holiday. South China is the main destination area in the Tomb-sweeping Day holiday, meaning that people in South China attach more importance to the tradition of returning to hometowns to honour the deceased relatives and satisfy the ancestors at this time.

The Spring Festival holiday's daily average population mobility is closer to that of the National Day holiday. For the Spring Festival holiday, the regions in descending order of population mobility are North China, South China, East China, Southwest China, Central China, Northeast China and Northwest China. For the National Day holiday, the regions in descending order of population mobility are North China, East China, South China, Central China, Southwest China, Northeast China and Northwest China. Though Fig. 2.19 shows that the amount of daily average inflows plus outflows during Spring Festival is smaller than the number of other holidays,

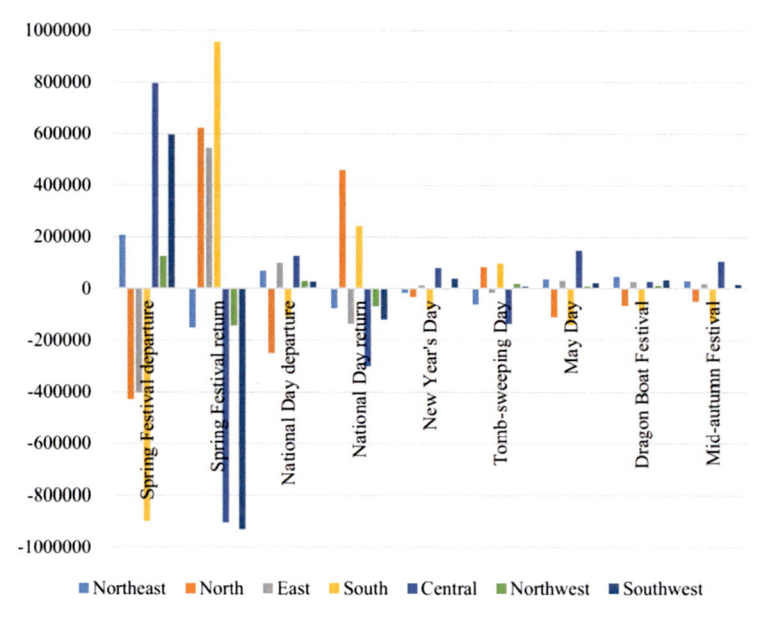

Fig. 2.20 Daily average net population inflows (persons) of different regions in different holidays in 2018

when considering the total amount of population flows (population inflows plus outflows throughout the holiday), it is found that the total travel scale of Spring Festival with a duration of 40 days is much larger than the other holidays, followed by National Day and May Day.

People in the south (South China and Southwest China) are more inclined to travel on traditional holidays than non-traditional holidays, while people in North China, East China, and Central China tend to travel on non-traditional holidays. Whether long holidays or short holidays, non-traditional holidays witness that Each China has more extensive population mobility than South China, while traditional holidays see the opposite situation. Although people in East China and South China both like travelling, they have completely different travel behaviours innon-traditional and traditional holidays. For another similar pair of regions-Central China and Southwest China, Central China exceeds Southwest China in terms of population mobility in all holidays, except in the Spring Festival holiday. It can be seen that the number of migrant workers from Southwest China is considerable.

The population flow directions during different holidays are displayed in Fig. 2.20. During the Spring Festival holiday, people mainly flow from East, North, and South China (the 3 biggest urban agglomerations) to Central, Southwest, Northwest, and Northeast China, from working places to their hometowns. People flow from North and South China to other leisure tourism regions during the National Day holiday and other short holidays (except Tomb-sweeping Day). In New Year's Day, Northeast and Northwest China witness net outflows of population, probably due to the influence of cold climates on tourism. In Tomb-sweeping Day, however, net population inflows occur in North, South, Southwest and Northwest China; net population outflows emerge in East, Central and Northeast China. This flow trend is opposite to the other holidays. Furthermore, people in the south attach more importance to the tradition in Tomb-sweeping Day and people from North China and South China like travelling, as previously mentioned. Therefore, Spring Festival and Tomb-sweeping Day are mainly for returning to hometowns according to tradition, while other holidays are more for leisure tourism.

(3) **Dialect divisions**

Language heterogeneity is an important cultural factor influencing population mobility because of cultural adaptation's expected cost [29]. Language competence can be regarded as a kind of human capital, and language differences will increase communication costs and cause individual identity problems. Thus, people tend to migrate to the same dialect region to work and live [77]. However, people like travelling to cities with different dialects to experience different customs and cultures for tourism purposes. Though Mandarin Chinese is the official language in China, significantly different dialects influence social-spatial segregation and agglomeration [76]. People speaking the same dialect usually share similar social and cultural backgrounds, thus leading to similar travel behaviours. Cities in China can be divided into 9 dialect divisions (Fig. 2.21).

It is evident in Fig. 2.22 that the Wu Dialect region and Cantonese region's population mobility is the largest, demonstrating that people in these regions are fond of travelling due to the relatively higher economic development level and higher living standards. The second level of population mobility occurs in the Xiang Dialect region, the third level in the Mandarin, Min Dialect, Gan Dialect and Jin Dialect regions, and the last in the Tibetan region. The Wu Dialect region's population mobility is larger than that of the Cantonese region during non-traditional holidays, while it is the opposite during traditional holidays, reflecting that people of the Cantonese region emphasize more on traditional holidays than those of the Wu Dialect region.

Similar to the above results, the population mobility during the Spring festival and National Day holidays is most muscular in the Wu Dialect and Cantonese regions. Net population outflows feature these 2 regions in the departure period and net population inflows in the return period (Fig. 2.23). This manifests that the Pearl River Delta Region (approximate to Cantonese region) and Yangtze River Delta Region (approximate to Wu dialect region) are the main employment areas. People who work there return to hometowns or travel during holidays and come back to workplaces after holidays. The population flow direction is reverse in Xiang Dialect, Gan Dialect, Mandarin, Jin Dialect and Min Dialect regions. Wu Dialect region and Cantonese region show net outflows and other regions present net inflows during all 3-day holidays except Tomb-sweeping Day, exhibiting that people in the Wu Dialect region and Cantonese region value the tradition of returning to hometowns to honour the deceased relatives and satisfy the ancestors in Tomb-sweeping Day. During the departure period of Spring Festival and 3-day holidays (except Tomb-sweeping Day), the Xiang and Gan Dialect regions are the main destination areas;

Fig. 2.21 Distribution of 9 dialect divisions in China

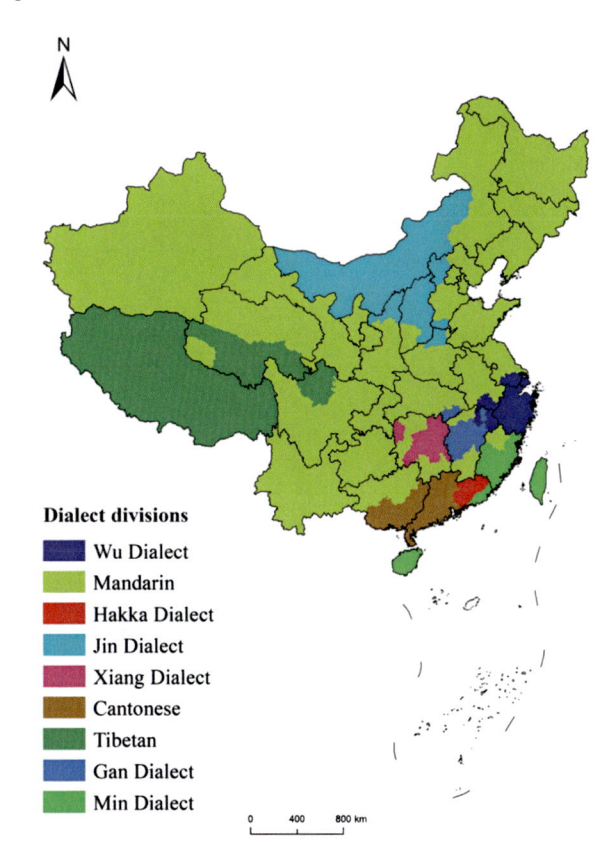

during the departure period of National Day, the Jin and Min Dialect regions become the main destination areas. The Xiang and Gan Dialect regions are geographically closer to the Wu Dialect and Cantonese regions, making the former become the main origin areas of migrant workers and tourist destinations of the latter during short holidays. However, the Jin and Min Dialect regions stand out during the National Day holiday for showing more attraction for tourists.

Travel Purposes

As it is known to all, travel purposes also have impacts on intercity mobility patterns. For non-traditional holidays, the travel purpose is mainly leisure tourism; for traditional holidays, the travel purpose is particularly returning home for visiting relatives and sacrificial activities, especially in the Spring Festival and Tomb sweeping Day. China's main employment areas are concentrated in the 3 biggest urban agglomerations and other regional central cities, which can be regarded as the primary origin areas during holidays based on the largest floating population. The main destination

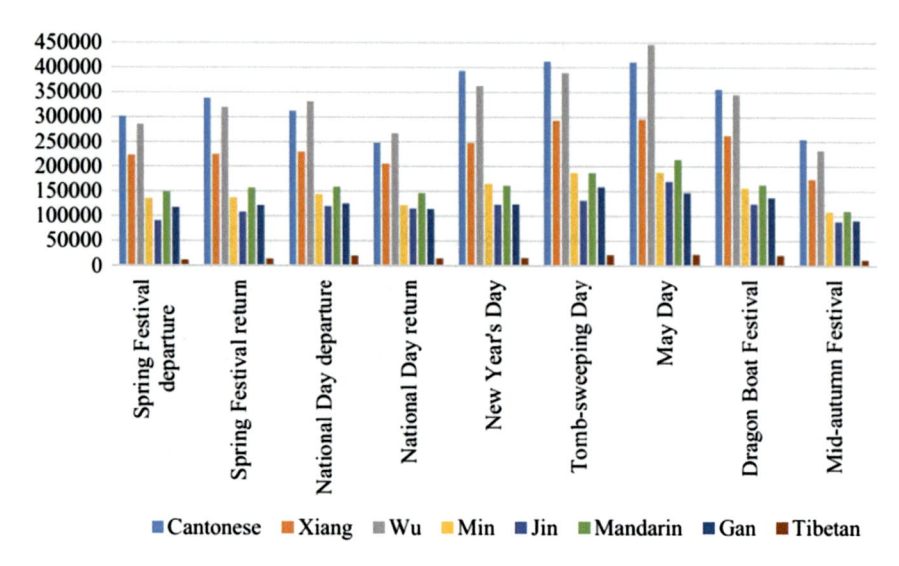

Fig. 2.22 Daily average population inflows + outflows (persons) of different dialect divisions in different holidays in 2018. *Notes:* Hakka region contains only 3 cities, so we do not calculate its average to avoid statistical bias

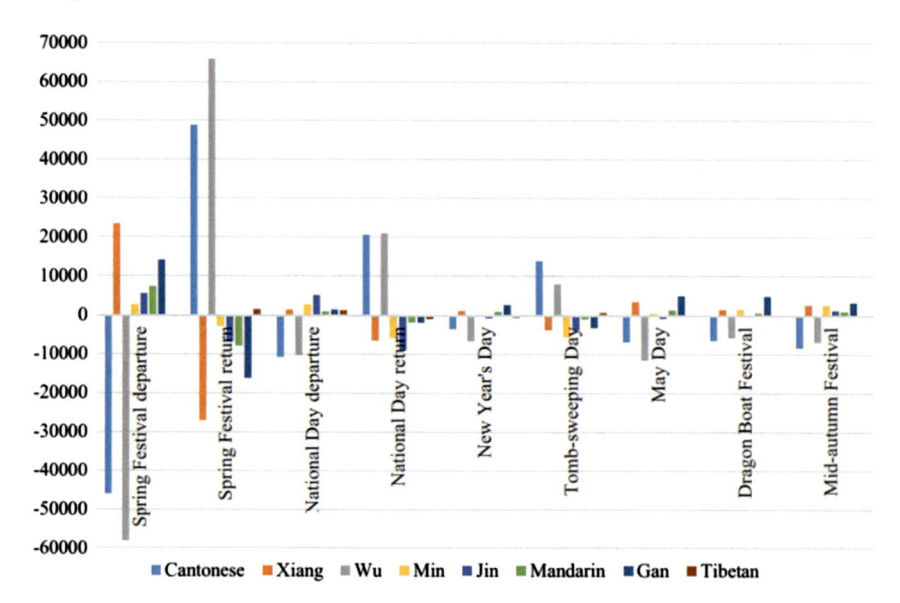

Fig. 2.23 Daily average net population inflows (persons) of different dialect divisions in different holidays in 2018

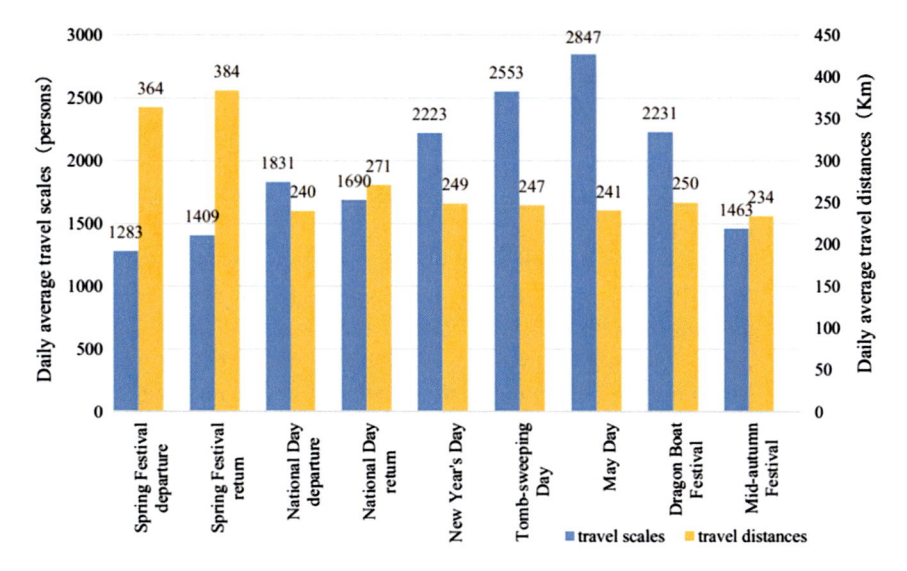

Fig. 2.24 Daily average travel scales and distances

areas of non-traditional holidays are surrounding cities of these origin cities and important tourism cities, owing to people's demands of tourism and relaxation and the consideration of limited time and convenience. Whereas the destination areas of traditional holidays usually spread throughout the country, the south of China predominates over the north, for tradition prevails in the south.

Travel Distances and Scales

As illustrated in Fig. 2.24, the largest daily average travel scales occur in the May Day holiday, followed by Tomb-sweeping Day, Dragon Boat Festival and New Year's Day. The Mid-autumn Festival's travel scale is relatively smaller because it is close to the long holiday (National Day). The daily average travel scales in Spring Festival and National Day holidays are also smaller due to the distribution over relatively long periods. From the perspective of travel distances, the daily average travel distance (over 300 km) is the longest in the Spring Festival holiday, on account of people's returning to their hometowns all over the country from where they work. The daily average travel distances in other holidays are similar to each other (around 250 km).

Other Factors at the City Level

The daily population mobility is primarily affected by the economic development level and tourism development level of cities. According to classical migration theories [78, 79], the economic development level (employment opportunities and income level) is critical in selecting workplaces. Therefore, for all travel purposes (visiting relatives or leisure trips) during different holidays, origin cities' attributes influencing population flows are mainly economic factors, including GDP, average wage, housing prices, industrial structures, and total retail sales of consumer goods. For the travel purpose of leisure tourism, the characteristics of destination cities that affect population mobility consist of the number of tourist attractions, hotels and employees in the tourism industry [70].

As shown in Table 2.6, economic and tourism factors are significantly and positively correlated with cities' daily average inflows in all holidays. When replacing the average daily inflows with net inflows of each city, among all holidays, housing prices and GDP have the highest positive correlation with the daily net inflows of cities during the Spring Festival return period (with the correlation coefficients as 0.797 and 0.744). Meanwhile, the employment figures of tourism-related industries, employment figures of the service industry, and numbers of hotels have the highest positive correlation with the daily net inflows of cities during the National Day departure period (with the correlation coefficients as 0.795, 0.821 and 0.768). This demonstrates that the primary origin areas during the Spring Festival holiday are comparatively developed cities. Due to their higher economic development levels, more employment opportunities and higher wage levels, cities in the Pearl River Delta, Yangtze River Delta, and Beijing-Tianjin-Hebei Urban Agglomerations are still the main attraction centres of population flows and the main employment regions [80]. In this period, the main direction of population flows is going home for a family reunion from workplaces, which are more influenced by city-level economic factors. However, during the National Day holiday, the main destination areas are major tourism cities, with tourists attracted more by the tourism industry's development levels of cities. Intercity leisure trips happen more frequently during non-traditional holidays, so a city's tourism resources and tourism reception capability exert a significant influence on the number of visitors [70].

2.1.3.5   Discussion

This comparative study of intercity mobility patterns among different holidays has made certain contributions to the extant literature. Firstly, intercity mobility studies based on big data usually neglect a critical perspective: the temporal heterogeneity of intercity mobility [70]. Existing research only compares the differences among weekdays, weekends, and certain national holidays [66, 70, 72], while the differences among various national holidays have been under-researched. Therefore, this study compares the spatial patterns of intercity mobility among different holidays, considering a complete holiday classification: long holidays versus short holidays, non-traditional holidays versus traditional holidays. We obtain fascinating discoveries by comparing the intercity mobility patterns between Spring Festival and National Day, between Tomb-sweeping Day, Dragon Boat Festival, Mid-autumn Festival and New Year's Day, May Day. Different holidays have different meanings for Chinese

Table 2.6 The correlation analysis between daily average population inflows of cities and influencing factors

	Spring festival departure period	Spring festival return period	National day departure period	National day return period	New year's day	Tomb-sweeping day	May day	Dragon boat festival	Mid-autumn festival
GDP	0.810	0.873	0.858	0.870	0.854	0.858	0.867	0.859	0.850
Housing price	0.600	0.777	0.696	0.749	0.737	0.727	0.731	0.738	0.728
Total retail sales of consumer goods	0.836	0.879	0.884	0.893	0.864	0.878	0.890	0.872	0.863
Employment figure of tourism-related industries	0.804	0.851	0.783	0.857	0.798	0.800	0.810	0.817	0.787
Employment figure of service industry	0.835	0.881	0.804	0.892	0.811	0.820	0.839	0.843	0.810
Number of hotels	0.823	0.834	0.821	0.854	0.812	0.842	0.842	0.831	0.811

Notes: The significance levels of all Pearson correlation coefficients in Table 2.6 are 0.001, meaning that they are highly statistically significant. The tourism-related industries include wholesale and retail sale trades, transportation, warehousing and postal service industry, and the lodging and catering industry. The data of housing prices in 2017 come from the Anjuke housing information website (https://www.anjuke.com/fangjia/quanguo2017/). The number of hotels in all cities is obtained from Ctrip's official website (http://www.ctrip.com/), China's leading hotel booking service centre. The other indicators are collected from China City Statistical Yearbook 2018, which records the data of 2017.

people, resulting in different travel purposes, travel distances, and travel destinations, leading to different travel behaviours and spatial patterns of intercity mobility.

Secondly, though some scholars have paid attention to the effects of regional features on intercity mobility [66, 76, 80], there is a lack of a systematic consideration of natural, political and cultural dimensions. Zhang et al. [76] produced an interaction-based regionalization based on the daily intercity mobility network in Yangtze River Delta and analyzed its forming reasons by comparing it with the attribute-based regionalization (including administrative divisions, landform regions and dialect divisions). At the national level, we further explore the critical role of regional attributes in affecting intercity mobility systematically from the perspectives of administrative divisions, geographical divisions and dialect divisions. The geographical divisions and dialect divisions are somehow associated with each other, with 2 related pairs of regions (East China and Wu Dialect region, South China and Cantonese region) having the highest population mobility. Though the rapid development of transportation and communication technology can somehow weaken the distance-decaying effect on population mobility (the effects of administrative divisions), some underlying social and cultural factors need to be considered in the destination selection in the human movement process (including geographic identity and social adaptation). The geographic identity is a psychological judgement, and the social adaptation is a psychological result, and they can be reflected in the natural conditions, cultural customs and living habits [80]. The huge disparity in natural conditions between the north and the south will lead to different cultural customs and living habits, embodied in the different importance attached to traditional holidays.

Thirdly, this study discovers that cultural factors are the potential causes of intercity mobility's spatial and temporal heterogeneity. The most important traditional holidays for Chinese people currently are Spring Festival and Tomb-sweeping Day. The travel purpose for the former is returning home for a family reunion, and for the latter is returning to hometowns to honour the dead relatives and the ancestors. Other traditional holidays still carry out the significance of inheriting traditional cultures and also blend into leisure tourism. The people in the south of China (South and Southwest China) or people from the Cantonese region lay more stress on tradition, embodied in the ancestral temples all over the south.

Finally, some policy implications can be drawn from this study: First, the spatial and temporal heterogeneity of intercity mobility discovered by this study can provide scientific evidence for governments and ministry of transports to rationally arrange for transportation resources, focusing more on main origin cities and destination cities, in order to satisfy people's various demands of travelling in diverse regions during different holidays. Second, Pearl River Delta, Yangtze River Delta, and Beijing-Tianjin-Hebei Urban Agglomerations still play a dominant role in China's city network system of population mobility, while central cities of other urban agglomerations have relatively lower functional levels except for Xi'an, which need to be further strengthened to correspond to the major national strategies of regional development (Belt and Road Initiative and Yangtze River Economic Belt). To a certain extent, the whole city network system of population mobility can be further improved by enhancing convenient transportation systems in other regions. Learning from the example of Xi'an, the active talent attraction policies and tourism publicity can also impact a city's population mobility.

Despite its contributions, this study still has some limitations. Tencent migration data only records the population flows between each city and its top 10 origin cities and destination cities, so we can only use this data for basic spatial pattern analysis rather than rigorous econometric analysis, not to mention the lack of statistical data in different periods of a year. Therefore, we can only discuss the possible influencing factors by a simple statistical analysis method. Future studies can combine this data with other data sources to investigate the influencing mechanism of intercity mobility and employ Tencent migration data of multiple years (such as 2016–2020) to reveal human movements' spatial–temporal dynamics deeply.

2.1.3.6 Conclusions

Based on the Tencent migration data of 2018 in China, we conduct a comparative study on spatial patterns of intercity mobility among different holidays and reveals underlying reasons. The main conclusions are demonstrated as follows.

Firstly, spatial patterns of intercity mobility in different holidays are different. The non-traditional holidays are distinct from traditional holidays. The cities in the 3 biggest urban agglomerations and several regional central cities rank the top in the city hierarchical structure of population mobility, functioning as the main origin cities during holidays. The cities of Pearl River Delta and Xi'an stand out. The main destination cities in traditional holidays are relatively scattered, while the main destination cities in non-traditional holidays are relatively concentrated in the surrounding cities of national and regional central cities and tourism cities. It is worth noting that the Tomb-sweeping Day holiday is an exceptional period for its reverse direction of population flows compared with other 3-day traditional holidays.

Secondly, regional attributes have remarkable effects on the spatial patterns of intercity mobility in different holidays. The largest intercity flows usually happen between central cities and their surrounding cities in the range of a province, signifying the important role of administrative divisions and geographical proximity. East China (approximate to Wu Dialect region) and South China (approximate to Cantonese region) stick out as the main origin areas with the highest population mobility in terms of geographical divisions and dialect divisions. The former's population mobility is larger than that of the latter during non-traditional holidays, and it is just the reverse during traditional holidays. It appears that people in the south of China (South and Southwest China) pay more attention to tradition.

Thirdly, travel purposes also exert impacts on intercity mobility among different holidays. During non-traditional holidays, the travel purpose is mainly leisure tourism, while the travel purpose of traditional holidays is mainly returning home for visiting relatives and sacrificial activities, leading to different distributions of main destination cities. Also, the travel distances and scales are different on different holidays. The largest daily average travel scale characterizes the May Day holiday, and the farthest daily average travel distance marks the Spring Festival holiday.

Last but not least, the city-level economic factors and tourism factors both affect intercity mobility patterns. Economic factors have more influence on job location choices, thus related correlation coefficients are highest during the Spring Festival holiday. However, the selection of main destination areas during the National Day holiday is more affected by cities' tourism factors.

2.1.4 Driving Factors of In-Migration in Coastal and Inland Cities in China

2.1.4.1 Introduction

Statistics of 2015 show that China's total population has reached 1.375 billion, the highest in the world. Since the reform and opening up, there have been dramatic changes in population migration between regions, largely due to the uneven development of socio-economic and infrastructural factors between regions, and the gradual relaxation of the *hukou* system. A large population have migrated from undeveloped rural areas to relatively developed urban areas in search of better living conditions and development opportunities.

According to the 6th national population census in 2010 (the 6th census), the number of in-migrants across China reached 169 million in 2010, accounting for nearly 12% of the total population, compared to the number of in-migrants in the 5th national population census in 2000 (the 5th census) (78.16 million), an increase of nearly 2.3 times. From the perspective of in-migration, it can be observed that economically developed coastal cities and regions have become main destination areas of population migration, while some less economically developed inland areas have become main origin areas of population migration.

The total number of coastal cities in China only accounts for 16.25% of the total number of prefecture-level cities in China, but the total number of in-migrants in coastal prefecture-level cities accounts for 42.01% of the total in-migrants in China, according to the 6th national population census data. A great development disparity between regions will lead to a significant difference between regions in the number of in-migrants.

From an economic perspective, Li [81] discovered that population migration is closely related to economic factors, such as the economic development level, wage level, the economic extroversion, employment opportunities and unemployment rates in different regions in China. From the geographic perspective, Wang et al. [4, 82] analysed the factors influencing the distribution patterns of in-migration and out-migration flows in 31 provinces in China, and found the distance between origin and destination places will affect the transportation costs and time costs of the migrants. Most extant studies on population migration in China have focused on a particular provincial unit or a region (northeastern, eastern, central, western regions or urban agglomerations), and some studies have discovered that the migration distance, regional economic development level (GDP, unemployment rates, salary and income levels, etc.) and the public service levels all exert impacts on in-migration, taking Jiangsu Province, Yangtze River Delta metropolitan area and Pearl River Delta metropolitan area as examples. Liu [83] employed the 5th and 6th census data to explore the changes in regional patterns and the characteristics of in-migration respectively. Li et al. [84] conducted an empirical study of in-migration within a province, and analyzed the spatial-temporal differences and spatial patterns of Guangdong Province and Hubei Province. In general, there are relatively few empirical studies focusing on the influencing factors on in-migration in prefecture-level cities [85]. This study attempts to investigate the economic factors affecting the in-migration of coastal cities and inland cities based on a negative binominal regression model, and propose policy recommendations for a balanced development among cities and a reasonable and orderly urbanisation pattern in China.

2.1.4.2 Data and Research Methods

Research Data

This study uses the 6th national population census data as the basis for a study of 346 administrative units (prefecture-level cities, autonomous prefectures, autonomous regions, and regions) at the prefectural level and above, and analyses which factors influence in-migration.

The regional divisions help to compare the variability of influencing factors between regions. Therefore, the prefecture-level cities in China are divided into coastal cities and inland cities [86], among which 53 prefectural-level units are regarded as coastal cities, including 2 municipality directly under the central government (Shanghai and Tianjin), 7 sub-provincial cities (Hangzhou, Guangzhou, Dalian, Qingdao, Ningbo, Xiamen and Shenzhen) and 44 prefecture-level cities, and the other units are deemed as inland cities.

The in-migrants refer to those who have lived in the current residence that is different from their registered permanent residence for more than six months at the census time of 2010. The data of influencing factors come from the *2010 China Statistical Yearbook for Regional Economy*, recording the data of 2009. As there is a lag effect in population migration, the migration in the current period is often affected by the factors of the previous period.

After data processing, some prefecture-level units are removed due to missing data, including Jiyuan, Enshi Tujia and Miao Autonomous Prefecture, Xiantao, Qianjiang, Tianmen, Shennongjia Forest Region, Zhongwei, Shihezi, Alar, Tumxuk, Wujiaqu, Guilin, Beihai, and prefecture-level units in Qinghai Province and Tibet Autonomous Region. Finally, 319 prefecture-level units are selected as the effective sample, consisting of 52 coastal cities and 267 inland cities.

Table 2.7 The data distribution test

	Number of samples	Z value	P value
Coastal cities	52	6.26	<0.001
Inland cities	269	11.18	<0.001

Table 2.8 Dispersion test for in-migration

	Number of samples	Mean	Variance
Coastal cities	52	136.65	46,467.75
Inland cities	267	36.24	6089.81

Research Methods

In general, most empirical studies in population economics use grey correlation analysis, panel data analysis and multiple linear regression as the main research methods [87–89], and set the dependent variable as the number of population migration, in-migration and out-migration, and the independent variables as economic and social factors.

The number of in-migration within a certain period is the number of events, which are discrete non-negative integers. Table 2.7 shows the result of the data distribution test, and the fact of P-values <0.05 indicates that the data follows a skewed distribution, and violates the normal distribution assumption of the OLS regression. Therefore, the Poisson or negative binomial regression model is employed to analyze the influencing factors of in-migration to deal with the discrete distribution.

The Poisson regression model is similar to the negative binomial regression model in that it is a mean regression of the count variables through maximum likelihood estimation. The Poisson regression assumes that the mean must be equal to the variance under the Poisson distribution assumption, and if the variance is greater than the mean, there is excessive dispersion in the data. Under this condition, the Poisson regression will underestimate the standard deviation of parameters and overestimate the significance level of independent variables, so it is necessary to employ the negative binomial regression model instead. Assuming that the in-migration data obeys a Poisson distribution, the mean of the in-migration data must be equal to the variance of the in-migration data, and the variance and mean of the dependent variable (in-migration) need to be further tested. Table 2.8 shows that the variance of both coastal cities and inland cities is much larger than the mean, contrary to the assumption of Poisson distribution, so we employ a negative binomial regression model to conduct an empirical analysis of the influencing factors of in-migration.

Table 2.9 Variable selection

Influencing factors	Indicators	Abbreviations
Per capita GDP	Per capita GDP	gdp
Employment opportunities	Number of employed persons in urban areas/(Number of employed persons in urban areas + Number of registered unemployed persons in urban areas)	empi
Wage	Average salary of employed persons	wage
Percentage of secondary industry	Total output value of the secondary industry/Total output value of the primary, secondary and tertiary industries	Ind2
Percentage of tertiary industry	Total output value of the tertiary industry/Total output value of the primary, secondary and tertiary industries	Ind3
Basic medical facilities	Number of beds in health institutions	med
Percentage of government welfare expenditure	(Social security and employment expenditure + Education expenditure + Health care expenditure)/Total financial expenditure	gov
Basic education facilities	Number of ordinary secondary schools/Land area	edu

Variable Selection

Based on the extant literature, the factors influencing in-migration consist of regional economic growth, employment, population, wages and income, basic medical facilities, education level, government expenditure, industrial structure, the distance between destination and origin regions [83, 90–92], etc. The selection of variables in this study is shown in Table 2.9, including the following aspects: firstly, per capita GDP and the percentage of secondary and tertiary industries are employed to explore the impact of regional economic development level on the population in-migration; secondly, the employment opportunities and salary levels in the destination cities have direct effects on the in-migration; thirdly, basic medical facilities, basic education facilities and the percentage of government welfare expenditure are applied to reflect the influences of public services.

Model Construction

In the negative binomial regression model, the independent variable does not satisfy the assumption of normal distribution in the OLS model, so the linear regression expectation value model is transformed into an exponential function as Eq. (2.1):

$$E(M_{it}|X_{it}) = Var(M_{it}|X_{it}) = \lambda_{it} = exp(\beta X_{it}) \tag{2.1}$$

The density function of the negative binomial regression model is shown in Eq. (2.2).

$$f(M_{it}|\mu,\alpha) = \frac{\Gamma\left(M_{it}+\alpha^{-1}\right)}{\Gamma(M_{it}+1)\Gamma(\alpha^{-1})}\left(\frac{\alpha^{-1}}{\alpha^{-1}+\mu}\right)^{\alpha^{-1}}\left(\frac{\mu}{\alpha^{-1}+\mu}\right)^{M_{it}}, \alpha \geq 0, \ M_{it} = 0,1,2,\ldots \tag{2.2}$$

of which $E(M_{it}|X_{it}) = \mu$, $Var(M_{it}|X_{it}) = \mu(1+\mu\alpha)$, $\Gamma(\cdot)$ is the gamma distribution function.

The log-likelihood function $\Gamma(\cdot)$ of the corresponding negative binomial regression model is Eq. (2.3), so that the maximum likelihood estimates β and α can be obtained by maximising the log-likelihood function in Eq. (2.3) through computer iteration.

$$\ln L(\alpha,\beta) = \sum_{i=1}^{n}\left\{\begin{array}{l}\sum_{j=0}^{M_{it}-1}\ln(j+\alpha^{-1}) - \ln M_{it}! - (M_{it}+\alpha^{-1})\ln(1+\alpha\exp(M_{it}\beta)) \\ +M_{it}\ln\alpha + M_{it}X_{it}\beta\end{array}\right. \tag{2.3}$$

2.1.4.3 Regression Results

This section include 2 regression analyses, the dependent variable of the first part is the total in-migration of coastal areas and inland areas, and the second part takes the interprovinicial in-migration as the dependent variable. The total in-migration can be divided into intraprovincial and interprovincial in-migration. General speaking, it takes higher migration costs (such as transportation costs, communication costs and social networks) to migrate within a province than beyond a province. However, the data displays that the interprovinicial in-migration of the coastal areas account for 57% of the country's interprovinicial in-migration, so we investigate the influencing factors on the total in-migration and the interprovinical in-migration from the perspectives of coastal cities and inland cities.

Total In-Migration

The results of the negative binomial regression are shown in Table 2.10. The employment opportunities, the percentage of secondary or tertiary industry, and basic medical facilities all have significantly positive impacts on the total in-migration

Table 2.10 The regression results of the total in-migration

	Coastal area	Inland area
Gdp	−9.45000*	0.000107***
Empi	33.37000***	2.557859*
Wage	4.280000	3.642000***
Ind2	8.272530***	1.394241**
Ind3	9.538043***	3.257248***
Edu	1.746973	0.3859631
Med	0.000034***	0.0000519***
Gov	−1.936000	−1.279292**
Constant	−36.61114***	−2.511661*
−2Log likelihood	−246.1910	−983.6346
Pseudo R^2	0.1943	0.1982
Sample observations	52	267

Note: * signifies $p < 0.1$, ** signifies $p < 0.05$, *** signifies $p < 0.01$

in the coastal cities, which is consistent with the expected hypothesis. The employment opportunities have the strongest impact on the in-migration in the coastal areas, followed by the industrial structure, among which the percentage of the tertiary industry is more influential than the percentage of the secondary industry, indicating that the tertiary industry has a relatively stronger employment absorption capacity than the secondary industry. In general, the economic incentives still play a dominant role in affecting migration behaviours. The basic medical facilities also matters in attracting the in-migration, demonstrating that besides economic factors, people also concern about the public services in their migration decision process.

Regarding the inland areas, the per capita GDP, the employment opportunities, the wage level, the percentage of secondary or tertiary industry, basic medical facilities and the percentage of government welfare expenditure all have significantly positive impacts on the total in-migration in the inland cities. Compared with the coastal areas, immigrants attach more importance to the economic development level (the per capita GDP and the wage level), probably due to the fact that the income level is more important for migrants to settle down in the relatively underdeveloped inland regions with a relatively imperfect job market and social security system.

There exists a significant negative relationship between government welfare expenditure and in-migration in inland areas, which is inconsistent with the expectation. The possible reason for this is that the governments of the inland cities do not function well in the provision of public services, which cannot satisfy the demands of floating population. In addition, a large in-migration population will exert a crowding effect on the local public services for the original inhabitants and cause social problems, if the government does not timely improve the local public services.

Table 2.11 The regression results of the interprovincial in-migration		Coastal area	Inland area
	Gdp	-0.000198^{***}	0.000177^{***}
	Empi	40.35872^{***}	6.215896^{***}
	Wage	13.584000^{***}	5.721000^{***}
	Ind2	11.44264^{***}	-0.156514
	Ind3	12.32019^{***}	2.4637780^{***}
	Edu	2.229133	-3.669140
	Med	0.0000279^{***}	0.0000414^{***}
	Gov	-1.390857	-0.515381
	_cons	-38.41013^{***}	1.668992^{*}
	-2Log likelihood	-700.22552	-3175.4341
	Pseudo R^2	0.0748	0.0646
	Sample observations	52	267

Note * signifies $p < 0.1$, ** signifies $p < 0.05$, *** signifies $p < 0.01$

In summary, the economic factors are still the critical driving force for in-migration in both coastal and inland areas, and public service levels also play a certain role in attracting floating population.

Interprovinical In-Migration

China's interprovincial in-migration population accounts for 50.46% of the total in-migration population, while the interprovincial in-migration population in coastal areas accounts for 57% of its total in-migration population. Therefore, the interprovincial in-migration is very important, and we will further investigate the influencing factors of the interprovincial in-migration, shown in Table 2.11. The employment opportunities, wage levels, the percentage of tertiary industry, and basic medical facilities all have significantly positive impacts on the total in-migration in both the coastal cities and inland cities, which is consistent with the expected hypothesis. Different from the inland areas, the per capita GDP has negative impacts on the interprovincial in-migration in coastal areas and the percentage of secondary industry has significantly positive effects. Migrants pay more attention to the economic factors that directly affect their work and life, such as the employment opportunities and wage levels, while the per capita GDP play a less important role. The tertiary industry have more influence on both the total in-migration and the interprovincial in-migration than the secondary industry, and the secondary industry are more attractive for floating population in the coastal area than in the inland area. In general, the economic factors have a greater impact on the interprovincial in-migration than on the total in-migration.

2.1.4.4 Conclusions and Discussion

This study discovers that, among the influencing factors, the employment opportunities and wage levels have the greatest impacts on in-migration, industrial structure and basic medical facilities also matter. For inter-provincial migrants, the employment opportunities and the wage level are more important, since the migration costs of inter-provincial migrants are higher than those of intra-provincial migrants, they urgently need a job with enough income to support their living expenses, otherwise they may return or choose to move to other areas.

According to the expected income theory, the employment opportunities and the wage levels are both key determinants in attracting in-migration, and the former is even more important than the latter, for it is the precondition of the latter. Furthermore, there exists a negative relationship between government welfare expenditure and in-migration, which indicates that there is a gap between the public services provided by the governments and the psychological expectations of the in-migrants.

This study has certain policy implications: Firstly, in cities with low in-migration, governments should moderately raise the minimum wage limit to provide safeguard mechanism for immigrants, and make an effort to raise the wage levels of migrant workers, which will further stimulate the in-migration. Secondly, the local government should provide more employment opportunities for migrants by promoting the development of the secondary and tertiary industry, and help improve the competitiveness in the job market by providing more free occupational training for migrant workers. Thirdly, the government should conduct a survey on the floating population's preference for public services in order to avoid unnecessary social losses, and actively advance the equalization of public services to ensure that the migrants can enjoy the same social benefits as local residents.

2.2 An Exploration into China's Urban System Evolution Forecast Based on Intercity Migration

2.2.1 Introduction

Since the 1990s, accompanying the rapid urbanization, an important feature of China's social change is its large-scale interregional migration, originating from not only the high demand for labor in the eastern coastal region due to its development policy but also the gradual loosening of migration and household registration policies. The migrant population has reached 247 million by 2015, accounting for approximately 1/6 of the total population, with an increase of approximately 8 million per year, according to the 2016 Report on China's Migrant Population Development released by the National Health and Family Planning Commission of China. With the rapid development of China's urbanization, intercity migration has directly led to the change of city numbers and sizes at all levels, thus affecting the city hierarchical structure and city spatial distribution, namely the urban system. The urban system is a spatial distribution structure in a region, country or the world consisting of cities of different types and sizes. As the connections between cities are becoming increasingly complex instead of containing purely vertical and horizontal linkages and the social network analysis method (Social network analysis (SNA) is the mapping and measuring of relationships and flows between people, groups, organizations, computers and other connected socioeconomic entities) is in wide use, urban system research has shifted gradually from the inspection of city attributes to the exploration of intercity relationships in networked societies in the form of "world city network research" [93, 94]. From the perspective of migration, all cities in the urban system form a network connected by intercity migration and this spatial linkage integrates the scattered cities into a whole. By conducting an associated exploration of migration and the urban system, both of which are important issues in the research fields of regional economics and urban geography, this study comprehensively and deeply reveals the interaction and co-evolution mechanism between the two, combining theories of demography and New Economic Geography.

Population represents regional competitiveness in current China and the diminishing of China's demographic dividend leads to a new round of population battle between cities [24]. China is now in a transition stage from the industrial society to the post-industrial society, in which the low-end manufacturing has been gradually replaced by the service industry, whose development needs sufficient labor force and domestic market demand, as well as high-quality talents, so megacities and urban agglomerations with large population have obvious advantages. This study investigates the direction of the future population battle and predicts which cities will stand out. The key research question in this study, therefore, concerns how China's migration network influences the urban system and what the distribution of China's future city sizes will be. This is of particular interest for several reasons. Firstly, urbanization has become a dominant tendency influencing China's future economic development and the clearest manifestation of urbanization is migration, which brings about the evolution of the urban system. Second, starting from the essence of China's urbanization—the migration network, this study analyzes the influencing factors of migration and the evolutionary process of the urban system and establishes an urban system model with an explicit intercity migration mechanism and a clear spatial reference, thus deepening the studies of the urban system and migration. Thirdly, the model is used as the basis for predicting the size changes of all cities, regarding the whole urban system as a network connected by intercity migration, with the prediction results providing scientific evidence for decision making in National New-Type Urbanization Planning, in terms of floating population management, public service improvement and urban system planning.

2.2.2   Literature Review

As there exists a close relationship between the urban system and migration, this study will review studies on migration and the urban system in a separate and integrated context. More specifically, it starts with migration theories, taking into account China's population projection methods, introduces theoretical models of urban system, further discusses the relationship between migration and the urban system and finally summarizes deficiencies of current research and the main contributions of this study.

Migration models, which are used to analyze and simulate the migration process and predict migration indices, can be divided into macro models, micro models and comprehensive models in terms of the research scale. This study investigates intercity migration, which can be viewed as a mechanism analysis at the macro level, so we will focus on macro models and comprehensive models (combining macro models with micro models). There are three main types of macro models. First, the basic idea of a gravity model [95–97] is that interregional migration is positively related to the population sizes and economic development levels of the origin and destination regions and inversely related to the distance between these two regions. Second, push–pull migration theory [78] holds that the push force of the origin region, the pull force of the destination region and intervening obstacle factors directly influence migration. This theory has been extended by other scholars [95, 98] to include a series of influencing factors: demographic, economic (such as income and unemployment rate), social, geographic, ecological factors, government policies (including migration policies, especially household registration system in China), housing indexes, previous interregional migration flow and interregional distance. Third, the Markov chain migration model [99, 100] assumes that migration is determined by the probability of interregional migration. Other classical microeconomic migration models incorporate the Dual Economy Model [101], the Expected Income Theory [102], the Hypothesis of the Mobility Transition [103], the Dual Labor Market Theory [104], New Economics of Migration [105], Network Theory [106], the Cost-Income Theory [107] and so on. Migration models are conventionally used to explain the migration process at the macro or micro levels only, although the construction of comprehensive migration models by combining macro and micro models has recently attracted attention from academia. Comprehensive models mainly consist of meso migration models [108], 2-stage migration models [109, 110], spatial choice models [111, 112], multiregional models [113] and NEG models [114]. Of these, NEG models are based on the hypothesis that spatial economic agglomeration is the main reason for migration aggregation and that the labor force tends to migrate to a region with a relatively high utility/wage level. Among these migration theories, Gries et al. [115] argue that three strands of theory that seem relevant for the migration process within China are identified as the classical rural–urban migration approach (in line with Harris/Todaro), the NEG and gravity approach and the new economics of labor migration (NELM).

Although theories proposed to explain internal migration posit different causal mechanisms at many levels of aggregation, the various propositions of the above migration theories all suggest that migration flows acquire a measure of stability and structure over space and time, allowing for the identification of stable internal migration systems [116]. An internal migration system is characterized by relatively large flows of migrants between certain regions compared to flows from outside the system, including a core destination region, which may be a city or group of cities and a set of specific origin regions linked to it by large flows of immigrants [117, 118]. Multipolar migration systems may exist and migration systems will evolve as social and economic conditions change. As the cities in the migration system are connected by intercity migration network, the review on migration systems theory will enlighten further studies.

In China, studies of population projection often adopt traditional research methods, such as Leslie Matrix Model [119], Keyfitz Model [99], Logistic Model [120], Population Dynamics Equation [121] and Grey System Method [122], whereas few studies use intercity migration to predict the population change of each city from the perspective of all cities. At present, the mechanical growth of population in China's cities is higher than the natural growth, so the fact that most of the existing prediction models do not take into account intercity migration causes a deviation in the prediction results. To overcome the lack of research into population spatial patterns in China, Deng et al. [123] constructed a new top-down, multiregional population projection method to predict the population at national and provincial levels in China from 2010 to 2050, considering both natural population growth and intercity migration as influencing factors. There are two problems with this: First, the assumption of the Markov chain migration model used in the prediction, that the transition probability is determined by the evolution of the system, is not consistent with the reality; Second, the prediction is on a macroscopic scale at the provincial level, while it is more helpful to predict the population of each city when making planning and policy decisions. Even more encouraging, the gravity modelling of migration has a promising future in a multiregional population projection system [124, 125], which will benefit China's future population projection.

Urban system theoretical models comprise classical urban system models and urban system models based on NEG theories. Classical urban system models include central place theory [126, 127], optimum city size theory [128] and urban growth theory. Central place theory was first put forward by Christaller [126] and Losch [127] developed this theory which suggests that a city's size depends on the economy scale of goods or services provided by the city, thus explaining how the location patterns of different industries form the regional urban system. As a classical model of urban economics, Henderson's [128] optimum city size theory explains the concentration of economic activities in cities and the formation of city size distribution and points out that a balanced city size will eventually form under the effects of external economies of scale (spatial agglomeration of specific industries in cities) and external non-economy (rising commuting and congestion costs caused by overlarge city sizes). Furthermore, urban growth theories also focus on the city size structure of urban systems, including random growth models [129] and endogenous growth models predicting deterministic, persistent, parallel growth of cities [130–135]. The random growth theory assumes that the city size growth process follows Gibrat's law (a stochastic process in which all cities have a common expected growth rate and a common standard deviation), then, in the steady state, the distribution of city sizes will follow Zipf's law [136, 137]. In regard to researches on China's urban system, many scholars have conducted empirical studies on the best approximation for China's city size distribution based on Zipf's Law and the patterns of urban growth and analyzed influences of economic and institutional factors on the urban system and urban growth [138–141], especially intercity migration in recent years as an important factor contributing to city growth in China.

Urban system models based on NEG theories incorporate the space factor into urban system evolution theories [142–144], effectively making up for the lack of spatial dimension and microeconomics basis in previous urban system evolution models. The initial conditions of locational characteristics play a crucial role in shaping the formation and evolution of the city size of that location, which is called the path dependence effect or the lock-in effect of self-reinforcing agglomeration forces. The basic agglomeration mechanism of the urban system is the same as that of basic NEG models, which consists of the diversity of consumer preferences, interregional transport costs and manufacturers' internal economies of scale and is embodied in the local market effect and the price index effect, with the spatial distribution of manufacturing activities determining the city number, sizes and locations in equilibrium. Urban system models based on NEG theories are represented by Krugman's [145] racetrack economy model and Fujita et al.'s [114] linear model of the urban system, which present a regular urban hierarchy through the self-organization of microeconomic entities. Under the theoretical framework of NEG models, the racetrack economy model comprises a circle of 12 equidistant locations, with goods only transported along the circle. In such a ring-shaped space, when the share of expenditure on manufacturing goods is large enough, or the elasticity of substitution is high enough, or the transportation cost is low enough, the originally evenly distributed areas change dramatically. Some locations with weak initial advantages tend to expand their population sizes because of self-reinforcement and eventually evolve into cities. The following two examples demonstrate that it is feasible to apply the extended racetrack economy model to empirical studies of urban system: Stelder [146] introduced geographical space into Krugman's [145] model to simulate the urban system of Europe; Ge et al. [147] integrated spatial heterogeneity into Stelder's [146] model, calculated the geographic advantage of each grid and simulated the evolution of the urban system of Zhejiang Province in China.

A certain amount of studies has discussed the close relationship between migration and the urban system. To begin with, the evolution of urban system (the process of urbanization) and migration have mutually caused and resulted from each other, working together as a positive feedback system [148]. Whether the internal migration flows are upward or downward within the urban hierarchy depends on the urbanization development stage of this country [149]. Other studies forecast dynamics of urban system based on migration flows between cities, linking the migratory behavior of individuals at the micro level to the dynamics of populations of cities at the macro level [150, 151].

Concerning the interrelationship between migration and the urban system, the perspective of network analysis is adopted, which regards the urban system as a network of industrial activities and social connection (including migration) and uses network models to explain city size distribution. The existing network models [152, 153] propose the preference attachment hypothesis, which is similar to Simon's [129] stochastic growth model, making the connection of the network obey the power law distribution. The preferential attachment theory proposed by Barabasi and Albert [152] can be used to analyze intercity migration. First, it is assumed in the theory that well-connected city nodes enjoying economies of scale can provide more reliable services and more switching opportunities at low costs, so a new city in the network always tends to establish connections with well-connected city nodes and people are inclined to migrate to well-connected (with a large population) cities; Second, it is assumed that the network connection cost increases along with the increasing geographical distance, so the possibility of connecting a new node with existing nodes decreases with the increasing geographical distance between them, indicating that intercity migration will gradually decline with the augment of spatial distance. However, very few network models take into account space factors [154]. Therefore, using the network model to explain city size distribution has a wide research potential and urban network theory is the key to studying complex connections between cities [155]. Mansury and Gulyas [156] adopted a bottom-up approach to construct a model and explained how migration behaviors of individual decision makers affect the formation of city size distribution. In summary, as intercity migration is one kind of city network and an important aspect of the research on urban system, it is feasible and necessary to combine the studies of migration and urban system to establish a comprehensive research framework and Krugman's [145] racetrack economy model provides a particular way to realize this goal, because city size distribution is determined by migration in this model.

In conclusion, to rectify the following problems in extant researches, this study makes the following contributions:

(1) Studies predicting China's population are mainly based on local population growth models of one city, with a lack of studies on population spatial pattern prediction regarding the urban system as a whole and the spatial scales of migration are relatively macro [3, 38, 81, 134, 157, 158]. This study establishes a global network model considering all cities and intercity migration linkages and predicts changes in each city's population viewing the whole urban system as a network connected by intercity migration, by introducing important influencing factors of migration into the NEG model to deepen its migration mechanism and expanding the spatial scale of migration studies from province-level to city-level.

(2) Current models of the urban system (classical urban system models and NEG models) are based on two or several regions, difficult to be used to conduct empirical tests in a real geographic environment. This study extends the NEG

model from two homogenous regions to heterogeneous multi-regions, to simulate and predict the evolution of China's actual urban system using empirical evidence based on real data, thus advancing the development of empirical research into NEG theories.

(3) Though current studies on urban system evolution and migration have formed a complete theoretical system separately, there is no systematic research framework combining them into a comprehensive analysis. Due to the close interconnection between migration and urban system, based on the urban system evolution model of NEG theory [145], this study establishes an integrated research framework for migration and urban system.

2.2.3 Description of the Simulation Process

In accordance with the key research question, this study attempts to focus efforts in the following three aspects: exploring the influence of intercity migration on urban system; modelling China's urban system by connecting all cities in the urban system by intercity migration; extending the extant theoretical models of urban system to make them applicable in empirical studies. The urban system model of Krugman [145, 159], Fujita et al. [114], can address the above problems, therefore it is chosen as the basic theoretical model. According to related migration theories and China's actual situation, this study presents such important factors influencing migration as population, economic development, public service, geographic advantage (including living conditions and environment quality), social network, spatial distance and policy elements, using the gravity model with econometric results shown in Table 2.12. Hence, we add a utility function containing public service level and an interregional spatial distance matrix to the basic model. In this model, to link the theoretical model to China's actual situation, each region's economic development level is represented by wage and income, geographic advantages are signified by heterogeneous numbers of peasants and the influence of policy elements on migration is indicated by its effect on the level of public service, while social network linkages are difficult to quantify directly in this model. Therefore, different from the basic model, the mechanism for migration influences on the urban system is embedded in the model with the above influencing factors of migration, with the basic theoretical framework under the case of 2 regions shown in Fig. 2.25. The utility level of each region is determined by the consumption of manufacturing goods, agricultural goods and public goods by local workers.

Our starting point is the basic multi-regional NEG model presented in Krugman [145], which builds a discrete urban system of n locations/cities and the economy is divided into two sectors of agriculture and manufacturing. Agriculture is assumed to be perfectly competitive under constant returns to scale, while manufacturing is taken to be monopolistic competitive with increasing returns to scale. In the short-run equilibrium, the producers' profits are all zero, with balanced supply and demand. To consumers, their living expenses equal labor income. Peasants of all regions

Table 2.12 Econometric analysis results of influencing factors of China's inter-provincial migration

Explanatory variable	Ratio index	1995–2000		2000–2005		2005–2010	
		B	t	B	t	B	t
Demographic variable	Population	−0.181 (0.000)	−4.73 (0.000)	−0.438 (0.000)	−9.49 (0.000)	−0.455 (0.000)	−12.57 (0.000)
Economic development	Urban residents' per capita disposable income	−0.376 (0.029)	−2.19 (0.029)				
	GDP per capita			0.163 (0.076)	1.78 (0.076)	0.247 (0.003)	2.98 (0.003)
Public service	Per capita expenditure on science, education, culture and health	0.636 (0.000)	6.24 (0.000)	0.283 (0.012)	2.52 (0.012)		
	Per capita expenditure on education					0.334 (0.007)	2.69 (0.007)
	Number of college students per 10,000 people	−0.148 (0.008)	−2.67 (0.008)				
Living conditions	House price	0.319 (0.003)	2.94 (0.003)				
Environment quality	Per capita public green area			0.106 (0.091)	1.69 (0.091)		
Social network	Migration chain index	0.703 (0.000)	29.14 (0.000)	0.844 (0.000)	28.54 (0.000)	0.627 (0.000)	31.09 (0.000)
Migration cost	Interregional distance	−0.511 (0.000)	−9.39 (0.000)	−0.653 (0.000)	−10.45 (0.000)	−0.646 (0.000)	−13.99 (0.000)
	Constant term	10.249 (0.000)	25.20 (0.000)	11.424 (0.000)	24.38 (0.000)	12.076 (0.000)	35.22 (0.000)
	Degree of fit	R^2	0.718	R^2	0.689	R^2	0.754

Notes: The significance levels of the regression coefficients (p-values) are shown in corresponding parentheses, and the ratio represents the relative difference of each factor between migration destination and origin (that is X_j/X_i), and only the regression coefficients reaching significant levels are listed

Data source: The Fifth National Population Census Data (2000), the Data of 1% Sampling National Population Survey (2005), the Sixth National Population Census Data (2010) and the China Statistical Yearbook (1999, 2004, 2009). Among the ratio indexes, the migration chain index is the ratio of an origin region's emigration in each destination region to the total emigration of this origin region (migration from province i to province j/total emigration of province i).

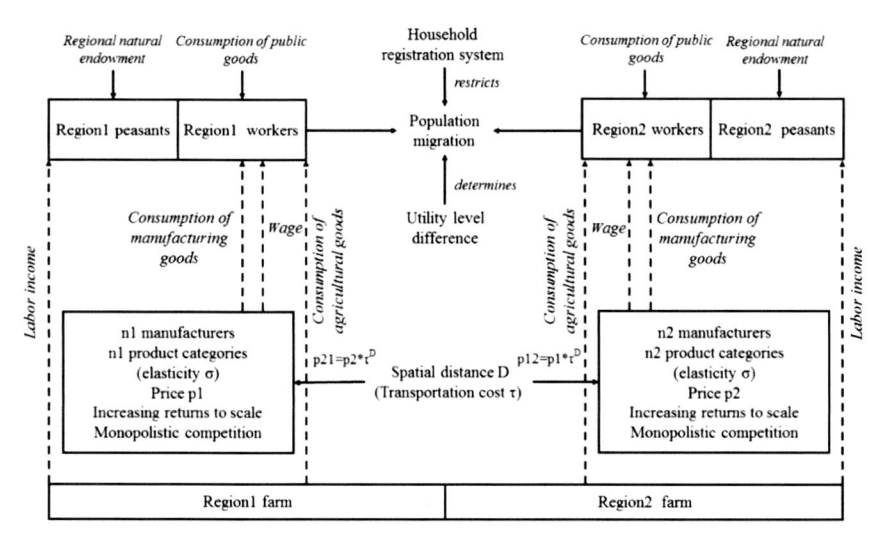

Fig. 2.25 The basic theoretical framework of the proposed NEG model (2 regions)

total L_A and each region's share of agricultural labor is exogenous, given as φ_i, while manufacturing labor is changing in time, meaning workers can migrate among regions. Manufacturing workers of all regions total L_M, with a region i's share of manufacturing labor represented by λ_i. Choose appropriate units to let $L_M = \mu$ and $L_A = 1 - \mu$.

Both agricultural and manufacturing workers consume products from other regions under the Samuelson iceberg assumption: when one unit of manufacturing goods travels from region i to region j, only a fraction of $1/T_{ij}$ arrives. The transportation cost between regions i and j is $T_{ij} = \tau^{D_{ij}}$, among which τ is unit transportation cost and D_{ij} is the distance between regions i and j. Agricultural goods are traded without cost, so peasants of all regions share the same wage. Both the wage of peasants and price of agricultural goods are set to unity, that is, $w_i^A = 1$ and $p_i^A = 1$. w_i is defined as the nominal wage of manufacturing workers in region i.

All individuals in this economy, then, are assumed to share a utility function of the form

$$U = \frac{M^\mu A^{1-\mu} S^\gamma}{\mu^\mu (1 - \mu)^{1-\mu} \gamma^\gamma (1 + \gamma)^{-(1+\gamma)}} \tag{2.4}$$

where M is the aggregate consumption of manufacturing, A is the consumption of agricultural goods, S is the consumption of public goods, μ refers to the share of expenditure on manufacturing goods and $(1 - \mu)$ refers to the share of expenditure on agricultural goods. γ denotes the elasticity of the consumers' utility to local public goods, meaning when the supply of public goods increases by one unit, how much the consumer welfare level will increase. Therefore, a higher value of

γ indicates that consumers are more sensitive to the supply of public goods, i.e. relatively preferring public goods in welfare preference. Dividing the product by $\mu^{\mu}(1-\mu)^{1-\mu}\gamma^{\gamma}(1+\gamma)^{-(1+\gamma)}$ aims to simplify the form of indirect utility function.

To simplify the computation, this model regards public goods as an exogenous variable [160], then Q_i, the supply of public goods in region i is also exogenous, manifested as an increasing function of region i's share of manufacturing labor—λ_i (urban population as city size). In most instances, the higher is the city grade (larger city size), the more exclusive public goods are enjoyed by the local residents. However, the city household registration system determines whether laborers can enjoy public goods, because a higher city grade means a stricter household registration system, which causes more difficulty in obtaining public goods for migrants [161]. For this reason, ε, the power exponent of λ_i is set to a number less than unity. So

$$Q_i = \lambda_i^{\varepsilon}, \quad 0 < \varepsilon < 1 \tag{2.5}$$

On the premise that the distribution of manufacturing labor is given and laborers cannot migrate among regions in the short-run, by introducing the above formulae into [145] urban system model (See Fujita et al. [114] for a full description of the basic model), the following 4 equations in the short-run equilibrium of city spatial pattern are derived.

$$Y_i = \mu\lambda_i w_i + (1-\mu)\varphi_i \tag{2.6}$$

$$G_i = \left[\sum_j \lambda_j \left(w_j \tau^{D_{ij}}\right)^{1-\sigma}\right]^{1/(1-\sigma)} \tag{2.7}$$

$$W_i = \left[\frac{1}{1+\gamma}\sum_j Y_j \tau^{D_{ij}(1-\sigma)} G_j^{\sigma-1}\right]^{1/\sigma} \tag{2.8}$$

$$U_i = Y_i^{1+\gamma} G_i^{-\mu} \left(p_i^S\right)^{-\gamma} = Y_i^{1+\gamma} G_i^{-\mu} \left[\frac{(\lambda_i+\varphi_i)\gamma Y_i}{(1+\gamma)Q_i}\right]^{-\gamma}$$

$$= Y_i^{1+\gamma} G_i^{-\mu} \left[\frac{(\lambda_i+\varphi_i)\gamma Y_i}{(1+\gamma)\lambda_i^{\varepsilon}}\right]^{-\gamma} \tag{2.9}$$

where Y_i denotes the consumer income of region i, G_i denotes region i's price index, U_i signifies region i's indirect utility function, σ signifies the constant elasticity of substitution between any two manufacturing varieties and p_i^S expresses region i's price of public goods.

The long-run equilibrium state of this model focuses on migration, i.e. the state of $(U_i - \overline{U})$ determines if migration is in a stable state. Due to the nature of migrants pursuing utility maximum, if a region's utility level is relatively high (higher than the average utility), manufacturing workers will migrate to this region.

Suppose workers will migrate from a region with utility lower than average to another region with utility higher than average, the average utility is defined as:

$$\overline{U} = \sum_i \lambda_i U_i \qquad (2.10)$$

then the dynamic equation of migration is expressed as:

$$d\lambda_i = \eta_i \lambda_i \left(U_i - \overline{U} \right) \qquad (2.11)$$

where η_i denotes migration speed and Eq. (2.11) indicates that region i's net immigration $(d\lambda_i)$ is proportional to region i's population size (λ_i), as stated by the preference attachment theory of network models. If region i's consumer utility is higher than the average utility of all regions, region i becomes a destination region, or vice versa.

Based on China's national conditions, each city's population is divided into urban population and rural population [113], actual city size is measured by urban population and the existence of cities in different sizes produces a complete urban hierarchy. The change of each city size (urban population) is mainly determined by inter-urban migration and rural–urban migration:

$$P_u(i, t) = [_u P_u(i, t) + d\lambda_i +_r P_u(i, t)] * (1 + b_i) \qquad (2.12)$$

where

$$_u P_u(i, t) + d\lambda_i = \lambda_{i,r} P_u(i, t) / P_u(i, t) = \alpha \qquad (2.13)$$

$P_u(i, t)$ denotes city i's urban population at a given time t, $_u P_u(i, t)$ denotes the population in city i's urban area both in the past and at the present, $_r P_u(i, t)$ denotes the population in city i's urban area at the present which used to be in rural areas and $d\lambda_i$ is the immigration from other cities' urban areas to city i's urban area. α refers to the ratio of immigration from rural areas to city i's urban area and b_i refers to city i's natural population growth rate. To simplify the computation process, α is set as a national uniform constant.

In this way, all cities in China can be divided into megalopolises, large cities, medium-sized cities and small cities in terms of city size and the urban growth momentum comes from 2 exogenous variables added here: α (the ratio of immigration from rural areas to city i's urban area) and b_i (natural population growth rate). Therefore, the urban system connotation and urban growth mechanism are embedded into the multiregional population projection model.

The simulation process of city spatial pattern includes two solution procedures: the short-run equilibrium and the long-run equilibrium, shown in Fig. 2.26. First,

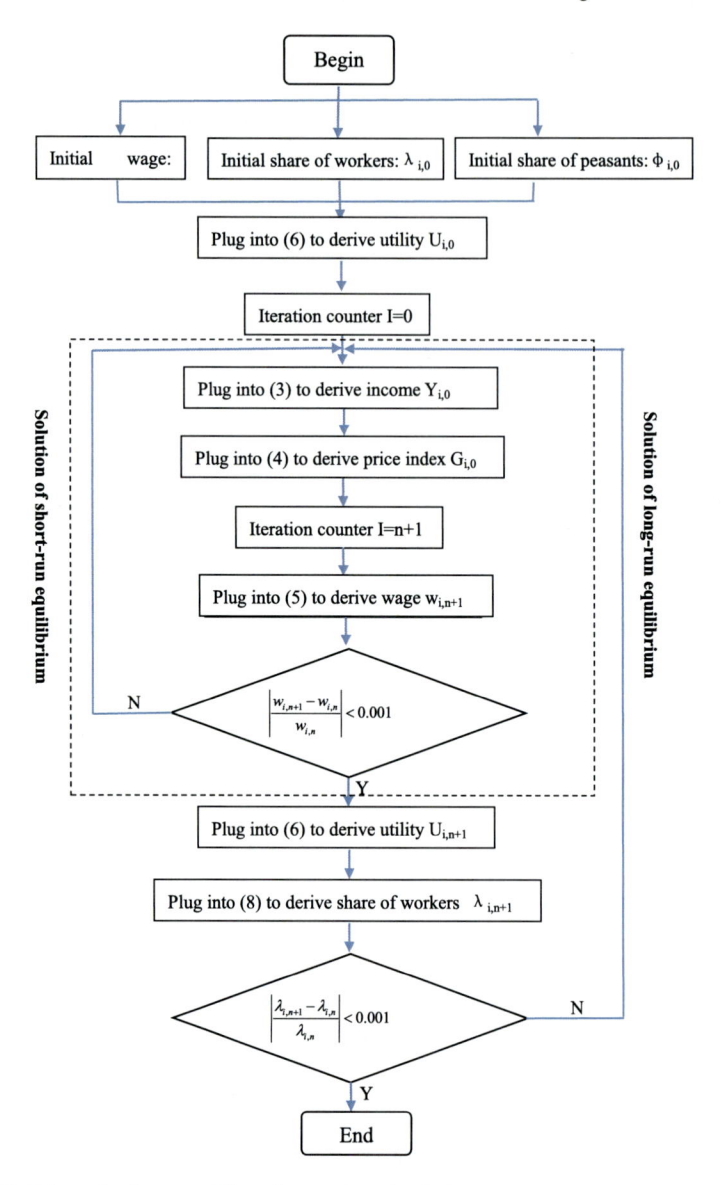

Fig. 2.26 Schematic diagram of the urban system simulation process

assign values to explanatory variables (λ_i, φ_i, w_i) and other variables (μ, σ, τ, γ, ε, η) and then solve the equations by sequential iterations. The detailed procedures are:

i.   Set the initial values of nominal wages of N regions ($w_i,0$), where the subscripted variable 0 denotes that iterations have not happened;

ii.   Plug the variable ($w_i,0$) into Eqs. (2.6) and (2.7) to compute the income ($Y_i,0$) and price index ($G_i,0$);

iii. Plug the income (Y_i,0) and price index (G_i,0) derived by Step (ii) into Eq. (2.8), to solve for the nominal wage (w_i,1);

iv. Repeat Steps ii and iii until $\left| \frac{W_{i,n+1} - W_{i,n}}{W_{i,n}} \right| < 0.001$, then the condition of short-run equilibrium is found, where the subscripted variables "n" and "n + 1" are the numbers of iterations.

v. Derive region i's utility (U_i) and the average utility of all regions ($\overline{U}$) from Eqs. (2.9) and (2.10).

vi. Plug U_i and $\overline{U}$ into Eq. (2.11) to solve for the distribution of manufacturing laborers among regions (λ_i), until $\left| \frac{\lambda_{i,n+1} - \lambda_{i,n}}{\lambda_{i,n}} \right| < 0.001$, then the condition of long-run equilibrium is found.

When these two judging conditions are met, the distribution of manufacturing laborers among regions (λ_i) in the equilibrium state is obtained; the solution process terminates only when the above steps hold for all regions.

2.2.4 Analysis of Simulation Results

Referring to the empirical parameter values of related studies, the parameter values in the model are set by repeated testing as $\mu = 0.4, \sigma = 5, \tau = 1.5, \gamma = 5, \varepsilon = 0.7$ and $\eta = 0.5$. The initial data is obtained from the *China City Statistical Yearbook*, where λ_i is the urban population of each spatial unit at prefecture level in 2000, w_i signifies the GDP per capita of each prefecture-level unit in 2000 that better represents a city's economic development level, the number of peasants φ_i is obtained by the weight assignment method based on geographic advantages (each region's number of peasants is proportional to its geographic advantage, the total number of which equals the number of national non-migrating peasants), D_{ij} denotes the geographic distance between 2 prefecture-level units. The geographic advantages are obtained by assigning values to each province according to the topographic, temperature, wet and dry climate zones to which it belongs and summarize them to obtain the score. The geographic advantage score of each prefecture is the same as each province to which it belongs: the first ladder in the topographic zone is assigned a value of 1, the second ladder of 2 and the third ladder of 3; the plateau climate and cold temperature zones are assigned a value of 0, mid temperature zone of 1, warm temperature zone of 2, subtropical zone of 3 and tropic zone of 4; the arid zone is assigned a value of 0, semi-arid zone of 1, semi-humid zone of 2 and humid zone of 3. According to actual needs, the above initial values are normalized or standardized. As shown in Eqs. (2.12) and (2.13), "$P_u(i, t) = [\lambda_i + {}_r P_u(i, t)] * (1 + b_i)$" demonstrates that city i's simulated urban population in 2010 ($P_u(i, t)$) can be derived by the sum of the initial share of workers λ_i (urban population) and the rural–urban migration ${}_r P_u(i, t)$, also taking the population growth rate (b_i) into consideration. To make the simulation result closer to the actual situation, the natural population growth rate of each city's urban area is determined by that of each city from 2009 to 2010 and the natural population growth rate of each city's rural area is determined by that of national rural area from 2009 to 2010, both of which come from the 6th national population census data in 2010. This study focuses on the urban system measured by urban population, so the rural population growth rate is simplified with a national index, due to the lack of data of rural population growth rate of each city. After multiple experiments and repeated modifications of the model and simulation program, the final simulation results show that the model fitting precision is high enough to pass the test. The simulation results will be compared with actual situations in terms of the model fit, intercity migration and hierarchical structure of the urban system.

2.2.4.1   Model Fit

The model fit is expressed as the ratio of the simulated value to the actual value (consistency rate), which implies a relatively high fit: its average, median, minimum, maximum and standard deviation values are 99.58, 101.62, 38.74, 134.10 and 14.00% respectively. As shown in Fig. 2.27, the fit presents a roughly normal distribution around the consistency rate 100% and most simulated values are in close proximity to their actual values (between 75 and 125%).

Furthermore, the actual population is positively correlated with the simulated population, with a coefficient of determination of 0.9586 in Fig. 2.28, which also indicates that the simulation results are very close to actual data.

Fig. 2.27 Histogram of consistency rates

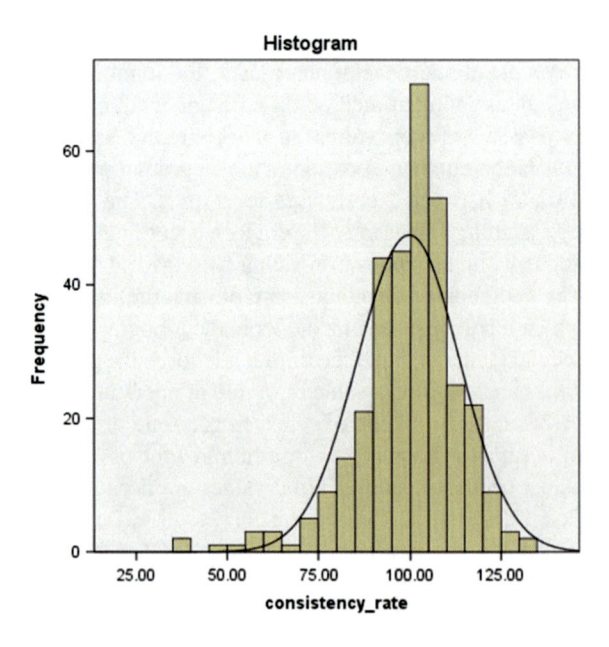

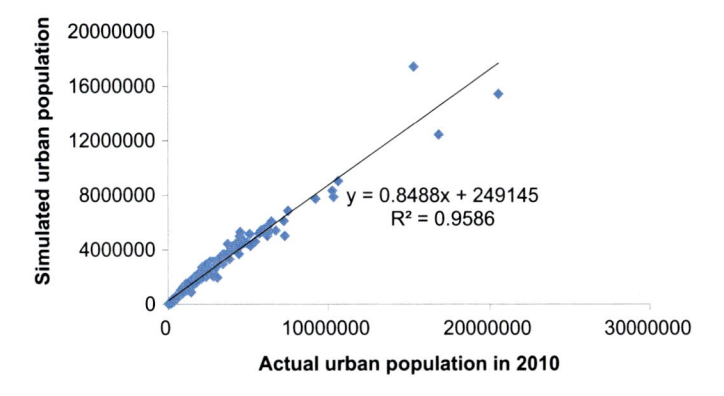

Fig. 2.28 Correlation analysis of actual to simulated population of each prefecture-level unit in 2010

2.2.4.2 Comparison Between the Actual and Simulated Results of Intercity Migration

There is a significant Pearson correlation coefficient of 0.699 (p-value $= 0.01$) between the simulated net immigration and actual immigration. Furthermore, the results of spatial autocorrelation analysis and hotspot analysis can be corroborative evidence. Moran's I of actual immigration is 0.122086 at a significance level of 0.001 and Moran's I of simulated net immigration is 0.071839 at a significance level of 0.001, meaning that both of them present a similar spatial agglomeration pattern with positive spatial correlation. The result of hotspot analysis shown in Fig. 2.29 also shows that the spatial agglomeration pattern of the actual immigration is similar to that of the simulated net immigration, with the core cities of the Beijing-Tianjin-Hebei

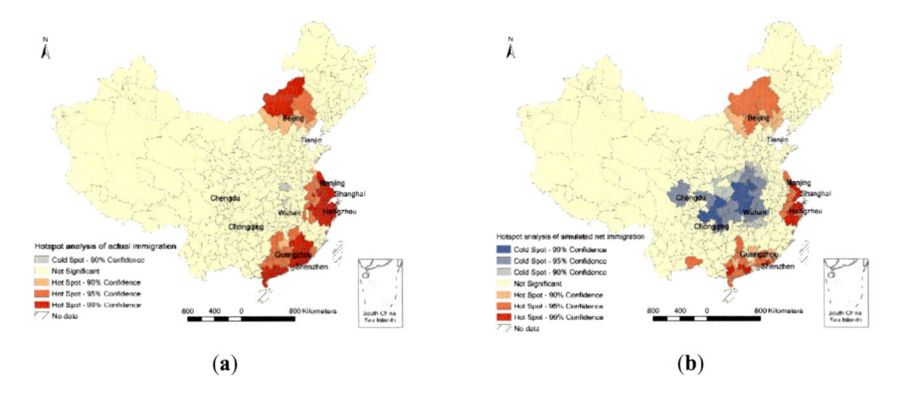

(a)   (b)

Fig. 2.29 Comparison between the actual and simulated immigration spatial distribution of all prefecture-level units in 2010 through hotspot analysis. **a** Actual immigration in 2010; **b** Simulated net immigration in 2010

Region, Yangtze River Delta Region, Pearl River Delta Region as main concentration areas of immigration (hot spot regions) and the central regions as main areas of emigration (cold spot regions).

2.2.4.3   Comparison Between the Actual and Simulated Results of the Urban System

In general, the simulated urban system of 2010 is consistent with the real situation in the following respects:

(1)   The hierarchical structure of the urban system (Table 2.13). At the prefecture level, there exists the smallest number of megalopolises, the largest number of large cities, a relatively smaller number of medium-sized cities and small cities. The number of megalopolises has increased significantly between 2000 and 2010, the number of large cities has also enjoyed fast growth, while the number of medium-sized and small cities has decreased because of their rapid promotion to large cities.

(2)   Law of the primate city. The city size distribution disobeys the law of the primate city and the primate city Shanghai has a limited effect of agglomeration and radiation. The urban system presents a double-center or multi-center structure, with the urban primacy index declining slightly from 2000 to 2010.

(3)   Rank-size distribution of cities. China's urban system is broadly in line with the rank-size rule and the city-size distribution remains relatively stable with the rank-size curve moving forward in parallel (Fig. 2.30), implying an incremental total urban population. The balanced degree of the urban system gradually strengthens from 2000 to 2010, which is consistent with the declining trend of the urban primacy index. Theoretically, from the perspective of the rationality of city size structure, high-order cities still have much room for further development.

(4)   Spatial distribution of city sizes. The spatial differences of city numbers and sizes are significant, especially in the eastern region, which possesses a distinct advantage in terms of city number, city size and the number of large cities and megalopolises, compared with the central and western regions (shown in Fig. 2.31).

2.2.5   Analysis of Prediction Results

As the simulation results indicate a good model fit, which verifies the robustness of the model, the initial data for the prefecture-level units of 2010 are plugged into the theoretical model and the simulation process is used to predict the evolution of China's urban system by 2020 under different urbanization development scenarios.

According to the objective of urbanization rate reaching 60% by 2020 proposed by the National New-Type Urbanization Planning (2014–2020), we suppose that

Table 2.13 Comparison between the actual and simulated city hierarchical structures in 2000 and 2010

Level of population (10,000 people)	City type	Number of cities						City size (urban population)					
		2000		2010		2010 (simulation)		2000		2010		2010 (simulation)	
		Number	%	Number	%	Number	%	10,000 People	%	10,000 People	%	10,000 People	%
>500	Megalopolises	10	3.00	21	6.31	21	6.31	7996.06	17.75	18,091.69	27.29	15,565.86	24.11
100–500	Large cities	153	45.95	195	58.56	207	62.16	27,894.11	61.92	41,272.68	62.26	43,265.99	67.01
50–100	Medium-sized cities	98	29.43	75	22.52	62	18.62	7373.33	16.37	5814.75	8.77	4724.02	7.32
<50	Small cities	72	21.62	42	12.61	43	12.91	1783.06	3.96	1110.73	1.68	1007.52	1.56
Total		333	100	333	100	333	100	45,046.56	100	66,289.85	100	64,563.39	100

Notes: According to A Notice on Adjusting the Standard of City Size Division issued by the State Council on 29 October 2014, China's prefectures can be divided into 5 categories of: cities with an urban resident population of fewer than 500 thousand as small cities; cities with an urban resident population between 500 thousand and 1 million as medium-sized cities; cities with an urban resident population between 1 and 5 million as large cities; and cities with an urban resident population of more than 5 million as megalopolises

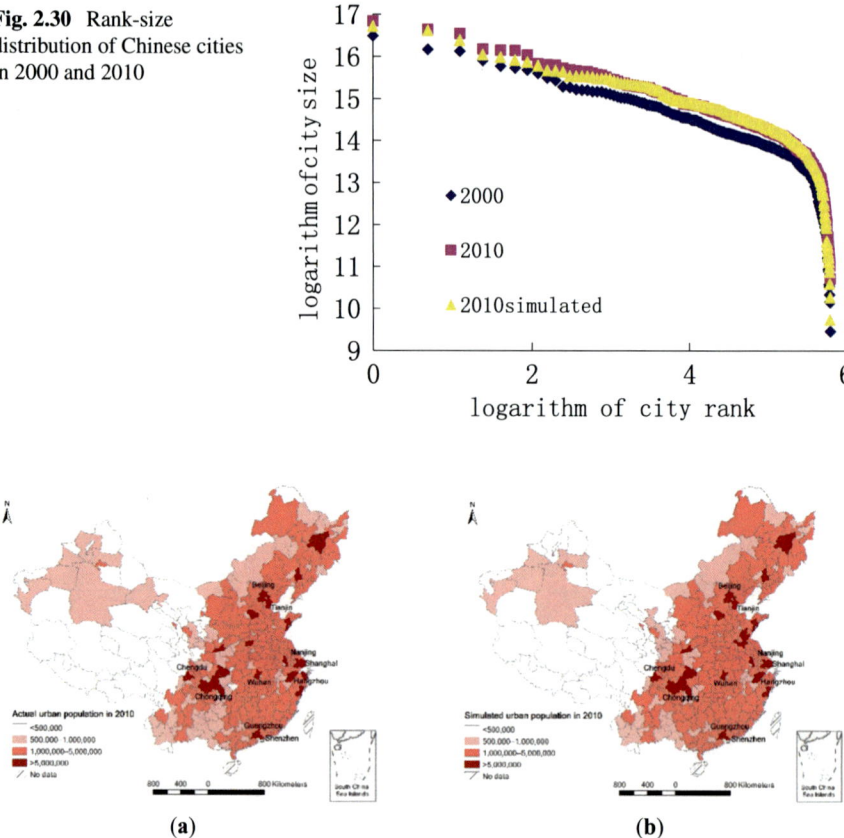

Fig. 2.30 Rank-size distribution of Chinese cities in 2000 and 2010

Fig. 2.31 Comparison between the actual and simulated city size spatial distribution of prefecture-level units in 2010. **a** Actual urban population in 2010; **b** Simulated urban population in 2010

the urbanization rate in 2020 will be 60%, increased by 10.32% compared with the national urbanization rate in 2010 (49.68%), meaning that 1.42 hundred million rural population migrate to urban area from 2010 to 2020, consistent with the current urbanization trend (the national urbanization rate is 57.35% in 2016). Based on the 1% national population sampling survey data of 2015, the national population is 13.73 billion and the national population in 2020 will be 14.08 billion increasing at the growth rate from 2010 to 2015. The natural growth rate of each city from 2010 to 2020 is also estimated with the natural growth rate of urban and rural areas from 2009 to 2010, due to the limited data accessibility and the relative stability of the natural growth rate in recent years.

2.2.5.1 Prediction Results Under the Baseline Scenario

This is therefore taken to be the baseline scenario of urban system evolution, that is, the evolution of the urban system in 2020 predicted according to current development trends. As can be seen in Table 2.14, the evolution of the urban system (2010–2020) still maintains its original development trend (2000–2010). First, the majority of city levels do not change. Second, there is a dramatic increase in the proportion of megalopolises in terms of both number and city size, with 13 large cities converting to megalopolises raising the city size proportion by 8.19%. Third, the number of large cities rises slightly while the city size proportion decreases. Fourth, although the number and the city size proportions of the small and medium-sized cities diminish, 35 medium-sized cities become large cities while 9 small cities grow into medium-sized cities. The prediction results indicate that the population growth rate of China's coastal large cities will be well above the national average level and the ratio of population in small and medium-sized cities will decline, in line with the international experience of urbanization [162]. From the perspective of prefecture-level cities, the evolution of China's urban system will still be dominated by cities with a population of over 1 million.

In general, assuming that the current trend of urban system evolution remains unchanged, the prediction results depict that the city hierarchical structure and city spatial distribution will stay relatively stable between 2010 and 2020. To be more specific, the sizes of most cities will expand slightly with their city levels unchanged. Only a few cities, especially the large ones, will be upgraded to a higher level. Furthermore, the less populated and undeveloped prefecture-level cities will undergo a sharp decrease in population. These cities either are located in the remote western inland region or cannot provide sufficient employment to attract enough people, hence they may gradually disappear over time.

2.2.5.2 Prediction Results Under "Dominated by Cities of Different Sizes" Scenario

There is always some disagreement over China's urbanization development models [163]. Those advocating a small-city-dominated model emphasize that basic national conditions determine that the process of urbanization in China should be dominated by small cities, which means that the sizes of large cities need to be severely restricted in favor of the development of small and medium-sized cities and small towns. In contrast, theoretical analysis suggests a large-city-dominated model to be more appropriate, placing more emphasis on the phasic rule of prioritizing large cities in the course of urbanization or the agglomeration economic effect of city size. In addition, another model is proposed concerning the coordinated development of cities of different sizes, which attempts to take into account the advantages of both the "large-city-dominated" and the "small-city-dominated" models in accordance with urban system theories. Overall, urbanization development models dominated by cities of different sizes lead to different urban system structures.

Table 2.14 Predicted city hierarchical structure in 2020 under the baseline scenario

Level of population (10,000 people)	Level of cities	Number of cities				City size (urban population)			
		2010		2020 (Prediction)		2010		2020 (Prediction)	
		Number	%	Number	%	10,000 People	%	10,000 People	%
>500	Megalopolises	21	6.31	34	10.21	18,091.7	27.29	29,619.5	35.48
100–500	Large cities	195	58.56	217	65.17	41,272.7	62.26	49,431.7	59.22
50–100	Medium-sized cities	75	22.52	48	14.41	5814.8	8.77	3607.4	4.32
<50	Small cities	42	12.61	34	10.21	1110.7	1.68	817.0	0.98
Total		333	333	333	333	100.00	66,289.85	100	83,475.7

Different speeds are set for migration to megalopolises, large cities, medium-sized cities and small cities, to generate different prediction results under the "large-city-dominated" scenario (the net immigration rate of large cities is the highest), the "small-medium-city-dominated" scenario (the net immigration rate of small and medium-sized cities is the highest) and the "coordinated development" scenario (the net immigration rates of cities at all levels are consistent). The results are shown in Table 2.15, revealing that the prefecture-level city hierarchical structures remain largely unchanged no matter what kind of urbanization development scenarios is adopted; the size proportions of megalopolises in these three scenarios decline slightly compared with the baseline scenario but they are still higher than that in 2010, reflecting an irreversible natural tendency; and the speed of large cities developing into megalopolises is also much lower than that of small and medium-sized cities converting to large cities.

The size proportions of cities at all levels under the "large-city-dominated" scenario are similar to those of the baseline scenario, except that the size proportion of megalopolises under the "large-city-dominated" scenario is slightly lower, while the size proportion of large cities is a little higher. This demonstrates that the prediction result under the "large-city-dominated" scenario is closest to the natural law of urban system evolution, in which the agglomeration economic effect plays a decisive role, while the other two scenarios are mainly affected by policies. Compared with the other scenarios, it is evident that the speed of small and medium-sized cities developing into large cities is a lot higher under the "small-medium-city-dominated" scenario (42 medium-sized cities becoming large cities), resulting in a larger number (224) and a higher size proportion (61.24%) of large cities. Relatively speaking, the development speeds of cities at all levels under the "coordinated development" scenario (such as the number of medium-sized cities changing into large cities and large cities changing into megalopolises) are between those in the "large-city-dominated" scenario and "small-medium-city-dominated" scenario.

2.2.5.3 Prediction Results Under "Different Strictness of Household Registration System" Scenario

The provisions of the National New-Type Urbanization Planning (2014–2020) are shown as followings: the limits to household registration in designated towns and small cities should be fully removed, cities with a population of 500 thousand–1 million orderly removed and cities with a population of 1 million–3 million reasonably removed; the requirements for household registration in cities with a population of 3 million–5 million are obliged to be defined rationally, while the population sizes of cities with over 5 million residents have to be rigidly controlled. Different household registration systems, therefore, are supposed to be established in accordance with different city sizes and overall carrying capacities. Under the guidance of the government's policies, the urbanization scenarios of "releasing all cities", "releasing small and medium-sized cities" and "limiting megalopolises" in terms of household registration system are designed in the simulations.

Table 2.15 City hierarchical structures in 2020 under the 'dominated by cities of different sizes' scenario

Level of population (10,000 people)	Baseline scenario		Large-city-dominated scenario		Small-medium-city-dominated scenario		Coordinated development scenario	
	Number of cities	Size proportion (%)	Number of cities	Size proportion (%)	Number of cities	Size proportion (%)	Number of cities	Size proportion (%)
I: >500	34	35.48	35	34.11	34	33.76	34	34.02
II: 100–500	217	59.22	219	60.77	224	61.24	220	60.72
III: 50–100	48	4.32	46	4.16	44	4.09	46	4.27
IV: <50	34	0.98	33	0.96	31	0.90	33	0.98
II to I	13		14		13		13	
III–II	35		38		42		38	
IV–III	9		10		12		10	

Notes: According to the net migration rate of cities at all levels and through repeated experiments, the migration speed η_i in Eq. (2.11) is set as following in the range of allowed values: $\eta_1 = 0.5$ for megalopolises, $\eta_2 = 3$ for large cities, $\eta_3 = 0.5$ for medium-sized and small cities, under the 'large-city-dominated' scenario; and $\eta_1 = 0.5$, $\eta_2 = 0.5$, $\eta_3 = 3$ under the 'small-medium-city-dominated' scenario. Cities of type I to IV are megalopolises, large cities, medium-sized cities and small cities respectively

Table 2.16 City hierarchical structures in 2020 under 'different strictness of household registration system' scenarios

Level of population (10,000 people)	'Releasing all cities' household registration system' scenario		'Limiting megalopolises' household registration system' scenario		'Releasing small and medium-sized cities' household registration system' scenario	
	Number of cities	Size proportion (%)	Number of cities	Size proportion (%)	Number of cities	Size proportion (%)
I: >500	34	35.30	35	34.10	34	33.85
II: 100–500	218	59.49	219	60.76	225	61.30
III: 50–100	47	4.23	46	4.18	43	3.95
IV: <50	34	0.99	33	0.96	31	0.90
II–I	13		14		13	
III–II	36		38		43	
IV–III	9		10		12	

Notes: In order to relate the household registration system to the public service level of cities, the initial public service levels of cities at all levels under scenarios with different household registration system restriction are multiplied by different registration difficulty coefficients. Under the 'releasing all cities' scenario, the registration difficulty coefficient of all cities is set to 1; under the 'releasing small and medium-sized cities' scenario, the registration difficulty coefficient of large cities and megalopolises is set to 0.5, and the coefficient of small and medium-sized cities is set to 1; and under the 'limiting megalopolises' scenario, the registration difficulty coefficient of large cities, small and medium-sized cities is set to 1, and the coefficient of megalopolises is set to 0.5. A lower registration difficulty coefficient means more difficulty in enjoying the local public service for immigrants, because it is multiplied by public service level of each city to measure the local public service level enjoyed by immigrants

The city hierarchical structures in 2020 under "different strictness of household registration system" scenarios, calculated based on the actual data of the prefecture-level units in 2010, are shown in Table 2.16. There is a greater size proportion of megalopolises under the "releasing all cities" scenario, while large cities account for a lower proportion, reflecting the aggregation of population towards megalopolises. Besides, small and medium-sized cities develop rapidly under the "releasing small and medium cities" scenario, with 43 cities developing into large cities, giving rise to a greater number and size proportion of large cities. Under the "limiting megalopolises" scenario, the size proportion of megalopolises and the development speed of small and medium-sized cities are between those under the other two scenarios and large cities grow relatively quickly, which causes a greatest number (14) of large cities to become megalopolises.

As can be seen from Table 2.16, the different household registration restrictions exert a certain influence on city hierarchical structures. To begin with, under the "releasing all cities" scenario in which all cities' immigration are not restricted, the population growth of megalopolises is faster from 2010 to 2020 than that of the other two scenarios, resulting from the natural law of China's internal migration that people tend to migrate to the highest-ranking cities. Meanwhile, the population growth in large cities is more rapid under the "limiting megalopolises" scenario than the corresponding values under the other two scenarios, because of the advantages of large cities over small and medium-sized cities in terms of their scale of economy and population. Finally, small and medium-sized cities have a higher population growth rate under the "releasing small and medium-sized cities" scenario than that under the other two scenarios, due to the restriction on immigration of megalopolises and large cities in that case.

2.2.6 Conclusions and Discussion

In response to the comment of Wahnschafft and Wei [162] that it is hard to accurately predict China's specific urban morphology in the future, this study builds a theoretical model based on the urban system models of NEG theories from the perspective of migration, intending to improve the prediction accuracy of China's urban system by explaining how intercity migration affects the urban system evolution. The simulated values of this model using data of China's prefecture-level units in 2000 are close to actual situation in 2010 with a high fitting accuracy, in terms of each city's urban population, intercity migration, city hierarchical structure and city spatial distribution, indicating that the model is feasible to predict the future urban system evolution after passing empirical tests.

The following main discoveries are obtained through applying the model to predicting the development of China's urban system by 2020 under a variety of urbanization scenarios.

(1) Under the baseline scenario, the city hierarchical structure and spatial distribution remain relatively stable, with most city sizes expanding slightly in spite of their unchanged city levels. There is a rapid growth in both the number and the size proportion of megalopolises, therefore the evolution of the urban system at prefecture level is still dominated by cities with a population of over 1 million. Small and medium-sized cities also develop rapidly, while less populated and less attractive cities are likely to gradually disappear in the future. To present the prognosis in a more clear way, the top 10 cities enjoying the largest population growth include Shanghai, Chongqing, Beijing, Shenzhen, Guangzhou, Tianjin, Chengdu, Wuhan, Dongguan and Wenzhou, mostly megalopolises, the cities in the second tier with large population growth are mainly provincial capitals and sub-provincial cities, followed by relatively developed cities with large populations mostly in eastern and central regions and small cities in the remote western region (Xinjiang, Xizang and Qinghai Provinces) are supposedly in the list of the shrinking cities.

(2) Under the "large-city-dominated" scenario, megalopolises take up the highest size proportion, as this scenario is closest to the natural law of urban system evolution, in which the market mechanism plays a decisive role. Urban systems

are mainly affected by policies under the "small-medium-city-dominated" and "coordinated development" scenarios and the high speed of small and medium-sized cities developing into large cities is the most prominent under the "small-medium-city-dominated" scenario, while the results under the "coordinated development" scenario are between those under the "large-city-dominated" scenario and "small-medium-city-dominated" scenario.

(3) Population tend to concentrate in high-level cities irrespective of changes in the restrictions on the household registration system, reflecting the lasting agglomeration forces from super cities [164]. The population growth of megalopolises, large cities, small and medium-sized cities are the fastest respectively under the "releasing all cities", "limiting megalopolises" and "releasing small and medium-sized cities" scenarios.

(4) The simulation and prediction results are essentially consistent with the results of Krugman's core-periphery model after the introduction of spatial heterogeneity and the construction of city hierarchical structure. This means that, with the continuous enhancement of cohesion, circulation and accumulated effect, regions with first-mover advantage (referring to a larger population) always attract an increasing amount of people and the core areas are gradually strengthened owing to the agglomeration economic effect while, on the contrary, population may decrease sharply in the rural areas around cities and small cities in marginal areas.

As we can see, the future development trend of centralized urbanization predicted by this study (dominated by large cities with a population of above 1 million) is consistent with the main standpoints of the following reports: World Bank [165] regards the law of scale economy as the basic law of the world economic development, which is clearly supported by our prediction that population tend to concentrate in larger cities, despite adoptions of different urbanization development paths and restrictions in the household registration system of larger cities. According to a recent report released by McKinsey Global Institute [166], centralized growth is the optimal solution for China's urbanization development, hence the urbanization development model dominated by megalopolises is the most economical, stating that targets including the highest per capita GDP, the lowest per capita energy consumption, intensive land use, more efficient public transportation, more powerful pollution control, knowledge spillovers and innovation development, will be achieved with this model. Wang [167] also points out that the active development of cities with a population of over 1 million will considerably improve economic performance, thus enhancing the speed and quality of economic growth. More importantly, the development of large cities emphasizes not only simply the expansion of existing cities but also the accelerating development of small and medium-sized cities into newer large cities. Conforming to this law of urban system evolution, China's urban system development should take the path of centralized urbanization pattern, rely on huge urban agglomerations and actively cultivate regional economic growth poles, to form urban agglomeration structures with megalopolises as growth poles, which enjoy a coordinated development of cities at all levels.

What's more, there exists a mismatch between the trend of population migrating to larger cities and strict household registration system restrictions on megalopolises and large cities. To resolve this conflict, firstly public service equalization among different levels of cities should be enhanced, making sure that most floating population can settle down and share the benefits of economic and social development in cities where they have made great contributions; furthermore, as main destination regions of immigration, the development of large cities and megalopolises should obey the natural law of scale economy to constantly aggregate population and economies, whereas in order to cope with the urban diseases of growing pollution, traffic jams and blistering house price growth, governments should gradually disperse functions (especially industrial functions) of large cities and megalopolises to surrounding cities, rather than simply control the population growth by setting higher entry hurdles for migrants.

Very few studies conduct an overall prediction of China's national population spatial pattern and city hierarchical structure and the prediction result of this study is roughly identical to research conclusions of Gu [168] and Deng et al. [123]: In the predicted urban system in 2020 by Gu [168], city proportions of large cities with a population of over 1 million will enjoy the largest increase between 2010 and 2020, Deng et al. [123] predicted that China's urbanization rate will be 61% in 2020, at that time, eastern coastal developed regions including Beijing, Tianjin, Shanghai, Jiangsu Province, Zhejiang Province and Guangdong Province are considered as net immigration dominated regions with rapid population changes, central regions consisting of Henan, Anhui and Hubei Provinces are deemed as net emigration dominated regions with rapid population changes, most northwestern and northeastern provinces belong to regions with steady population growth.

In contrast with extant studies, this study establishes a theoretical model to predict the evolution of China's urban system based on the internal migration network, with the embedded mechanism of how migration influences the urban system, while also expanding the empirical studies of NEG models. In regard with research limitations, further studies are needed to develop the data source to a longer time scale and more micro spatial units, which will also benefit from increasing refined scenarios (such as considering various natural population growth rates, urbanization levels, economic development levels and transportation conditions) in line with China's recent development trends to improve the ability of the model in terms of prediction accuracy and government decision support; moreover, a systematic sensitivity analysis will make the empirical approach more convincible; to rectify this situation, the methodology based on the integration of GIS technology, scenario approach in urban planning and sensitivity analysis [169–172], will represent a useful tool to support decisions on China's floating population management, public service improvement and urban system planning, which can be integrated into our model in the future research.

References

1. Plane DA, Mulligan GF (1997) Measuring spatial focusing in a migration system. Demography 34(2):251–262
2. Ding J, Liu Z, Cheng D, Liu J, Zou J (2005b) Areal differentiation of inter-provincial migration in China and characteristics of the flow field. Acta Geogr Sin 60:106–114
3. Ding J, Liu Z, Cheng D, Liu J, Zou J (2005a) Areal differentiation of inter-provincial migration in China and characteristics of the flow field. Acta Geogr Sin 1(11):106–114 (in Chinese)
4. Wang G, Pan Z, Lu Y (2012a) China's inter-provincial migration patterns and influential factors: evidence from year 2000 and 2010 population census of China. Chin J Popul Sci 5:2–13 (in Chinese)
5. He S, Tang C, Zhou G (2014) Research on spatial interaction of the urban agglomeration in the middle reaches of the Yangtze River. Econ Geogr 04:46–53 (in Chinese)
6. Wang T, Zeng X (2014) Spatial patterns and development strategy of competition-integration between cities in urban agglomeration in the middle reaches of the Yangtze River. Trop Geogr 03:390–398 (in Chinese)
7. Wang S, Zhai C, Gu Y (2016) Analysis on spatial network structure's dynamic evolution of urban agglomerations in the middle Yangtze river basin. Resour Environ Yangtze Basin 03:353–364 (in Chinese)
8. Bai J (2012) Analysis on the basic conditions of industrial division of labor and cooperation in the urban agglomeration in the middle reaches of the Yangtze River. Hubei Soc Sci 06:61–64 (in Chinese)
9. Wang L, Wu Y (2014) Research on the economic connection of urban agglomerations in the middle reaches of the Yangtze River based on urban flow. Jianghuai Trib (03):62–69. (in Chinese)
10. Gong S, Zhang T, Ding M, Mei L, Wu Q, Ge L, Chu H (2014) A study on the cooperation mechanism in urban agglomeration in the middle reaches of the Yangtze River. China Soft Sci (01):96–104. (in Chinese)
11. Liang B (2015) Research on the process and path of building a world-class smart city agglomeration in the middle reaches of the Yangtze River. Jianghuai Trib 03:25–31 (in Chinese)
12. Liu Y, Yan T (2013) Types of the return migrations from mega-cities to local cities in China: a case study of Zhumadian's return migrants. Geogr Res 07:1280–1290 (in Chinese)
13. Peng J, Sun C (2014) The evolutionary game theory analysis and strategy to the population flows of Yanbian District. Popul J (05):96–104. (in Chinese)
14. Duan C, Yang G, Zhang F, Lu X (2008) Nine major trends of China's floating population changes since the reform and opening up. Popul Res 06:30–43 (in Chinese)
15. Liu Y, Feng J (2014) Characteristics and impact factors of migration in China: based on the analysis of the sixth census data. Hum Geogr 02:129–137 (in Chinese)
16. Li Y, Liu H (2010) Research progresses on migration spatial structure modeling. Prog Geogr 10:1162–1170 (in Chinese)
17. Qian X, Huang Y (2013) Floating populations across provinces in China-analysis based on the sixth census. Popul Dev 01:13–28 (in Chinese)
18. Lao X, Shen T (2015) Spatial pattern changes of China's internal migration to prefectural and higher level cities: evidence from the 2000 and 2010 population census data. Chin J Popul Sci (01):15–28+126. (in Chinese)
19. Li W (2008b) An analysis on the spatial pattern of China's interprovincial migration. Popul Res 32:86–96
20. Li W (2008a) An analysis of the spatial pattern of inter-provincial migration of population in China. Popul Res 04:86–96 (in Chinese)
21. Yu T (2012) Spatial-temporal features and influential factors of the China urban floating population growth. Chin J Popul Sci (04):47–58+111–112. (in Chinese)
22. Zhang Y, Cen Q (2014) Spatial patterns of population mobility and determinants of inter-provincial migration in China. Popul Res 05:54–71 (in Chinese)

23. Cai F (2010a) Demographic transition, demographic dividend and Lewis turning point. Econ Res J 45(4):4–13 (in Chinese)
24. Cai F (2010b) Demographic transition, demographic dividend, and Lewis turning point in China. Econ Res J 3:107–119
25. Cai F (2011) How long can China's demographic dividend last? Econ Perspect 06:3–7 (in Chinese)
26. Li J (2016) Recognition of demographic dividend: the origin, the structure and the mechanism. J Guizhou Univ Financ Econ 06:1–6 (in Chinese)
27. Chen Y (2005) Demographic bonus and demographic debt: quantitative delimitation, empirical observation and theoretical thinking. Popul Res 06:23–29 (in Chinese)
28. Fan CC (2005b) Modeling interprovincial migration in China, 1985–2000. Eurasian Geogr Econ 46:165–184
29. Zhang W, Chong Z, Li X et al (2020) Spatial patterns and determinant factors of population flow networks in China: analysis on Tencent location big data. Cities 99:102640
30. Liu Z, Gu H (2020) Evolution characteristics of spatial concentration patterns of interprovincial population migration in China from 1985 to 2015. Appl Spat Anal Policy 13(2):375–391
31. Liu Y, Shen J (2017) Modelling skilled and less-skilled interregional migrations in China, 2000–2005. Popul Space Place 23(4):e2027
32. Liu Y, Xu W (2017) Destination choices of permanent and temporary migrants in China, 1985–2005. Popul Space Place 23(1):e1963
33. Shen J (2012b) Changing patterns and determinants of interprovincial migration in China 1985–2000. Popul Space Place 18:384–402
34. Zhou T, Huang B, Liu X et al (2020) Spatiotemporal exploration of Chinese spring festival population flow patterns and their determinants based on spatial interaction model. ISPRS Int J Geo Inf 9(11):670
35. Shen J (2012a) Changing patterns and determinants of interprovincial migration in China 1985–2000. Popul Space Place 18(3):384–402
36. Kwan MP, Schwanen T (2016) Geographies of mobility. Ann Am Assoc Geogr 106(2):243–256
37. Gu H, Liu Z, Shen T (2020) Spatial pattern and determinants of migrant workers' interprovincial hukou transfer intention in China: evidence from a national migrant population dynamic monitoring survey in 2016. Popul Space Place 26(2):e2250
38. Sheng G (2018) Study on the evolution and explanation of inter-provincial population fow network in China. China Popul Resour Environ 28(11):1–9 (in Chinese)
39. Gu H, Jie Y, Li Z et al (2021) What drives migrants to settle in Chinese cities: a panel data analysis. Appl Spat Anal Policy 14:297–314
40. Lao X, Gu H (2020) Unveiling various spatial patterns of determinants of hukou transfer intentions in China: a multi-scale geographically weighted regression approach. Growth Chang 51(4):1860–1876
41. Lin L, Zhu Y (2016) Spatial variation and its determinants of migrants' Hukou transfer intention of China's prefecture- and provincial-level cities: evidence from the 2012 national migrant population dynamic monitoring survey. Acta Geogr Sin 71:1696–1709 (in Chinese)
42. Liu Y, Deng W, Song X et al (2018) Influence factor analysis of migrants' settlement intention: considering the characteristic of city. Appl Geogr 96:130–140
43. Deng Y, Liu S, Cai J et al (2015) Spatial pattern and its evolution of Chinese provincial population: methods and empirical study. J Geogr Sci 25(12):1507–1520
44. Gu H, Liu Z, Shen T et al (2019) Modelling interprovincial migration in China from 1995 to 2015 based on an eigenvector spatial filtering negative binomial model. Popul Space Place 25(8):e2253
45. Shen J (2015) Explaining interregional migration changes in China, 1985–2000, using a decomposition approach. Reg Stud 49(7):1176–1192
46. Hu M (2019) Visualizing the largest annual human migration during the spring festival travel season in China. Environ Plan A 51(8):1618–1621

47. Pan J, Lai J (2019) Spatial pattern of population mobility among cities in China: case study of the National day plus mid-autumn festival based on Tencent migration data. Cities 94:55–69
48. Wang Y, Dong L, Liu Y et al (2019) Migration patterns in China extracted from mobile positioning data. Habitat Int 86:71–80
49. Wei Y, Song W, Xiu C et al (2018) The rich-club phenomenon of China's population flow network during the country's spring festival. Appl Geogr 96:77–85
50. Lao X, Zhang X, Shen T, Skitmore M (2016) Comparing China's city transportation and economic networks. Cities 53:43–50
51. Derudder B, Witlox F (2008) Mapping world city networks through airline flows: context, relevance, and problems. J Transp Geogr 16(5):305–312
52. Li E, Lu Y, Yang X et al (2020a) Spatio-temporal evolution on connection strength of global city network based on passenger fight data from 2014 to 2018. Sci Geogr Sin 40(1):32–39 (in Chinese)
53. Mahutga MC, Ma X, Smith DA et al (2010) Economic globalisation and the structure of the World City system: the case of airline passenger data. Urban Stud 47(9):1925–1947
54. Matsumoto H (2004) International urban systems and air passenger and cargo flows: some calculations. J Air Transp Manag 10(4):239–247
55. Zhang F, Yang C, Ning Y et al (2016) The changing structure of Chinese transnational urban network: an analysis through air passenger flow. World Reg Stud 25(3):1–11 (in Chinese)
56. Derudder B, Taylor PJ, Ni P et al (2010) Pathways of change: shifting connectivities in the world city network, 2000–08. Urban Stud 47(9):1861–1877
57. Pereira RO, Derudder B (2010) Determinants of dynamics in the World City network, 2000–2004. Urban Stud 47(9):1949–1967
58. Sheng K, Wang Y, Fan J (2019) Dynamics and mechanisms of the spatial structure of urban network in China: a study based on the corporate networks of Top 500 public companies. Econ Geogr 39(11):84–93 (in Chinese)
59. Zhao X, Li Q, Rui Y et al (2019) The characteristics of urban network of China: a study based on the Chinese companies in the fortune global 500 list. Acta Geogr Sin 74(4):694–709 (in Chinese)
60. De Montis A, Caschili S, Chessa A (2011) Time evolution of complex networks: commuting systems in insular Italy. J Geogr Syst 13(1):49–65
61. Limtanakool N, Dijst M, Schwanen T (2007) A theoretical framework and methodology for characterising national urban systems on the basis of flows of people: empirical evidence for France and Germany. Urban Stud 44(11):2123–2145
62. Neal Z (2014) The devil is in the details: differences in air traffic networks by scale, species, and season. Soc Netw 38(3):63–73
63. Chen W, Xiu C, Ke W et al (2015) Hierarchical structures of China's city network from the perspective of multiple traffic flows. Geogr Res 34(11):2073–2083 (in Chinese)
64. Wang J, Jing Y (2017) Comparison of spatial structure and organization mode of inter-city networks from the perspective of railway and air passenger flow. Acta Geogr Sin 72(8):1508–1519 (in Chinese)
65. Yang H, Dobruszkes F, Wang J et al (2018) Comparing China's urban systems in high-speed rail- way and airline networks. J Transp Geogr 68:233–244
66. Li T, Wang J, Gao X (2020b) Comparison of inter-city travel network during weekdays and holiday in China. Acta Geogr Sin 75(4):833–848 (in Chinese)
67. Li J, Ye Q, Deng X et al (2016) Spatial-temporal analysis on spring festival travel rush in China based on multisource big data. Sustainability 8(11):1–16
68. Xu J, Li A, Li D et al (2017) Difference of urban development in China from the perspective of passenger transport around spring festival. Appl Geogr 87:85–96
69. Li T, Wang J, Huang J (2020c) Research on travel pattern and network characteristics of inter-city travel in China's urban agglomeration during National day week based on Tencent migration data. J Geo-Inf Sci 22(6):1240–1253 (in Chinese)
70. Cui C, Wu X, Liu L, Zhang W (2020) The spatial-temporal dynamics of daily intercity mobility in the Yangtze River Delta: an analysis using big data. Habitat Int 106:102174

71. Wu S, Wang L, Liu H (2021) Study on tourism flow network patterns on May Day holiday. Sustainability 13(2):947
72. Liu W, Shi E (2016) Spatial pattern of population daily flow among cities based on ICT: a case study of "Baidu migration." Acta Geogr Sin 71(10):1667–1679 (in Chinese)
73. Gao Y, Nan Y, Song S (2021) High-speed rail and city tourism: evidence from Tencent migration big data on two Chinese golden weeks. Growth Change
74. Lai J, Pan J (2019) Spatial pattern of population flow among cities in China during the spring festival travel rush based on "Tencent migration" data. Hum Geogr 34(03):108–117 (in Chinese)
75. Yang Z, Gao W, Zhao X, Hao C, Xie X (2020) Spatiotemporal patterns of population mobility and its determinants in Chinese cities based on travel big data. Sustainability 12(10):4012
76. Zhang W, Derudder B, Wang J et al (2018) Regionalization in the Yangtze River Delta, China, from the perspective of inter-city daily mobility. Reg Stud 52(4):528–541
77. Huang Z, Yang J (2020) The impact of dialect on inter-provincial migration in China. Popul Res 44(04):89–101 (in Chinese)
78. Lee ES (1966) A theory of migration. Demography 3(1):47–57
79. Todaro M (1980) Internal migration in developing countries: a survey[M]//population and economic change in developing countries. University of Chicago Press, pp 361–402
80. Feng Z, Zhang Y, Wei Y et al (2019) Spatial-temporal pattern and dynamic mechanism of population flow of Changchun City during Chunyun period based on Baidu migration data. Econ Geogr 39(05):101–109 (in Chinese)
81. Li Y (2013a) The research about provincial population migration and regional economic development in china-based on analysis on the sixth census data. Jinlin University. (in Chinese)
82. Wang G, Qin Z, Cheng L (2012b) Spatial distribution of population migration in China in the 1990s. Sci Geogr Sin 32(3):273–281 (in Chinese)
83. Liu S (2014) Factors analysis of interprovincial migration in China. J Quant Tech Econ 31(04):83–98 (in Chinese)
84. Li Y, Yang X, Cai H (2015) Spatiotem-poral characteristics and influencing factors of inflow popula-tion in Guangdong from 2000 to 2010. Prog Geogr 34(1):110–117 (in Chinese)
85. Zhang Q (2008) A study on China's population migration and regional economic development differences. Fudan University. (in Chinese)
86. Zhang Y, Ren Z (2012) Population change and its spatial distribution patterns of coastal cities based on GIS. Areal Res Dev 31(4):152–156 (in Chinese)
87. Kang W, Shao J, Guo Y (2016) Spatial-temporal distribution and influence factors of population migration in typical mountainous area. Trop Geogr 36(01):132–141 (in Chinese)
88. Li S, Mei Z, Zhang R et al (2017) Analyze of spatial characteristics and its influencing factors of China's interprovincial migration. J South China Norm Univ (Nat Sci Ed) 03:84–91 (in Chinese)
89. Lu C, Sun W (2014) Impacting factors of population agglomeration areas on migration: a case study in Dongguan City. Prog Geogr 33(5):593–604 (in Chinese)
90. Lei G, Fu C, Zhang L et al (2013) The changes in population floating and their influencing factors in china based on the sixth census. Northwest Popul J 34(05):1–8. (in Chinese)
91. Li P, Deng H (2007) The characteristics and influence factors of migration in Beijing-Tianjin-Hebei region. Popul Econ 6:59–63 (in Chinese)
92. Zhang S, Zhu Y, Jin X et al (2013) The spatial patterns of intra-provincial migration and their determinants in Anhui province. Econ Geogr 33(5):24–30 (in Chinese)
93. Camagni RP (1993) From city hierarchy to city network: reflections about an emerging paradigm. In: Lakshmanan TR, Nijkamp P (eds) Structure and change in the space economy. Springer, Berlin/Heidelberg, Germany
94. Castells M (1996) The rise of the network society. Blackwell Press, Malden, MA, USA
95. Lowry IS (1966) Migration and metropolitan growth: two analytical models. Chandler Press, San Francisco, CA, USA
96. Stouffer SA (1960) Intervening opportunities and competing migrants. J Reg Sci 2:1–26

97. Zipf GK (1946) The P1P2/D hypothesis: on the intercity movement of persons. Am Sociol Rev 11:677–686
98. Rogers A (1967) A regression analysis of interregional migration in California. Rev Econ Stat 49:262–267
99. Keyfitz N (1968) Introduction to the mathematics of population. Addison-Wesley, Old Tappan, NJ, USA
100. Rogers A (1966) A Markovian policy model of interregional migration. Reg Sci 17:205–224
101. Lewis WA (1954) Economic development with unlimited supplies of labour. Manch Sch 22:139–191
102. Todaro MP (1969) A model of labor migration and urban unemployment in less developed countries. Am Econ Rev 59:138–148
103. Zelinsky W (1971) The hypothesis of the mobility transition. Geogr Rev 61:219–249
104. Piore MJ (1979) Birds of passage: migrant labor in industrial societies. Cambridge University Press, Cambridge, UK
105. Stark O, Bloom DE (1985) The new economics of labor migration. Am Econ Rev 75:173–178
106. Taylor JE (1986) Differential migration, networks, information and risk. In: Stark O (ed) Migration, human capital, and development, vol 4. Research in human capital and development. JAI Press, Greenwich, CT, USA
107. Schultz TP (1990) Testing the neoclassical model of family labor supply and fertility. J Hum Resour 25:599–634
108. Cadwallader MT (1992) Migration and residential mobility: macro and micro approaches. University of Wisconsin Press, Madison, WI, USA
109. Fotheringham AS, Rees P, Champion T, Kalogirou S, Tremayne AR (2004) The development of a migration model for England and Wales: overview and modelling outmigration. Environ Plan A 36:1633–1672
110. Office of the Deputy Prime Minister (ODPM) (2002) Development of a migration model. Office of the Deputy Prime Minister, London, UK
111. Fotheringham AS (1986) Modelling hierarchical destination choice. Environ Plan A 18:401–418
112. Fotheringham AS (1991) Statistical modelling of spatial choice: an overview. In: Ghosh A, Ingene C (eds) Spatial analysis in marketing: theory, methods, and applications. JAI Press, Greenwich, CT, USA
113. Rogers A (1979) Multiregional methods for subnational population projections. J Biochem 120:1247–1252
114. Fujita M, Krugman P, Venables AJ (1999b) the spatial economy: cities, regions and international trade. MIT Press, Cambridge, MA, USA
115. Gries T, Kraft M, Simon M (2016) Explaining inter-provincial migration in China. Reg Sci 4:709–731
116. Massey DS, Arango J, Hugo G, Kouaouci A, Pellegrino A, Taylor JE (1993) Theories of international migration: a review and appraisal. Popul Dev Rev 13:431–466
117. Fawcett JT (1989) Networks, linkages, and migration systems. Int Migr Rev 23:671–680
118. Hania Z (1992) Empirical identification of international migration systems. In: Kritz M, Lim LL, Zlotnik H (eds) International migration systems: a global approach. Clarendon Press, Oxford, UK
119. Leslie PH (1945) On the use of matrices in certain population mathematics. Biometrika 33:183–212
120. Malthus TR, Flew A (2007) An essay on the principle of population and a summary view of the principle of population, vol 41. Penguin, Harmondsworth, UK, pp 114–115
121. Song J (1982) Population projection and population control. People's Publishing House, Beijing, China
122. Deng J (2005) The primary methods of Grey system theory. Huazhong University of Science and Technology Press, Wuhan, China
123. Deng Y, Liu S, Cai J, Lu X, Nielsen CP (2014) Spatial pattern and its evolution of Chinese provincial population and empirical study. Acta Geogr Sin 69:1473–1486

124. Kumo K (2017) Interregional migration: analysis of origin-to-destination matrix. Palgrave Macmillan, London, UK
125. Poot J, Alimi O, Cameron MP, Maré DC (2016) The gravity model of migration: the successful comeback of an ageing superstar in regional science. J Reg Res 63–68. http://ftp.iza.org/dp10329.pdf. Accessed 20 Feb 2018
126. Christaller W (1933) Central places in Southern Germany. Prentice-Hall Press, Englewood Cliffs, NJ, USA
127. Losch A (1954) The economics of location. Yale University Press, New Haven, CT, USA
128. Henderson JV (1974) The types and size of cities. Am Econ Rev 64:640–656
129. Simon H (1955) On a class of skew distribution functions. Biometrika 44:425–440
130. Black D, Henderson V (1999) A theory of urban growth. J Polit Econ 107:252–284
131. Duranton G (2002) City size distributions as a consequence of the growth process. CEPR discussion paper, vol 1, pp 477–501
132. Duranton G (2006) Some foundations for Zipf's law: product proliferation and local spillovers. Reg Sci Urban Econ 36:542–563
133. Eaton J, Eckstein Z (1997) Cities and growth: theory and evidence from France and Japan. Reg Sci Urban Econ 27:443–474
134. Glaeser EL, Scheinkman JA, Shleifer A (1995) Economic growth in a cross-section of cities. J Monet Econ 36:117–143
135. Glaeser EL, Kahn ME, Rappaport J (2008) Why do the poor live in cities? The role of public transportation. J Urban Econ 63:1–24
136. Córdoba JC (2008) On the distribution of city sizes. J Urban Econ 63:177–197
137. Gabaix X (1999) Zipf's Law for cities: an explanation. Q J Econ 114:739–767
138. Anderson G, Ge Y (2005) The size distribution of Chinese cities. Reg Sci Urban Econ 35:756–776
139. Chen X, Greene R (2012) The spatial-temporal dynamics of China's changing urban hierarchy (1950–2005). Urban Stud Res 2012:1–13
140. Schaffar A, Dimou M (2012) Rank-size city dynamics in China and India, 1981–2004. Reg Stud 46:707–721
141. Song S, Zhang K (2002) Urbanisation and city size distribution in China. Urban Stud 39:2317–2327
142. Fujita M, Krugman P (1995) When is the economy monocentric? Von Thünen and Chamberlin unified. Reg Sci Urban Econ 25:505–528
143. Fujita M, Mori T (1997) Structural stability and evolution of urban systems. Reg Sci Urban Econ 27:399–442
144. Fujita M, Krugman P, Mori T (1999a) On the evolution of hierarchical urban systems. Eur Econ Rev 43:209–251
145. Krugman P (1993) On the number and location of cities. Eur Econ Rev 37:293–298
146. Stelder D (2005) Where do cities form? A geographical agglomeration model for Europe. J Reg Sci 45:657–679
147. Ge Y, Zhu G, Wu Y (2013) Simulation on Krugman's urban system in geographic environments. Sci Geogr Sin 33:273–281
148. Riddell JB, Harvey ME (2018) The urban system in the migration process: an evaluation of step-wise migration in Sierra Leone. Econ Geogr 1972, 48:270–283. Sustainability 10, 654 21 of 21
149. Plane DA, Henrie CJ, Perry MJ (2005) Migration up and down the urban hierarchy and across the life course. Proc Natl Acad Sci USA 102:15313–15318
150. Brown LA, Odland J, Golledge RG (1970) Migration, functional distance, and the urban hierarchy. Econ Geogr 46:472–485
151. Haag G, Munz M, Pumain D, Sanders L, Saint-Julien T (1992) Interurban migration and the dynamics of a system of cities: 1. The stochastic framework with an application to the French urban system. Environ Plan A 24:181–198
152. Barabasi AL, Albert R (1999) Emergence of scaling in random networks. Science 286:509–512

153. Menczer F (2004) Evolution of document networks. Proc Natl Acad Sci USA 101:5261–5265
154. Andersson C, Hellervik A, Lindgren K, Hagson A, Tornberg J (2003) Urban economy as a scale-free network. Phys Rev E Stat Nonlinear Soft Matter Phys 68:999–1005
155. Batty M (2001) Cities as small worlds. Environ Plan B Plan Des 28:637–638
156. Mansury Y, Gulyas L (2007) The emergence of Zipf's Law in a system of cities: an agent-based simulation approach. J Econ Dyn Control 31:2438–2460
157. Fan CC (2005a) Interprovincial migration, population redistribution, and regional development in China: 1990 and 2000 census comparisons. Prof Geogr 57(2):295–311
158. Sun Q, Tang F, Tang Y (2015) An economic tie network-structure analysis of urban agglomeration in the middle reaches of Changjiang river based on SNA. J Geogr Sci (06):739–755
159. Krugman P (1997) Development, geography, and economic theory. MIT Press, Cambridge, MA, USA
160. Pflüger M, Südekum J (2008) Integration, agglomeration and welfare. J Urban Econ 63:544–566
161. Liang Q, Chen Q, Wang R (2013) Household registration reform, labor mobility and optimization of the urban hierarchy. Soc Sci China 12:36–59
162. Wahnschafft R, Wei F (2015) Urban China: toward efficient, inclusive, and sustainable urbanization. The World Bank and the Development Research Center of the State Council, Beijing, China
163. Sheng G (2011) A literature review on the research of urbanization pattern. Urban Dev Stud 7:13–19
164. Tian M, Tian Z, Cushing B (2016) Inter-city migration in China: a recurrent-event duration analysis of repeat migration. Camb J Reg Econ Soc 9:551–569
165. World Bank (2009) Reshaping economic geography. Oxford University Press, New York, NY, USA
166. Woetzel J, Mendonca L, Devan J, Negri S, Hu Y, Jordan L, Li X, Maasry A, Tsen G, Yu F (2009) Preparing for China's urban billion. McKinsey Global Institute Report. McKinsey & Company, New York, NY, USA
167. Wang X (2010) Urbanization path and city scale in China: an economic analysis. Econ Res J 10:20–32
168. Gu C (2009) Prospect on China's urban system in 2020. Future Dev 6:2–7
169. Del Giudice V, De Paola P, Torrieri F (2014) An integrated choice model for the evaluation of urban sustainable renewal scenarios. In: Advanced materials research, vol 1030. Trans Tech Publications, Zürich, Switzerland, pp 2399–2406
170. Oppio A, Corsi S, Torrieri F, Mattia S (2017) Infrastructure development and territorial vulnerability. The role of composite indicators for addressing siting decisions. In: Appraisal: from theory to practice. Springer, Berlin, Germany, pp 277–290
171. Torrieri F, Nijkamp P (2005) Scenario analysis in spatial impact assessment: a methodological approach. In: Sustainable urban development, 3rd edn. Routledge, London, UK
172. Verburg PH, Tabeau A, Hatna E (2013) Assessing spatial uncertainties of land allocation using a scenario approach and sensitivity analysis: a study for land use in Europe. J Environ Manag 127:132–144

Part II
Migration Intentions of Floating Population

Chapter 3
The Overall Situation of the Floating Population in China

3.1 The Total Amount and Structures of the Floating Population

This part describes the changes in the total amount of floating population and analyzes the structures of the floating population in terms of personal attributes, migration features, family characteristics, socio-economic factors and regional properties, based on the annual data of the China Migrants Dynamic Survey (CMDS) released by National Health Commission of PRC, as well as the data from national population censuses and 1% national population sampling surveys.

3.1.1 The Total Amount and Growth Rates of Floating Population

Since the 1980s, the changing process of China's floating population size has gone though 3 stages:

The first stage is from the beginning of 1980s to the beginning of the 1990s. At this stage, with the publication of *Notices on the issue of farmers settling down in towns* issued by State Council, governments gradually relaxed the restriction on the rural population migrating to urban areas to work and live, which accelerated the rural–urban migration of rural population. China's floating population size increased from 6.57 million in 1982 to 21.35 million in 1990, with an annual growth rate of 7%.

The second stage is from 1990 to 2010, during which the floating population size grew at a more rapid speed, increasing from the 21.35 million in 1990 to 221.43 million in 2010, with an annual growth rate of 12%.

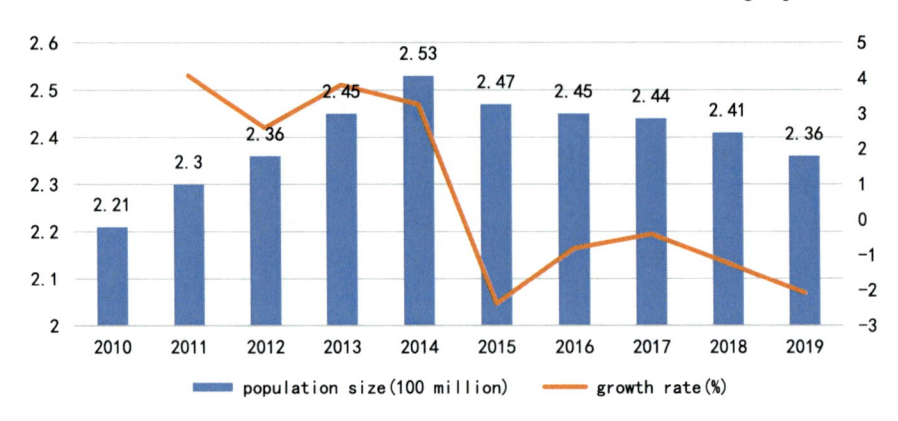

Fig. 3.1 The total amount of floating population and its growth rate from 2010 to 2019. *Data sources:* China Migrants Dynamic Survey (CMDS)

The third stage is from 2010 to now, the growth of the floating population size has slowed down. With the development of new-type urbanization, the transformation of economic development mode and the readjustment of regional economic structure, the total amount of floating population from 2010 to 2019 presented a development trend of rising first and falling later. From 2010 to 2014, the number of floating population increased from 221 to 253 million with an annual increase of 8 million people, and the average annual growth rate was 3.39%. Since 2015, the number of floating population begun to decline slowly, the size of 2015 (247 million) decreased by 6 million compared with that of 2014. From 2014 to 2019, the number of floating population decreased from 253 to 236 million with an annual decrease of 3.4 million people. The possible reasons of the reduction in the amount of floating population include the following aspects: the citizenization promotion of floating population, the industrial transfer from the eastern coastal region to the central and western region, the low inclusiveness of employment in megacities, the decrease of the proportion of labor forces in floating population (Fig. 3.1).

3.1.2 The Gender Structure of Floating Population

From 2009 to 2012, the proportion of females in the floating population presented a downward trend. Since 2012, the proportion of females rose from 47.2% in 2012 to 48.3% in 2017. In contrast, the proportion of males in the floating population showed a trend of rising first and falling later. The ratio of males to females in the floating population are featured by rising first and falling later, which reached the peak value of 111.8 in 2012 and began to decrease after that (Fig. 3.2).

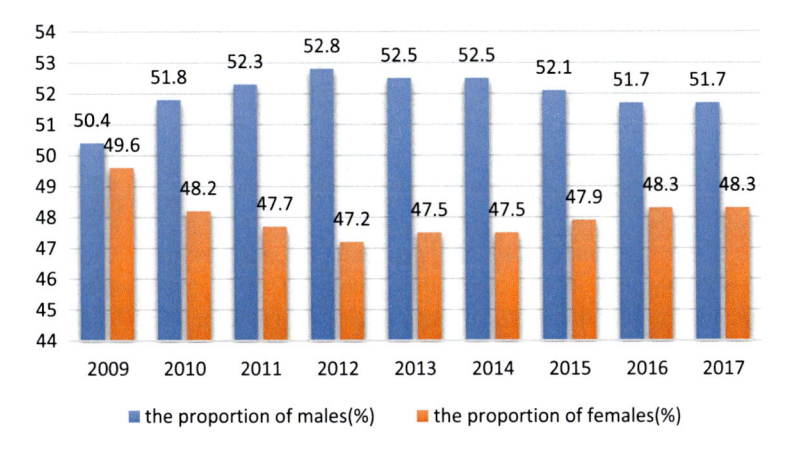

Fig. 3.2 The gender structure of floating population from 2009 to 2017. *Data sources:* China Migrants Dynamic Survey (CMDS)

3.1.3 The Age Structure of Floating Population

China's floating population are mainly labor forces (16–59 years old), especially the youth and middle-aged group, whereas the proportions of children and older adults are relatively low. The proportion of labor forces in the floating population has increased from 53.3% in 1982 to 84.1% in 2015. With the changing process of the demographic dividend (rising first and falling later), the proportion of young and middle-aged labor forces (16–44 years old) in the floating population experienced the following stages: a period of rapid growth in the 1980s with an increase of 24.1% from 1982 to 1990, a stabilization stage from 1990 to 2010 with the proportion stabilizing at around 70%, a period of decline from 2010 to 2015 with a decrease of 1.6%. In recent years, the average age and median age has increased significantly. From 1982 to 2015, the average age of floating population increased by 4 years, and the median age increased by 8 years (Table 3.1).

Table 3.1 The age structure of floating population from 1982 to 2015

Age structure (%)	1982	1990	2000	2005	2010	2015
0–15 years old	35.4	17.3	14.9	13.5	11.6	10.6
16–44 years old	45.7	69.8	70.2	71.1	71.1	68.5
45–59 years old	7.6	7.6	9.7	10.0	12.5	15.6
60 years and above	11.3	5.3	5.3	5.4	4.8	5.3
Total	100	100	100	100	100	100
Average age (years)	27.3	28.2	29.0	30.4	30.8	31.0
Median age (years)	23	25	27	29	29	31

Data sources: National population censuses and 1% national population sampling surveys

Among different age groups, the proportion of the 0–14 years old group to the total floating population presented a overall upward trend, which increased from 19.8% in 2012 to 21.1% in 2017. The proportion of the 15–59 years old group to the total floating population were on a decline, from 79.7% in 2012 to 75.4% in 2017, indicating the reduction in labor forces. Whereas, the proportion of the over 60 years old group to the total floating population rose from 0.5% in 2013 to 3.5% in 2017, corresponding to the population aging process.

The age structure change of floating population are characterized by 3 major characteristics: the new generation floating population has gradually replaced the old generation floating population; the amount of older migrants has been on a rapid rise; the amount of the floating children has grew quickly, while presenting a downward trend since 2010.

Firstly, with the continuous process of population replacement, the new generation floating population (born in 1980 and after 1980) have gradually replaced the old generation floating population, and become the backbone force of industrial workers and the main body of new citizens. From 2000 to 2015, the proportion of the new generation floating population in the labor-age floating population rose from 17.2 to 62.3%, and the new generation labor-age floating population increased from 14.08 million to nearly 130 million, becoming the main force of the labor-age floating population (shown in Fig. 3.3). With the return migration of the old generation floating population and the continuous outflows of the added rural labor forces, the new generation floating population size will continue to grow, and its proportion in the total floating population will also improve continuously (Table 3.2).

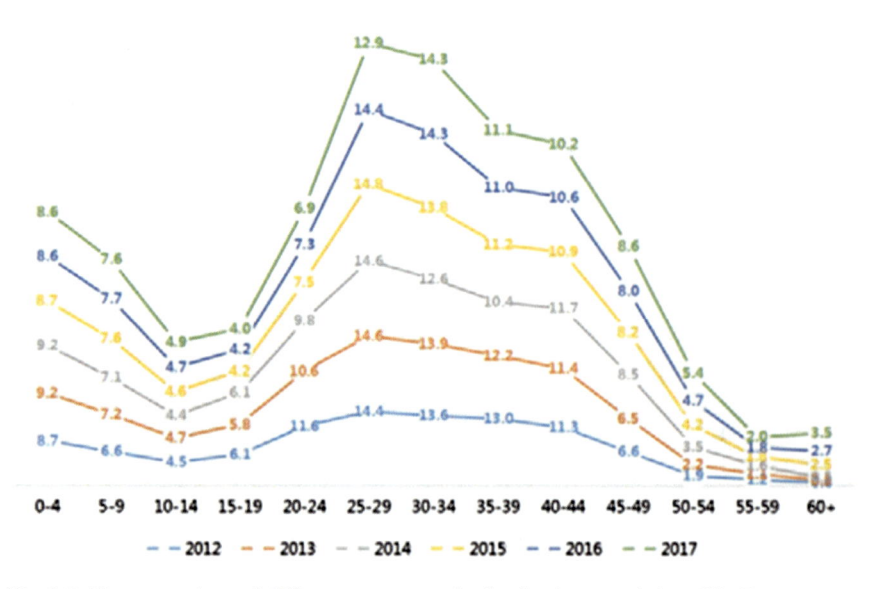

Fig. 3.3 The proportions of different age groups in the floating population (%). *Data sources:* China Migrants Dynamic Survey (CMDS)

Table 3.2   The sizes and proportions of the new generation floating population from 2000 to 2015

	2000	2005	2010	2015
The floating population size of 16–59-years-old group (ten thousand)	8167	11,952	18,510	20,677
The proportion of the new generation floating population (%, born in 1980 and after 1980)	17.2	33.0	49.8	62.3
The size of the new generation floating population (ten thousand, born in 1980 and after 1980)	1408	3943	9216	12,878
The total floating population size (ten thousand)	10,229	14,735	22,143	24,597
The proportion of the new generation floating population (%, born in 1980 and after 1980)	28.7	40.2	53.6	62.2
The size of the new generation floating population (ten thousand, born in 1980 and after 1980)	2931	5929	11,878	15,289

Data sources: National population censuses and 1% national population sampling surveys

Secondly, the population aging develops rapidly, with the proportion of older adults over 60 years old increasing from 10.5% in 2000 to 16.1% in 2015. Meanwhile, there has been a rapid growth in the interregional migration, with the percentage of the floating population to the national total population increasing from 7.9% in 2000 to 18% in 2015. Under the influence of the rapid growth of population aging and internal migration, the migration of older adults has become one of the hot research topics currently.

The older floating population size has grew rapidly since 2000, increasing from 5.03 million in 2000 to 13.04 million in 2015, with an annual increase of 6.6%. The proportion of the middle-aged and older floating population to the national floating population increased slightly from 4.9% in 2000 to 5.3% in 2015.

The older floating population are mainly composed of 4 groups: labor migrants, disabled migrants, healthy retired migrants and family-support migrants. In recent years, the retired migrants and disabled migrants among the older floating population increased rapidly. Meanwhile, with the population aging, the migrants that worked outside in the early days have become a large migrant group of older labor forces. Different older migrant groups have different socio-economic characteristics, which needs different supports and services for the older adults.

Thirdly, the rapid growth of floating children began from 1990s, rising from 4.59 million in 1990 to 19.82 million in 2000. From 2000 to 2010, it continued to grow to 35.81 million in 2010, with an increase of more than 40%. The results of the 1% national population sampling survey data of 2015 show that the amount of floating children decreased by 1.55 million compared with that of 2010, with a reduction of 4% (shown in Table 3.3). This trend is contrary to the growth of national floating population size (increasing from 221 million in 2010 to 247 million in 2015). The reduction of floating children amount from 2010 to 2015 is due to the change of population age structure: the decreasing birth rate causes the amount of the national

Table 3.3 The floating children sizes at different school ages from 1982 to 2015 (ten thousand)

Education stage	1982	1990	2000	2005	2010	2015
Infant stage (0–2 years old)	26	56	287	321	386	463
Preschool education stage (3–5 years old)	45	82	377	388	512	590
Primary education stage (6–11 years old)	104	139	709	764	929	934
Junior high school stage (12–14 years old)	46	66	332	361	464	412
Post-compulsory education stage (15–17 years old)	33	115	276	699	1290	1026
The total amount of floating children (0–17 years old)	254	459	1982	2533	3581	3426

Data sources: National population censuses and 1% national population sampling surveys

children to decline from 279 million in 2010 to 271 million in 2015, decreasing by
8 million.

3.1.4 The Marriage Structure of Floating Population

The floating population are mainly first-married people, accounting for about 80%
of the total floating population, followed by unmarried people, and the proportion of
divorced and widowed people occupy a very small proportion (Fig. 3.4).

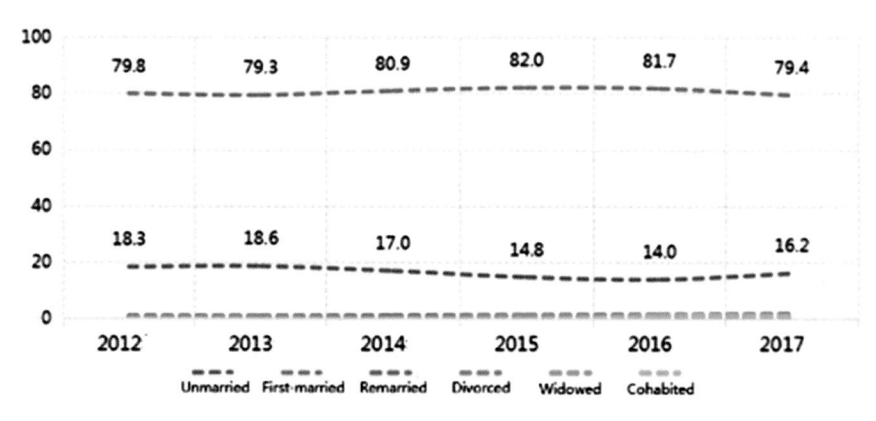

Fig. 3.4 The marriage structure of floating population (%). *Data sources:* China Migrants Dynamic
Survey (CMDS)

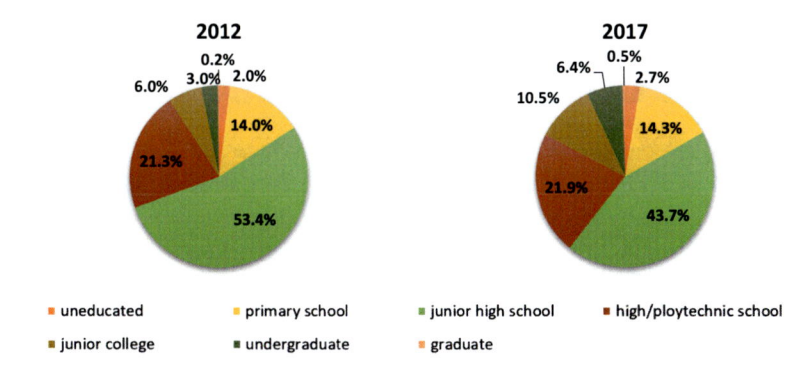

Fig. 3.5 The education attainment structure of floating population in 2012 and 2017 (%). *Data sources:* China Migrants Dynamic Survey (CMDS)

3.1.5 The Education Attainment Structure of Floating Population

From 2012 to 2017, the proportion of the floating population with the education level of junior high school and below to the total floating population decreased, while that of the floating population with the education level of high school and above increased. It is worth noting that the floating population with the education level of junior high school always account for the largest proportion of the floating population (over 40%), indicating that the education attainment level of floating population is relatively low. However, their education level has been improved a lot, reflected by the proportion of the floating population with the education level of junior college rising obviously from 6.0% in 2012 to 10.5% in 2017 (Fig. 3.5).

3.1.6 The Household Size Distribution of Floating Population

From 2012 to 2017, the floating population with a family size of 2 or 3 persons took up 50% of the total floating population. The proportion of people migrating alone showed a downward trend, while the percentage of migrants with a family size of 4 or 5 persons were on a rise. This demonstrates that the floating population tend to migrate more based on a family unit (Fig. 3.6).

3.1.7 The Hukou Structure of Floating Population

The *hukou* types are divided into the following 4 types: agricultural, non-agricultural, resident and others. Since the release of "Opinions on Further Improving the *hukou*

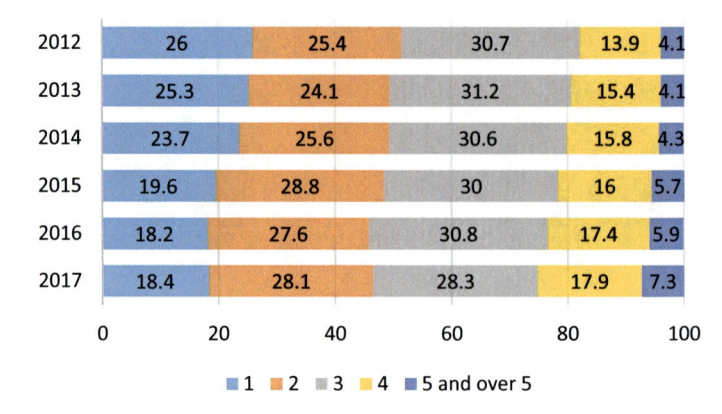

Fig. 3.6 The proportions of different family sizes in floating population (%). *Data sources:* China Migrants Dynamic Survey (CMDS)

System Reform" by State Council in 2014, the distinction between the agricultural *hukou* and non-agricultural *hukou* and the derived blue-print *hukou* have been gradually abolished, and these types of *hukou* have been gradually replaced by the resident *hukou*. The floating population mainly have agricultural *hukou*, and the proportion of migrants having agricultural *hukou* slightly decreased from 2012 to 2017, with the continuous progress of urbanization development (Fig. 3.7).

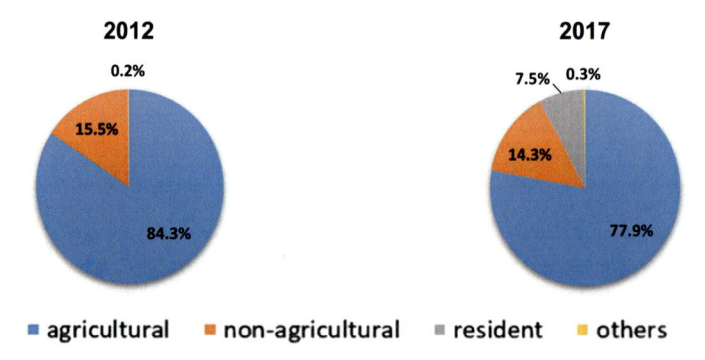

Fig. 3.7 The proportions of floating population with different *hukou* types in 2012 and 2017 (%). *Data sources:* China Migrants Dynamic Survey (CMDS)

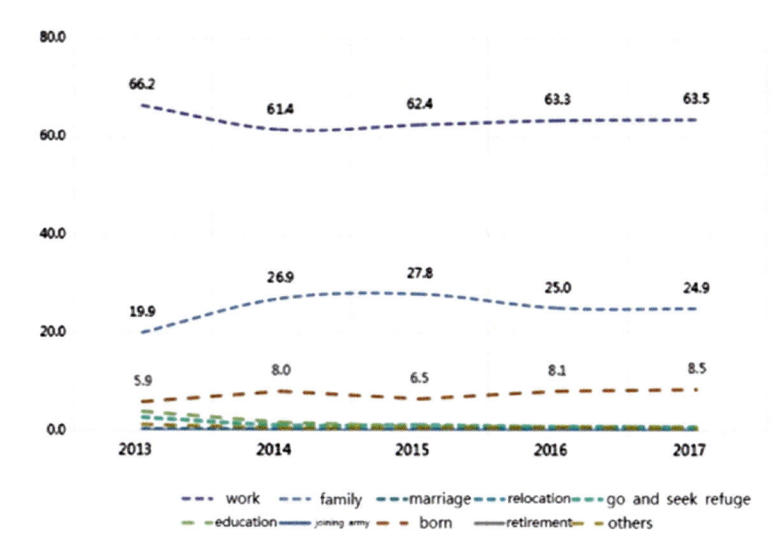

Fig. 3.8 The distribution of flow reasons of floating population (%). *Data sources:* China Migrants Dynamic Survey (CMDS)

3.1.8 The Distribution of Flow Reasons of Floating Population

In recent years, the flow reasons of floating population presented a diversifying trend, among which doing business or seeking jobs occupied a proportion of over 60% and tended to be stable (Fig. 3.8).

3.1.9 The Regional Structure of Floating Population

The early internal migration was mainly intraprovincial migration, and 3/4 of the floating population were intraprovincial migration in 1990. Subsequently, the proportion of interprovincial migrants increased rapidly and reached a peak (46.1%) in 2005. Since 2005, the proportion of interprovincial migrants began to decline (3.5% from 2005 to 2010, 3.2% from 2010 to 2015).

The distribution of floating population in the eastern, central and western regions gone through a process of first concentration and later dispersion. Before 2005, the floating population significantly agglomerate in the eastern region, increasing from 40.7% in 1982 to 64.6% in 2005. This trend reached a peak in 2005, and the proportion of floating population in the eastern region rapidly decreased by nearly 10% from 2005 to 2015. At the same time, the dispersion of floating population to central and western regions became increasingly obvious. From 2005 to 2015, the proportion of

Table 3.4 The proportions of floating population in the eastern, central and western regions from 1982 to 2015 (%)

Region		1982	1990	2000	2005	2010	2015
All	Eastern region	40.7	49.2	57.0	64.6	59.2	54.8
	Central region	42.9	29.0	20.4	17.2	19.3	21.7
	Western region	16.4	21.8	22.7	18.3	21.5	23.5
	Total	100	100	100	100	100	100
Interprovincial migration	Eastern region	–	58.5	77.8	84.6	82.5	78.2
	Central region	–	22.0	7.3	5.4	5.9	8.7
	Western region	–	19.6	14.9	10	11.6	13.1
	Total	–	100	100	100	100	100

Notes: The data of 1982 cannot distinguish the interprovincial floating population

floating population in the central region increased by 4.5%, and that of the western region increased by 5.2%.

The distribution of interprovincial migrants significantly reflects the change of the regional distribution of floating population. The eastern region still has the largest attractiveness for interprovincial floating population, with its proportion of floating population increasing from 58.5% in 1990 to 84.6% in 2005, and decreasing slowly to 78.2% in 2015. The proportions of interprovincial floating population gradually grew in central and western regions from 2005 to 2015 (Table 3.4).

3.2   The Migration Intentions of Floating Population

This part describes the 3 kinds of subjective migration intentions of floating population: *hukou* transfer intentions, settlement intentions and return intentions, based on the CMDS data. The *hukou* transfer intention can be regarded as permanent migration intentions, derived by asking a migrant whether he/she has a propensity to change his/her *hukou* to the destination region if possible. The settlement intention, deemed as temporary migration intention, is based on the question of the willingness to live in the destination region for a long time. The return intention denotes whether a migrant has the intention to return to his/her hometown. These migration intentions of the floating population all reflect the tolerance and attractiveness of destination cities and provide significant evidence for future *hukou* system reform. Each migration intention is discussed from the differences in demographic characteristics, economic factors and regional features.

3.2.1 Hukou *Transfer Intentions*

The *hukou* transfer intentions of floating population were only 39.38% in 2017, and remained relatively stable. There were only 37.2% of floating population that were willing to not only live in the destination area but also obtain local *hukou*; 45.5% of floating population have settlement intentions rather than *hukou* transfer intentions; 1.9% of floating population have *hukou* transfer intentions rather than settlement intentions; 7.1% of floating population haven't made a decision on these two issues (Table 3.5).

3.2.1.1 Differences in Gender

Regarding the impacts of gender on the *hukou* transfer intentions, it is found that the *hukou* transfer intentions of female migrants were relatively higher than those of the male migrants, and the proportions of male and female migrants with *hukou* transfer intentions decreased from 48.67% and 51.4% to 38.16% and 39.92%, respectively (Fig. 3.9).

Table 3.5 The *hukou* transfer intentions and settlement intentions of floating population in 2017

Hukou transfer intentions	Settlement intentions			Total
	Plan to	Not plan to	Haven't decided	
Willing	37.2	0.2	1.7	39.0
Unwilling	26.4	1.9	6.1	34.5
Haven't decided	19.1	0.3	7.1	26.5
Total	82.6	2.5	14.9	100.0

Fig. 3.9 The proportions of migrants with *hukou* transfer intentions in different genders (%)

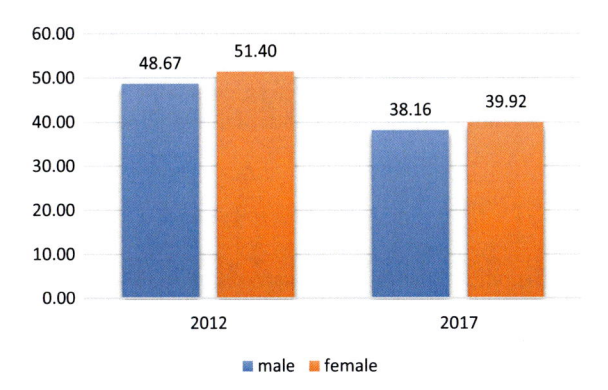

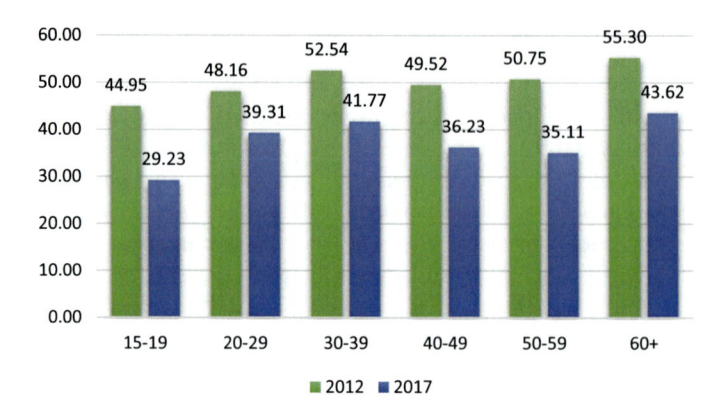

Fig. 3.10 The proportions of migrants with *hukou* transfer intentions at different ages (%)

3.2.1.2 Differences in Age

The older the migrant is, the more willing he is to transfer his *hukou* to the locality, embodied in the fact that the age group of over 60 years old had the highest *hukou* transfer intentions (43.62%), and the groups of 30–39, 40–49 and 50–59 were all around 40%. From 2012 to 2017, the *hukou* transfer intentions of floating population at different ages were all on a fall. The age groups of 15–19 and 50–59 had the largest decrease (15.72 and 15.64%) (Fig. 3.10).

3.2.1.3 Differences in Education Attainment

From 2012 to 2017, the *hukou* transfer intentions of floating population with different education levels were on a decline, among which the primary school level group and the uneducated group had the largest decrease (16.35 and 15.36%). The migrant with a higher education level will be more willing to transfer his *hukou* to the destination area. It is reflected by the highest *hukou* transfer intentions among the groups with the education levels of graduate, undergraduate and junior college (Fig. 3.11).

3.2.1.4 Differences in *Hukou* Types

On the whole, the *hukou* transfer intentions of floating population with agricultural *hukou* were lower than those with non-agricultural *hukou*. The floating population with non-agricultural *hukou* had the highest *hukou* transfer intentions (over 50%). From 2012 to 2017, the *hukou* transfer intentions of floating population with agricultural *hukou* decreased significantly from 48.22 to 35.09%, and those of floating population with non-agricultural *hukou* decreased slightly from 59.4 to 56.86% (Fig. 3.12).

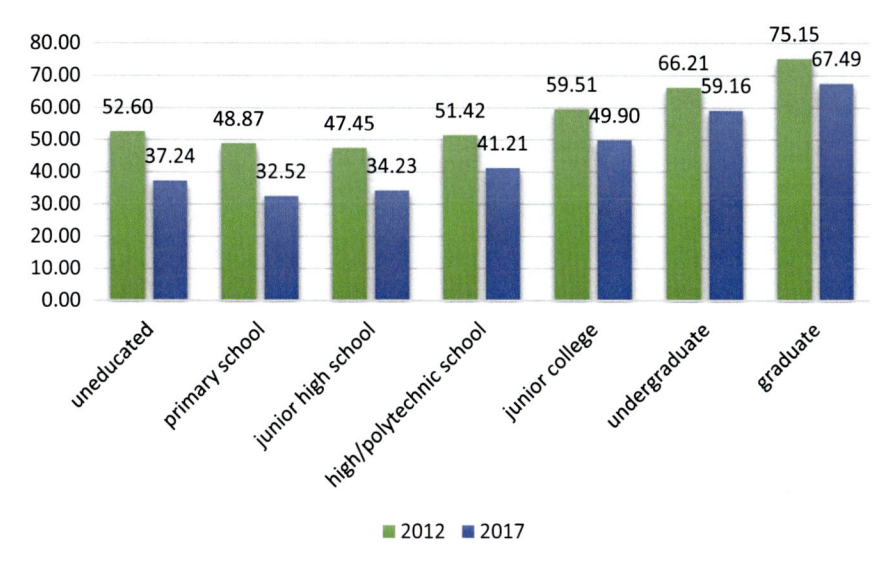

Fig. 3.11 The proportions of migrants with *hukou* transfer intentions at different education levels (%)

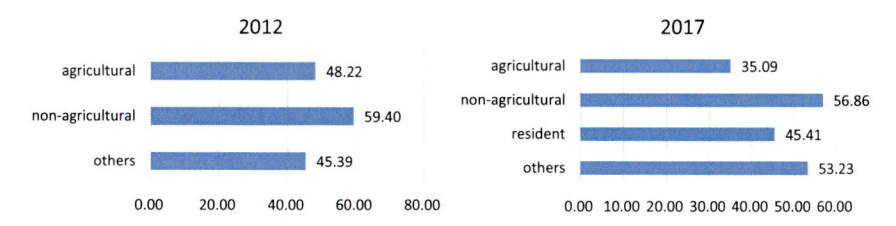

Fig. 3.12 The proportions of migrants with *hukou* transfer intentions with different types of *hukou* (%)

3.2.1.5   Differences in Occupation Types

Among different occupation types, the migrants engaged in agriculture, forestry, animal husbandry, fishery and water conservancy production had the highest *hukou* transfer intentions, followed by migrants who were heads of state organs, party/mass organizations, enterprises and institutions as well as civil servants, clerks and related personnel. The lowest *hukou* transfer intentions existed among production and transportation equipment operators and relevant personnel, as well as business and service personnel and others. From 2012 to 2017, the *hukou* transfer intentions of different occupations all presented a downward trend (Fig. 3.13).

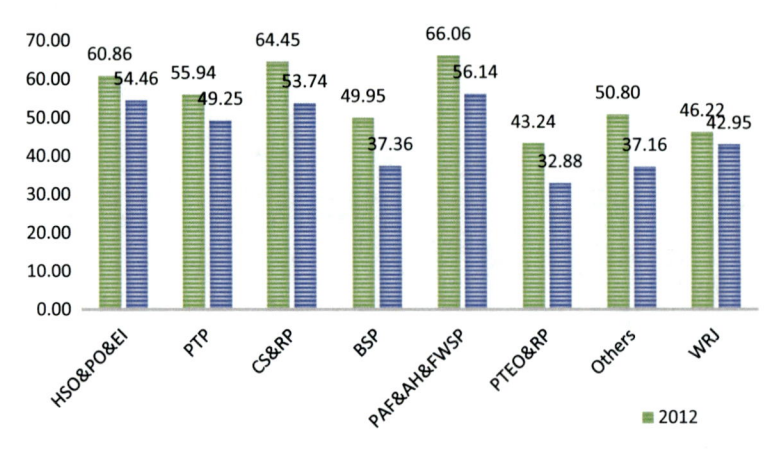

Fig. 3.13 The proportions of migrants with *hukou* transfer intentions engaged in different occupations (%). *Notes:* The abbreviations in the Figure represent the followings: heads of state organs, party/mass organizations, enterprises and institutions (HSO&PO&EI); professional and technical personnel (PTP); civil servants, clerks and related personnel (CS&RP); business and service personnel (BSP); personnel in agriculture, forestry, animal husbandry, fishery and water conservancy production (PAF&AH&FWSP); production and transportation equipment operators and relevant personnel (PTEO&RP); without regular jobs (WRJ)

3.2.1.6 Differences in Income Levels

The results demonstrate that the migrants with higher income levels tend to have higher *hukou* transfer intentions. From 2012 to 2017, the proportions of migrants with *hukou* transfer intentions at different income levels all decreased obviously, except for the migrants with the average monthly income more than 20,000 RMB. The migrants with the income levels of 8000–12,000, 6000–8000 and 4000–6000 experienced the largest decrease in the *hukou* transfer intentions (Fig. 3.14).

3.2.1.7 Regional Disparity

Concerning different city levels, the *hukou* transfer intentions were highest in megacities, followed by larger cities, and the medium and small cities had the lowest intentions. The *hukou* conversion intentions in megacities were close to the settlement intention, while there existed a large difference between them in relatively smaller cities. In small and medium cities, the difference was 50.56% (81.45% of floating population were willing to live for a long time in the destination city, while only 30.89% of floating population wanted to obtain local *hukou*) (Fig. 3.15).

In terms of cities that belong to different urban agglomerations, though the settlement intentions of floating population in the 3 major urban agglomerations were not significantly higher than those in cities outside the 3 major urban agglomerations, the *hukou* transfer intentions of the former were much higher than the latter. There were

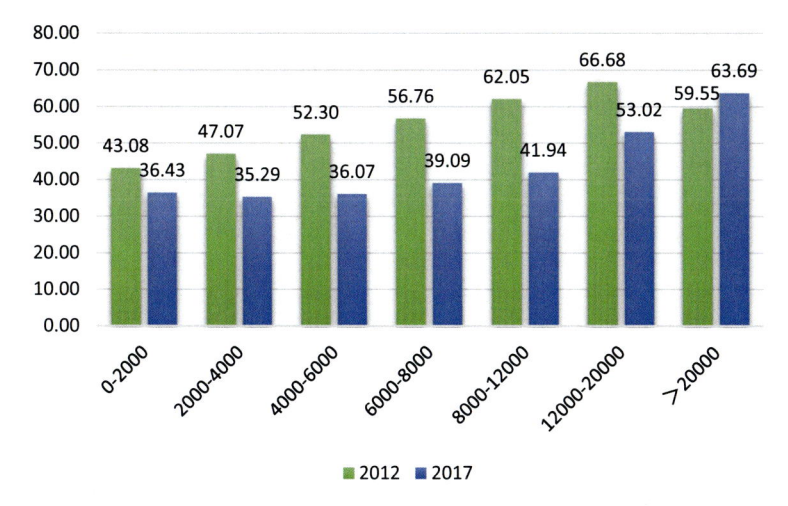

Fig. 3.14 The proportions of migrants with *hukou* transfer intentions with different income levels (%)

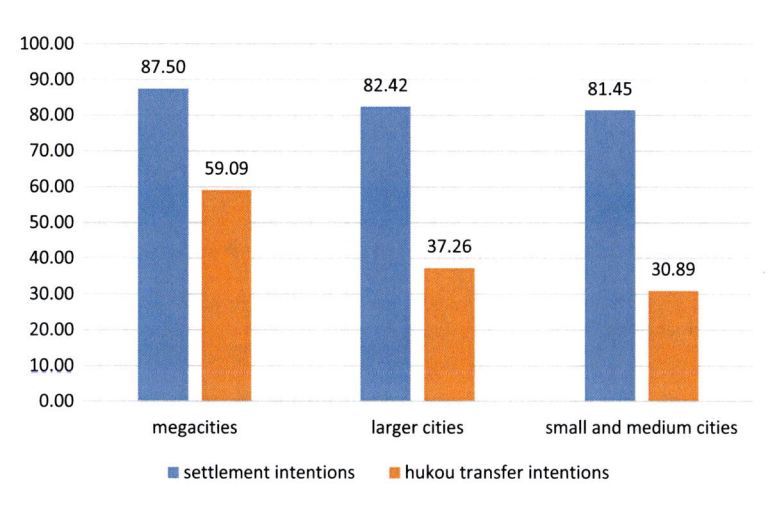

Fig. 3.15 The proportions of floating population with settlement intentions and *hukou* transfer intentions in cities of different levels in 2017 (%). *Notes:* The megacities refer to the cities with the permanent population in the urban area more than 10 million; the larger cities signify the cities with the permanent population in the urban area of 3–10 million; the small and medium cities represent the cities with the permanent population in the urban area fewer than 3 million

58.41% of floating population in Beijing-Tianjin-Hebei urban agglomeration that had *hukou* transfer intentions, with counterparts as 43.79% in Yangtze River Delta and 41% in Pearl River Delta, while only 34.75% of floating population were willing to transfer their *hukou* to the locality in cities outside the 3 major urban agglomerations.

The largest difference (47.77%) between the settlement intentions and *hukou* transfer intentions occurred in the cities outside the major urban agglomerations (Fig. 3.16).

At the province level, the *hukou* transfer intentions of floating population in Beijing and Shanghai (over 70%) were much higher than the other provinces, while Hunan Province and Anhui Province had the lowest *hukou* transfer intentions (20.84 and 21.92%). From 2012 to 2017, the *hukou* conversion intentions of floating population in most provinces showed a drop. The largest decrease happened in Liaoning Province (from 62.73 to 41.6%), followed by Henan Province and Heilongjiang Province. The *hukou* conversion intentions only increased in Hainan Province and Tianjin (Fig. 3.17).

Regarding the regional disparity, the eastern region had the highest *hukou* transfer intentions (47.42%), followed by the northeastern region (38.67%) and western

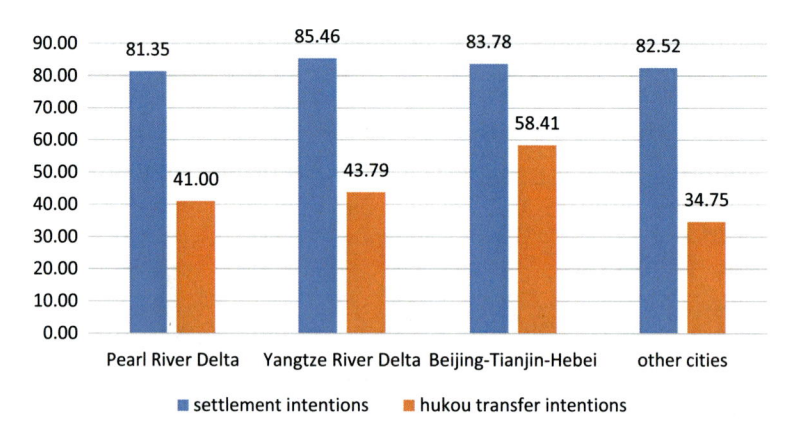

Fig. 3.16 The proportions of floating population with settlement intentions and *hukou* transfer intentions in cities of different urban agglomerations in 2017 (%)

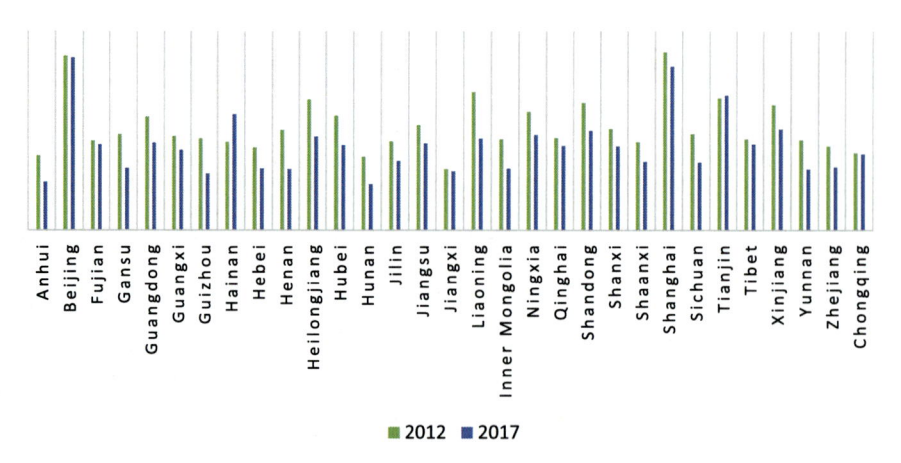

Fig. 3.17 The proportions of migrants with *hukou* transfer intentions in different provinces (%)

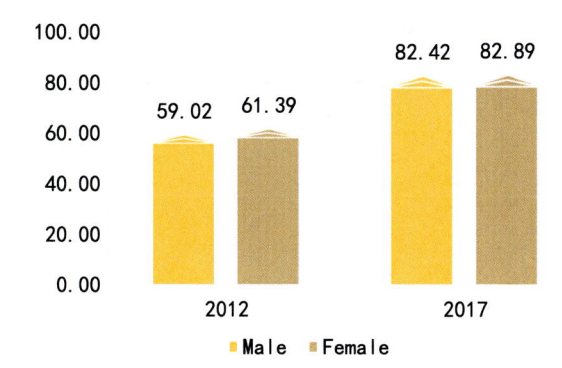

Fig. 3.18 The proportions of migrants with *settlement* intentions in different genders (%)

region (33.92%), and the central region was in the last place (33.92%). This result is consistent with the main trend of interregional population migration in China, that is, from the central, western and northeastern regions to the eastern region, with the eastern region as the main destination area of floating population and the central region as the main origin area of floating population.

3.2.2   Settlement Intentions

3.2.2.1   Differences in Gender

In 2017, the male and female floating population with settlement intentions both occupied around 80% of the total male and female floating population. Compared with 2012, the settlement intentions of male and female floating population were improved a lot in 2017 (23.4% and 21.5% respectively) (Fig. 3.18).

3.2.2.2   Differences in Age

Among different age groups, the settlement intention of the aged 30–39 group was the strongest (85.49%) in 2017, followed by the group of aged 60 years or more, 20–29 and 40–49. The lowest settlement intention occurred in the group of aged 15–19, due to the fact that young migrants lacked enough working experience and social capital to settle down in the destination city. From 2012 to 2017, the settlement intentions of floating population at different ages all had a significant growth (Fig. 3.19).

3.2.2.3   Differences in Education Attainment

The results showed that the migrants with higher education levels were more inclined to live and work for a long time in the destination city. The migrants with the graduate

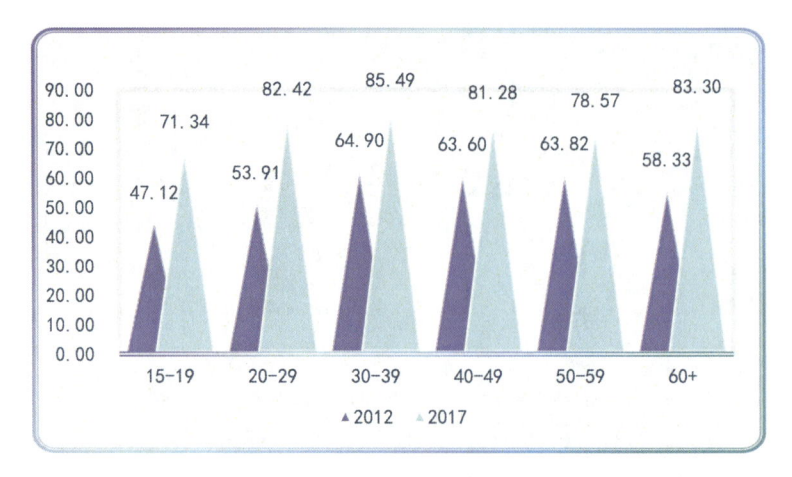

Fig. 3.19 The proportions of migrants with *settlement* intentions at different ages (%)

education level had the strongest settlement intentions (89.91%), followed by the migrants with the education levels of undergraduate and junior college (89.83 and 87.91%), and the uneducated migrants had the lowest settlement intentions (76.20%). From 2012 to 2017, the settlement intentions of migrant groups of different education levels were all on a rise (Fig. 3.20).

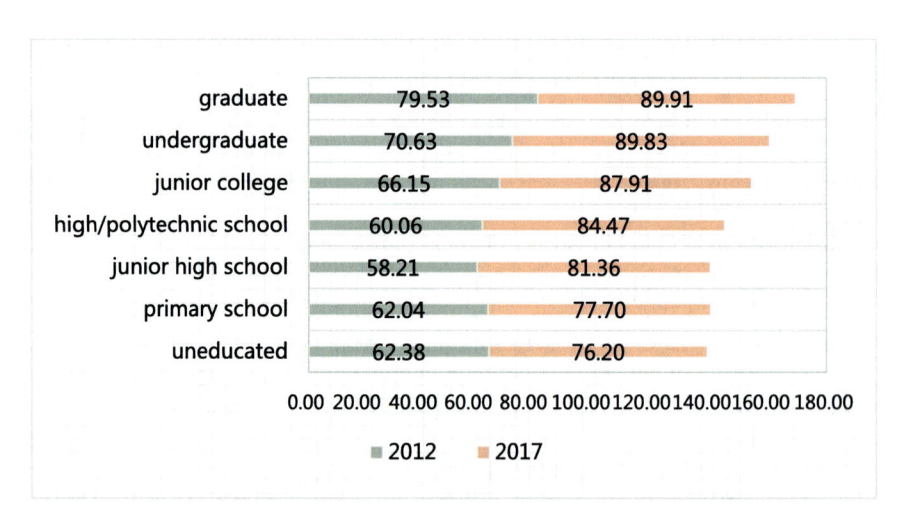

Fig. 3.20 The proportions of migrants with *settlement* intentions at different education levels (%)

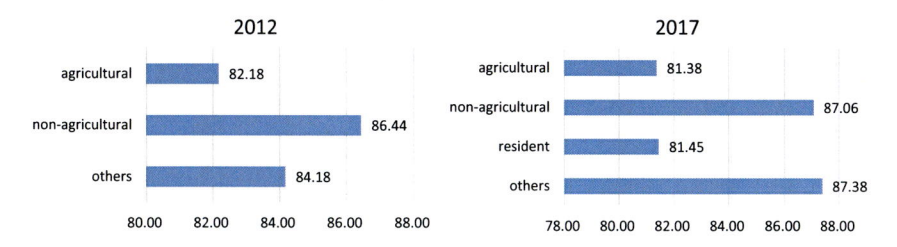

Fig. 3.21 The proportions of migrants with *settlement* intentions with different types of *hukou* (%)

3.2.2.4   Differences in *Hukou* Types

On the whole, the settlement intentions of floating population with agricultural *hukou* were lower than those with non-agricultural *hukou*. The floating population with non-agricultural *hukou* had the highest settlement intentions (over 85%). From 2012 to 2017, the settlement intentions of floating population with different types of *hukou* all increased slightly (Fig. 3.21).

3.2.2.5   Differences in Occupation Types

In 2017, the highest settlement intentions existed among the migrant groups of civil servants, clerks and related personnel (88.88%), heads of state organs, party/mass organizations, enterprises and institutions (88.64%), professional and technical personnel (87.87%), which had relatively stable jobs and a reliable living security. In contrast, the migrant groups without regular employment had the lowest settlement intentions (77.01%). From 2012 to 2017, the migrant groups of different occupations all experienced an evident increase in settlement intentions (Fig. 3.22).

3.2.2.6   Differences in Income Levels

The results demonstrated that migrants with a higher income level tended to have a higher settlement willingness. However, the highest settlement intentions (97.25%) existed in the migrant group with the average monthly income of 12,000–20,000 RMB, even higher than that with the income level of over 20,000 RMB. From 2012 to 2017, the migrant groups with different income levels all went through a rise in settlement intentions.

3.2.2.7   Regional Disparity

Regarding the city levels, the megacities had the strongest settlement intentions of floating population (87.5%), the larger cities took the second place (82.42%), and

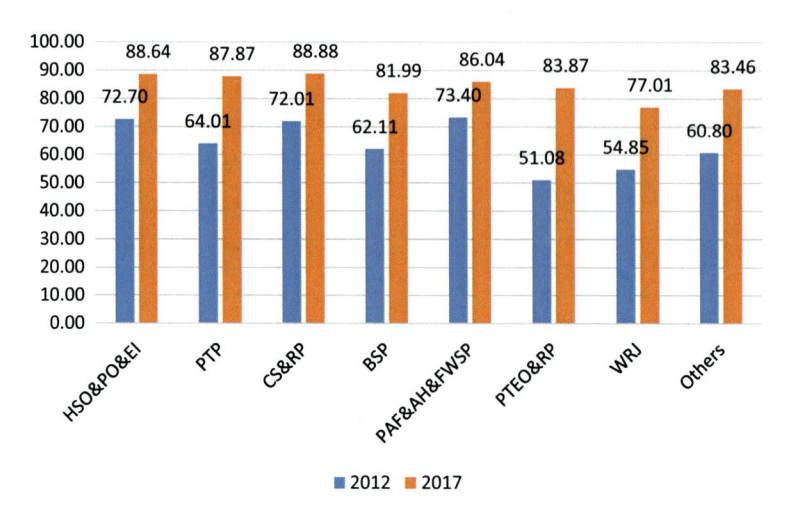

Fig. 3.22 The proportions of migrants with *settlement* intentions engaged in different occupations (%). *Notes:* The abbreviations in the Figure represent the followings: heads of state organs, party/mass organizations, enterprises and institutions (HSO&PO&EI); professional and technical personnel (PTP); civil servants, clerks and related personnel (CS&RP); business and service personnel (BSP); personnel in agriculture, forestry, animal husbandry, fishery and water conservancy production (PAF&AH&FWSP); production and transportation equipment operators and relevant personnel (PTEO&RP); without regular jobs (WRJ)

the small and medium cities had the weakest settlement intentions (81.45%). The floating population are more inclined to settle down in larger cities, caused by the higher wage levels, more employment opportunities and better public services in larger cities (Fig. 3.23).

In respect to the cities that belong to different urban agglomerations, the floating population in Yangtze River Delta and Beijing-Tianjin-Hebei urban agglomeration had the highest settlement intentions (85.46 and 83.78%), followed by the cities outside the major urban agglomerations (82.52%), while floating population in Pearl

Fig. 3.23 The proportions of floating population with settlement intentions in cities of different levels (%)

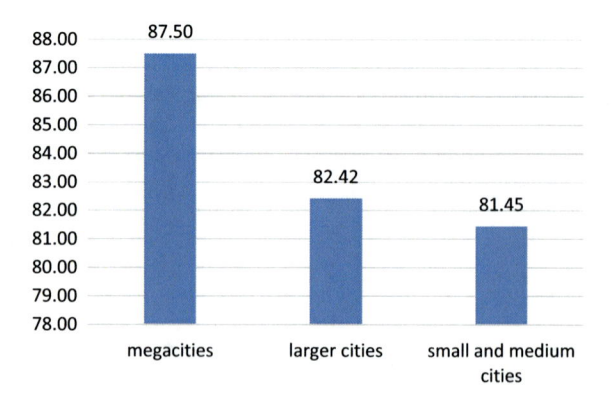

River Delta had the lowest settlement intentions (81.35%). As the main national employment center, the Pearl River Delta had attracted a large number of floating population, whereas its attraction for the floating population to stay here for a long time was not enough compared with the other two urban agglomerations (Fig. 3.24).

At the province level, Beijing, Shanghai and Shandong Province had the strongest settlement intentions (over 90%) in 2017, while Tibet, Hebei and Gansu Provinces had the weakest settlement intentions (below 75%). All provinces experienced an evident growth in the settlement intentions from 2012 to 2017 (Fig. 3.25).

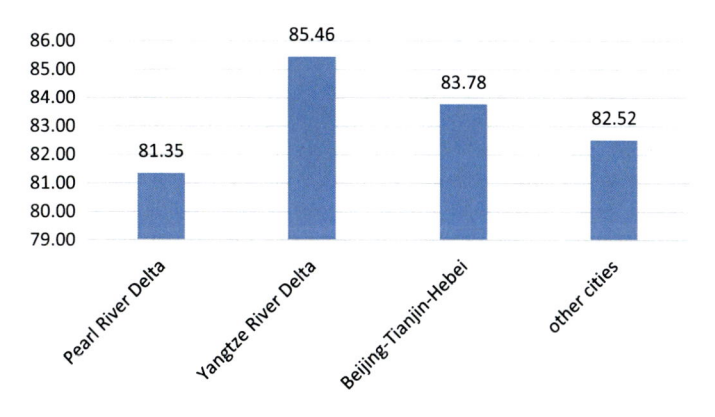

Fig. 3.24 The proportions of floating population with settlement intentions in cities of different urban agglomerations (%)

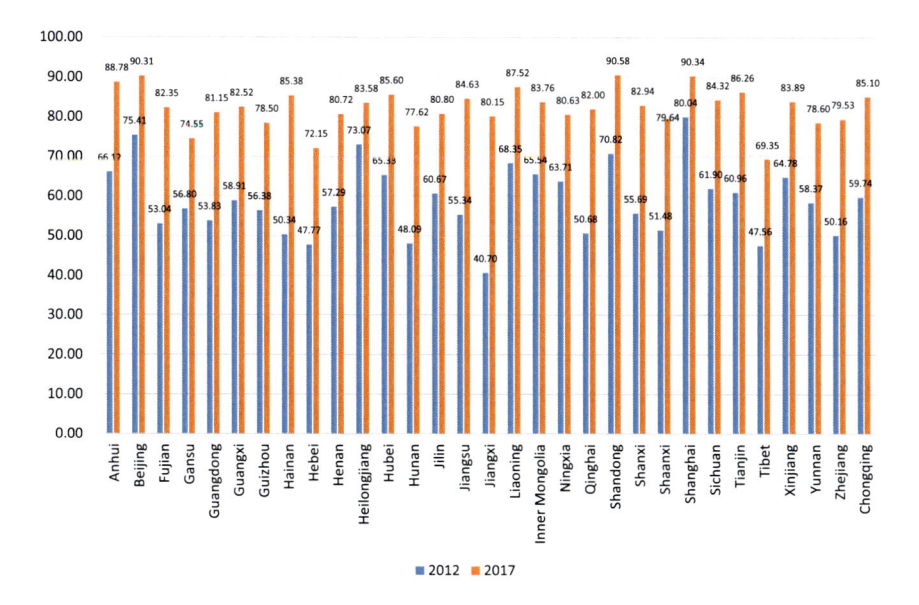

Fig. 3.25 The proportions of migrants with *settlement* intentions in different provinces (%)

   In terms of the regional disparity, the regions in the descending order of settlement intentions were the eastern region (84.15%), northeastern region (83.6%), central region (82.71%) and western region (81.72%). The possible reason was that the higher socio-economic development levels in the eastern region were more attractive for floating population, and that there were more intra-provincial migrants in the northeastern region than other regions, thus increasing its overall settlement intentions.

3.2.3   Return Intentions

Among all the floating population, some of them will choose to settle down in the destination cities, some of them will choose to migrate to another city, and part of them will decide to return to their hometowns. The China Migrants Dynamic Survey conducted by the National Health Commission didn't investigate the return intentions of floating population until 2016, to keep the time consistency with the above analysis, we only analyze the return intentions of 2017 below. The return intentions of floating population in 2017 was very low (1.64%), only accounting for 4.16 and 1.99% of the *hukou* transfer intentions and settlement intentions.

3.2.3.1   Differences in Gender

The return intention of the female floating population (1.66%) was higher than that of the male floating population (1.61%), and the overall return intentions were relatively low (only around 1.6%).

3.2.3.2   Differences in Age

Among different age groups, the return intentions of the age groups of 50–59 and over 60 were the strongest (over 3%) in 2017, followed by the groups of aged 40–49 and 15–19. It indicated that the older migrants (over 50) tended to come back to their hometowns to spend one's remaining years in comfort, influenced by the Chinese traditional idea "Falling leaves settle on their roots". The lowest settlement intention occurred in the group of aged 30–39, due to the fact that migrants at this age stage had accumulated enough working experience, social capital and savings to settle down in the destination city (Fig. 3.26).

3.2.3.3   Differences in Education Attainment

The results indicated that the migrants with higher education levels were less willing to return to their hometowns, due to the fact that they had more competitiveness in the

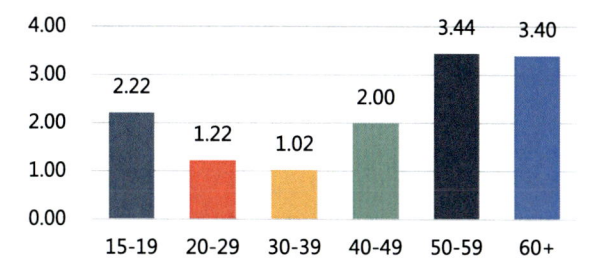

Fig. 3.26 The proportions of migrants with return intentions at different ages (%)

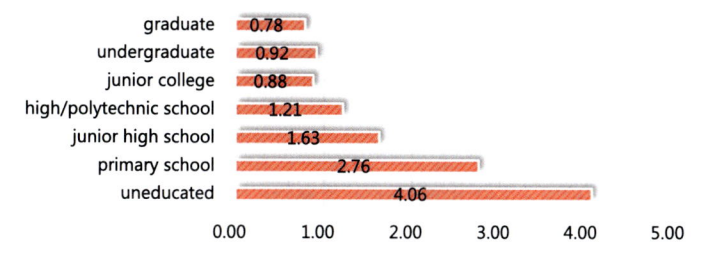

Fig. 3.27 The proportions of migrants with return intentions at different education levels (%)

job market and would be easier to settle down in the destination cities. The highest return intentions existed among the uneducated migrants (4.06%), and the lowest return intentions was only 0.78%, which emerged among the floating population with the education level of graduate (Fig. 3.27).

3.2.3.4 Differences in *Hukou* Types

On the whole, the return intentions of floating population with agricultural *hukou* were the highest, and migrants with non-agricultural *hukou* had the lowest return intentions. It indicated that the rural floating population were more likely to return to their hometowns, under the influence of the rural contracted lands and homesteads in hometowns (Fig. 3.28).

3.2.3.5 Differences in Occupation Types

Among floating population in different occupation types, the highest return intentions existed in production and transportation equipment operators and relevant personnel, personnel in agriculture, forestry, animal husbandry, fishery and water conservancy production, as well as migrants without regular jobs, which were over 1.9%. The lowest return intentions occurred in civil servants, clerks and related personnel, professional and technical personnel, as well as business and service personnel, which

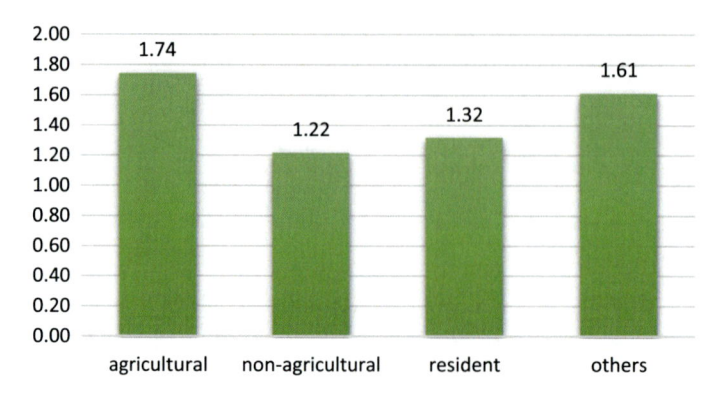

Fig. 3.28 The proportions of migrants with return intentions with different types of *hukou* (%)

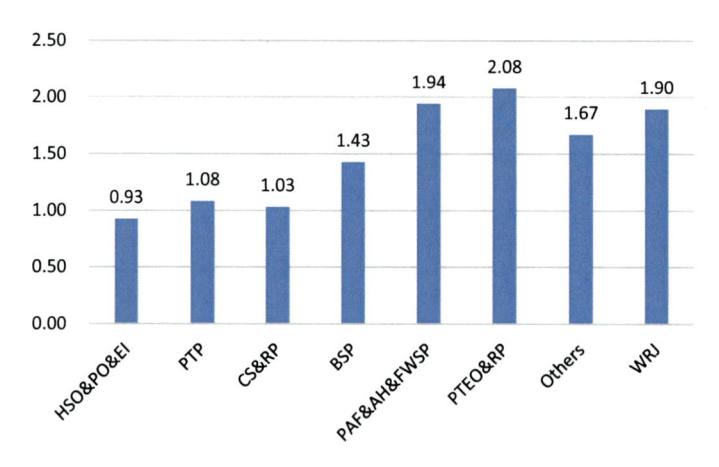

Fig. 3.29 The proportions of migrants with return intentions engaged in different occupations (%). *Notes:* The abbreviations in the Figure represent the followings: heads of state organs, party/mass organizations, enterprises and institutions (HSO&PO&EI); professional and technical personnel (PTP); civil servants, clerks and related personnel (CS&RP); business and service personnel (BSP); personnel in agriculture, forestry, animal husbandry, fishery and water conservancy production (PAF&AH&FWSP); production and transportation equipment operators and relevant personnel (PTEO&RP); without regular jobs (WRJ)

were only around 1%. This results show that the migrants with relatively unstable jobs were more inclined to return to their hometowns, while those with relatively stable jobs were more likely to settle down in the destination cities (Fig. 3.29).

3.2.3.6 Differences in Income Levels

Contrary to the settlement intentions, the migrants with a higher income level tended to have a lower return willingness, as they had a higher capacity to bear the high

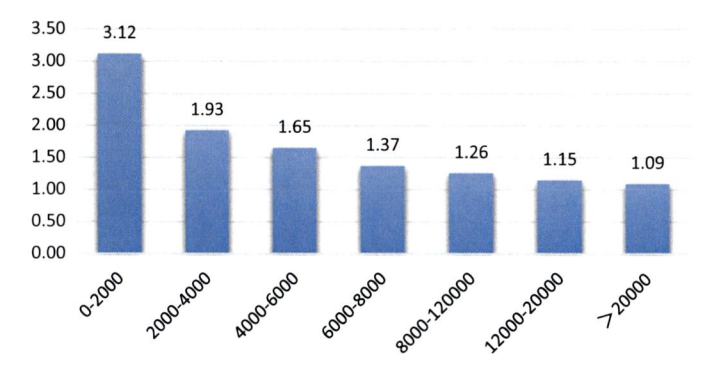

Fig. 3.30 The proportions of migrants with return intentions with different income levels (%)

living costs and settle down in the destination cities. The floating population with the average monthly income of 0–2000 RMB had the highest return intentions (3.12%), while those with the average monthly income of over 20,000 RMB had the lowest return intentions (1.09%) (Fig. 3.30).

3.2.3.7 Regional Disparity

Concerning the city levels, the small and medium cities had the strongest return intentions of floating population (1.74%), the megacities took the second place (1.49%), and the larger cities had the weakest return intentions (1.42%). The order of the return intentions in cities at different levels was contrary to that of the settlement intentions, because migrants with higher settlement intentions were less willing to return to their hometowns (Fig. 3.31).

Regarding the cities that belong to different urban agglomerations, the floating population in Yangtze River Delta had the highest return intentions, followed by those in Pearl River Delta and the cities outside the major urban agglomerations,

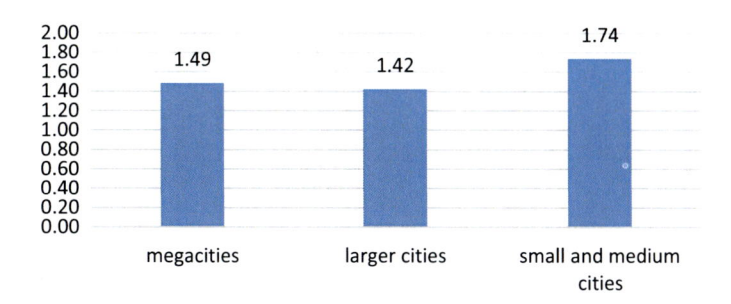

Fig. 3.31 The proportions of floating population with return intentions in cities of different levels (%)

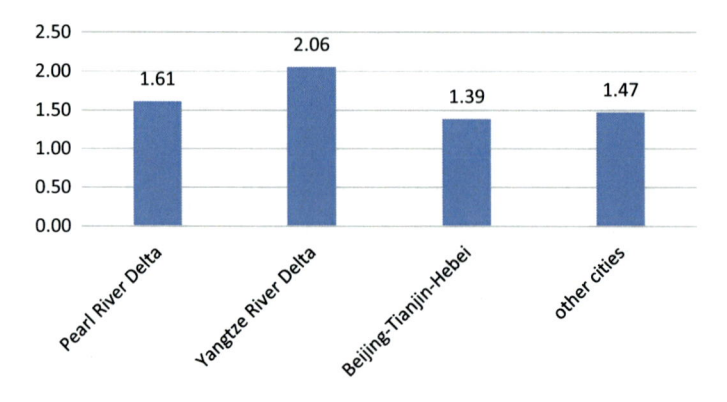

Fig. 3.32 The proportions of floating population with return intentions in cities of different urban agglomerations (%)

while the floating population in Beijing-Tianjin-Hebei urban agglomeration had the lowest return intentions (Fig. 3.32).

With respect to floating population in different provinces, Tibet, Zhejiang and Gansu Provinces had the highest return intentions (over 2.5%), while Guangxi, Liaoning and Heilongjiang Provinces had the lowest return intentions (below 0.8%) (Fig. 3.33).

In regard to the regional disparity, the regions in the descending order of the return intentions were the eastern region (1.75%), western region (1.54%), central region (1.47%) and northeastern region (0.94%). The probable reason was that there were more inter-provincial migrants in the eastern region than other regions, thus

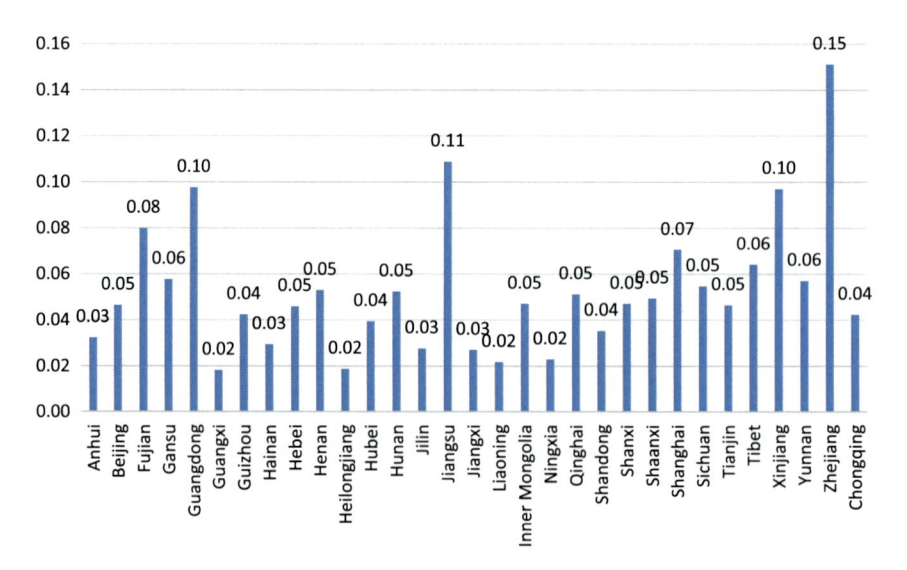

Fig. 3.33 The proportions of migrants with return intentions in different provinces (%)

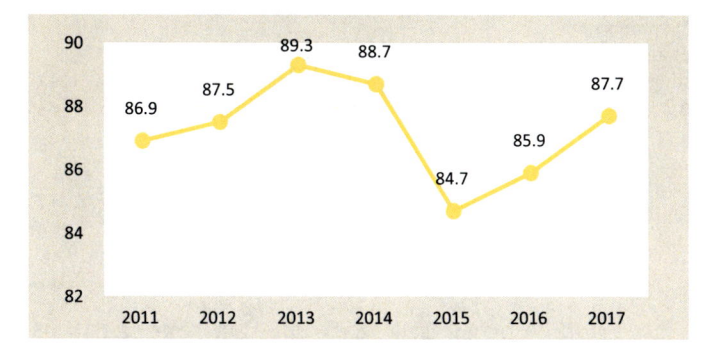

Fig. 3.34 The change of employment proportion of floating population from 2011 to 2017 (%)

increasing its overall return intentions, and the situation of the northeastern region was exactly contrary to that of the eastern region.

3.3   The Economic Conditions of Floating Population

This part analyzes the overall working and living conditions of the floating population, including employment conditions and income levels, based on the CMDS data.

3.3.1   The Employment Proportions of Floating Population

The change of the employment proportion of flowing population fluctuated from 2011 to 2017. Overall, the employment proportion of floating population increased by 0.8% from 2011 to 2017, and became 87.7% in 2017, signifying that the overwhelming majority of floating population had acquired a job and obtained certain income in the destination cities (Fig. 3.34).

3.3.2   The Employment Status of Floating Population

The floating population that were employees accounted for the majority (more than 60%) of the total floating population, followed by those with the employment status of employers, and the floating population who were self-employed and others occupied a very small proportion. From 2010 to 2017, the proportions of migrants with different employment status remained relatively stable, among which the proportion of floating

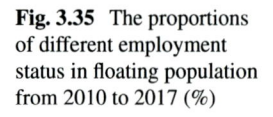

Fig. 3.35 The proportions of different employment status in floating population from 2010 to 2017 (%)

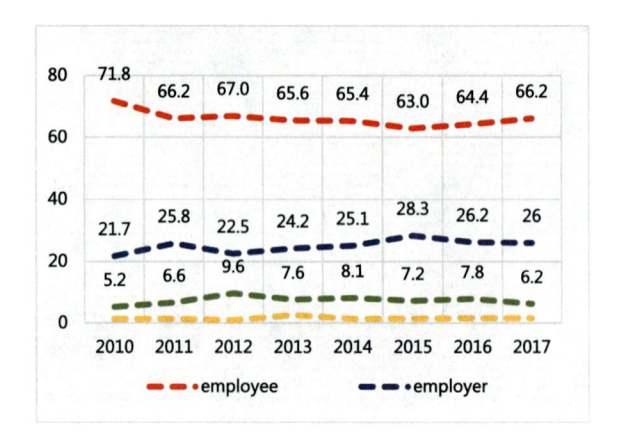

population as employees decreased from 71.8% in 2010 to 66.2% in 2017, while those who were employers and self-employed increased (Fig. 3.35).

3.3.3 The Income Levels of Floating Population

From 2012 to 2017, the average monthly income of floating population increased from 3196 to 4872 RMB, with a growth rate of 52.4%. The floating population with the income levels of 4000–6000 and 2000–4000 accounted for the largest proportions, displaying that their income levels were relatively low. The increase in the proportion of migrants with 4000–6000 income and the decrease in the proportion of migrants with 2000–4000 income also demonstrated a significant growth in the total income level of floating population (Figs. 3.36 and 3.37).

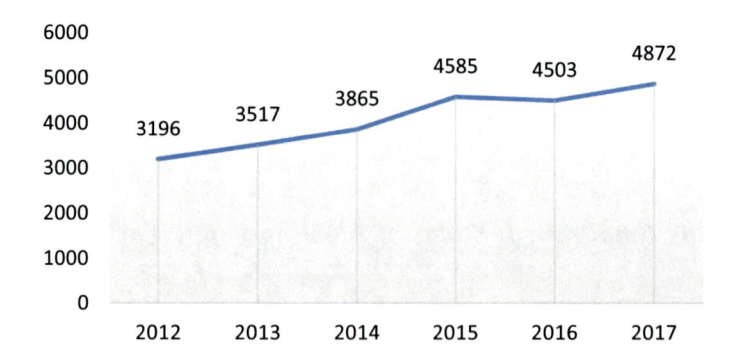

Fig. 3.36 The average monthly income of floating population from 2012 to 2017 (RMB)

Fig. 3.37 The distribution of floating population with different income levels in 2012 and 2017 (%)

3.4 The Public Services for Floating Population

This part analyzes the public service levels enjoyed by the floating population, including medical insurances, health records and health education, based on the CMDS data.

3.4.1 The Health Record Establishment Situations of Floating Population

A very small part of floating population had established health records in the destination cities, which was only 22.7% in 2017. There were 31.1% of the floating population who had heard of the health records, but never established one in the destination cities, and 30% of the floating population never heard of the health records in the destination cities. The proportion of floating population who had established health records decreased from 29.1% in 2015 to 22.7% in 2017. Therefore, it is necessary to publicize the importance of health records in destination cities to the floating population and help them to establish health records (Fig. 3.38).

3.4.2 The Health Education Receiving Situations of Floating Population

The proportions of floating population who had received health education were not very high, among which the migrants receiving health education in terms of smoking

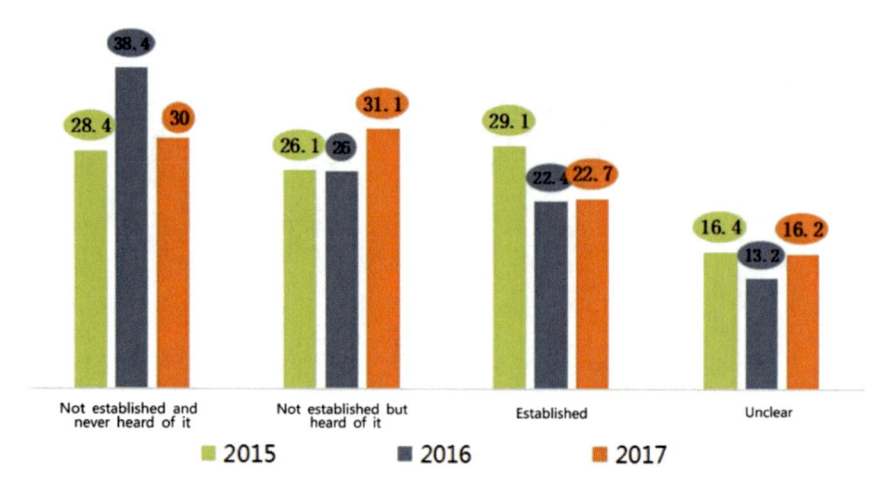

Fig. 3.38 The health record establishment situations of floating population (%)

control, maternal and children health care, as well as reproduction health and contraception occupied the highest proportion (over 50%), while occupational disease prevention and control, tuberculosis prevention and cure, as well as psychological health attracted the lowest proportions of floating population (below 36%). The results showed that the floating population were more willing to accept the health education closely related to themselves (the reproduction issues) (Fig. 3.39).

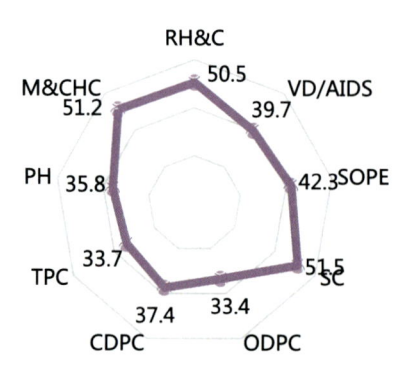

Fig. 3.39 The proportion of floating population that have accepted health education in 2017 (%). *Notes* The abbreviations in the Figure represent the followings: maternal and children health care (M&CHC); psychological health (PH); tuberculosis prevention and cure (TPC); chronic disease prevention and cure (CDPC); occupational disease prevention and cure (ODPC); smoking control (SC); save oneself in public emergencies (SOPE); venereal disease/AIDS prevention and cure (VD/AIDS); reproduction health and contraception (RH&C)

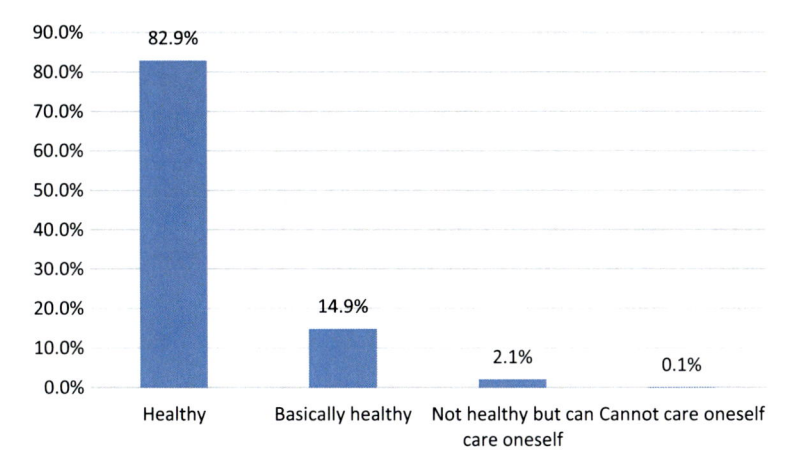

Fig. 3.40 The self-evaluation health results of floating population (%)

3.4.3 The Health Status of Floating Population

In the self-assessment of migrants' health status, more than 95% of floating population evaluated themselves as being in a health condition (healthy and basically healthy), while the proportions of non-healthy floating population were very low (Fig. 3.40).

3.4.4 The Insurance Participation of Floating Population

The medical insurance participation rates of floating population were very low. Among all kinds of medical insurances, the highest participation rate of floating population existed in the new rural cooperative medical insurance (more than 60%), followed by the medical insurance for urban employees (21.5%), while the other medical insurance types only covered fewer than 10% of the total floating population. Therefore, it is necessary to promote the medical insurance participation rate of floating population, especially the medical insurance for urban residents and the free medical care, in order to help the floating population enjoy the same social benefits as the local residents (Fig. 3.41).

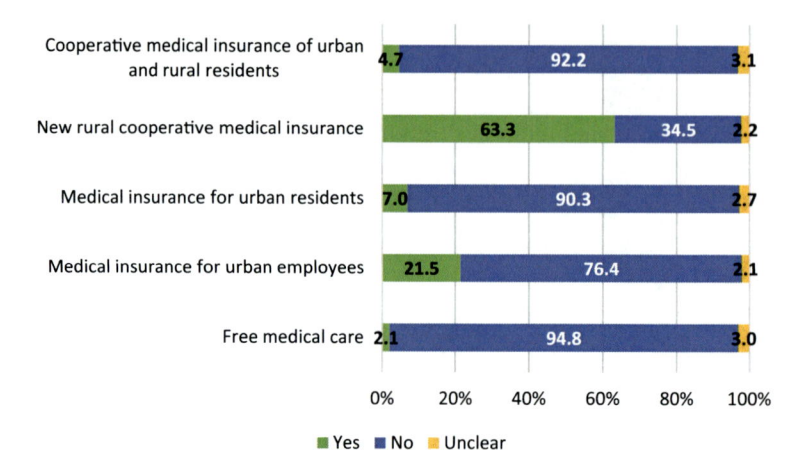

Fig. 3.41 The participation rate of floating population in various medical insurances in 2017 (%)

3.5 The Generalized Theoretical Framework for the Analysis of Migration Intentions

Based on extant literature, we established the following theoretical framework for the analysis of migration intentions (composed of *hukou* transfer intentions, settlement intentions and return intentions) shown in the Figure below, and the main influence factors include internal drivers (individual-level factors) and external drivers (city-level factors) (Fig. 3.42).

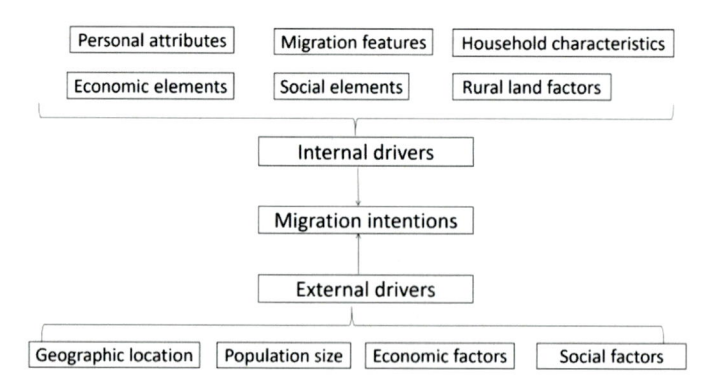

Fig. 3.42 The theoretical framework for the analysis of migration intentions

Chapter 4
Hukou Transfer Intentions of Floating Population

4.1 Interprovincial *Hukou* Transfer Intentions

Population mobility and migration are the key factors affecting the construction of new urbanization and regional sustainable development in China. In 2016, China's floating population reached 245 million [1]. How to promote the rural floating population with ability to work and live in urban areas to realize in situ urbanization and nearby urbanization is a key action. The future trend of permanent migration (with *hukou* transfer) and the driving forces of migration attracted constant attention from scholars. Interprovincial floating population's *hukou* transfer intention refers to the willingness of transferring *hukou* to the destination areas when the local conditions of obtaining *hukou* are met. In previous studies, population migration data based on census or sample survey only reflect the results of permanent migration at a certain time or survey time, and it is difficult to characterize the future trend of migration with *hukou* transfer. Interprovincial floating population's *hukou* transfer intention is closely related to the social and economic development levels of the origin and destination provinces, as well as the social and cultural factors of the floating population. What is the current situation of interprovincial floating population's *hukou* transfer intention in China? What kind of spatial characteristics does it represent and whether it has significant spatial autocorrelation? What are the factors affecting the *hukou* transfer intention of the interprovincial floating population? Answering the above questions has important theoretical and practical significance for reasonably formulating regional population management and planning strategies.

Studies on inter-regional population migration have accumulated many theories, such as the neoclassical economics migration theory [2–4], new migration economics [5], "push–pull migration theory" [6], the dual labor market segmentation theory [7], and the social network theory [8]. Since the turn of the century, as the micro survey data on the floating population was open for application, the academic community has begun to carry out empirical research on the migration intentions (settlement intentions and *hukou* transfer intentions) of the floating population. The impact of the characteristics of floating population on their migration intentions has attracted the most attention in the existing studies. ① Personal attributes such as age, sex, marital status, and educational attainment are regarded as key factors. Migration can be considered as an investment of social capital and human capital, and thus, younger, unmarried, and better educated floating population are more likely to settle down in destination regions [9]. ② From the perspective of family linkages, the family is the basic unit for China's floating population's migration decisions, so that floating population can diversify and maximize economic opportunities while counteracting economic risks to the whole family. As a result, having more family members at their destinations increases their willingness to settle down [10]. ③ Economics factors exert a substantial influence on people's migration intentions. Generally speaking, floating population with higher incomes and lower expenditures on housing and living are more willing to settle down at destinations [11–13]. ④ Social conditions (social status, employment industry, employment status, social network, social security, etc.) also influence the migration decisions of individuals. Those with higher social and employment status and those with social insurance tend to stay at destinations [14, 15].

The external characteristics of origin and destination places also affect the migration process of population [16, 17]. From the perspective of destination place, the characteristics of urban income level and unemployment rate are unavoidable factors when considering the settlement of floating population. On the other hand, the origin place has the social, cultural and family conditions familiar to the floating population, which is usually the preferred destination for the floating population with weak willingness to settle down in the destination place [17]. In addition, for the interprovincial floating population, the migration distance also affects their willingness to stay and move, and a longer distance migration will consume a higher migration cost. At the same time, the integration cost of survival in areas with different cultures will be higher [18]. Nevertheless, due to the limitations of data and other reasons, extant studies mainly focus on the effect of destination characteristics on the willingness of floating population to stay and move [10, 19], while ignoring the impact of origin areas, resulting in a lack of convincing force in the research results.

When considering the characteristics of the location of the origin and destination places, the interprovincial *hukou* transfer intentions of the floating population will be transformed into a network composed of origin–destination flows. When analyzing its pattern, the network autocorrelation (NA) [18, 20, 21] should be considered. Meanwhile, when using gravity model to analyze the factors influencing the *hukou* transfer intention, ignoring the network autocorrelation (NA) information will cause a deviation of the estimated results [18, 22]. Since 2015, the spatial econometric models have been used to deal with the impact of NA in China's interprovincial population migration and its influencing factors, such as spatial OD model [23] and Eigenvector Spatial Filtering (ESF) model [18]. Gu et al. [24]'s research, for the first time, focused on the migrant worker' interprovincial *hukou* transfer intentions, while the interprovincial *hukou* transfer intentions of the total floating population had not been investigated. Therefore, this study will depict the spatial pattern of the Interprovincial floating population's *hukou* transfer intention in China in 2016 with the exploratory spatial data analysis (ESDA) such as spatial autocorrelation, and measure the effects of various factors on interprovicial floating population's *hukou* transfer intentions through a spatial filtering gravity model.

4.1.1 Data Source and Methodology

4.1.1.1 Data Source

The data comes from the China Migrants Dynamic Survey (CMDS) in 2016 conducted by the National Health Commission of China. In this survey, multistage stratified random sampling method was adopted to extract sampling points from target areas with high concentration of floating population in 31 provincial units in China [10]. In total, this database contains 169,000 samples. Respondents of CMDS were floating population over 15 years old who had lived in the destination cities for more than a month without local *hukou*. One of the key questions was "If it is possible, are you willing to transfer your *hukou* to the destination area?" The floating population who chose "Yes" as the answer are defined as floating population with *hukou* transfer intentions, whereas the rest, who chose "No" or "Unsure," are defined as floating population without *hukou* transfer intentions. Furthermore, the regression analysis took into account regional socio-economic factors from *China Statistical Yearbook in 2017* [25] and other provincial statistical yearbooks. The data of the migration distance came from Baidu Map (http://map.baidu.com), measured in the minimum road distance between two provincial capitals (excluding Tibet, Hong Kong and Macau).

4.1.1.2 Construction of Interprovincial Floating Population's *Hukou* Transfer Intention Matrix

Our research subject is the interprovincial floating population's *hukou* transfer intentions, and the matrix construction method is shown as follows: First, we selected samples of interprovincial floating population, and deleted missing data. Eventually, we obtained 71,194 micro-observations, with the proportion of floating population with *hukou* transfer intentions as 41.46%. Second, based on the Python platform, we built up the intention matrix, using the information of the origin area and the destination area of every migrant. Specifically, we summed up floating population with *hukou* in the origin region i but staying in region j at the time of survey, and then, for each flow, we calculated the proportion of floating population with *hukou* transfer intentions. The matrix of interprovincial *hukou* transfer intentions in China is shown below:

$$\begin{pmatrix} * & Y_{2-1} & Y_{3-1} & \cdots & Y_{30-1} \\ Y_{1-2} & * & Y_{3-2} & \cdots & Y_{30-2} \\ Y_{1-3} & Y_{2-3} & * & \cdots & Y_{30-3} \\ \vdots & \vdots & \vdots & \ddots & \vdots \\ Y_{1-30} & Y_{2-30} & Y_{3-30} & \cdots & * \end{pmatrix} \tag{4.1}$$

Y_{i-j} in the matrix denotes the proportion of floating population with *hukou* transfer intentions from region i to region j. We set up a threshold of 10, and consider a specific flow with less than 10 samples as unrepresentative, which is subject to undue influence from extreme values. Hence, we deleted these flows. Finally, we obtained 543 flows of interprovincial *hukou* transfer intentions.

4.1.1.3 Methodology

(1) Exploratory spatial data analysis. ① Moran's I Coefficient (MC), which measures the NA of the interprovincial *hukou* transfer intention network and *hukou* attractiveness and exclusion in different provinces, is an important aspect of understanding the spatial pattern of interprovincial *hukou* transfer intentions. MC is the most widely used spatial autocorrelation method, and its idea comes from Pearson correlation coefficient formula [22]. If the spatial weight matrix in Moran formula is row standardized, MC can be expressed as a more concise standard Moran's I coefficient (SMC); ② Getis-Ord G_i* statistics can be used to measure the hot spot and cold spot characteristics of the spatial patterns of *hukou* attractiveness and exclusion in the provincial administrative units. Getis-Ord G_i* can detect whether each spatial element belongs to high-value aggregation or low value aggregation, thus hot spot areas and cold spot areas are obtained [26].

(2) Eigenvector spatial filtering. Spatial filtering can reduce the estimation error of the model and make the model result more robust. The eigenvectors in filtering come from the network weight matrix representing spatial structure information. The filtered eigenvectors will be directly incorporated into the regression model as a proxy variable of NA effect in explanatory variables to achieve the effect of "filtering" [18].

Each element in the eigenvectors can represent the spatial structure information in the corresponding geographical unit, and the Moran's I Coefficient (MC) corresponding to each eigenvector can be calculated based on each element [18]. The influence of NA in dependent variables can be regarded as a linear combination of NA information reflected by each eigenvector to a certain extent [22].

4.1.2 Spatial Distribution of Interprovincial Hukou *Transfer Intentions*

4.1.2.1 The Topological Pattern of Interprovincial *Hukou* Transfer Intentions

The SMC of interprovincial floating population's *hukou* transfer intention network reached 0.661 ($P \leq 0.001$) in 2016. Its strong NA showed a spatial pattern of agglomeration, indicating a *hukou* transfer intention flow had similar value with the flows of neighboring provinces, which is similar to the NA of migrant workers' interprovincial *hukou* transfer intentions [24]. The flows of *hukou* transfer intention greater than 0.7 were extracted and charted in Fig. 4.1. It demonstrates that the flows with high interprovincial *hukou* transfer intentions in China were mainly from the northeast, central and western underdeveloped regions to the eastern developed areas (such as Beijing, Shanghai, Guangdong and Tianjin). However, there also existed a few flows with high interprovincial *hukou* transfer intentions in the northwest region, such as the floating population from Qinghai Province to Xinjiang Province.

The top 10 *hukou* transfer intention flows were "Guangdong-Shanghai" (0.956), "Heilongjiang-Shanghai" (0.953), Jilin-Shanghai (0.948), Inner Mongolia-Shanghai

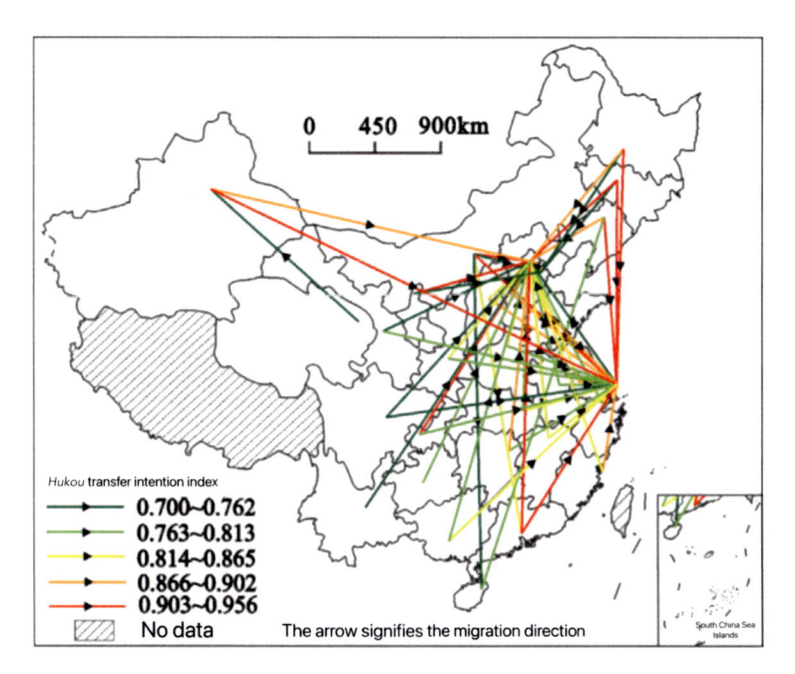

Fig. 4.1 Spatial distribution of interprovincial *hukou* transfer intentions in China

(0.947), Inner Mongolia-Beijing (0.940), Xinjiang-Shanghai (0.938), Liaoning-Shanghai (0.932), Jilin-Beijing (0.923), "Chongqing-Beijing" (0.915), Ningxia-Beijing (0.909). From the perspective of destination places, Beijing and Shanghai, as developed megacities in China, were the preferred places of *hukou* immigration for the floating population from all provinces. From the perspective of origin places, Heilongjiang, Jilin and Liaoning provinces in Northeast China were the main origin places of *hukou* emmigration, which reflected the problem of population outflows in Northeast China to a certain extent. The origin places and destination places of flows with high interprovincial *hukou* transfer intentions were relatively concentrated, which showed the uneven pattern of interprovincial *hukou* transfer intentions of floating population.

4.1.2.2   Geographical Pattern of Interprovincial *Hukou* Transfer Intention

(1)   The spatial pattern of *hukou* attractiveness. The *hukou* immigration index of a province was measured by the average of the *hukou* transfer intentions of floating population in this province from the other 29 provinces, which reflected the *hukou* attractiveness of each province and was demonstrated on the map by using ArcGIS software (Fig. 4.2), and the characteristics of its spatial pattern were analyzed. First, the provinces with the highest *hukou* attractiveness included Beijing, Shanghai, Tianjin, Hainan and Guangdong, most of which are economically developed provinces in the eastern region with a relatively higher amenity. The lowest ranking provinces consisted of Jiangxi, Guizhou, Hunan, Henan and Yunnan. Most of them were economically underdeveloped provinces in the central and western regions. Secondly, the SMC of *hukou* attraction showed a random distribution ($P = 0.427$), indicating that the *hukou* transfer intentions of floating population in a province were not related to those in neighboring provinces.

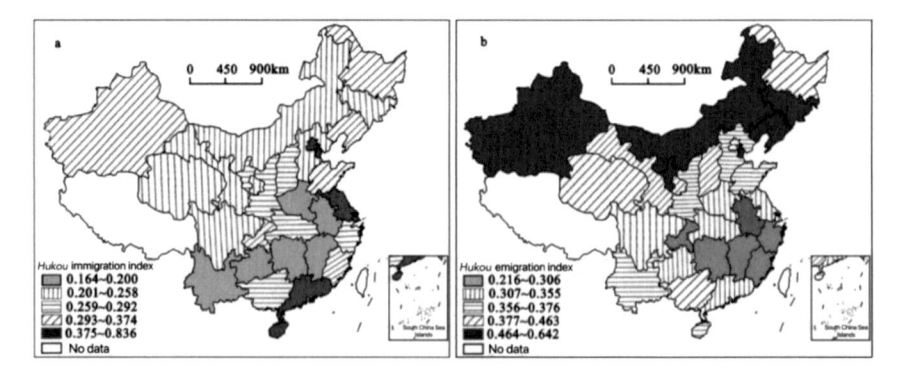

Fig. 4.2 Spatial pattern of *hukou* immiration (**a**) and emigration intention (**b**) of provincial-level units in China

(2) The spatial pattern of *hukou* emigration indexes. The *hukou* emigration index of a province was measured by the average of the *hukou* transfer intentions of floating population in the other 29 provinces from this province. The provinces with the highest *hukou* emigration indexes contained Xinjiang, Ningxia, Jilin, Tianjin and Liaoning, mainly distributed in the northeast and northwest regions, while the lowest ranking provinces incorporated Zhejiang, Jiangxi, Fujian, Hunan and Anhui, mainly distributed in the central and eastern regions. Unlike the *hukou* attraction indexes, the provinces with the lowest *hukou* emigration indexes had no obvious relationship with the level of economic development. The *hukou* emigration indexes showed significant spatial autocorrelation characteristics, indicating a spatial pattern of agglomeration, with SMC of 0.331 ($P \leq 0.001$). The results of Getis-Ord $G_i{}^*$ were shown in Fig. 4.3, and the areas in blue, cyan and yellow were low value agglomeration areas, namely, the cold spots of *hukou* emigration. Meanwhile, the areas in orange, pink and purple were high value agglomeration areas, which were hot spots of *hukou* emigration. The area in earthy yellow represented the area where existed no significant cold spots or hot spots. We can see that the hot spots of China's *hukou* emigration included Inner Mongolia, the three provinces in the northeast region (Heilongjiang, Jilin, Liaoning), Xinjiang and Qinghai, concentrated in the eastern and northwest regions. The cold spots of the *hukou* emigration consisted

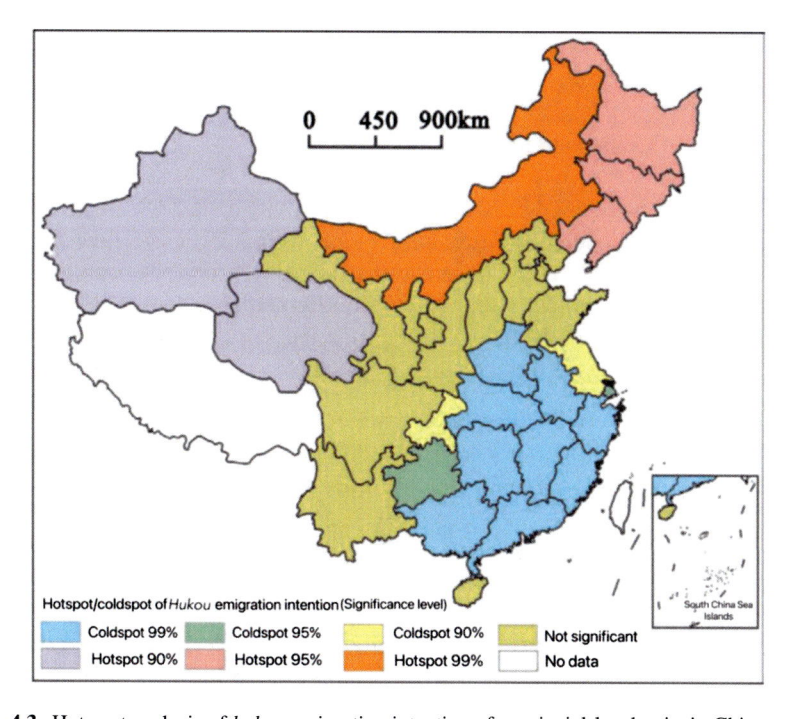

Fig. 4.3 Hot spot analysis of *hukou* emigration intention of provincial-level units in China

of Henan, Anhui, Hubei, Hunan, Jiangxi, Zhejiang, Jiangsu, Shanghai, Fujian, Guangdong, Guangxi, Guizhou and Chongqing, concentrated in the central and eastern regions.

4.1.3 The Influencing Mechanism of Interprovincial Floating Population's Hukou Transfer Intentions

4.1.3.1 Selection of Variables

This study selected 16 explanatory variables, of which the macro-level regional variables included the population sizes of the origin and destination, the per capita GDP of the origin and destination, the unemployment rate of the destination, the average wages of urban employees of origin and destination, the total export volume of foreign-invested enterprises in destination, and the shortest distance between the two provincial capitals. Micro-level individual factors consisted of average years of education, average age, proportion of male floating population, average family size in destination, proportion of floating population with house purchase intention in destination, proportion of floating population migrating for business, and average income level. Micro-level individual variables were obtained by summarizing the micro data of individuals in a specific migration direction to the migration flow level, through calculating the corresponding average value or proportion (Table 4.1).

4.1.3.2 Model Construction and Regression Results

The econometric model used in this study was the gravity model, which is a classical and widely applied model [27]. After linearization, the model can be directly used in the traditional least squares (OLS) regression. Due to the strong NA in the explained variable of this study, in order to extract the NA information in the data and improve the estimation accuracy of the model, we constructed an eigenvector spatial filtering gravity model based on the traditional gravity model:

$$\ln Y_{i,j} = \sum_{l=1}^{\lambda} \beta_\lambda \ln X_\lambda + \sum_{l=1}^{k} \gamma_k E_k + \varepsilon_{i,j} \tag{4.2}$$

where $Y_{i,j}$ denotes the interprovincial floating population' *hukou* transfer intention from region i to j, X_λ is the λth influencing factor, β_λ represents its corresponding regression coefficient, and $\varepsilon_{i,j}$ is the error term, E_k denotes the kth selected eigenvector, and γ_k is its corresponding regression coefficient. $\sum_{l=1}^{k} \gamma_k E_k$, a linear combination of eigenvectors, represents spatial autocorrelation information in the error term.

Table 4.1 Variable types, names, descriptions and expected effects

Classification		Variable	Description of variable	Expected effects
Macro-level factors	Population factors	Pop_i	Population size of the origin (ten thousand)	+
		Pop_j	Population size of the destination (ten thousand)	+
	Economic factors	GDP_i	Per capita GDP of the origin (RMB/person)	−
		GDP_j	Per capita GDP of the destination (RMB/person)	+
		$Export_j$	Total export volume of foreign-invested enterprises in destination (10^3 dollars)	+
	Employment and income factors	$Unemploy_j$	Unemployment rate of the destination (%)	−
		$Wage_i$	Average wage of urban employees in the origin (RMB)	−
		$Wage_j$	Average wage of urban employees in the destination (RMB)	+
	Distance factor	D_{ij}	Minimum road distance between the provincial capitals of the origin and the destination (km)	−
Individual-level factors	Personal attributes	Edu_{ij}	Average education level of floating population (a)	+
		Age_{ij}	Average age of floating population (years)	−
	Family factors	$Male_{ij}$	Proportion of male floating population (%)	−

(continued)

Table 4.1 (continued)

Classification		Variable	Description of variable	Expected effects
		Family$_{ij}$	The average family size of the floating population in the destination (person)	+
Housing and income factors		House$_{ij}$	Proportion of floating population intending to purchase a local house (%)	+
		Income$_{ij}$	The average income of floating population (RMB/month)	+
Migration reason		Bus$_{ij}$	Proportion of floating population migrating for business (%)	−

The regression results of Model 1 and 2 were shown in Table 4.2. After the multicollinearity test of the model, it is found that the VIF didn't reach 4, indicating that there existed no serious multicollinearity problem in the model. The White test was used to test the heteroscedasticity of the model. The results showed that there were significant heteroscedasticity problems in Model 1 and 2, indicating that it was necessary to employ robust standard errors in regression models. Compared with the traditional gravity model, the improvement of the spatial filtering gravity model can be judged by the values of Akaike information criterion (AIC), Bayesian information criterion (BIC) and SMC in the residual. First, by comparing Model 1 and 2, it is found that after filtering, the AIC and BIC values of Model 2 decreased to varying degrees, from 585.901 and 658.952 to 446.88 and 601.576, respectively. Secondly, the SMC value in the residual also decreased from 0.186 ($P \leq 0.001$) to 0.037 ($P = 0.103$), indicating that the eigenvector completely filtered the significant NA information in the model error term. In addition, the adjusted R^2 of the model increased from 0.601 to 0.701, indicating that the spatial filtering model (Model 2) had a stronger data interpretation ability. The above results showed that the spatial filtering gravity model can improve the fitting ability and estimation accuracy of the traditional gravity model. Through model analysis, the following conclusions were discovered:

(1) The basic variables of the gravity model, such as the population sizes of desti-nation and origin, the distance of migration, had a weak impact on the *hukou* transfer intentions of the floating population. The population size of the origin and migration distance were not significantly related to the floating population's

Table 4.2 Regression results of interprovincial *hukou* transfer intentions in China

Variable	Model 1: Gravity model		Model 2: Eigenvector spatial filtering gravity model	
	Coefficient	P value	Coefficient	P value
Pop_j	−0.070**	0.047	0.035	0.289
Pop_i	−0.157***	0.000	−0.139***	0.002
GDP_j	−0.040	0.639	0.148*	0.064
GDP_i	0.293***	0.006	0.167*	0.094
$Export_j$	0.046***	0.002	0.063***	0.000
$Unempoly_j$	−0.288***	0.000	−0.231***	0.001
$Wage_i$	−1.016***	0.000	−0.874***	0.000
$Wage_j$	0.707***	0.000	0.524***	0.003
D_{ij}	0.008	0.790	−0.011	0.722
Edu_{ij}	0.825***	0.000	0.594***	0.003
Age_{ij}	−0.048	0.859	−0.670**	0.011
$Male_{ij}$	−0.133	0.198	−0.131	0.104
$Family_{ij}$	0.113	0.420	0.283**	0.032
$House_{ij}$	0.243***	0.000	0.205***	0.000
$Income_{ij}$	−0.256**	0.015	−0.114	0.243
Bus_{ij}	−0.057***	0.000	−0.051***	0.000
Constant	1.419	0.621	1.340	0.628
Eigenvectors	0		19	
AIC	585.901		446.880	
BIC	658.952		601.576	
Residual Moran's I	0.186***		0.037	
Observations	543		543	
Adj R^2	0.601		0.701	

Notes $* p < 0.1$, $** p < 0.05$, $*** p < 0.01$

intentions to obtain *hukou* in the destination province, while the population size of the destination had a negative impact on the *hukou* transfer intention.

Regarding the population factors, the population size of the origin area had no significant impact on the *hukou* transfer intentions of floating population, which was not consistent with the expectation. The possible reason was that in previous studies, the explained variable was mostly the number of interprovincial population migration, which was closely related to the population size of the origin area. For the interprovincial *hukou* transfer intention in this study, the population size of the origin area didn't mean that the emigration population had a stronger inclination of *hukou* conversion. On the other hand, the population size of the destination area had a negative effect on the *hukou* transfer intentions of floating population, and the *hukou* transfer intention decreased by about 0.139% with the 1% increase in the population size of the destination area. For the immigrants, the increase of population size caused more fierce competition for employment, and living congestion led to an increase in the costs of urban life and commuting, and further aggravated the difficulty of obtaining local *hukou*. In terms of distance factor, after incorporating into the eigenvectors, the regression coefficient of migration distance changed from positive to negative, which showed the necessity of dealing with the spatial autocorrelation effect. From the perspective of coefficient significance, the road distance between two regions had no significant effect on *hukou* transfer intentions of migrants. The development of communication technology such as Internet and the infrastructure construction such as high speed rail had produced a "time–space compression" effect, resulting in a gradually weakening effect of the distance on *hukou* conversion [18].

(2)   Under the market conditions, socioeconomic conditions were the primary cause of the *hukou* transfer intentions of floating population [11, 12, 28]. The economic factors, employment and income factors of the destination areas and origin areas had significant effects on the interprovincial *hukou* transfer intention. Among them, the average wage of the urban employees had a greater impact on the *hukou* transfer intention.

In terms of the economic factors, the average GDP per capita in destination areas had a significantly positive effect on *hukou* transfer intention. When GDP per capita in the destination area increased by 1%, the floating population's *hukou* transfer intention would increase by about 0.167%. The economic development of the region would increase the "gold content" of the local *hukou*, and led to the increase in benefits associated with the local *hukou*, thus exerting a "pull" effect on the *hukou* conversion of floating population. Contrary to expectations, the GDP per capita of the origin areas also had a positive effect on the *hukou* transfer intention. When the GDP per capita of the origin area increased by 1%, the *hukou* transfer intention of the floating population would increase by about 0.148%. The probable reason was that the regional economic development led to a more fierce competition for settlement and greater difficulty in obtaining local *hukou*, thus "pushing" part of the population away from this area. Moreover, the export of foreign-invested enterprises in the destination areas had a weak positive effect on the interprovincial *hukou* transfer intention. The expansion of foreign-invested enterprises' exports can bring more revenues and improve the performance of enterprises themselves and upstream and downstream affiliated enterprises, resulting in the improvement of regional economic level and more floating population that choose to settle down in the destination area.

In respect of employment and income factors, the average wage increased by 1%, the *hukou* immigration intention increased by about 0.524%, and the *hukou* emigration intention decreased by about 0.874%. It is indicated that the income level was still the primary concern in the *hukou* transfer decision process of floating population: higher wages would bring greater migration benefits to destination provinces, leading to an increase in the *hukou* immigration. For the origin provinces, the decline in the wage level caused the growth in the costs of the return migration of floating population in terms of re-employment and living. The interprovincial floating population's *hukou* transfer intention was more influenced by the average wage level of origin areas than destination areas, which was opposite to the result of migrant workers' interprovincial *hukou* transfer intention [24]. The job stability of the destination areas also affected the *hukou* conversion decision of the floating population. The increase of the regional unemployment rate often meant that the employment opportunities in the destination area decreased, and the immigration population would face greater unemployment probabilities and could not get stable income sources, thereby reducing the *hukou* attractiveness of the destination area.

(3) Concerning micro-level factors, the individual characteristics and family factors of floating population were closely related to their *hukou* transfer intentions. Migrants with higher education level, younger age and larger family size tended to have higher *hukou* transfer intentions.

Age and average education years had negative and positive effects respectively on *hukou* transfer intention: as the average age of migrants increased by 1%, their *hukou* transfer intentions decreased by 0.67%; as the average education years of migrants increased by 1%, their *hukou* transfer intentions increased by 0.594%. The *hukou* transfer behaviors of floating population was a kind of investment in human capital. Floating population with younger age and higher education level often had higher competitive advantages in the job market. From the perspective of social network, the older floating population were more influenced by the social network of the origin area, and the social integration cost of reconstructing social networks in the destination area was relatively high, so their *hukou* transfer intention would be relatively lower. As the average family size of floating population in the destination area increased by 1%, their *hukou* transfer intention increased by 0.283%. The accompanied family members reduced the cost of migration and integration into the new environment, which exerted a positive incentive effect on the settlement behaviors of migrants [10].

(4) The housing conditions and migration reasons of the floating population also had an nonnegligible impact on their *hukou* transfer intention. Migrants with lower housing purchase willingness in the destination area and migrants who migrated for business, usually had relatively weaker *hukou* transfer intention.

From the aspect of housing factors, floating population with higher housing purchase intention in the destination areas had higher *hukou* transfer intention, increasing by 0.205% with the 1% increase of housing purchase intention. Under the background of the general rise of real estate prices in large cities, housing prices had played an increasingly important role in the settlement decision-making of floating population. For China's floating population, housing is their spiritual support and material security, so the floating population with housing purchase intention tend to settle down in the destination area. From the aspect of migration reason, as the proportion of floating population migrating for business increased by 1%, their *hukou* transfer intention decreased by 0.051%. This result was related to the high mobility in the job market of floating population migrating for business. Businessmen needed to contact suppliers and customers, and with the expansion of business scope, their scope of activities would expand accordingly, not limited to one place. In terms of income factors, the average income of floating population had nothing to do with *hukou* transfer intention, due to the fact that the average wage had been included in the model as the macro-level explanatory variable. On the other hand, although the floating population with higher personal income would get higher returns when settling down in the destination area, for some floating population whose family members were in other places, their migration decision was based on the development of the whole family. Once they achieved the economic goals in the destination area, they would return to their hometowns rather than settle down here [5].

4.1.4 Conclusions and Discussion

This study constructed China's interprovincial floating population's *hukou* transfer intention matrix, employed GIS spatial analysis method to analyze the topological structure and geographical pattern of interprovincial *hukou* transfer intentions, and then established a spatial filtering gravity model to examine their influencing factors. The main conclusions are as follows:

(1) China's interprovincial *hukou* transfer intention network showed a spatial pattern of agglomeration. The higher-ranking flows of *hukou* transfer intentions were mainly from the less developed areas to the eastern developed areas. The *hukou* attractiveness at the provinical level presented a random spatial pattern, among which provinces with higher economic and social development levels were attractive to floating population whereas less developed provinces were comparatively less attractive. In contrast, the *hukou* emigration patterns were spatially concentrated, with the western and northeast provinces as hot spots, central and eastern provinces as cold spots.

(2) The spatial filtering gravity model completely filtered the NA information in the error term of the model. The regression results showed that the population size of the destination areas had a negative impact on the interprovincial *hukou* transfer intention, while the population size of the origin area and the migration distance were not related to the interprovincial *hukou* transfer intention. The economic factors, employment and income factors of the destination areas and origin areas had a significant influence on the interprovincial *hukou* transfer intention. GDP per capita of destination and origin and the export of foreign-invested enterprises in the destination area exerted a positive effect on the interprovincial *hukou* transfer intention.

(3) The floating population's individual characteristics and family factors were closely related to their *hukou* transfer intention. The floating population with higher education level, younger age and larger family size in the destination area

had higher *hukou* transfer intentions. The housing conditions and migration reasons of the floating population also had an important influence on their *hukou* transfer intention. The floating population who had a lower willingness to buy a local house and migrated for business, were less willing to obtain local *hukou* in destination areas.

In summary, China's interprovincial floating population's *hukou* transfer intentions are affected by the external factors of the destination areas and origin areas and the internal factors of the floating population, which is a complex decision-making process. Under the influence of market conditions, the socio-economic factors of the destination areas and origin areas are the primary reasons affecting the *hukou* conversion willingness of floating population. The imbalance of social and economic development levels between the eastern region and the central and western regions, as well as large cities and small cities, has led to a unbalanced spatial distribution pattern of interprovincial floating population's *hukou* transfer intention, with the high intention flows mainly from the less developed areas to the developed areas. It can be predicted that China's internal migration network will maintain this unbalanced spatial pattern for a long time, and Beijing, Shanghai and other development poles are still the first choices for the settlement of floating population. Under this context, comprehensively implementing the new-type urbanization strategy and promoting the in situ urbanization or nearby urbanization of floating population will face more severe challenges. On the one hand, it is necessary to improve the job market of the floating population in the origin area, promote the transfer of high-quality educational resources from developed areas to underdeveloped areas, and encourage floating population to return to their hometowns to start their own businesses. On the other hand, it is of great significance to formulate feasible regional development strategies, adjust the urban income levels of different regions, and rationally regulate the future trend of interprovincial migration by influencing floating population's *hukou* transfer intention.

4.2 *Hukou* Transfer Intentions at the City Level

4.2.1 Introduction

China's floating population, referring to migrants (mainly migrating from rural areas to urban areas) without local household registration (*hukou*) status, not only accounts for a large proportion of the mobile population in the world but also becomes an important issue influencing China's economic and social development. According to the 2018 Report on China's Migrant Population Development released by the National Health and Family Planning Commission of China, China's floating population reached 244 million by 2017, accounting for approximately 1/6th of the total population. The total floating population had enjoyed a sustainable growth from 2011 to 2014, while a slow decline that began in 2015, indicating that the *hukou* system reform has transformed part of the floating population into new citizens (permanent residents) in places of destination [29, 30]. Unlike permanent migrants, the floating population cannot gain the local and settle down permanently in the place of migration work. The vast majority of rural-urban migrants in China keep circulating between the places of destination (city) and origin (hometown village), taking a temporary form of migration. The National New-Type Urbanization Plan (2014–2020) issued by China's government aims at enabling migrant workers to settle in the cities where they work by granting 100 million new urban *hukou* from 2015 to 2020, thus helping floating population integrate into China's urbanization process. The new trend to relax restrictions on the *hukou* system and promote people-oriented urbanization elevates the importance of *hukou* transfer intentions of the floating population, an important indicator of migration behaviors [31–33]. The *hukou* transfer intentions of the floating population denote whether migrants want to obtain an urban *hukou* and settle down permanently in the city, which also reflects the tolerance and attractiveness of destination cities and provides significant evidence for the future *hukou* system reform.

People intend to move to big cities that can offer them better-living conditions, while social benefits are tied to what kinds of *hukou* they have [24]. It is the "screening and moderating effect" of China's *hukou* system that excludes the floating population from civil rights and benefits [34–38]. Since a large population migrates from rural to urban areas to make a living, while they cannot settle down in the destination cities due to the limitations of the *hukou* system, it is reasonable to assume that rural migrants have a strong desire to transfer their *hukou* from their hometowns to destination cities and live permanently in cities. However, dozens of recent studies have discovered that the *hukou* transfer intentions of migrants are not as strong as expected [19, 39, 40], the reasons for which are complicated. During the current process of promoting people-oriented new-type urbanization in China, it is the top priority to advance the orderly citizenization of migrants who steadily work and live in the destination cities. Under this context, it has been transformed into practical policies and measures in more cities to accelerate the *hukou* system reform, relax the *hukou* transfer policies, advance the citizenization of migrants through *hukou* localization and ensure that migrants can share the basic public services in cities. However, the implementation of any policies needs support from relevant stakeholders and should respect their choice. Therefore, in the course of promoting new-type urbanization and *hukou* system reform, it is of great significance to investigate the *hukou* transfer intentions of the floating population in destination cities on a national scale. The studies on *hukou* transfer intentions can also provide evidence for related studies on migration intentions and social integration of international migrants and internal migrants in other countries. Therefore, this study focuses on the intention of migrants to convert their *hukou* to the places where they work and its influence factors.

As spatial data, information about *hukou* transfer intentions in different cities and their determinants are composed of a series of site and situational attributes that are based on the location and may exhibit spatial effects, including spatial dependence (similarities in position) and spatial heterogeneity (the tendency for the relationships among variables to vary across space), which violate the classic assumptions of non-spatial regression methods (such as ordinary least squares or "OLS") and cause estimation bias [41, 42]. Although there is a considerable literature on the determinants on *hukou* transfer intentions [39, 40, 43, 44], only a few studies hitherto have paid attention to the spatial dependence and spatial heterogeneity of this relationship. Nevertheless, recent research has shown the existence of spatially varying effects [31, 45]. With a substantial floating population and a vast territory, China's floating population and related resources are unevenly distributed in space along with unbalanced economic development, which leads to an apparent spatial disparity of *hukou* transfer intention and its determinants. Consequently, it may be that different contextual influences cause the spatial variations in this relationship, which can further provide support for location-based migration policies when combined with visualized maps.

Therefore, to rectify the deficiencies of extant studies based on the data of China Migrants Dynamic Survey (CMDS) in 2016, we employ the multi-scale geographically weighted regression (MGWR) method to examine the underlying spatial variations in modeling *hukou* transfer intentions, thus providing empirical evidence for local governments on how they should formulate and adopt customized migration management strategies in response to China's new-type urbanization process, as well as guide the migration in the direction of narrowing the gap in regional economic development.

4.2.2 Literature Review

As far as China is concerned, migrants can be divided into two types: temporary migrants, also known as the floating population, who migrate to the destination cities without local *hukou*, while permanent migrants migrate to the destination cities with their *hukou* transferring to localities [29]. Accordingly, the settlement intentions of the floating population in urban areas also fall into two categories [43]: *hukou* transfer intention and residence intention. The former intention can be regarded as permanent migration intention, derived by asking a migrant whether he/she has a propensity to change his/her *hukou* to the destination region if possible, while the latter intention, deemed as temporary migration intention, is based on the question of the willingness to live in the destination region for a long time. Migrants can minimize risks and maximize the economic benefits of immigration by adopting the strategy of temporary migration to maintain original rural *hukou*, which explains their cautious attitude toward obtaining local *hukou*. Most studies focus on the residence intention, while a relatively fewer pay attention to the *hukou* transfer intention [14, 39, 40, 46–48], discovering significant influences of different factors on settlement intentions, such as geographic factors (including city sizes and location), socio-demographic factors and the possession of farmland and housing land in rural areas. Studies of temporary migration in other countries also concern permanent and temporary settlement intentions [49–52]. However, *hukou* conversion intention only occurs in China due to the unique *hukou* system.

There exist significant differences between residence intention and *hukou* transfer intention: First, permanent migration with *hukou* conversion is a much longer, more complicated, and more sophisticated process, thus leading to more opportunity costs when leaving origin places, compared with temporary migration [53]. Second, temporary migrants can enjoy the benefits of both origin and destination places, instead of giving up benefits from original *hukou* (such as contracted farmland and rural homestead) [54]. Third, the residence intention is a comprehensive consideration based on the evaluation of economic benefit-cost and payment capacity, which is more influenced by competence factors including human capital, socio-economic status, and social integration level [31], while the *hukou* transfer intention is a decision process based on the social benefit-cost measurement with diverse expected return forms, which is more affected by pull forces of migration, such as the abundance of public services (including employment, welfare, education) in destination cities, as well as the family demands of bringing children to the destination cities to live and accept formal education [19].

The settlement intentions of the floating population, in terms of either the *hukou* conversion or the place of residence, present significant differences in different groups and different regions, which are nevertheless both influenced by a combination of similar factors [19, 31–33]. Scholars have conducted studies on the determinants on settlement intentions, including individual factors and geographic factors, among which the individual factors contain personal attributes, migration features, household characteristics, economic elements, and social elements, and the geographic factors comprise the urbanization rate, population size, GDP per capita and geographic location of destination regions [55–57].

Regarding the individual-level factors, Yue et al. [9] pointed out that personal attributes such as gender, age, educational attainment, and marital status affect settlement intention. Migration can be conceived as an investment of social capital and human capital, hence younger, unmarried, and higher-educated migrants are more inclined to settle down in destination regions [14, 56]. Fan [54] and You et al. [55] stated that migrants who have more migrant work experience with a longer flow time and better integrate into the local society due to a shorter distance between the destination areas and their hometowns are more likely than other migrants to intend to stay. Some scholars mentioned that rural-urban migrants in China continue to circulate between their hometown villages and the places they undertake migrant work to maintain a split-household arrangement where some family members are left behind, so they can diversify and maximize economic opportunities and counteract economic risk to the whole family, viewing the family as a single body of migration decision-making [39, 54]. Besides, having more family members (spouse, children, parents, and siblings) in a city motivates one to settle down permanently [55–57].

Furthermore, the empirical studies of China also demonstrated that economic incentives have a significant positive impact on rural migrants' urban settlement intentions [58, 59], which are consistent with traditional migration theories that economic opportunities and achievements (such as employment type and income level) are among the most important determinants of migration decision. Recent studies have also discovered that the self-employed migrants tend to have a stronger intention for permanent urban settlement [33, 60], and higher household income, as well as longer working contracts, are factors enhancing settlement willingness [56]. Social elements are found to be gaining significance in determining the long-term settlement plan [59, 61], including the social security status of migrants in destination regions (whether they are covered by endowment insurance, unemployment insurance, and employment injury insurance), and living conditions [11, 12, 62–64]. Some scholars also lay stress on the positive influence mechanism of social networks on settlement intentions, stating that the long-term residence of migrants is a process of social integration [13, 54, 65].

In regard to the geographic factors or city-level variables, economic and social contexts of both origins and destinations also matter [45, 58]. At the macro level, migration is triggered by the regional development disparity between origin and destination areas. In China, there exist substantial regional differences, and migrants are prone to migrate to larger cities with more job opportunities, higher wages, and better public services [56]. However, as largest cities usually take various measures to control population migration and introduce the strict implementation of the *hukou* system, migrants find it increasingly difficult to settle down in larger cities and obtain local *hukou*, thus decreasing their settlement intention [45, 46]. Among those who have a long-term plan to stay in cities, most migrants tend to settle in small towns or small cities instead of larger cities [57]. Therefore, the city-level variables affect the residency willingness of migrants in a very sophisticated way, in which various determinants, including institution factors (*hukou* system), have to be taken into consideration [40].

As many scholars discover that individual factors and geographic factors are important determinants of settlement intentions, we propose the 1st research hypothesis that *hukou* transfer intentions of the floating population are both influenced by individual characteristics and city-level variables.

Though lots of studies focus on the determinants of settlement intention, little attention has been paid to the spatial difference of settlement intention and its influence factors [19, 45]. Some studies consider geographic factors (city-level variables) in the regression model or investigate regional differences of determinants by conducting a comparative analysis of several representative regions and cities [65, 66]. Besides, through GIS spatial analysis and statistical modeling methods, Lin and Zhu [19] investigated the spatial pattern and its determinants of migrants' *hukou* transfer intention of China's 276 prefecture- and provincial-level cities, revealing that the overall level of migrants' *hukou* transfer intention of the cities was not high, and varied significantly among different cities. Similarly, Liu et al. [45] examined the influence of city-level variables on settlement willingness and the relationship between the city-level and individual-level variables, by spatial analysis method of GIS and hierarchical linear regression model, discovering that there existed remarkable regional differences in settlement intentions, and Eastern China attracted the most migrants with a relatively low settlement willingness. Gu et al. [53] described the spatial difference of the settlement willingness of floating people in China, built up spatial econometric models to analyze its influencing factors, and discovered that the settlement intention of the floating population is higher in the south than in the north and presents a U-shaped trend in the east-west direction, and internal influencing factors on settlement intention play more critical roles than external factors. Gu et al. [67] used the Semi-parametric Geographically Weighted Regression (SGWR) model and K-means clustering method to detect the zonal spatial differentiation patterns of the factors influencing floating population's settlement intention and divided all cities into four influencing zones. Gu et al. [24] employed spatial analysis methods and the eigenvector spatial filtering gravity model to examine the spatial pattern and determinants of the interprovincial *hukou* transfer intention network.

According to the above literature review, remarkable spatial variances do occur in settlement intention and its determinants, while lacking enough attention. Therefore, we propose the second research hypothesis that there exist significant spatial differential features in determinants on *hukou* transfer intentions of the floating population.

In conclusion, scholars conduct a series of studies on determinants of settlement intention of the floating population in China, using diverse data sources and various methods and considering different aspects of factors. However, there is a lack of studies on the spatial disparity of settlement intention and its determinants, which employ spatial analysis and spatial econometrics methods on a national scale, especially for *hukou* conversion intension. To rectify this deficiency, we employ the GIS spatial analysis method and the MGWR model to examine the spatially varying effects of the influence factors on the *hukou* transfer intention of the floating population at the preffecture-level, based on the CMDS data in 2016.

4.2.3 Data and Methodology

4.2.3.1 Data Declaration and Variable Selection

The primary data set used in this study is from CMDS in 2016, initiated by the National Health and Family Planning Commission. Since its first release by National Health and Family Planning Commission in 2009, CMDS has the largest sample size of floating population (representative of all cities in China) with a complete-time series and the most scientific sampling survey method, making it possible to conduct a nationwide study at the city level. According to the principle of randomization, this survey collects data by extracting sampling points from destination areas with a high concentration of floating population in 31 province-level units in China, using a multi-stage stratified random sampling method with probability-proportional-to-size. The respondents are the floating population aged from 15 to 69 in the destination regions of in-migration (county, district, or city), who have been residing here for over one month without local *hukou*. The full sample size in 2016 is 169,000. By the end of 2016, there are 297 prefecture-level cities in China, among which the following cities are not included in the CMDS database: Changdu, Danzhou, Fushun, Fuxin, Hami, Heze, Huai'an, Linzhi, Maoming, Mudanjiang, Shigatse, Sansha, Shannan,

Shangluo, Suqian, and Yichun. Besides, Jiyuan is not included in China City Statistical Yearbook in 2016, there is a lack of data in Turpan and Qujing. Therefore, the research units of this study are 279 prefecture-level cities, making the final sample size 153,320.

Meanwhile, the CMDS microdata are aggregated to the prefecture-level macro data because prefecture-level cities are considered to be the main geographical units affecting the decision-making processes of the floating population and the policy-making processes of local governments [53]. The floating population with *hukou* transfer intentions can be defined as migrants who intend to give up their original *hukou* and obtain local *hukou* where they work. The dependent variable is signified as the ratio of the floating population with *hukou* transfer intention to the total sample.

This study attempts to explain the *hukou* conversion intentions of the floating population in urban China from different perspectives. Centering on features of floating population (including demographic, migration, economic and social variables) and characteristics of destination cities as stated in the literature review, we list a series of explanatory variables that may exert effects on *hukou* transfer intentions of the floating population (shown in Table 4.3). First, the economic variables of the floating population (such as income) are derived from Todaro's theory that migrants make long-term settlement decisions based on expected revenue maximization and cost minimization [68]. Furthermore, the migration feature variables and social factors of the floating population are drawn from social integration theory [69]. Finally, the socio-economic variables of destination cities come from push-pull theory [70], holding that the social and economic situations of destination cities will act as driving forces to promote the settlement choice of migrants. The variables of floating population features are collected from the CMDS database, while the variables of destination city characteristics come from China City Statistical Yearbook 2017.

4.2.3.2 MGWR Model

The studies on determinants of *hukou* conversion intentions of the floating population at the city level are mainly based on the traditional multiple linear regression model (OLS). However, there implies a hypothesis of spatial homogeneity in the OLS model that the regression coefficient of each sample point is the same. If there exists spatial non-stationarity in the relationship between the dependent variable and independent variables of each sample point, the global regression model represented by OLS cannot measure the differential influences of independent variables on dependent variables in different regions. In this study, because of the existence of spatial heterogeneity, the effects of explanatory variables may vary across space and on different scales. Therefore, this study analyzes the spatially varying effects of determinants on *hukou* transfer intentions of the floating population with an improved multi-scale GWR (MGWR) model.

The MGWR is the latest improvement of GWR that could make the bandwidths of independent variables differ from each other [71]. As a better fitting model, MGWR

Table 4.3 Variable descriptions and their expected effects on settlement intention

	Variable name	Description of variables	Expected effect
Demographic attributes	AGE	The average age of the floating population	+
	EDUCATION	Average education years of floating population	+
	MARRY	The ratio of married migrants (%)	+
Migration features	STAY	Average residence time in destination cities (years)	+
	AGRI	The ratio of rural *hukou* holders (%)	−
	TIMES	The average number of flows	+
Economic factors	PAYMENTS	The ratio of family income to family expenditure (%)	+
	HIRER	The ratio of self-employed migrants (%)	-
	SINDUS	The ratio of migrants in the secondary industry (%)	+
Social factors	INSURE	The ratio of sharing town employees' social insurance (%)	+
	CHILD	The ratio of floating population accompanied by children in destination cities (%)	+
Destination city factors	WAGE	The average wage of employed workers (RMB)	+
	DENSITY	Population density of municipal districts (persons/km^2)	+

can tell us the varying scales of each variable. An MGWR model is formulated as

$$y_i = \sum_{j=1}^{k} \beta_{ij} x_{ij} + \varepsilon_i \tag{4.3}$$

where for the observation at location $i \in \{1, 2, \ldots, n\}$, y_i is the response variable, x_{ij} is the jth predictor variable, $j \in \{1, 2, \ldots, k\}$, β_{ij} is the jth parameter estimate, and ε_i is the error term. MGWR can also be expressed as a Generalized Additive Model (GAM) format:

$$y = \sum_{j=1}^{k} f_j + \varepsilon \tag{4.4}$$

where f_j is a smooth function applied to the jth predictor variable. In the context of MGWR, each smooth function f_j is a spatial GWR parameter surface that is calibrated by using a known bandwidth. This bandwidth can be varying over j in MGWR. The estimation and inference processes of MGWR are demonstrated in [71].

The criteria for selecting the bandwidths in MGWR is derived from the same procedure used in the traditional GWR models: the corrected Akaike information criteria (AICc). The AICc can be written as:

$$AICc = 2nln(\sigma) + nln(2\pi) + n\frac{n + tr(S)}{n - 2 - tr(S)} \tag{4.5}$$

where n denotes the number of observations, σ is the standard deviation of residuals, $tr(S)$ is the trace of the *hat matrix* in MGWR.

In this study, the bi-square kernel function suggested by Fortheringham and Oshan [72] is employed for calculating the optimal bandwidth. The convergence criterion for the MGWR back-fitting algorithm using the residual sum of squares (RRS) is given by:

$$SOC_{RSS} = \left| \frac{RSS_{new} - RSS_{old}}{RSS_{new}} \right| \tag{4.6}$$

where SOC_{RSS} denotes the convergence criterion, RSS_{new} stands for the RRS in the last step's calculation, and RSS_{old} represents the RRS in the next step's calculation.

4.2.4 *Spatial Variation Analysis of Influence Factors on Hukou Transfer Intentions*

4.2.4.1 Model Comparison

As shown in Table 4.4, we construct three models to analyze the influence factors on *hukou* transfer intentions of the floating population in prefecture-level cities in China. Model 1 is a traditional OLS model; Model 2 is a traditional GWR model that takes into consideration the spatial variances of the relationship between *hukou* conversion intention and its determinants with the same bandwidth; Model 3 is an MGWR model, which incorporates different bandwidths of different variables into the model to depict the spatially varying relationship.

The result of the multicollinearity test with VIF has shown that there exists no multicollinearity among variables, and the result of the White test has also shown that there exists no heteroscedasticity. In order to make better choices of bandwidths in the MGWR model, we standardize the dependent variable and the independent variables (Yu et al. 2020). The chosen bandwidths of the GWR model and MGWR

Table 4.4 Regression results of OLS, GWR and MGWR Model

	Model 1: OLS		Model 2: GWR		Model 3: MGWR	
	β	t	$\bar{\beta}$	Bandwidth	$\bar{\beta}$	Bandwidth
AGE	−0.137*	−1.826	−0.102	248	−0.027	278
EDUCATION	−0.066	−0.823	0.012	248	−0.127	53
MARRY	−0.047	−0.790	0.012	248	0.027	275
STAY	0.311***	5.103	0.175	248	0.062	241
AGRI	−0.014	−0.180	0.033	248	0.020	79
TIMES	0.002	0.040	−0.045	248	−0.016	122
PAYMENTS	0.170***	2.904	0.168	248	0.166	278
HIRER	0.184**	2.327	0.185	248	0.161	278
SINDUS	−0.255***	−3.052	−0.244	248	−0.240	278
INSURE	0.271***	3.639	0.300	248	0.372	278
CHILD	0.206***	3.371	0.180	248	0.170	278
WAGE	0.254***	4.316	0.222	248	0.276	224
DENSITY	0.112*	1.957	0.129	248	0.185	274
Intercept	0.000	0.000	−0.074	248	−0.118	53
Obs	279		279		279	
AICc	710.456		689.400		653.570	
R^2	0.333		0.468		0.620	
Adj. R^2	0.301		0.400		0.532	
Moran I in residual	0.043***		0.001		−0.016	

Notes: * $p < 0.10$; ** $p < 0.05$; *** $p < 0.01$

model are both adaptive bandwidths, and the chosen kernel function is the bi-square kernel function.

As shown in Table 4.4, the OLS regression model without spatial variability has the highest AICc value and the lowest R^2 value, the MGWR model with spatial variability and variable bandwidths has the lowest AICc value and the highest R^2 value, and the AICc and R^2 of the GWR model with spatial variability and invariable bandwidths are between these two models. Therefore, the MGWR model has the best model fitting capacity. Furthermore, strong spatial autocorrelation in the residual will cause the endogeneity problem, thus affecting the estimation effects of models [67]. In the OLS model, the residual has the strongest spatial autocorrelation (Moran's I is significantly positive). Nevertheless, the spatial autocorrelation of residuals in the GWR and MGWR models becomes non-significant when incorporating spatial variability into models. The chosen bandwidth of GWR model is 248 for all variables, while different variables have different bandwidths in the MGWR model: the average education years of the floating population (EDUCATION), the ratio of rural *hukou* holders (AGRI), the average number of flows (TIMES) and the intercept have relatively smaller bandwidths, while other variables have relatively larger bandwidths. In conclusion, the goodness of fit of the MGWR model is better than the GWR model and OLS model, so we employ the MGWR model to examine the spatial variances.

4.2.4.2 Analysis of Regression Results

First, the abovementioned hypothesis that *hukou* conversion intentions are affected by a combination of individual-level and city-level variables is verified. Among the 13 variables passing significance tests, 11 variables are individual-level variables representing the features of the floating population, only WAGE (the average wage of employed workers) and DENSITY (population density of municipal districts) are city-level variables, reflecting the economic development level and city sizes of destination cities. The higher average wage of employed workers hints that the destination city has a higher economic development level, which is an important driving force to enhance the intentions of the floating population to obtain local *hukou* [19]. Besides, the floating population in larger cities (with higher population density) tends to have higher *hukou* transfer intentions, because cities with a larger population are also high-level cities having stronger agglomeration economic power, which possess more job opportunities, higher wages, and better public services, due to the resource allocation among cities based on China's urban administrative hierarchy [19].

Second, economic factors are closely related to the *hukou* transfer intention of the floating population. Regarding economic factors of the floating population, migrants with a higher ratio of family income to family expenditure tend to have a stronger willingness to convert *hukou*. As the floating population incline to maximize the returns for the whole family, higher household income exerts positive impacts on settlement tendency as an essential economic incentive [53]. The self-employed migrants are more likely to permanently settle in cities than informally employed migrants, due to the reason that self-employment is more helpful for rural-to-urban migrants to realize upward mobility [35, 60]. The higher the ratio of migrants in the secondary industry, the lower the *hukou* conversion intention of migrants will be. The possible reason may be that migrants in the secondary industry are often employed in the secondary labor market with lower wages and job stability, who are difficult to migrate to the primary labor market, according to the labor market segregation theory [7].

Third, among the social elements, the more floating population is covered by town employees' social insurance, the more of them are likely to transfer their *hukou* to the current cities. It is notable that migrants who take part in social insurance in the destination cities feel more security and share more benefits in terms of life and job, which has a positive effect on permanent migration [31]. Household characteristics also play a nonnegligible role in the intention to change *hukou* status. Floating population with children migrating with them are more likely to transfer their *hukou*, as bringing children to the city ("family migration") increases migrant parents' sense of integration to the city [73] and the need to solve the education issues of their children will act as a positive incentive.

Fourth, demographic attributes and migration features also matter. For the demographic attributes, a negative correlation exists between the age of the floating population and the probability of permanent settlement in destination cities. In contrast with the younger generation of the floating population who tend to value development opportunities and acquire more experiences in big cities, the older generation of the floating population is more inclined to pursue stable life conditions by returning hometown, which maximizes the welfare of the entire family [47]. Longer residence time in destination cities is closely related to the high propensity to settle in terms of migration features. In general, the more time migrants spend in the current cities, the more work experience and social capital they will accumulate and more integrated they will become into the local society [24, 53].

4.2.4.3   Spatial Patterns of Influence Factors

To reveal the spatial pattern of spatial non-stationary variables, we only select explanatory variables with statistical significance ($|\bar{t}| \geq 1.64$), and divide each variable into five levels in terms of influence degree through Jenks classification method: highest, relatively higher, medium, relatively lower, lowest. The significant spatial differences of influencing effects of various explanatory variables on *hukou* transfer intentions are revealed in Fig. 4.4, which proves the second research hypothesis tenable. Taking spatial heterogeneity into consideration, the effect of the average age (AGE) becomes insignificant, and the ratio of rural *hukou* holders (AGRI) and the average number of flows (TIMES) become significant.

To begin with, regarding the migration features, the average residence time in destination cities (STAY) has positive impacts in northeastern and northwestern China, and the strongest influence emerges in northeastern China. The average residence time in destination cities indicates the social network of migrants in destination cities, and this strong social network effect of northwestern China is related to its cultural traits. The ratio of rural *hukou* holders (AGRI) mostly have positive effects on *hukou* conversion intentions, concentrated in some parts of western China (Sichuan Province and Gansu Province). This is mainly because the urban–rural gap in this region is relatively huge, and migrants in this region are usually intra-provincial migrants with a relatively shorter migration distance, who prefer to transfer *hukou* to urban areas. Furthermore, the number of flows (TIMES) exerts positive impacts in northeastern China and negative impacts in north China. More times of flows have improved the social integration of migrants in northeastern China, thus increasing their likelihood of converting *hukou*, while the opposite situation occurs in north China with fiercer competitions for jobs.

Concerning the economic factors, the ratio of family income to family expenditure (PAYMENTS) generates a positive impact on the willingness to change *hukou*

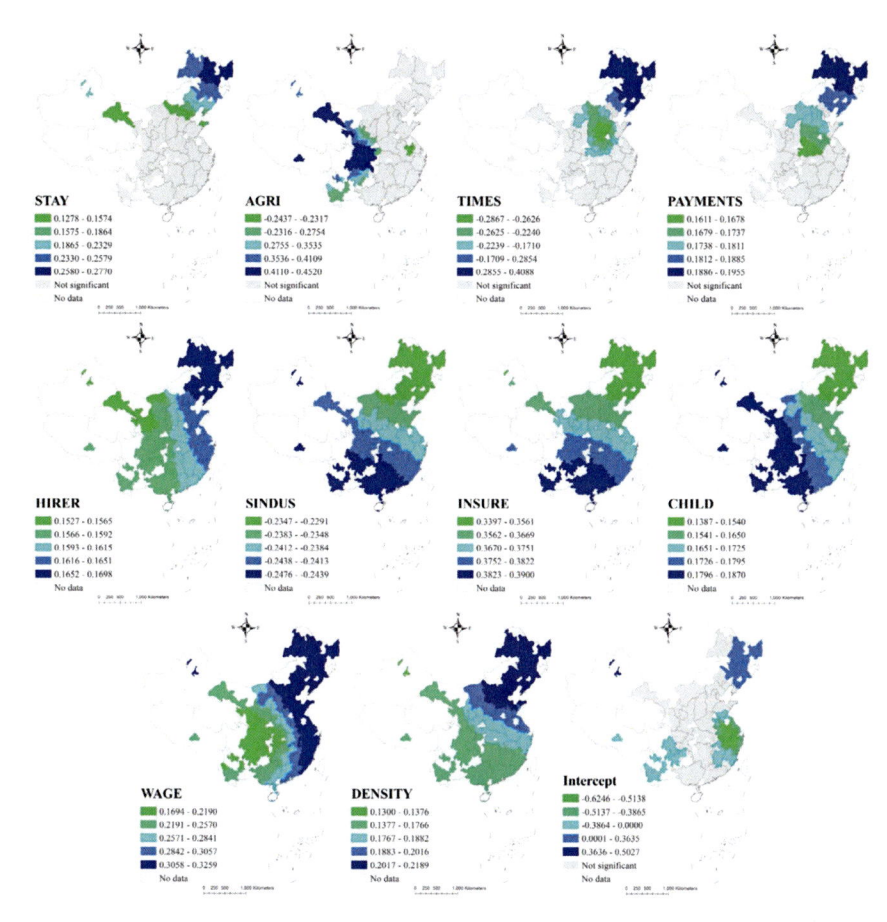

Fig. 4.4 Spatial patterns of regression coefficients of explanatory variables. *Notes: Only significant variables (p < 0.1) are mapped*

status in some parts of northeastern China and north China, with the strongest influence also appearing in northeastern China. The positive effect of the ratio of self-employed migrants (HIRER) decreases from east to west, and the negative effect of the ratio of migrants in the secondary industry (SINDUS) presents a similar trend of declining from northeast to southwest. The cause of this phenomenon may be related to the economic development disparity between the eastern and western regions: the self-employed migrants have more economic opportunities and higher wages in the eastern region, thus increasing the probability of permanent migration; the job market of the western region is less perfect than the eastern region, leading to relatively lower job stability of floating population employed in the second industry and a weaker *hukou* conversion intention.

With respect to the social factors, the positive effects of the ratio of sharing town employees' social insurance (INSURE) and the ratio of floating population accompanied by children in destination cities (CHILD) both present a spatial pattern of diminishing from southwest to northeast. The reason for the former may be that the job market in the western region is more imperfect, so social insurance can provide migrants with greater security relatively, helping them permanently settle down in urban areas. The reason for the latter could be that migrants in the western region depend more on family factors when making settlement decisions.

It is found that city-level factors also play a significant role in influencing *hukou* transfer intentions. The East–West pattern shows that the average wage of employed workers (WAGE) has stronger influences in the eastern coastal region since the average wage level is much higher in the eastern developed region, which brings more benefits and higher utility, owing to the agglomeration effect. The NE-SW pattern of the population density of municipal districts (DENSITY) demonstrates that the positive impacts are the strongest in the northeastern region and the weakest in the southwestern region.

Finally, the intercept of the MGWR model represents the geographical effect, meaning that it can reflect the influencing effect of geographical location on *hukou* transfer intentions of the floating population [74]. It is demonstrated in Fig. 4.4 that the geographical location factors of the two cities in Xinjiang Province and some cities in northeastern China, exert positive impacts on *hukou* transfer intentions, while those of cities in eastern China (Shanghai, Zhejiang, and Jiangsu) and southwest China (including Yunnan and Guizhou) may decrease *hukou* transfer intentions. The above results indicate that there also exist spatially varying effects of geographical location on *hukou* conversion willingness, which also suggest significant spatial heterogeneity of *hukou* conversion willingness.

In general, the results of MGWR indicate that the effects of migration features, economic factors, social factors, and city-level variables on *hukou* transfer intentions all present spatial variation characteristics, except individual-level factors.

4.2.5   Conclusions and Discussion

Drawing on the CMDS data in 2016, this study analyzes the determinants of *hukou* transfer intention and their spatial patterns through the MGWR model. It contributes to the growing literature on the *hukou* conversion intentions of the floating population in China from the following aspects.

First, our study employs nationally representative data at the prefecture-level to prove that individual-level variables (including demographic attributes, migration features, economic factors, and social elements) and city-level variables both have significant influences on the *hukou* transfer intentions of floating population.

Second, via the MGWR model, the spatial patterns of determinants on *hukou* conversion intentions are revealed: For the average residence time in destination cities, the number of flows and the ratio of family income to family expenditure, the significant positive effects only occur in the northeastern region. Similarly, the significant positive influences of the ratio of rural *hukou* holders only emerge in part of the western region. Regarding the ratio of self-employed migrants and the average wage of employed workers, the positive influences diminish from east to west. The positive effects caused by the ratio of sharing town employee' social insurance and the ratio of floating population accompanied by children in destination cities, as well as the negative impacts exerted by the ratio of migrants in the secondary industry demonstrate a spatial pattern of decreasing from southwest to northeast, and the population density of municipal districts presents an opposite trend in terms of its positive influences on *hukou* transfer intentions. It is evident that the northeastern region has distinct features compared with other regions, especially in terms of migration features and economic factors, and the economic and social development disparity between the eastern and western regions still plays an important role in the above various spatial patterns. In addition, the geographical location also has a spatially varying effect on *hukou* conversion intentions.

Finally, the findings of this study have some policy implications. In consideration of important determinants, the accompanying children of the floating population significantly contribute to the intention of converting *hukou*. Therefore, the focus should be on making efforts to ensure that these children gain equal access to education with local children; the social security status also matters, leading to the necessity of increasing social insurance coverage among the floating population.

Due to the spatial disparity of influence effects of determinants on *hukou* transfer intentions, cities of different conditions should formulate policies that are sensitive to their contexts. Larger cities with higher population density and wage levels are usually more attractive for the floating population than smaller cities, so there exists an apparent mismatch between the trend of floating population migrating to larger cities and strict *hukou* system restrictions on larger cities (especially megacities). Although China's government has issued many *hukou* reform initiatives in the past decade, many of them are limited and even nominal. It is necessary to take measures to relax the *hukou* system in megacities and big cities where migrants can truly benefit step by step. At the present stage, the possible solution is to promote the moderate functional dispersal in megacities through the industrial transfer to surrounding medium-sized and small cities, thus improving their industrial cluster development and employment absorptive capacity to attract more floating population. More importantly, targeted migration policies should be crafted to take into consideration different appeals of the floating population in different cities. For the economic factors-dominated cities, it is urgent to raise the income levels of the floating population by providing more job training for them and guaranteeing wage payments on time via legal labor contracts. For the social factors-dominated cities, more attention should be paid to increasing the coverage of social insurance among the floating population, enhancing financial inputs in education and medical treatment for accompanying family members of the floating population, and promoting equalization of public services among different levels of cities. The educational issues of the accompanying children of the floating population should be incorporated into the overall urban planning of destination cities by taking the following measures: strengthening the management and registration of accompanying children of floating population, raising more funds for their compulsory educational expenses in destination cities from central governmental finance and social funds, expanding enrollment of public schools and improving educational conditions of private schools.

This study has made contributions by revealing the spatially varying relationship between *hukou* transfer intention and its determinants, based on the latest improved version of GWR-the MGWR model, which can offer support for local governments to formulate place-tailored migration strategies. From the theoretical perspective, the results of this study can provide further evidence for traditional migration theories, including Todaro's [68] theory, social integration theory [69], and the push–pull theory [70]. Based on the MGWR model, this study uses both individual-level and city-level data in China, which also contributes to the combination of micro-level and macro-level migration theories. Compared with the most relevant studies on *hukou* transfer intentions of floating population, this study is basically consistent with them in terms of the results that the spatial variances of *hukou* transfer intentions of the floating population are influenced by both individual-level factors and city-level factors, and the influencing effects of the latter are stronger than the former [19], furthermore, this study deepens the extant studies by examining the spatially varying effects of determinants on *hukou* transfer intentions. Compared with the closely related studies on settlement intentions of floating population, this study agrees with them that the effects of migration features, economic factors, social factors and city-level variables on *hukou* transfer intentions and settlement intentions all present spatial variation characteristics [31], moreover, this study improves the existing research based on GWR and SGWR models by employing the MGWR model with multi-scale effects.

Regarding the connection of this study with the international literature, there are different patterns of international and internal migration across the world, which can also be divided into permanent migration and temporary migration, similar to China's situation. Internal migration in China is often compared to international migration across the world because China's migrants are limited by the *hukou* system restrictions, similar to those encountering barriers to transnational immigration [75]. Those who have moved to a new place but do not possess local citizenship (e.g., *hukou* in China) are referred to as temporary migrants (e.g., floating population in China). By analyzing the influencing factors on *hukou* transfer intentions from the perspective of settlement intention instead of *hukou*-centered approach, this study can provide empirical evidence for migration policy making of other countries toward international and internal migrants, thus contributing to the better integration of temporary migrants into local society, in terms of both economic and social status.

Nevertheless, there still exist limitations in this study. Since the *hukou* transfer intention of the floating population is a complex issue affected by various factors in different ways, the results of this study based on the cross-section data and the MGWR model need examination and further research.

4.3 *Hukou* Transfer Intentions at the Individual Level

4.3.1 Introduction

The urban–rural dualism in the People's Republic of China was codified in 1958 with the issue of the Regulations on Registration. Since then, Chinese citizens have been classified as either rural (agricultural) or urban (non-agricultural) on their household registration, or *hukou* [76, 77]. The types of *hukou* correspond to particular arrangements relating to the welfare system and land property rights [29, 34, 78, 79]. China's reform and opening-up in the late 1970s unleashed a massive interregional population migration [18, 80]. Under these circumstances, the breaking of barriers established by the *hukou* system allowed for the transfer of a significant portion of the population from rural areas to cities in step with the ongoing industrialization and modernization in China's cities [29, 79]. In 2014, the implementation of the New-type Urbanization policy blurred the urban–rural distinction, giving greater freedom for migration from rural to urban areas and leading to a new surge in urban development [29, 81]. By 2017, the stock of rural–urban migration had climbed to 280 million [82]. Reform of the *hukou* system in the present decade is expected to loosen restrictions on migration further. However, the nature and extent of these reforms, particularly in relation to the permanent residences of rural–urban migrants, remain largely unexplored.

Despite the reforms undertaken thus far, strict controls on the movement of people still exist in some of China's large developed cities, especially megacities such as Beijing and Shanghai [79]. While it is common for a rural–urban migrant to transfer *hukou* to a large city [19, 79, 83], many find it more feasible to acquire urban *hukou* from a small- or medium-sized city. Thus, the decision regarding whether to exchange agricultural *hukou* for urban *hukou* has turned into something of a gamble [79, 84]. On the one hand, the rural contracted land and homesteads associated with agricultural *hukou* can be sufficient to earn a living; on the other hand, urban *hukou* may lead to higher wages, improved social status, and wider access to public services [85].

China's system of rural collective land ownership grants to members of the agricultural population the right to use contracted land and homesteads [86, 87]. Contracted land is allocated by the village collective to each household for agricultural purposes, while rural homesteads are the portions allotted to rural households from the lands collectively owned by village governments for the purpose of building homes [88, 89]. *Hukou* grants the legal right to use contracted land and rural homesteads, and the extent and nature of rural residents' landholdings appear to correlate closely with their likelihood of engaging in rural–urban migration [90, 91]. As just discussed, agricultural *hukou* serves as a prerequisite for the tenure of both rural homesteads and contracted land. Legally, the contracted land of a rural–urban migrant who has transferred *hukou* to an urban area cannot be redistributed by the village collective once the contracted period is over [92]. China's land contracting system stipulates the legality of contracting land to farmers. The first round of land contracting began in 1983 and lasted for fifteen years, at which point (i.e., in 1998) a second, thirty-year round began [93]. The expiration of the arrangements made during this second round in 2028 will result in significant economic losses for rural–urban migrants who have decided to transfer their *hukou*.

Compared with contracted land, the tenure of a rural homestead is more complicated when a rural–urban migrant transfers *hukou*. When such a transfer takes place, according to the Land Management Law and the Property Law, the migrant is permitted to use the rural homesteads until the buildings on the land disappear, for instance, because of a natural disaster. However, a migrant cannot repair or remodel buildings on a rural homestead or transfer or lease the property, a restriction that may also result in economic loss (Kong et al. 2018) [94]. A further consideration is that homesteads, as the sites of dwellings, have significant sociocultural associations for members of China's rural population, such as contributing to a sense of belonging [95]. To promote *hukou* transfer by rural–urban migrants, some areas have conducted a pilot program of targeted compensation for these migrants' loss of their rural homesteads [94]. However, a uniform and universal compensation mechanism has not yet been formulated [94, 96]. The issue is significant because, as has been seen, rural homesteads play a significant role in rural–urban migrants' decisions regarding whether to transfer *hukou* and, therefore, in the progress of urbanization.

As an indicator measuring the *hukou* transfer tendency for migrants, the *hukou* transfer intention has gained increasing discussion from Chinese scholars in the past decade [19, 40, 79]. Some of this research has explored the underlying determinants of transfer intention, including housing prices [11, 12], social integration [32], public services [97], and employment status [60]. However, relatively little attention has been paid to the extent to which the rural homesteads of rural–urban migrants factor into their *hukou* transfer intentions. Now, however, the issue can be addressed using data gathered in the 2017 China Migrants Dynamic Survey (CMDS). The purpose of the present study is to help fill this gap in the literature on the *hukou* transfer intentions of rural–urban migrants, and it is hoped that the findings presented here will inform policies targeting Chinese rural–urban migrants.

4.3.2 Hukou *Transfer Intentions of Chinese Rural–Urban Migrants*

Economists, demographers, and geographers have done considerable work investigating the massive rural–urban migration in China that, as just noted, was touched off by the reform and opening-up policies that began to be implemented in the latter twentieth century. Since the 2000s, researchers have been drawing on existing classical theories of population migration (e.g., [2–5]) to model the interregional migration of Chinese rural–urban migrants from economic, social, and employment perspectives as well as from the perspective of decisions made by individuals [14, 80, 98–102].

Numerous researchers have taken advantage of the access to relevant micro-level data for Chinese floating migrants since 2009 to assess the migration and settlement intentions of rural–urban migrants [10, 31, 32, 39, 56, 58, 90, 103] as well as their *hukou* transfer intentions [19, 79] and return intentions [18, 104]. Many of these studies have considered the settlement intentions of specific sub-groups of migrants (e.g., rural–urban, aging, female) [9, 32, 33, 43, 55, 58, 64]. However, migrants' *hukou* transfer intentions have received relatively little attention (exceptions include [19, 79]). In the work that has been done, the factors that influence *hukou* transfer intentions include: individual characteristics, migration characteristics, economic concerns, employment factors, and hometown factors. Migration has been described as the investment of an individual's human and social capital [105], from which perspective it is understandable that migrants who are relatively young, unmarried, and educated tend to transfer their *hukou* to cities [9, 19, 79]. In order to maximize individual and family's utilities, migrants with a higher income level and employment status in destination cities or with fewer children and elderly care in hometowns have a strong willingness to transfer *hukou* [58]. Various aspects of destination cities also play a role, thus, *hukou* from a city with a high-administrative level is associated with high economic value and elevated social status and, therefore, is appealing to rural–urban migrants [19]. Besides the destination factors, existing research indicates the influence of places of origin. *Hukou* transfer intentions of rural–urban migrants from different places are differential in their characteristics [31, 79]. Overall, then, the *hukou* transfer intentions of migrants involve a complex decision-making process affected by multiple factors.

4.3.3 *Whether to Transfer* Hukou *or Continue Using Rural Homestead: A Dilemma*

As discussed, the *hukou* system has had a significant impact on the migration patterns of China's rural population. The highly clustered regional development in contemporary China has combined with the country's longstanding urban–rural dichotomy to create vast differences between urban and rural areas in terms of economic activity and the availability of public services [80, 101, 102]. In general, an urban floating migrant who transfers agricultural *hukou* to urban *hukou* enjoys access to better public services (e.g., medical care, schools, and housing subsidies), a higher income, and higher social status than before the transfer [34]. Conversely, as has been seen, migrants need to balance such rewards from rural-to-urban *hukou* transfer with the loss of the right to use the contracted rural land and homesteads [94, 96].

In China, collective land ownership is the material and economic basis of the rural economy [87]: inhabitants of rural areas have the right to use rural homesteads and contracted land, but the village maintains ownership rights. A rural-to-urban *hukou* transfer involves changes in both the rural homestead and contracted land (see Table 4.5). The Rural Land Contracting Law set the period for land contracts and, in the process, ensured that the transfer of *hukou* would entail economic loss. The more complicated situation with rural homesteads is at least in part a product of the "one household one homestead" policy limiting each rural household to a single rural homestead of a given size [96]. Since rural homesteads can be transferred among members of a household, a rural family's homestead tenure can be, at least theoretically, permanent [90]. Moreover, in cases in which a rural homestead is appropriated by the local, regional, or national government, the previous holder may receive compensation for both the land and buildings thereon [96].

Under the legal regime outlined above, a rural–urban migrant with a rural homestead who transfers *hukou* to an urban area can continue to use the homestead until the buildings disappear but cannot make improvements on, transfer, or receive compensation for it (Table 4.5). The housing units on rural homesteads in such circumstances can still be leased, but a proportion of the proceeds must be returned to the village. In some parts of China, rural–urban migrants are encouraged to transfer their *hukou* and withdraw their homesteads in exchange for compensation [90]. At the same time, the aforementioned sense of belonging associated with these homesteads may also influence *hukou* transfer intentions [95].

The previous discussion argues that rural homesteads function as an essential factor that affects the *hukou* transfer intentions of Chinese rural–urban migrants, yet the influencing mechanism of homesteads is still underexplored. A few of the studies that have been done on these issues have found that access to rural homesteads tends to have a negative effect on *hukou* transfer intentions [40, 62, 63, 106]. According to Yu et al. [94], the living conditions of rural–urban migrants in destination cities play a key role in their rural homestead withdrawal processes, which economic compensation promotes. Some research also suggests that rural homesteads play a psychological as well as a material role in the well-being of rural–urban migrants [40, 62, 63, 106]. The intention in the present study is to use the 2017 CMDS data to fill gaps in the current understanding of *hukou* transfer intentions.

4.3.4 Research Data, Variables, and Methods

4.3.4.1 Data

The data used in this study are drawn from the 2017 China Migrants Dynamic Survey (CMDS) of non-native floating migrants (without local *hukou*) over the age of 15 years who had been in their current place of residence for more than one month. The CMDS survey relies on a stratified probability-proportional-to-size (PPS) criterion for sampling and consists of individual questionnaires. The total number of respondents to the 2017 survey is 169,000; of these respondents, 101,735 are rural-urban migrants, making this the sample size for the present study. The data of migrants relevant to this study are selected based on whether they held rural *hukou* and whether they were migrating in search of employment.

Table 4.5 Changes in rural homesteads and contracted land when transferring *hukou* status

	Rural homestead	Contracted land
Holding agricultural *hukou*	Each agricultural household can only be allocated one homestead, owned by the village collective	Enjoy the right to land contracted and the right to operate
	Enjoy the right to use the homestead and the right to the proceeds of the building on the homestead	Allowed to transfer the right to operate the land
	Allowed to transfer or lease the homestead (but not allowed to be allocated new homestead after)	
	Get compensation when the homestead is requisitioned	
Agricultural *hukou* transferred to urban *hukou*	Allowed to use the homestead until the housing property on the land disappear	During the contract period, allowed to enjoy land withdrawal
	Not allowed to repair or remodel the building on the homestead	Compensation or transfer the right to operate the land
	Not allowed to enjoy homestead acquisition compensation (but still enjoy the housing acquisition compensation)	Once the land is withdrawn or the contract period ends, not allowed to have the land contract right
	Not allowed to transfer or lease the homestead	
	Allowed to transfer or lease the house on the homestead, with a proportion of the income handing over to the village collective	
	Voluntarily enjoy homestead withdrawal compensation (partial areas), but will lose the homestead use right	

4.3.4.2 Variables

The dependent variable for this study is the *hukou* transfer intention of rural-urban migrants, which is assessed based on the answer to the survey question "Are you willing to transfer your *hukou* to the destination city if you meet the necessary preconditions?" The possible responses to this question are "willing to transfer," "unwilling to transfer," or "undecided," representing 34.26% (34,852 respondents), 38.53%

(39,201 respondents), and 27.21% (27,682 respondents) of the sample, respectively. The analysis omits responses classified as "undecided." A binary variable of *hukou* transferring decision is coded "1" for those answering "unwilling to transfer" and "0" for those answering "willing to transfer."

The key independent variable in the study is the dummy variable based on answers to the question "Do you have a rural homestead in your hometown?" Responses classified as "unclear" are excluded. While all rural households have the right to be allocated a rural homestead from the village government, the limited availability of rural homesteads in some villages means that not all of the applicants for a homestead actually receive one. Thus, farmers who become eligible must wait until land is made available after the retreat of the homesteads from other inhabitants [96], in this respect, the tenure of rural homesteads is independent of their holders' characteristics (i.e., *hukou* transfer intentions). In this sense, the rural homestead variable is exogenous.

Previous literature provides guidance for control factors that may affect the *hukou* transfer intentions of migrant workers [39, 56, 58, 79, 90, 94]. Individual factors include gender, age, marital status, and education level. It has been reported that the age of rural-urban migrants correlates negatively with their job opportunities in destination cities and that their education level correlates positively with their job opportunities [94].

Migration factors include distance and the size of the destination city. The migration distance variable covers the three situations that occur in China: intra-city, intra-provincial, and inter-provincial migration [107]. Simply put, the *hukou* transfer intentions of rural-urban migrants are affected by both the individual characteristics of the migrants and the features of the destination city [19]. Chinese cities vary greatly in their economic and social-cultural environments as well as in size. Following Gu et al. [18], the migrants' destinations in this study are categorized as either small cities (those with fewer than 1 million residents), medium-sized cities (1–5 million residents), large cities (5–10 million residents), and megacities (more than 10 million residents).

Economic variables relating to rural-urban migrants, specifically income and cost of living, are represented by two proxies, respectively, the income-expenditure ratio and the share of total family expenditures devoted to housing. Rural-urban migrants naturally weigh the expected income and chance of securing gainful employment when determining where to settle [32, 39], thus, when facing higher living costs, they are more inclined to return to their hometowns [31, 108]. Employment status, industrial classification, and labor contract coverage serve as proxies for employment conditions. Self-employed migrants, those engaged in tertiary industries, and those with a labor contract appear to be more willing to settle in cities [60, 109]. Lastly, several variables relate to migrants' hometowns, including the hometown location, whether respondents are raising children, and whether they have elders to support in their places of origin. All of the variables are described in Table 4.6.

Table 4.6 Variable description

Variable	Description	Mean	Std. Dev.
Dependent variable: *hukou* transfer intention	Whether to transfer *hukou* into urban areas. (dummy: willing = 0; unwilling = 1)	0.529	0.499
Key variable: Homestead	Whether the respondent has a rural homestead. (dummy: have = 1; do not have = 0)	0.745	0.436
Individual factors: Gender	Gender of the respondent. (dummy: female = 0; Male = 1)	0.591	0.492
Age	Age of the respondent. (continuous; years)	35.921	9.162
Education level	Education years of the respondent. (continuous; years)	9.767	3.164
Marital status of the respondent	Marital status of the respondent.(dummy: married = 1; single = 0)	0.832	0.374
Migration factors: City size	Size of the destination city. (categorical variable: small city = 1, fewer than 1 million residents; medium-sized city = 2, 1–5 million residents; large city = 3, 5–10 million residents; megacity = 4, more than 10 million residents)	2.003	1.031
Migration distance	Scope of migration. (dummy: intra-city = 1; intra-province = 2; inter-province = 3)	2.362	0.751
Employment factors: Employment status	Whether the respondent is self-employed. (dummy: self-employed = 1, employers and self-employed workers; employed = 0, employees with and without regular employers)	0.418	0.493
Industrial classification	Whether the respondent is engaged in a tertiary industry. (dummy: tertiary = 1; non-tertiary = 0)	0.610	0.488
Labor contract coverage	Whether the respondent has a labor contract. (dummy: have = 1; not have = 0)	0.316	0.465
Economic factors: Income-Expenditure ratio	The proportion of family monthly income to the monthly family expenditure of the respondent.(continuous; rate)	2.306	1.861
Housing expenditure ratio	The share of total family expenditures devoted to housing of the respondent. (continuous; rate)	0.212	0.206

(continued)

Table 4.6 (continued)

Hometown factors: Hometown location	The location of hometown (dummy: village = 0; non-village = 1)	0.098	0.297
Raise children	Whether the respondent has children in the hometown. (dummy: have = 1; do not have = 0)	0.243	0.429
Support the elderly	Whether the respondent has elders in the hometown. (dummy: have =1; do not have = 0)	0.716	0.451

4.3.4.3 Methodology

As has been seen, the *hukou* transfer intentions of rural-urban migrants are classified as either "willing" or "unwilling." A binary logistic model serves to fit the data and explore the impacts of rural homesteads on these intentions. The model assesses how the ceteris paribus changes in the independent variables affect the response probabilities of the dependent variable, represented as P (y=j|x), when the dependent variable takes values $j \in \{0, 1\}$. The response probabilities can thus be written as

$$P(y = 1|x) = \frac{\exp(x\beta)}{1 + \exp(x\beta)} \tag{4.7}$$

where y denotes the dependent variable, x the set of independent variables, and β the estimated coefficients of the independent variables. Generally, the partial effect of x_k can be written as

$$\frac{\partial P(y = 1|x)}{\partial x_k} = P(y = 1|x)\{\beta_k - [\beta_k \exp(x\beta)]/[1 + \exp(x\beta)]\} \tag{4.8}$$

where the estimator β_k indicates the direction of the partial effect of x_k on the response probability of *hukou* transfer. The odds ratio of those unwilling to transfer *hukou* to those willing to do so (the reference group) is given by

$$\frac{p_1(x, \beta)}{1 - p_1(x, \beta)} = \exp(\beta_k) \tag{4.9}$$

where $p_1(x, \beta)$ denotes the response probability of the option of "unwilling to transfer *hukou*." The regression model is carried out by maximum likelihood estimation (MLE).

4.3.5 *Results*

A descriptive statistical analysis is first applied to detect the latent relationship between rural homesteads and *hukou* transfer intentions, followed by a regression based on the logistic model. Another logistic model with interaction terms is constructed to analyze the mechanisms of rural homesteads. Several robustness checks are employed to verify the accuracy of the main findings.

4.3.5.1 Descriptive Statistical Analysis

Table 4.7 reports the results of the descriptive statistical analysis. Compared with rural-urban migrants who do not have a rural homestead, those with a rural homestead show a 12% lower *hukou* transfer intention. The results also shed light on other factors influencing *hukou* transfer intentions (e.g., individual characteristics, migration factors, and economic considerations). Considering the impact of rural homesteads, the differences in the *hukou* transfer intentions relating to the various characteristics of rural-urban migrants merit greater attention. Specifically, while migrants with a rural homestead across all age groups are less willing to transfer their *hukou* than those without a rural homestead. Likewise, compared with less-educated rural-urban migrants, a larger proportion of better-educated migrants report an intention to transfer *hukou*, while those without a rural homestead have stronger transfer intentions than those with a rural homestead across education levels. Rural-urban migrants who migrate relatively long distances, relocate to large cities, have labor contracts, who are employed or engaged in tertiary industries, and whose hometowns are in non-village areas (townships, counties, or cities) are especially inclined to transfer their *hukou*. However, their *hukou* transfer intentions turn out to be lower when they own rural homesteads. In addition, migrants with children in their hometowns have weaker *hukou* transfer intentions; by contrast, those with elders in their hometowns are more willing to transfer *hukou*. At the same time, rural homestead tenure weakens migrants' transfer intentions irrespective of whether they have children or elders in their hometowns. These findings support the possible influences of the rural homestead on rural-urban migrants' *hukou* transfer intentions. However, more statistical evidence needs to be provided based on the econometric analysis.

4.3.5.2 Basic Regression Results

The main results of the logistic model (Model 1) are presented in Table 4.8. To begin with, these results indicate the influence of a significant pulling effect of rural homesteads on rural–urban migrants' *hukou* transfer intentions. Compared with migrants who are willing to transfer (hereafter, the "willing" group), access to rural homesteads increases the odds ratio for migrants who are unwilling to do so (the "unwilling" group) by 1.419 times. The finding that those with rural homesteads have significantly weaker *hukou* transfer intentions is consistent with previous literature [62, 63, 94, 106] and is in part attributable to the fact that rural homesteads offer a place of retreat for rural–urban migrants who are struggling in destination cities [40]. Also, having a rural homestead increases rural–urban migrants' opportunity cost when they consider to be granted for urban *hukou* and abandon their rural *hukou* [96].

Table 4.7 Descriptive statistical analysis

Variables		Full sample		Own homestead		Do not own homestead	
		U (%)	W (%)	U (%)	W (%)	U (%)	W (%)
Homestead ($p =$ 0.00)	Have	56	44				
	Do not have	44	56				
Gender ($p =$ 0.00)	Male	54	46	56	44	46	54
	Female	52	48	56	44	42	58
Age ($p = 0.00$)	15–20	60	40	64	36	46	54
	21–30	50	50	52	48	42	58
	31–40	51	49	54	46	43	57
	41–50	57	43	60	40	47	53
	51–60	51	49	63	37	48	52
Education level ($p = 0.00$)	Primary school and blew	60	40	64	36	48	52
	High school	54	46	56	44	46	54
	College and beyond	39	61	42	58	31	69
Marital status ($p = 0.00$)	Single	51	49	54	46	42	58
	Married	53	47	56	44	45	55
City size ($p =$ 0.00)	Small city	61	39	66	34	50	50
	Medium-sized city	57	43	60	40	48	52
	Large city	45	55	48	52	37	63
	Megacity	50	50	53	47	42	58
Migration distance ($p =$ 0.00)	Inter-provincial	50	50	53	47	42	58
	Intra-provincial	52	48	55	45	42	58
	Intra-city	63	37	67	33	55	45
Employment status ($p = 0.00$)	Employed	51	49	54	46	42	58
	Self-employed	57	43	59	41	50	50
Industrial classification ($p = 0.00$)	Tertiary	52	48	55	45	44	56
	Non-tertiary	56	44	58	42	47	53
Labor contract coverage ($p = 0.00$)	Have	48	52	51	49	38	62
	Do not have	55	45	58	42	47	53
Hometown location ($p = 0.00$)	Village	54	46	56	44	45	55
	Non-village	47	53	52	48	37	63
Raise children ($p = 0.00$)	Have	56	44	58	42	49	51
	Do not have	53	47	55	45	46	54
Support the elderly ($p = 0.00$)	Have	53	47	55	45	46	54
	Do not have	55	45	57	43	48	52

Table 4.8 Basic regression results and robustness checks

Variable	Unwilling versus Willing (Willing = reference group)			
	Model 1: *hukou* transfer intention		Model 2: *hukou* transfer intention	
	Odds ratio	Robust S. E.	Odds ratio	Robust S. E.
Homestead (do not have = base)				
Have	1.491***	0.048		
Homestead area			1.091***	0.002
Gender (female = base)				
Male	0.969	0.025	0.968	0.025
Age	1.005***	0.002	1.005***	0.002
Education level	0.955***	0.005	0.954***	0.005
Martial status (single = base)				
Married	1.032	0.046	1.033	0.046
Destination city size (small city = base)				
Medium-sized city	0.918**	0.037	0.919**	0.037
Large city	0.562***	0.025	0.562***	0.025
Megacity	0.233***	0.013	0.233***	0.013
Migration distance (intra-city = base)				
Intra-provincial	0.739***	0.041	0.739***	0.041
Inter-provincial	0.694***	0.036	0.694***	0.036
Employment status (employed = base)				
Self-employed	1.144***	0.040	1.143***	0.040
Industrial classification (non-tertiary = base)				
Tertiary	0.834***	0.024	0.833***	0.024
Labor contract coverage (do not have = base)				
Have	0.917**	0.033	0.916**	0.033
Income-expenditure ratio	1.027***	0.008	1.027***	0.008
Housing expenditure ratio	0.664***	0.044	0.661***	0.044
Hometown location (village = base)				
Non-village	0.822***	0.036	0.819***	0.036
Raise children (do not have = base)				
Have	1.203***	0.038	1.205***	0.038
Hometown-clustered standard error	Yes		Yes	
Obs	28,981		28,981	
Pseudo R-square	0.060		0.059	

The results of the control variables show that age increases the odds ratio for the "unwilling" group compared with the "willing" group by 1.005 times, indicating a negative relationship between the age of migrants and their *hukou* transfer intentions. Results also illustrate a positive association between education level and *hukou* transfer intentions. This finding reflects the human capital that migrants possess and their bargaining power in transferring *hukou*. Regarding factors associated with migration, rural–urban migrants living in medium-sized cities, large cities, and megacities are more willing to transfer their *hukou* than those in small cities. Likewise, the odds ratios decrease as the sizes of the destination cities increase, indicating that larger cities have a greater effect on *hukou* transfer intentions than smaller ones. These findings are evidence of a correlation between rural–urban migrants' *hukou* transfer intentions and the size of the cities to which they relocate. Also, migrants whose hometowns are located in non-village areas have stronger *hukou* transfer intentions than those whose hometowns are villages, primarily since the model controls for the migration distance factor. Thus, in the context of logistic regression, intra-city migrants (the base group) are more inclined to transfer their *hukou* to nearby cities so as to reduce their migration costs, enjoy socio-cultural similarities, and receive higher compensation for giving up their homesteads [96]. In addition, the results reveal a distance effect in *hukou* transfer intentions; as expected, the intentions of inter- and intra-provincial migrants are stronger than those of intra-city migrants.

The regression results also provide evidence for the influence of employment factors on *hukou* transfer intentions. Thus, self-employed migrants are more reluctant to transfer *hukou* than those who work for an employer. Conversely, engagement in a tertiary industry strengthens migrants' transfer intentions, as does the coverage of a labor contract. Similarly, regarding economic factors, the income-expenditure ratio correlates negatively with rural–urban migrants' *hukou* transfer intentions, while the proportion of housing expenditures to total expenditures correlates positively, results that are consistent with those of [24, 31]. Lastly, raising children and supporting elders in hometowns also play a role when rural–urban migrants decide whether to transfer *hukou* to urban areas. Migrants raising children in their hometowns have weaker *hukou* transfer intentions while those supporting elders have stronger intentions, which is in part on account of issues relating to access to education for children and to medical services for the elderly in rural and urban areas.

4.3.5.3 Analysis of the Mechanisms

The findings from the descriptive statistical analysis and basic regression just presented suggest that rural homesteads do indeed influence rural–urban migrants' *hukou* transfer intentions. There appear to be three mechanisms behind this influence: (1) the opportunity cost effect (OCE), (2) the revenue effect (RE), and (3) the direct effect (DE). The OCE represents possible losses (e.g., access to better urban public services, social identity as an urban resident) that rural–urban migrants may incur should they decide not to transfer their rural *hukou* but rather to maintain it so as to preserve their full rights to their rural homesteads. The analysis presented earlier indicates that the age variable has an inhibitory effect on *hukou* transfer intentions, since workers' human capital decreases with age, while the coverage of labor contract strengthens *hukou* transfer intentions because of the associated employment security for migrants. This being the case, older rural–urban migrants and those without a labor contract tend to incur lower opportunity costs when they choose not to transfer their *hukou* to urban areas. Therefore, interaction terms between the rural homestead variable and the variables of age and labor contract coverage serve as proxies for the OCE.

Turning to the RE of homesteads, this mechanism comprises the absolute revenue effect (ARE), which can be defined as the absolute economic value of rural homesteads (e.g., the right to use, transfer or lease the homestead and the compensation when requisitioned), and the relative revenue effect (RRE), which is a product of relative changes in the revenue of rural homesteads attributable to characteristics of migrants' destination cities, while the absolute return on their homesteads remains unchanged [96]. Since its geographical location correlates, to some extent, with a homestead's absolute economic returns, the expectation is that the right to use a rural homestead will reduce the positive influence of non-village hometowns on *hukou* transfer intentions. In this case, the interaction terms between the rural homestead variable and the variable of the hometown location serve as the proxy variable for the ARE. On the other hand, larger cities with socioeconomic advantages over smaller locales are expected to lessen the relative revenue of homesteads, so the interaction terms between the rural homestead and city size variables serve as proxies for the RRE.

Lastly, the DE refers primarily to the direct impact of rural homesteads on *hukou* transfer intentions after controlling for the OCE and RE. In some cases, the DE of homesteads can be interpreted as the spiritual belongingness and basic material guarantee that they provide [95]. Controlling for the interaction terms for OCE and RE, then, the residual effect of the rural homestead variable can be considered equivalent to the DE.

The regression results from testing the three possible mechanisms behind the influence of rural homesteads in binary logistic models are reported in Table 4.9. These results provide evidence, in the first place, for the existence of the OCE (Model 3). Specifically, the odds ratio of the interaction term between the rural homestead variable and the age variable for the "unwilling" group compared with the "willing" group is 1.009, indicating that the access to a rural homestead strengthens the negative effect of age on rural–urban migrants' *hukou* transfer intentions. Rural homesteads also play a role in the relationship between the coverage of labor contract and *hukou* transfer intentions. By contrast, access to a rural homestead appears to weaken the positive effect of the coverage of labor contract on rural–urban migrants' *hukou* transfer intentions. As expected, these findings reveal differences in the opportunity costs of rural homesteads associated with migrants' age and labor contract status; specifically, relatively older migrants and those without a labor contract incur lower opportunity costs associated with their homesteads than younger migrants and those with a labor contract should they decide not to transfer their *hukou* to an urban area.

Table 4.9 Results of mechanism analysis

Variable	Unwilling versus Willing (Willing = reference group)					
	Model 3: Opportunity cost effect		Model 4: Revenue effect		Model 5: Direct effect	
	Odds ratio	Robust S. E.	Odds ratio	Robust S. E.	Odds ratio	Robust S. E.
Homestead (do not have = base)						
Have	0.958	0.141	1.528***	0.079	1.042	0.143
Homestead*Age	1.009***	0.004			1.009***	0.004
Homestead*Labor contract coverage	1.220***	0.081			1.248***	0.083
Homestead*Medium-sized city			0.813***	0.064	0.803***	0.064
Homestead*Large city			0.890	0.078	0.870	0.077
Homestead*Megacity			0.807*	0.096	0.770**	0.092
Homestead*Hometown location			1.222**	0.081	1.215**	0.121
Individual factors	Yes		Yes		Yes	
Migration factors	Yes		Yes		Yes	
Employment factors	Yes		Yes		Yes	
Economic factors	Yes		Yes		Yes	
Hometown factors	Yes		Yes		Yes	
Hometown-clustered standard error	Yes		Yes		Yes	
Constant	3.238***	0.516	2.253***	0.267	3.720***	0.742
Obs	28,981		28,981		28,981	
Pseudo R-square	0.060		0.060		0.060	

Notes: * $p < 0.1$, ** $p < 0.05$, *** $p < 0.01$

Second, the results provide evidence verifying the ARE of rural homesteads (Model 4). Absolute economic revenues from rural homesteads realized through (semi-permanent) use, transfer, rental, and expropriation are vital for out-migrants. The location of rural homesteads serves as a measure of the ARE. As shown in Table 4.9, the odds ratio of interaction terms between the homestead variable and the hometown location variable for the "unwilling" group compared with the "willing" group reaches 1.222, indicating, once more as expected, that rural homesteads decrease the positive impact of non-village hometowns on *hukou* transfer intentions.

Third, the results attest to the role played by the RRE as well (Model 4). The basic model shows a positive effect of city size on *hukou* transfer intentions (Model 1, Table 4.8), and the results reported in Table 4.9 further support the conclusion that access to a rural homestead strengthens the positive effect of city size on transfer intentions.

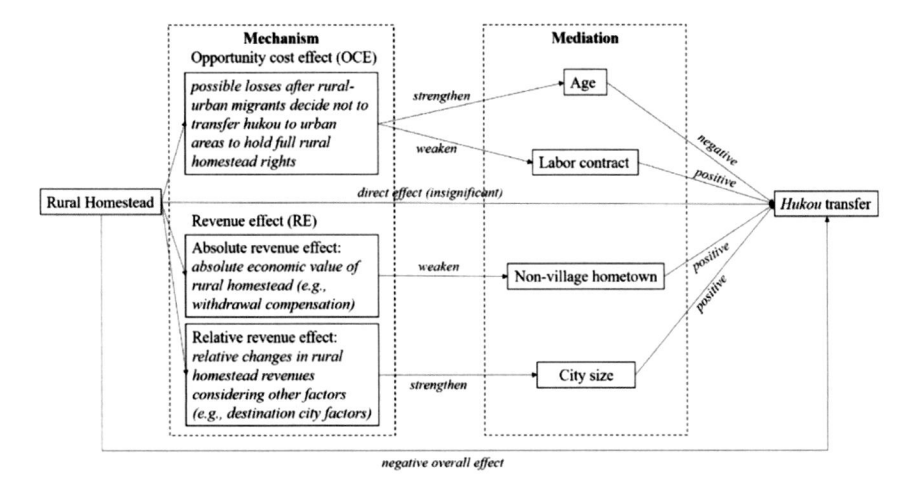

Fig. 4.5 Mechanisms of rural homesteads on the *hukou* transfer intentions of rural–urban migrants

Specifically, the odds ratio of the interaction term between the homestead variable and the variable of a medium-sized city for the "unwilling" group compared with the "willing" group is 0.813, and the corresponding odds ratio of the interaction term between the homestead variable and the variable of a megacity is 0.807. Economic resources and employment opportunities naturally tend to be concentrated in larger cities, which are destinations for rural–urban migrants seeking improved economic prospects. When the absolute revenues from rural homesteads remain unchanged, the relative revenues from these homesteads for migrants in larger cities decrease, with the result that the rural homesteads exert a weaker pull on them.

The results do not, however, provide evidence of the DE of rural homesteads (Model 5), for, after controlling for all possible influencing factors and the interaction terms for OCE and RE, the residual effect of rural homesteads on rural–urban migrants' *hukou* transfer intentions is insignificant. This finding suggests that access to a rural homestead primarily influences *hukou* transfer intentions through interaction with other factors (i.e., a mediating effect) and, again, exerts little in the way of a DE. In general, then, these findings point to the OCE and the RE as the two mechanisms behind the influence of rural homesteads on rural–urban migrants' *hukou* transfer intentions (Fig. 4.5).

4.3.5.4 Robustness Checks

As an indication of the robustness of previous findings, replacement of the key independent variable with the homestead area variable (Model 2, Table 4.8) yields results similar to those obtained with the basic logistic model (Model 1). This result supports the conclusion that access to rural homesteads weakens rural–urban migrants' *hukou* transfer intentions. In other words, the findings from the basic model are robust.

Second, to test the robustness of the analysis of the mechanisms, since the DE of homesteads is insignificant, our robustness checks shed light on the existence of the OCE and RE. We divide our samples into two groups based on their access to rural homesteads (i.e., whether or not they have such access), and the basic regression strategy is reapplied separately to the two sample sets. Note that the rural homestead variable is omitted from the two regressions. The results reported in Table 4.10 provide evidence for the OCE (Models 6 and 7). For migrants with a rural homestead, age increases the odds ratio for the "unwilling" group compared with the "willing" group by 1.007 times, while age has no impact on rural migrants without a rural homestead. Meanwhile, for migrants without a rural homestead, labor contract coverage weakens the odds ratio for the "unwilling" group compared with the "willing" group by 0.796 times. However, this effect is insignificant for migrants with a homestead. That is, access to a rural homestead strengthens the negative effect of age on *hukou* transfer intentions and weakens the positive effect of labor contract coverage.

Table 4.10 Robustness checks of mechanism analysis

Variable	Unwilling versus Willing (Willing = reference group)			
	Model 6: With a homestead		Model 7: With a homestead	
	Odds ratio	Robust S. E.	Odds ratio	Robust S. E.
Age	1.007***	0.002	0.996	0.004
Labor contract coverage (do not have = base)				
Have	0.950	0.038	0.796***	0.059
Destination city size (small city = base)				
Medium-sized city	0.860***	0.039	1.140*	0.084
Large city	0.534***	0.026	0.652***	0.054
Megacity	0.220***	0.013	0.287***	0.034
Hometown location (village = base)				
Non-village	0.866***	0.044	0.721***	0.062
Homestead variable	No		No	
Individual factors	Yes		Yes	
Migration factors	Yes		Yes	
Employment factors	Yes		Yes	
Economic factors	Yes		Yes	
Hometown factors	Yes		Yes	
Hometown-clustered standard error				
Constant	2.968***	0.370	3.959***	0.834
Obs	22,776		6205	
Pseudo R-square	0.057		0.059	

Our results also verify the RE of rural homesteads. A robust RE is indicated by different impacts of city size and hometown location on *hukou* transfer intentions when migrants with and without homesteads are compared. The results reported in Table 4.10 are consistent with those of the mechanism analysis (Table 4.9). Specifically, compared with migrants without access to a rural homestead, the odds ratios for those with such access are lower for all of the city size variables, indicating that access increases the positive effect of city size on *hukou* transfer intentions. In addition, the odds ratio for the hometown location variable is higher for those with a homestead than for those without. This result further reveals the weakening of the positive effect of non-village hometowns on *hukou* transfer intentions. Overall, then, these findings demonstrate the significance of the ARE and RRE.

4.3.6 Conclusions and Discussion

In China, access to a rural homestead can be a critical factor in decisions by rural–urban migrants regarding whether to transfer their *hukou* from a rural to an urban area. Due to limited data availability, few prior studies have examined the role of rural homesteads in the *hukou* transfer intentions of these migrants. The newly released nationwide CMDS data for 2017, however, make it possible to explore these issues in a systematic way. In general, results from the descriptive statistical analysis and the econometric models demonstrate that a significant relationship does indeed exist between access to a rural homestead and a migrant's *hukou* transfer intention. Specifically, rural–urban migrants with a rural homestead are less likely to transfer their *hukou*. Other significant factors in *hukou* transfer intentions identified here include individual characteristics, migration factors, economic conditions, employment opportunities, and hometown factors.

The results indicate that two mechanisms are responsible for the influence of rural homesteads on rural–urban migrants' *hukou* transfer intentions, the opportunity cost effect (OCE) and the revenue effect (RE). The OCE strengthens the negative effect of age on *hukou* transfer intentions but decreases the positive effect of labor contracts. The RE of rural homesteads comprises the absolute revenue effect (ARE) and the relative revenue effect (RRE). The former is reflected in weakening of the positive effect of migrants coming from non-village hometowns on *hukou* transfer intentions, and the latter is reflected in strengthening of the positive effect of city size on *hukou* transfer intentions. The results further suggest that rural homesteads have a mediating effect on *hukou* transfer rather than exert a direct effect on them.

The Chinese government considers it essential to promote urbanization [89, 107, 110]. The *hukou* transfer intentions of migrants is a key factor to be taken into account in the formulation of evidence-based population management policies intended to stimulate rural–urban migration and thereby accelerate regional urbanization. Rural–urban migrants weigh the advantages and disadvantages of transferring their *hukou* to destination cities when deciding where to settle [79, 84]. The findings presented here show that access to a rural homestead may influence these migrants' *hukou* transfer intentions, suggesting that policymakers should take measures to convince migrants to cede their rights to homesteads in rural areas [94, 96], such as offering financial compensation for migrant workers who voluntarily withdrawal from their homesteads and thus promote their *hukou* transfer intentions in destination cities. Also, the laws regarding the proper use of rural homesteads need to be enforced more vigorously and uniformly than has been the case.

Regarding other factors associated with *hukou* transfer intentions, to begin with, the governments in destination cities should work to provide more job opportunities for migrants who are willing to transfer their *hukou*. Housing subsidies could also help rural–urban migrants to support themselves in cities; in addition, high-quality public services, such as health care and schooling, are also clearly important to migrants. At the same time, in the places where these migrants originate, local governments should develop policies for those who return, such as encouraging them to settle in small and medium-sized cities in proximity to their hometowns.

The findings presented here, then, offer novel insights by modeling the mechanism of the influence of rural homesteads on rural–urban migrants' *hukou* transfer intentions. There is a need for further empirical research (e.g., multi-level modeling or longitudinal data analysis) that goes beyond individual-level, cross-sectional analysis. In addition, attention should be directed to specific areas of China in order to identify further aspects of the relationship between access to rural homesteads and *hukou* transfer intentions.

References

1. Department of Migrant Population, National Health and Family Planning Commission of the People's Republic of China (2017) Report on China's migrant population development. China Population Publishing House, Beijing (in Chinese)
2. Lewis WA (1954) Economic development with unlimited supplies of labour. Manch Sch 22(2):139–191
3. Todaro MP (1969) A model of labor migration and urban unemployment in less developed countries. Am Econ Rev 59(1):138–148
4. Todaro MP (1969) A model of labor migration and urban unemployment in less developed countries. Am Econ Rev (1):138–148 (in Chinese)
5. Stark O, Bloom DE (1985) The new economics of labor migration. Am Econ Rev 75(2):173–178
6. Lao X, Shen T, Gu H (2018) Prospect on China's urban system by 2020: evidence from the prediction based on internal migration network. Sustainability 10(3):654
7. Piore MJ (1979) Birds of passage: migrant labor and industrial societies. Cambridge University Press, Cambridge
8. Massey DS, España FG. The social process of international migration. Science 237(4816):733–738
9. Yue Z, Li S, Feldman MW, Du H (2010) Floating choices: a generational perspective on intentions of rural-urban migrants in China. Environ Plan A 42(3):545–562
10. Gu H, Xiao F, Shen T, Liu Z (2018) Spatial difference and influencing factors of settlement intention of urban floating population in China: evidence from the 2015 national migrant population dynamic monitoring survey. Econ Geogr 38(11):22–29 (in Chinese)
11. Liu Z, Wang Y, Chen S (2017) Does formal housing encourage settlement intention of rural migrants in Chinese cities? A structural equation model analysis. Urban Stud 54(8):1834–1850

12. Liu Y, Deng W, Song XQ et al (2017) Spatial pattern of interprovincial population migration from the comprehensive urbanization perspective. Scientia Geographica Sinica 37(8):1151–1158 (in Chinese)
13. Zheng S, Long F, Fan CC, Gu Y (2009) Urban villages in China: a 2008 survey of migrant settlements in Beijing. Eurasian Geogr Econ 50(4):425–446
14. Hu F, Xu Z, Chen Y (2011) Circular migration, or permanent stay? Evidence from China's rural-urban migration. China Econ Rev 22(1):64–74
15. Haug S (2008) Migration networks and migration decision-making. J Ethn Migr Stud 34(4):585–605
16. Goodkind D, West LA. China's floating population: definitions, data and recent findings. Urban Stud 39(12):2237–2250
17. Khoo SE, Hugo G, Mc Donald P (2008) Which skilled temporary migrants become permanent residents and why? Int Migr Rev 42(1):193–226
18. Gu H, Liu Z, Shen T, Meng X (2019) Modelling interprovincial migration in China from 1995 to 2015 based on an eigenvector spatial filtering negative binomial model. Popul Space Place 25(8):e2253
19. Lin L, Zhu Y (2016) Spatial variation and its determinants of migrants' hukou transfer intention of China's prefecture-and provincial-level cities: evidence from the 2012 national migrant population dynamic monitoring survey. Acta Geogr Sin 71(10):1696–1709
20. Lesage JP, Pace RK (2008) Spatial econometric modeling of origin-destination flows. J Reg Sci 48(5):941–967
21. Zhu Y, Lin LY (2016) Studies on the temporal processes of migration and their spatial effects in China: progress and prospect. Scientia Geographica Sinica 36(6):820–828 (in Chinese)
22. Griffith DA (2013) Spatial autocorrelation and spatial filtering: gaining understanding through theory and scientific visualization. Springer Science & Business Media, Berlin
23. Lian L (2016) An empirical study on the spatial effects in the migration. Popul Econ 2:30–39 (in Chinese)
24. Gu H, Qin X, Shen T (2019) Spatial variation of migrant population's return intention and its determinants in China's prefecture and provincial level cities. Geogr Res 38(8):1877–1890 (in Chinese)
25. National Bureau of Statistics of China (2018) 2017 migrant workers monitoring survey report. http://www.stats.gov.cn/tjsj/zxfb/201704/t20170428_1489334.html (in Chinese)
26. Cui NN, Feng CC, Song Y (2017) Spatial pattern of residential land parcels and determinants of residential land price in Beijing since 2004. Acta Geogr Sin 72(6):1049–1062 (in Chinese)
27. Zhao ZY, Yang R, Wei Y et al (2018) Quantitative estimation and spatial heterogeneity of the regression coefficient of the population flow gravity model in China. Scientia Geographica Sinica 38(9):1439–1448 (in Chinese)
28. Xu S, Deng Y, Wang KY (2016) Interprovincial migration model, spatial pattern and citizenization path of floating population in China. Scientia Geographica Sinica 36(11):1637–1642 (in Chinese)
29. Liu Y, Xu W (2017) Destination choices of permanent and temporary migrants in China, 1985–2005. Popul Space Place 23(1):e1963
30. Liu Z, Gu H (2020) Evolution characteristics of spatial concentration patterns of interprovincial population migration in China from 1985 to 2015. Appl Spat Anal Policy 13:375–391
31. Gu H, Meng X, Shen T, Cui N (2020) Spatial variation of the determinants of China's urban floating population's settlement intention. Acta Geogr Sin 75(2):240–254 (in Chinese)
32. Huang Y, Guo F, Cheng Z (2018) Market mechanisms and migrant settlement intentions in urban China. Asian Popul Stud 14(1):22–42
33. Huang X, Liu Y, Xue D, Li Z, Shi Z (2018) The effects of social ties on rural-urban migrants' intention to settle in cities in China. Cities 83:203–212
34. Chan KW (2009) The Chinese hukou system at 50. Eurasian Geogr Econ 50(2):197–221
35. Huang Y (2010) In: Urbanization, Hukou system and government land ownership: effects on rural migrant workers and on rural and urban Hukou residents. OECD Development Center, Paris, France

36. Liu Z (2005) Institution and inequality: the hukou system in China. J Comp Econ 33(1):133–157
37. Nielsen I, Smyth R, Liu Y (2011) The moderating effects of demographic factors and hukou status on the job satisfaction-subjective well-being relationship in urban China. Int J Hum Resour Manag 22(6):1333–1350
38. Whalley J, Zhang S (2004) Inequality change in China and (Hukou) labour mobility restrictions (No. w10683). National Bureau of Economic Research, Cambridge, MA
39. Zhu Y (2007) China's floating population and their settlement intention in the cities: beyond the Hukou reform. Habitat Int 31(1):65–76
40. Hao P, Tang S (2015) Floating or settling down: the effect of rural landholdings on the settlement intention of rural migrants in urban China. Environ Plan A 47(9):1979–1999
41. Jang S, Kim J (2018) Remedying food policy invisibility with spatial intersectionality: a case study in the Detroit Metropolitan Area. J Public Policy Mark 37(1):167–187
42. Kim J, Jang S, Kang S, Kim SJ (2020) Why are hotel room prices different? Exploring spatially varying relationships between room price and hotel attributes. J Bus Res 107:118–129
43. Tang S, Hao P (2018) Floaters, settlers, and returnees: settlement intention and hukou conversion of China's rural migrants. China Rev 18(1):11–34
44. Meng L, Zhao M (2018) Permanent and temporary rural-urban migration in China: evidence from field surveys. China Econ Rev 51:228–239
45. Liu Y, Deng W, Song X (2018) Influence factor analysis of migrants' settlement intention: considering the characteristic of city. Appl Geogr 96:130–140
46. Tang S, Feng J (2012) Understanding the settlement intentions of the floating population in the cities of Jiangsu Province, China. Asian Pacific Migr J 21(4):509–532
47. Tang S, Feng J (2015) Cohort differences in the urban settlement intentions of rural migrants: a case study in Jiangsu Province, China. Habitat Int 49:357–365
48. Tao L, Hui EC, Wong FK, Chen T (2015) Housing choices of migrant workers in China: beyond the Hukou perspective. Habitat Int 49:474–483
49. De Vroome T, van Tubergen F (2014) Settlement intentions of recently arrived immigrants and refugees in the Netherlands. J Immigr Refug Stud 12(1):47–66
50. Ette A, Heß B, Sauer L (2016) Tackling Germany's demographic skills shortage: permanent settlement intentions of the recent wave of labour migrants from non-European countries. J Int Migr Integr 17(2):429–448
51. Hosnedlova R (2017) Embedded settlement intentions: the case of Ukrainians in Madrid. Soc Netw 49:48–66
52. Khoo SE (2003) Sponsorship of relatives for migration and immigrant settlement intention. Int Migr 41(5):177–199
53. Gu H, Jie Y, Li Z, Shen T (2020) What drives migrants to settle in Chinese cities: a panel data analysis. Appl Spat Anal Policy
54. Fan CC (2011) Settlement intention and split households: findings from a survey of migrants in Beijing's urban villages. China Rev 11(2):11–41
55. You Z, Yang H, Fu M (2018) Settlement intention characteristics and determinants in floating populations in Chinese border cities. Sustain Cities Soc 39:476–486
56. Zhu Y, Chen W (2010) The settlement intention of China's floating population in the cities: recent changes and multifaceted individual-level determinants. Popul Space Place 16(4):253–267
57. Yang C, Xu W, Liu Y, Ning Y, Klein KK (2016) Staying in the countryside or moving to the city: the determinants of villagers' urban settlement intentions in China. China Rev 16(3):41–68
58. Chen J, Wang W (2019) Economic incentives and settlement intentions of rural migrants: evidence from China. J Urban Aff 41(3):372–389
59. Chen S, Liu Z (2016) What determines the settlement intention of rural migrants in China? Economic incentives versus sociocultural conditions. Habitat Int 58:42–50
60. Cao G, Li M, Ma Y, Tao R (2015) Self-employment and intention of permanent urban settlement: evidence from a survey of migrants in China's four major urbanising areas. Urban Stud 52(4):639–664

61. Tan S, Li Y, Song Y, Luo X, Zhou M, Zhang L, Kuang B (2017) Influence factors on settlement intention for floating population in urban area: a China study. Qual Quant 51(1):147–176
62. Guo J (2016) Influencing factors on the urban residence intention of floating population-based on the perspective of residence time. J Fujian Agric For Univ (Philos Soc Sci) 21(5):40–48
63. Guo M (2016) Residential difference and settlement intention: based on ordered logit model. Open J Bus Manag 4(3):513–518
64. Xie S, Chen J (2018) Beyond homeownership: housing conditions, housing support and rural migrant urban settlement intentions in China. Cities 78:76–86
65. Zhang H, Cao Y, Wang M (2015) The influence of social integration on the migrants' willingness of long-term residence in Guangzhou City. Northwest Population 36(1):7–11 (in Chinese)
66. Wei Z (2013) A region-specific comparative study of factors influencing the residing preference among migrant population in different areas: based on the dynamic monitoring & survey data on the migrant population in five cities of China. Popul Econ 4:12–20 (in Chinese)
67. Gu H, Meng X, Shen T, Wen L (2020) China's highly educated talents in 2015: patterns, determinants and spatial spillover effects. Appl Spat Anal Policy 13:631–648
68. Todaro MP (1980) Internal migration in developing countries: a survey. In: Easterlin RA (ed) Population and economic change in developing countries. University of Chicago Press, Chicago, IL, pp 361–402
69. Gordon M (1964) Assimilation in American life: the role of race, religion, and national origins. Oxford University Press, New York, NY, pp 26–52
70. Lee ES (1966) A theory of migration. Demography 3(1):47–57
71. Fotheringham AS, Yang W, Kang W (2017) Multiscale geographically weighted regression (MGWR). Ann Am Assoc Geogr 107(6):1247–1265
72. Fotheringham AS, Oshan TM (2016) Geographically weighted regression and multicollinearity: dispelling the myth. J Geogr Syst 18(4):303–329
73. Wang C, Zhang C (2017) Migrant children and rural-urban migrant's integration to the city. Sociol Study 32(2):199–224+245–246
74. Shen T, Yu H, Zhou L, Gu H, He H (2020) On hedonic price of second-hand houses in Beijing based on multi scale geographically weighted regression: scale law of spatial heterogeneity. Econ Geogr 40(3):75–83 (in Chinese)
75. Guo F, Iredale R (2015) Current trends, emerging issues and future perspectives. In: Iredale R, Guo F (eds) Handbook of Chinese migration, identity and well-being. Edward Elgar Publishing, Cheltenham, pp 297–318
76. Fan CC (2002) The elite, the natives, and the outsiders: migration and labor market segmentation in urban China. Ann Assoc Am Geogr 92(1):103–124
77. Fan CC (2007) China on the move: migration, the state, and the household. Routledge
78. Chan KW, Buckingham W (2008) Is China abolishing the hukou system? China Q 195:582–606
79. Gu H, Liu Z, Shen T (2020) Spatial pattern and determinants of migrant workers' interprovincial hukou transfer intention in China: evidence from a national migrant population dynamic monitoring survey in 2016. Popul Space Place 26(2):e2250
80. Fan CC (2005) Modeling interprovincial migration in China, 1985–2000. Eurasian Geogr Econ 46(3):165–184
81. Liu Z, Gu H (2019) Evolution characteristics of spatial concentration patterns of interprovincial population migration in China from 1985 to 2015. Appl Spat Anal Policy 1–17
82. National Bureau of Statistics (2018) 2017 migrant workers monitoring survey report
83. Liu T, Wang J (2019) Bringing city size in understanding the permanent settlement intention of rural-urban migrants in China. Popul Space Place e2295
84. Chen C, Fan CC (2016) China's hukou puzzle: why don't rural migrants want urban hukou? China Rev 16(3):9–39
85. Zhang L, Tao L (2012) Barriers to the acquisition of urban hukou in Chinese cities. Environ Plan A 44(12):2883–2900

86. Long H, Tu S, Ge D, Li T, Liu Y (2016) The allocation and management of critical resources in rural China under restructuring: problems and prospects. J Rural Stud 47:392–412
87. Pei X (2002) The contribution of collective landownership to China's economic transition and rural industrialization: a resource allocation model. Mod China 28(3):279–314
88. Liao H (2007) The stabilization and perfection of the collective ownership of the land in China's rural areas. Manag World 11:63–70
89. Long H, Liu Y, Hou X, Li T, Li Y (2014) Effects of land use transitions due to rapid urbanization on ecosystem services: implications for urban planning in the new developing area of China. Habitat Int 44:536–544
90. Tang S, Hao P, Huang X (2016) Land conversion and urban settlement intentions of the rural population in China: a case study of suburban Nanjing. Habitat Int 51:149–158
91. Tao R, Xu Z (2007) Urbanization, rural land system and social security for migrants in China. J Dev Stud 43(7):1301–1320
92. Li L (2008) The reform of the rural-urban dualism. J Peking Univ (Philos Soc Sci) 2:5–11
93. Huang Z, Wang P (2008) Farmland transfer and its impacts on the development of modern agriculture: status, problems and solutions. J Zhejiang Univ: Humanit Soc Sci 38(2):38–46
94. Yu W, Liu B, Song J (2016) A study on farmers' willingness to quit rural residential lands and its influencing factors. Geogr Res 35(3):551–560
95. Guan JH, Huang CX, Hu YG (2013) The affecting factors of farmers' willingness of rural residential land circulation based on logistic regression model under microscopic welfare perspective. Econ Geogr 33(8):128–133
96. Chen H, Zhao L, Zhao Z (2017) Influencing factors of farmers' willingness to withdraw from rural homesteads: a survey in Zhejiang, China. Land Use Policy 68:524–530
97. Liu Z, Wang Y (2014) Housing access, sense of attachment, and settlement intention of rural migrants in Chinese cities: findings from a twelve-city migrant survey. In: Housing inequality in Chinese cities, pp 123–138. Routledge
98. Gu H, Liu Z, Shen T (2019) Spatial pattern and determinants of migrant workers' interprovincial hukou transfer intention in China: evidence from a national migrant population dynamic monitoring survey in 2016. Popul Space Place 26(2):e2250
99. Li B (2006) Floating population or urban citizens? Status, social provision and circumstances of rural-urban migrants in China. Soc Policy Adm 40(2):174–195
100. Liu Y, Shen J (2017) Modelling skilled and less-skilled interregional migrations in China, 2000–2005. Popul Space Place 23(4):e2027
101. Shen J (2012) Changing patterns and determinants of interprovincial migration in China 1985–2000. Popul Space Place 18(3):384–402
102. Shen J (2017) Modelling interregional migration in China in 2005–2010: the roles of regional attributes and spatial interaction effects in modelling error. Popul Space Place 23(3):e2014
103. Huang X, He D, Liu Y, Xie S, Wang R, Shi Z (2020) The effects of health on the settlement intention of rural-urban migrants: evidence from eight Chinese cities. Appl Spat Anal Policy 1–19
104. Mohabir N, Jiang Y, Ma R (2017) Chinese floating migrants: rural-urban migrant labourers' intentions to stay or return. Habitat Int 60:101–110
105. Faggian A, McCann P (2009) Human capital, graduate migration and innovation in British regions. Camb J Econ 33(2):317–333
106. Li J (2016) Willingness of rural migrant workers to settle in cities and towns: a case study of sichuan province. On Econ Probl 7:65–69
107. Gu H, Shen T, Liu Z, Meng X (2019) Driving mechanism of interprovincial population migration flows in China based on spatial filtering. Acta Geogr Sin 74(2):222–237 (in Chinese)
108. Yang D (2016) A comparative study on settlement intention of the floating population in northeast China. Popul Res 38(5):34–44
109. Zuiker VS (1998) Hispanic self-employment in the southwest: rising above the threshold of poverty. Taylor & Francis
110. Li T, Long H, Liu Y, Tu S (2015) Multi-scale analysis of rural housing land transition under China's rapid urbanization: the case of Bohai Rim. Habitat Int 48:227–238

Chapter 5
Settlement Intentions of Floating Population

5.1 Settlement Intentions at the City Level

5.1.1 Introduction

Interregional population migration exerts enormous impacts on regional economic and social development [1–3]. In China, the household registration (*hukou*) system has restricted the free movement of people between regions since the 1950s [4]. According to the status of the *hukou* possession for migrants, scholars have divided China's migrants into two types: permanent migrants and temporary (floating) migrants [5–8]. Floating migrants represent those who have not obtained local urban *hukou* in destination cities despite staying for a stipulated period (e.g., 6 months), while permanent migrants refer to those who have stayed in destination places and have been granted with urban *hukou* [9]. Realizing that the *hukou* restrictions of regional migration had hindered regional economic development and prevented the progress of urbanization, the Chinese government has promoted the reform of the *hukou* system. Since the 1980s, limitations on interregional migration has gradually diminished, and China has witnessed a surge in the scale of rural–urban migration, providing sufficient labor force to industries in those developed regions, and thus, in turn, stimulating local economic development [9, 10]. In 2014, the Chinese government set forth "the National New Urbanization Plan (2014–2020)", enforcing further loose of *hukou* restrictions, promoting China's urbanization, and guiding more floating migrants to settle in cities (especially those small and medium-sized cities). The later formulated policy "the Key Tasks of New-Type Urbanization Construction" in 2019 claimed that the settlement restrictions for floating migrants in small and medium-sized cities should be fully liberalized shortly.

Local *hukou* of the city guarantees citizens' social rights and access to public services, and it is also regarded as a representation of social status for citizens [10, 11]. However, in most cases, floating migrants are not fully covered by the rights and benefits bound to local *hukou*. In contemporary China, the increasing size of the floating population in cities has caused a state of semi-urbanization, which leads to some problematic social issues, such as the over-occupation of urban public service resources and the crowding in the local job market [11]. Despite these social issues, China has been still witnessing massive volumes of the floating population in cities. By the end of 2017, the size of the floating migrants had reached 245 million, accounting for 17.6% of the total population [12]. However, China has been slowing down its pace in urbanization in recent years, reflecting the fact that a considerable number of migrants have returned home or migrated to other cities rather than settled in destination cities. With this regard, the research on the characteristics and drivers of the settlement of floating migrants in cities is of vital practical significance in China during the transition period.

In China, due to limited data availability, indicators measuring the migration tendency of floating migrants at the city level used to be relatively lacking. Since 2009, the access to some survey data of the floating population has enabled the research on related issues of floating migrants' migration behaviors. Numerous studies have been conducted on the urban settlement intention of floating migrants [13–19]. Although the settlement intention cannot fully represent the final migration decision [9], it measures possible settlement tendencies of migrants, which are determined by both external constraints of the city and subjective preferences of migrants [13, 15, 20]. Extant studies have tended to adopt a static cross-sectional approach providing novel insights into how the drivers shape the distribution pattern of the urban settlement of the floating population. Yet, changes in the influence of the determinants on the shifts in the spatial dynamics of the settlement intention over time have remained largely underexplored. Understanding these changes is of great significance in guiding evidence-based policies and regulations on the management of the urban floating population.

Drawing on China Migrants Dynamic Survey (CMDS) data, this study contributes to previous studies by using four-year city-level data of the urban settlement intention of floating migrants from 2014 to 2017. Several spatial data analyses are applied to elaborate on the spatial–temporal patterns of settlement intentions, and a fixed-effects panel model is employed to examine how these factors, including internal and external drivers, affect the spatial distribution of urban settlement intentions. The longitudinal data analysis widens our knowledge of the dynamics in the changes of settlement intentions over time and thus providing novel references for the policymakers.

5.1.2 Literature Review

Interregional migration is a complex decision-making process affected by multiple factors [21]. Classical theories have explained the motivations of migrants from the perspective of economic factors, such as the wage disparity [22], relocation of industries [23], and family utility maximization [24]. Another group of scholars, however, have given their attention to the supply of public goods and urban natural amenities [25–27]. Graves [26] argued that the city's wage income and the city's amenities were in a complementary relationship, with the sum as the urban rent. Glaeser et al. [25] further pointed out that urban amenities, including urban consumption levels, transportation, physical facilities, and public services, were positively related to urban immigration. Previous theories and empirical studies of interregional migration in western countries have provided references for the migration research in China on the role of economic factors, urban amenities, and institutional factors in shaping the migration pattern [3, 8, 28–32].

The unique *hukou* system in China has led to massive volumes of the floating population in cities, which has drawn much attention from policymakers, national and international firms, media, and academia [9]. Since 2009, supported by national or regional survey data of the floating population, a burgeoning body of literature has been conducted on depicting the subjective intentions of migration for floating migrants, including settlement intentions, *hukou* transfer intentions, and return intentions [9, 13, 14, 16, 18, 19, 28, 33–38]. Among existing studies, the settlement intention of floating migrants in cities has received widespread concerns. It is found that the internal motivations of the floating population are significantly associated with their settlement intentions in cities [18, 19]. Regarding individual and family factors of migrants, scholars discovered that younger and married migrants had a higher intention to settle in the city, so were those with more family members living together [18, 19, 35]. Economic conditions and migration factors are also found to have an impact on settlement intentions [39]. In general, migrants with a lower income level, a longer migration distance and shorter duration of staying are less willing to settle down. In addition, social factors including employment status, insurance coverage, etc. play a crucial part in the decision-making of migrants [14, 17, 40]. Researchers found that those with higher employment status, covered with insurance of employees or better integrated into the destination city were more possible to settle down.

Apart from internal drivers, external constraints of the destination city are also significantly related to the settlement intention of migrants, although these factors have received limited attention in earlier research. Gu et al. [13] and Lin and Zhu [15] examined the influence of characteristics of the destination city on settlement intentions. Prior studies have also focused on the impact of urban factors on the *hukou* transfer intention and return intention of urban floating migrants in China [9, 34]. Research has confirmed that urban economic factors predominantly affect the settlement intentions of floating migrants [36]. High wage levels, optimized industrial structures, and low unemployment rates of the city are found to enhance the floating population's settlement intentions [20, 41]. However, the existing literature has not arrived consistent conclusions on the impact of urban amenities (public services, air pollution, etc.). This may be related to the situation that urban residents' right to enjoy public services is largely bound to their *hukou* status [11].

Furthermore, the influencing factors of floating migrants' settlement intentions have differential characteristics in various regions of China [15, 20, 38, 41]. Using a Geographically Weighted Regression (GWR) method, Gu et al. [41] verified a spatially-varying effect of the urban factors on floating migrants' settlement intentions. Besides, it is found that the factors that affect settlement intentions are mutually influential and interrelated among neighboring regions, thus the settlement intentions may possess strong spatial autocorrelation across space [13]. Based on the CMDS data, Gu et al. [13] found strong and positive spatial autocorrelation in the spatial distribution of settlement intentions at the city level, and the spatial autocorrelation was mainly caused by unobservable factors (e.g., cross-regional policies). To sum up, research has partially demonstrated the characteristics of spatial heterogeneity and spatial autocorrelation in the distribution pattern of settlement intentions.

Several studies have compared the influence between internal and external drivers on the migration intentions of floating migrants. Gu et al. [13, 41] suggested that internal motivations are more influential than external constraints in the choice of the urban settlement of migrants. Other studies, however, argued that the urban settlement intention of the floating population is affected simultaneously by both individual factors and characteristics of the city [15, 20]. Overall, an increasing body of literature on the determinants of the urban settlement intention of migrants have begun to take into account the impact of the destination city. Yet, due to the data limitation, existing studies fail to model the determinants of settlement intentions using longitudinal city-level data,thus, their conclusions from cross sectional analysis are sometimes less rigor and robust. The study attempts to make up for existing research by employing a four-year longitudinal data analysis.

5.1.3 Conceptual Framework, Data, and Model Specification

5.1.3.1 Conceptual Framework

This study assumes that urban floating migrants' migration decisions depend on their migration utilities. The settlement intention in a city is defined as the proportion of floating migrants with settlement intentions in the city, which reflects the attractiveness of the city to floating migrants. The settlement intention of floating migrants is mainly determined by the internal motivations of the individuals and families, as well as the external constraints of the city [15, 20]. Following previous literature [13, 15, 20, 41], the twofold factors can be summarized explicitly into six categories: individual and family factors (I), migration characteristics (M), socioeconomic factors (S), urban economic factors (E), urban public service supply (P), and urban natural amenities (A). Then, the utility function for migrants in a particular city i at time t is expressed as: $U_{it} = U(I_{it}, M_{it}, S_{it}, E_{it}, P_{it}, A_{it})$. This framework also needs to controls time fixed-effects (T) and individual fixed-effects (C) to avoid the problem of potential missing variables. Given a particular city i and any other city j, the prerequisite for urban floating migrants to settle in the city i at time t is $U_{it} > U_{jt}$ for $\forall i \neq j$. This framework implies the assumption that internal motivations and external constraints jointly affect migrants' urban settlement intentions.

5.1.3.2 Research Data

The research units in the study are prefecture-level administrative units (hereafter, cities) in China, including prefecture-level cities, autonomous prefectures, and municipalities. Due to data availability, Hong Kong, Macau, and Taiwan are excluded. Cities are usually the primary formulation and implementation units of floating population and regional development policies, and thus floating migrants' settlement intentions are inevitably affected by external constraints of destination cities [13]. Considering the changes in China's administrative divisions and data sources over the years, the number of selected cities in our final dataset in 2014, 2015, 2016, and 2017 are 285, 297, 298, and 306, respectively.

Data used in this study are derived from the CMDS of 2014, 2015, 2016, and 2017, conducted by the National Health Commission of China. In CMDS datasets, a multi-stage stratified random sampling method with probability proportional to size is adopted to extract sampling points from target areas with a high concentration of floating population in 31 provincial units in China [42]. Respondents of the CMDS are migrants over 15 years old who have lived in their destinations for more than a month without being granted local urban *hukou*. Whether a migrant has the willingness to settle in the city depends on the answer to the question "Do you intend to stay here for five years or more in the future?". Migrants who answered "Yes" are defined as those who have settlement intentions, while those who answered "No" or "Not sure" are defined as those without the intention of urban settlement. The dependent variable used by us is the proportion of migrants who have settlement intentions in the total migrants in the city [13, 20]. By doing so, original micro-level data are aggregated to the city-level.

The econometric analysis in our study considers regional socioeconomic factors selected from the China City Statistical Yearbook of 2014, 2015, 2016, and 2017, which provide variables of Chinese cities in 2013, 2014, 2015, and 2016, respectively. The independent variables of the city lag the dependent variable by 1 year, which conduces to mitigate the endogeneity of reverse causality to some degree [43, 44]. Variables revealing characteristics of the floating population are derived from CMDS datasets from 2014 to 2017, where micro-level variables are aggregated to the city-level by average computation. The description and descriptive statistics of the variables are listed in Table 5.1.

5.1.3.3 Model Specification

Our model specification follows the logic of the conceptual framework. The individual and family factors include the average age (Age), marriage rate (Marry), and the number of family members living together (Family). Some previous studies show a negative relationship between age and settlement intentions [18, 19]. According to social network theory, family as a guarantee of individual survival shares the risks of employment and income for the individual, and thus we expect the effects of marriage

Table 5.1 Description and descriptive statistics of variables

Variable	Abbr	Exp	Mean	SD	Min	Med	Max	n
Dependent variable								
Settlement intention (%)	Int		62.186	20.093	0	63.720	100	1136
Internal drivers:								
Average age of urban floating migrants (years)	Age	NS	36.182	2.679	27.634	35.900	47.550	1103
Average marriage rate if urban floating migrants (%)	Marry	+	81.022	9.288	40	81.700	100	1103
Number of family members living together (persons)	Family	+	2.894	0.507	1.175	2.950	4.419	1107
Proportion of interprovincial floating migrants (%)	Dist	–	37.274	24.278	0	31.566	100	1103
Duration of stay (years)	Stay	+	5.434	2.070	1.325	5.090	21.100	1103
Coverage of basic medical insurance foe urban floating migrants (%)	Insure	+	13.344	11.563	0	10.526	59,330	1107
Ratio of the annual family income of floating migrants to the average annual wage of urban employees (%)	Income	+	1.422	0.605	0.582	1.351	17.036	1104
External drivers:								
Unemployment rate (%)	Unemp	–	5.328	3.479	0.298	4.779	35.901	1136
Average annual wage of employees (standardized with CPI, in log, yuan)	Wage	+	10.804	0.226	8.495	10.798	11.698	1133
Proportion of output value of the tertiary industry in GDP (%)	Tindus	+	39.635	9.037	16.440	38.640	80.230	1136
Proportion of employees in the education industry (%)	Edu	NS	4.992	6.548	0.233	3.292	73.042	1119
Per capita road area in a city (persons/km^2)	Road	NS	4.992	6.548	0.233	3.292	73.042	1119
Per capita fiscal expenditure (in log, 10,000 yuan)	Exp	NS	0.90	0.72	0.19	0.720	10.94	1136
Sulfur dioxide emissions (in log, tons)	Air	–	10.352	1.053	0.693	10.463	13.111	1116
Greening coverage rate in built-up areas in a city (%)	Green	+	39.111	7.724	1	40.396	95.250	1109

Notes: "+" denotes a positive expected effect, "−" denotes a negative expected effect, and NS means that the expected effect is not sure rate and the number of family members living together are positively correlated with migrants' settlement intentions.

The migration characteristics include the proportion of floating migrants across provinces (Dist) and the average duration of stay (Stay). Longer migration distance brings evident cultural differences and weaker senses of belonging, yet a longer stay duration may promote the social integration of migrants [45]. Therefore, it is expected that cross-province migration weakens the settlement intention, but the duration of stay positively correlates with the settlement intention. Socioeconomic factors include the coverage of basic medical insurance of urban floating migrants (Insure) and the ratio of the annual family income of floating migrants to the average annual wage of urban employees (Income), and we expect positive effects of both variables.

Urban economic factors are characterized by the urban unemployment rate (Unemp), the average annual wage of urban employees (Wage), and the proportion of tertiary industry output (Tindus). Since one of the motivations for floating migrants is to obtain more employment opportunities and higher economic incomes in the city, we expect the average annual wage of employees is positively related to the settlement intention, while the effect of the unemployment rate is the opposite. We also expect the estimates of the proportion of tertiary industry output to be positive.

The following three variables measure public service supply: per capita government annual expenditure on public services (Exp), proportion of employees in education-related industries (Edu), and per capita road area in the city (Road). In general, better public services provide more convenience for urban floating migrants; thus, the improvement of the supply of public services in a city increases migrants' willingness to stay. However, the *hukou* restrictions may prevent migrants from acquiring public services, thus, the expected effects of the public service variables are not very clear.

Not only that, this study considers the impacts of urban natural amenities on the settlement intention. They are measured by urban sulfur dioxide emissions (Air) and the urban greening rate in the built-up area (Green). The effect of the former is expected to be positive, while that of the latter is negative.

Considering the effects of external and internal drivers, we build a two-way fixed-effects panel model to investigate the factors affecting the settlement intention of floating migrants, with time fixed effects and individual fixed effects controlled. The model specification is as follows:

$$y_{i,t} = \alpha_0 + \alpha_1 I_{i,t} + \alpha_2 M_{i,t} + \alpha_3 S_{i,t} + \alpha_4 E_{i,t} + \alpha_5 P_{i,t}$$
$$+ \alpha_6 A_{i,t} + T_t + C_i + \varepsilon_{it} \tag{5.1}$$

where $y_{i,t}$ is the settlement intention of floating migrants in the city i at time t. $I_{i,t}$, $M_{i,t}$, $S_{i,t}$, $E_{i,t}$, $P_{i,t}$, and $A_{i,t}$ represent individual and family factors, migration characteristics, socioeconomic factors, urban economic factors, urban public service supply, and urban natural amenities of the city i at time t, with $\alpha_1 \ldots \alpha_6$ as corresponding coefficients. α_0 denotes the constant term. T_t and C_i refer to the time fixed and individual fixed effects. ε_{it} is the error term.

5.1.4   Settlement Intention of Floating Migrants in Chinese Cities

This section investigates spatial–temporal patterns of floating migrants' settlement intentions in Chinese cities. As shown in Fig. 5.1, we map the settlement intention of China's urban floating migrants from 2014 to 2017 in GIS software and classified the values by natural breaks criteria. The result illustrates a persistent pattern of high spatial heterogeneity of settlement intentions during the 4 years. Migrants in northern cities of China had higher inclinations to settle down, while those in southern cities had lower settlement intentions. Cities with higher settlement intentions were located primarily in the Shandong Peninsula, Northeast China, and Inner Mongolia, while southeastern cities had lower settlement intentions. It further indicates that cities with higher settlement intentions were not limited to those attractive megacities (e.g., Beijing and Shanghai) and second-tier emerging cities (e.g., Qingdao). However, quite a few small and medium-sized cities in the inland or remote region also appealed to a large percentage of floating migrants. This finding is consistent with the results of Liu et al. [20]. Not only less-competitive labor markets in these small and medium-sized cities but the formulation of favorable settlement policies have attracted more floating migrants in recent years.

Measures of inequality are employed to describe the degree of spatial unevenness in the distribution of settlement intentions. As reported in Table 5.2, results from the Gini index and coefficient of variation suggest that the degree of inequality of the spatial patterns of settlement intentions was relatively low between 2014 and 2017. Floating migrants had propensities to settle in a larger quantity of cities rather than to concentrate in a small set of developed cities, which is in part related to strict settlement policies in large cities in China. Besides, we examine positive spatial autocorrelation in the spatial patterns of settlement intentions. Results from the Moran's I reveal significant and positive spatial autocorrelation in the spatial patterns of settlement intentions during the 4 years, indicating that the settlement intention in a particular city was closely associated with that of the surrounding cities. This is partly on account of positive spatial dependence among factors influencing settlement intentions (e.g., agglomeration economies, cross-city social network, and mutually responsive regional development policies).

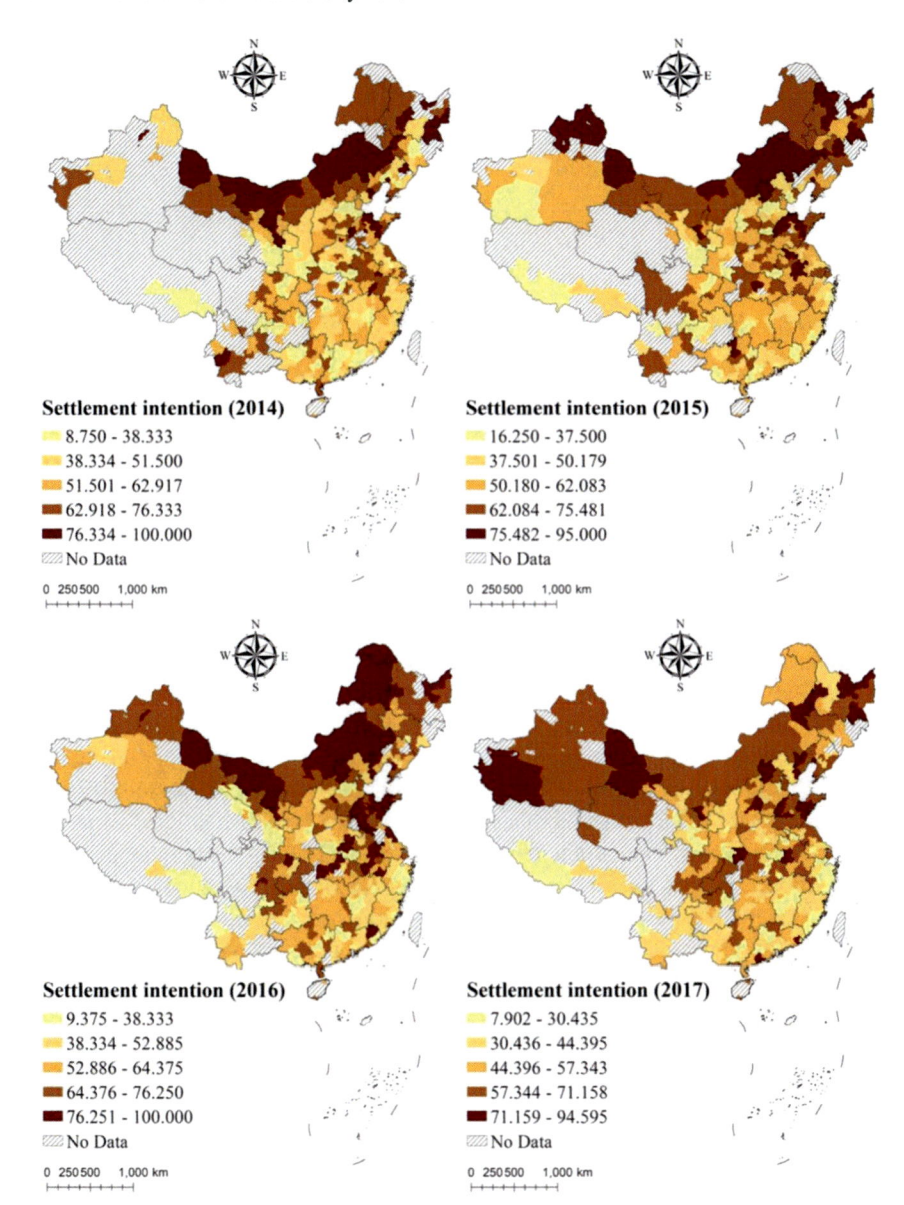

Fig. 5.1 Spatial–temporal patterns of urban settlement intentions from 2014 to 2017

Table 5.2 Results from measures of inequality spatial autocorrelation analysis

Year	Gini index	Coefficient of variation	Moran's I
2014	0.1719	0.3054	0.2192***
2015	0.1507	0.2697	0.2759***
2016	0.1655	0.2977	0.2321***
2017	0.1901	0.3365	0.2424***

*** $p < 0.01$, ** $p < 0.05$, * $p < 0.1$

5.1.5 Driving Forces of the Settlement Intention of Floating Migrants

5.1.5.1 Model Procession

This section begins with discussing the model processing in our study. Our independent variables are divided into two categories: external constraints and internal motivations. The standard error in our model is corrected by White heteroscedasticity to make the result more robust. Hausman test is conducted prior to the empirical analysis for the choice between a fixed-effects model and a random-effects model. Hausman test result shows that chi2 = 86.62, rejecting the null hypothesis that "independent variables are not related to random effects"; thus, the fixed-effects model is more appropriate to use in our case. Our regression strategy is to add independent variables of various aspects by step. Individual variables firstly enter the model (Model 1), followed by migration characteristic variables (Model 2), socioeconomic variables (Model 3), urban economic variables (Model 4), public service variables (Model 5), and urban natural amenity variables (Model 6). To further compare the effects of external and internal drivers, we construct Model 7, which only incorporates variables of the city. By using this regression strategy, we shed light on the effects of different influencing factors and test the robustness of the results (Table 5.3).

5.1.5.2 Results

Results from Model 1 indicate a negative relationship between the average age of migrants (Age) and their urban settlement intentions, but the coefficient is not significant. The estimates of the marriage rate (Marry) and the number of family members living together (Family) are significantly positive, which confirms the role of the family factors on floating migrants' settlement choices [46]. Stronger family nexus in destination cities reduces the risk of social integration and entering the local labor market for new migrants [14, 33].

Table 5.3 Results from regression model

Variable	(1) Intention	(2) Intention	(3) Intention	(4) Intention	(5) Intention	(6) Intention	(7) Intention
Age	−0.348 (0.292)	−0.552* (0.295)	−0.434 (0.292)	−0.347 (0.292)	−0.356 (0.273)	−0.341 (0.285)	−0.340 (0.287)
Marry	0.251*** (0.074)	0.284*** (0.071)	0.265*** (0.071)	0.270*** (0.072)	0.277*** (0.074)	0.293*** (0.076)	
Family	8.349*** (1.446)	7.431*** (1.311)	8.413*** (1.397)	7.460*** (1.463)	7.400*** (1.490)	7.210*** (1.489)	
Dist		−0.231*** (0.048)	−0.204***(0.049)	−0.230***(0.047)	−0.215*** (0.047)	−0.222*** (0.049)	
Stay		1.007** (0.395)	0.954** (0.398)	0.968** (0.382)	1.081*** (0.379)	1.075*** (0.389)	
Insure			0.210*** (0.050)	0.200*** (0.049)	0.190*** (0.050)	0.198*** (0.051)	
Income			−0.541 (1.211)	1.410 (1.376)	1.765 (1.355)	1.671 (1.376)	
Unemp				−0.463** (0.224)	−0.387* (0.230)	−0.392* (0.232)	
Wage				14.98** (7.301)	17.52** (7.173)	16.56** (7.210)	10.78** (4.212)
Tindus				−0.113 (0.168)	−0.086 (0.169)	−0.089 (0.174)	−0.092 (0.231)
Edu					0.414** (0.192)	0.478** (0.201)	0.362 (0.249)

(continued)

Table 5.3 (continued)

Variable	(1) Intention	(2) Intention	(3) Intention	(4) Intention	(5) Intention	(6) Intention	(7) Intention
Road					−0.074 (0.170)	0.034 (0.203)	−0.230 (0.282)
Exp					3.294 (3.593)	6.255* (3.387)	4.851 (7.939)
Air						−0.381 (0.906)	−1.270 (1.281)
Green						−0.028 (0.065)	0.034 (0.109)
Constant	27.29*** (9.314)	38.43*** (8.573)	30.72*** (9.007)	−125.4 (81.35)	−154.2* (79.98)	−139.1* (82.9)	−40.93 (51.54)
Time fixed effects	Yes	Yes	Yes	Yes	Yes	Yes	Yes
Individual fixed effects	Yes	Yes	Yes	Yes	Yes	Yes	Yes
Observations	1103	1103	1100	1100	1079	1046	1076
R-squared	0.627	0.647	0.654	0.661	0.665	0.647	0.445

Notes: Robust standard errors in parentheses, *** $p < 0.01$, ** $p < 0.05$, * $p < 0.1$

Model 2 incorporates migration factors. Results show that the proportion of inter-provincial migrants (Dist) has a significantly negative relationship with settlement intentions, while the duration of stay (Stay) negatively correlates with settlement intentions. Interprovincial migration usually has a long-distance movement compared with intra-provincial migration, which brings differences in living habits and cultures between origins and destinations [1, 2]. A closer migration distance implies similar socio-cultural conditions for migrants, which in turn increases their settlement intentions [14]. A long duration of staying also reflects better social integration for migrants, which enhances their settlement intentions [47]. It also illustrates an association relationship between average age (Age) and settlement intentions, whereas this relationship is not very robust across the models.

Socioeconomic factors are added in Model 3. The results indicate that a city with a higher percentage of floating migrants covered with employee medical insurance has a higher settlement intention. This finding confirms the effect of the social security system on migrants' settlement intentions, which is in line with some previous empirical studies (e.g., [41]). Also, we discover that there is no relationship between family income to urban wage ratio (Income) and their settlement intentions, which is against our expectations. A possible reason is that a large percentage of floating migrants move away from their hometowns to cities to earn money and improve their total family incomes by remittances. Once they achieve their income expectations, they will return to their hometowns [48].

Model 4 considers the effects of the urban economy. There is a significant negative relationship between the urban unemployment rate (Unemp) and settlement intentions, while the estimate of urban employees' average wage (Wage) is positive. A low unemployment rate reflects better employment security and a more stable job market in the city, which increases migrants' settlement intentions. However, not as expected, it is found that the estimate of the proportion of output value of the tertiary industry in a city (Tindus) is insignificant, implying that the industrial structure has no relationship with settlement intentions.

We further put variables of urban public services into the model. The results only confirm a significant relationship between the proportion of employees in the education industry (Edu) and the settlement intention in a city, which illustrates the role of a city's basic education resources. However, the coefficients of per capita road area in a city (Road) and per capita fiscal expenditure (Exp) are insignificant. This is partly because the public services in destination cities do not fully occupy floating migrants without local *hukou*.

Results from Model 6 reveals that there is an insignificant relationship between urban natural amenities and settlement intentions of floating migrants. Estimates of the Sulfur dioxide emissions of a city (Air) and the greening coverage rate in built-up areas (Green) fail to pass the significance test. The findings are not consistent with previous studies arguing that the improvement of urban amenities can appeal to more migrants [49, 50]. However, it is found that with the urban natural factors considered, the estimate of Exp becomes significant.

In Model 6, all variables are taken into consideration, and thus we can make a quantitative description of the influences of various factors. Generally speaking, floating migrants' settlement intentions are affected by both internal motivations (family connection, social integration, and social security) and external constraints (urban economy, education, and fiscal expenditure). Among the internal drivers, the family nexus and social integration of migrants significantly correlate with their settlement intentions. One more family member living together increases the settlement intention by 7.21%, and one more year of staying in destination cities promotes the settlement intention by 1.075%. As for the impact of medical insurance coverage, it is found that a 1% increase in the coverage rate of employee medical insurance increases the settlement intention by 0.198%. When it comes to external drivers, our results show the role of the urban economy. To be specific, a 1% increase in the average annual wage of urban employees triggers a 16.56% increase in the settlement intention of the city, while a 1% increase in the unemployment rate decreases the settlement intentions by 0.392%. The proportion of employees in education industries and per capita fiscal expenditure also play a role. Their coefficients reach 0.478 and 6.255, respectively.

Furthermore, we construct Model 7, which only incorporates the external factors, to investigate the relationship of external constraints and the settlement intention of floating migrants. By comparing the results between Model 7 and Model 3, we find that when external constraints are not controlled, the variables of internal drivers are still significant, whereas most of the variables of external drivers are insignificant when internal motivations are not included in the model. This implies that internal motivations are a prerequisite for external constraints to make a difference. This finding also echoes the conclusion in some previous literature arguing that urban factors play an less important role in China's urban floating population's settlement intention than individual characteristics [41] since benefits brought by the city may matter more for permanent residents who are granted urban *hukou* than the floating population.

5.1.6 Discussion

Our results have indicated a spatially differentiated pattern of floating migrants' settlement intentions during 2014–2017 where some small and medium-sized cities in several northern parts of China have higher settlement intentions. Interestingly, some cities with high settlement intentions are not limited to those megacities such as Beijing and Shanghai. The interpretation of this distribution pattern has a close relationship with the findings from the econometric models. Internal drivers are a prerequisite for external drivers in the decision-making of the choice of urban settlement for migrants. Family nexus, degree of social integration, and social security system coverage of the floating population are usually not affected by factors of destination cities. Yet, they may play a more crucial role in shaping the pattern of urban settlement intentions than external drivers. For example, cities in Northeast China may share similar cultural practices, thus lowers the cost of social integration of migrants originating from northeastern cities and enhances their willingness to settle down. Our finding of the distribution pattern of urban settlement intention is analogous with that of Liu et al. [20], but we provide evidence for the interpretation of the spatial pattern from the differences between internal and external drivers.

However, our results do not deny the role of urban factors. Yet, it is found that the economic conditions and public services in destination cities are closely associated with settlement intentions. In response to the future tendency of urban settlement for floating population, those small and medium-sized cities that have higher settlement intentions are suggested to consummate the employment market for floating migrants and provide sufficient employment and housing securities. Also, these cities need to develop their economies further, especially raise the income level of urban residents. For cities with a lower attraction to floating migrants, to promote their urbanization rates, they are suggested to focus more on the characteristics of the local floating population and strive to establish a closer family and social connections for floating migrants. In addition, local governments should provide better social security for these non-local migrants and ensure that they have equal rights to urban public services.

5.1.7   Conclusions

Due to data availability, previous literature primarily gives limited attention to the spatial pattern and determinants of floating migrants' settlement intentions in Chinese cities through longitudinal data analysis. The present study contributes to previous research by employing the city-level four-year panel data to assess the drivers of urban settlement of the floating population in 2014–2017. Our results have indicated a persistent and spatially differentiated pattern of urban settlement intentions of migrants where some small and medium-sized cities in several northern parts of China have higher values. There is positive spatial autocorrelation in the spatial patterns of settlement intentions, but the degree of inequality is relatively low.

Results from the fixed-effects panel model have indicated that the settlement intention of floating migrants is driven simultaneously by both internal motivations (family nexus, social integration degree, and social security) and external constraints (urban economy, education level, and fiscal expenditure). Among internal drivers, marriage rate, number of family members living together, duration of stay, and coverage of basic medical insurance are positively associated with floating migrants' settlement intentions, while the proportion of interprovincial floating migrants has a negative relationship with the settlement intentions. Among external drivers, the average annual wage of urban employees, per capital fiscal expenditure, and the proportion of employees in the education industry are positively related to floating migrants' settlement intentions, while the urban employment rate negatively correlates with urban settlement intentions. Further, we compare the effects of internal and external drivers. It reveals that internal motivations are a prerequisite for external constraints to play a role.

5.2   Network Characteristics of Intercity Settlement Intentions

5.2.1   Introduction

With the in-depth reform of China's *hukou* system and the gradual relaxing of restrictions on urban settlement, large-scale floating population have migrated among regions [28]. According to the Report on China's Floating Population Development 2018 released by the National Health Commission, by the end of 2015, the size of China's floating population had reached 247 million [51]. At the end of 2017, the size of China's floating population decreased to 244 million. On the one hand, the continuous decline in the size of the floating population reflects the citizenization process under the context of China's *hukou* system reform and the new urbanization policy; on the other hand, the large-scale floating population foreshadows that the future governance of the floating population is still a key challenge for cities in the transition period [9]. How to promote the reasonable *hukou* conversion of floating population has become an important task for the construction of new-type urbanization in the future. *The Key Tasks of New-type Urbanization Construction and Integrated Urban–Rural Development in 2020* states that it is necessary to promote the full abolition of restrictions on obtaining local *hukou* in cities with a permanent population of fewer than 3 million in urban areas, and the basic abolition of restrictions on obtaining local *hukou* for key groups in cities with a permanent population of more than 3 million in urban areas. Settlement intention is an indicator that reflects the tendency of the floating population to stay in the destination city for a long period of time. Settlement intention reflects the subjective feelings of individual migrants for long-term residence in the destination city, which is also influenced by various factors of the destination city, such as economic and social factors. It can provide an important reference for the future migration tendency of migrants [41]. The study on the settlement intention of the floating population is of great importance to the *hukou* system reform deepening and the urbanization quality improvement in China [9].

Population migration in China can be divided into two categories: temporary migration and permanent migration [6, 7]. Temporary migrants refer to the population that have worked and lived in the destination areas for a period of time but have not obtained local *hukou*, i.e., the floating population; permanent migrants refer to the population that have worked and lived in the destination areas and have obtained local *hukou* [52]. The imbalanced pattern of China's economic development resulted in a large number of floating population who cannot obtain local *hukou* and still choose to temporarily migrate to the destination city. So far, studies on population migration have mainly employed data from national censuses and sample surveys, and focused on the population that have migrated at the interprovincial level [1, 2, 28, 53, 54]. Since 2009, the National Health Commission has been conducting an annual national sampling survey (China Migrants Dynamic Survey, CMDS) on the floating population. The settlement intention of the floating population is an important indicator in the CMDS data and has received extensive research attention since its publication [13–15, 18, 20, 34, 36, 37, 41, 42, 55–57]. The personal characteristics, family features, and social-economic characteristics (such as housing and employment) of the floating population are closely related to their settlement intentions [13–15, 18, 20, 34, 36, 37, 41, 42, 55–57]. In general, floating populations with higher human capital and wage levels, lower costs of living, higher employment status, and stronger family and social network ties in the destination cities will have higher settlement intentions.

Geographical factors are a key part of influencing the settlement intention of the floating population [13, 15, 20, 34, 41, 42]. Gu et al. [13, 41], Lin and Zhu [15], and Liu et al. [20] investigated the spatial distribution of settlement intention and its influencing factors from the perspective of the destination cities. These studies showed that the external factors (city characteristics) had an important influence on the settlement intention of the floating population, and factors such as economic development levels, public service provision, the value of *hukou*, and employment opportunities of the destination city became key determinants in shaping settlement intention [15, 41]. In addition, the factors influencing the settlement intention produced spatial nonstationarity among cities [9].

In addition to the destination areas, it is also necessary to examine the interregional floating population's settlement intention from the perspective of the origin areas [34]. Gu et al. [34] constructed a *hukou* transfer intention network of the interprovincial floating population and found that the characteristics of the origin areas and the destination areas, and the characteristics of the floating population themself all affected their *hukou* transfer intentions. Gu et al. [42] further focused on the interprovincial *hukou* transfer intention network of the migrant workers. However, it is obviously difficult to finely portray the migration network only at the interprovincial level. Cities are precisely the main subjects to implement policies on floating population management and the main subjects to consider in the migration decision process of floating population [15]. In fact, even the data from decennial census and population sampling surveys in China cannot depict the population migration behaviors at the intercity level. In this sense, it is urgent to understand the intercity migration in China.

From the network perspective, a population migration network is often a complex network, reflecting certain complexity characteristics [58]. With the introduction of multi-source big data, more and more scholars use social network analysis method to investigate the population migration network in China [58–62]. To rectify the deficiencies of previous studies, this study uses the newly published data of China Migrants Dynamic Survey (CMDS) in 2017 to construct an intercity migration network, and employs geographic visualization and social network analysis methods to investigate the characteristics and spatial organization of intercity migration networks in China.

5.2.2 Research Design

5.2.2.1 Research Data

The data of this study from CMDS in 2017 consisted of 169,000 samples. The intercity network of the settlement intention of the floating population was constructed based on the information of the individuals including their destination cities and origin cities. The migrants who answered "Yes" to the question "Do you plan to stay in the destination city in the future?" were defined as those who had the settlement intention, while the migrants who answered "No" and "Undecided" were defined as those who did not have the settlement intention. The settlement intention flow between city i and city j was defined as the proportion of migrants who had the settlement intention among migrants from city i to city j. Referring to the existing literature [15, 34] and considering the representativeness of the sampling data, a threshold value of 10 was set to delete the settlement intention flows with the sample size smaller than 10. Finally, a total of 2209 intercity settlement intention flows involving 289 cities in China were obtained. Overall, the average settlement intention of intercity floating population in 2017 was 0.826.

5.2.2.2 Research Methodology

This study mainly investigates the network of settlement intention of floating population based on the social network analysis method, and uses Gephi software to calculate the in-migration degree, out-migration degree, total migration degree and net migration degree of each city node, as well as clustering coefficient and modularity in the network.

In-migration Degree, Out-migration Degree, Total Migration Degree and Net Migration Degree

For a weighted directed intercity settlement intention network, the in-migration degree of city node i characterizes the sum of the values of all settlement intention flows directing to city i, and the out-migration degree of city node i characterizes the sum of the values of all settlement intention flows from city i to other cities. The total migration degree is defined as the sum of the in-migration degree and the out-migration degree, and the net migration degree is defined as the difference between the in-migration degree and out-migration degree. The formulae are shown as follows:

$$Wd(i)_{in} = \sum_i w_{ji} \qquad (5.2)$$

$$Wd(i)_{out} = \sum_j w_{ij} \tag{5.3}$$

$$Wd(i)_t = Wd(i)_{in} + Wd(i)_{out} \tag{5.4}$$

$$Wd(i)_n = Wd(i)_{in} - Wd(i)_{out} \tag{5.5}$$

where w_{ji} is the settlement intention of city node j to city node i in the network; $Wd(i)_{in}$ is the in-migration degree of city node i; $Wd(i)_{out}$ is the out-migration degree of city node i; $Wd(i)_t$ is the total migration degree of city node i; and $Wd(i)_n$ is the net migration degree of city node i. The higher the total migration degree of a city node has, the greater the total influence it will have in the network.

Average Clustering Coefficient

The clustering coefficient is a measure of the aggregation degree used to describe the phenomenon of the aggregation of nodes into community in the complex network [59], while the average clustering coefficient characterizes the clustering of the whole network. The formula is as follows:

$$CC_i = \frac{1}{Wd(i)(d_i - 1)} \sum_{(j,k)} \frac{w_{ij} + w_{ik}}{2} a_{ij} a_{jk} a_{ik} \tag{5.6}$$

where CC_i is the clustering coefficient of city node i; $Wd(i)$ is the total migration degree of city node i; d_i is the degree of node i; w_{ij} and w_{ik} denote the weights of the edges between city nodes i and j and city nodes i and k, i.e., the intercity settlement intention of floating population; a_{ij}, a_{jk}, a_{ik} are the adjacency relations of nodes i, j, and k to each other in the network adjacency matrix, with the value of 1 representing adjacency, and the value of 0 signifying no adjacency. For the network as a whole, assuming that its total number of nodes (cities) is N, the expression of its average clustering coefficient is as follows:

$$\overline{CC} = \frac{1}{N} \sum CC_i \tag{5.7}$$

Modularity

In this study, the clusters in the intercity settlement intention network is identified by means of community modularity [63]. The modularity is employed to a detect a community by connecting the network nodes that are tightly linked to each other in the network. The process of dividing clusters is transformed into the process of solving the maximum modularity [64], which can be calculated as follows:

$$Q = \frac{1}{2m} \sum_{i,j} \left[w_{ij} - \frac{k_i k_j}{2m} \right] \delta(c_i, c_j) \qquad (5.8)$$

where Q is the modularity value; w_{ij} is the weight of the edge between cities i and j (settlement intention); k_i and k_j are the degree values of cities i and j in the unweighted network; c_i and c_j are the communities in which cities i and j are included; and $m = \frac{1}{2} \sum_{i,j} w_{ij}$ is the sum of all weights in the network. The Fast-unfolding algorithm is applied in the calculation of modularity in this study [65].

5.2.3 Analysis of Results

5.2.3.1 Analysis of Intercity Settlement Intention Network Characteristics

The intercity flows with settlement intention greater than 0.9 were extracted (a total of 694 settlement intention flows) and shown in Fig. 5.2. The high-value settlement intention flows were mainly from cities with relatively lower levels of economic development in the central, western and northeastern regions to the first-tier developed cities with higher administrative levels and larger population sizes. Cities in the eastern coastal region also presented a higher-value agglomeration pattern in terms of attractiveness to floating population. First-tier cities such as Beijing, Shanghai,

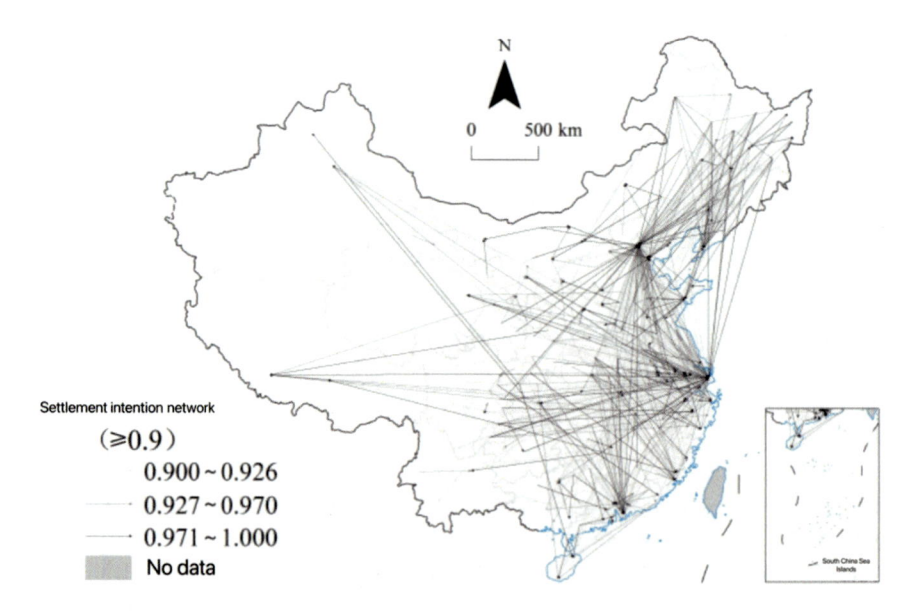

Fig. 5.2 Visualization of high-value settlement intention flows

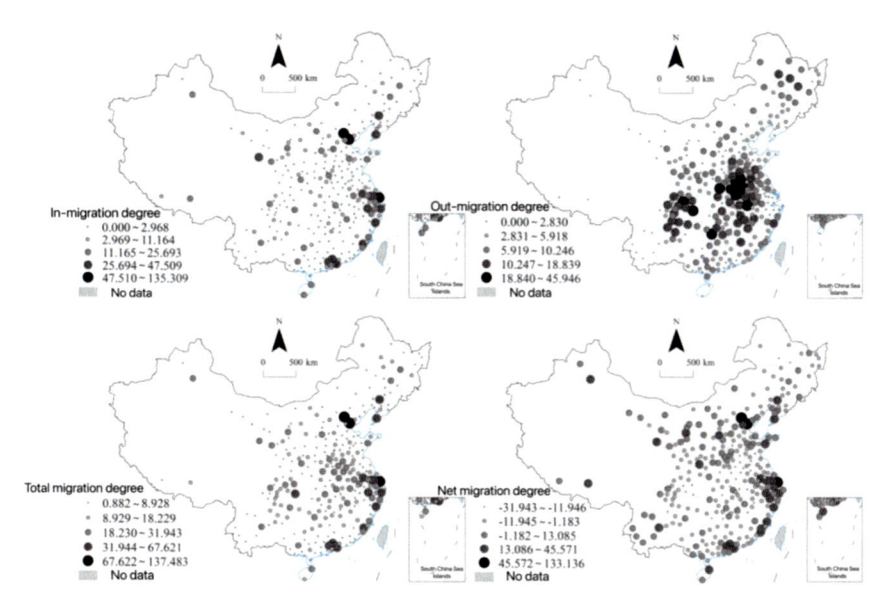

Fig. 5.3 Spatial patterns of in-migration degree, out-migration degree, total migration degree and net migration degree at the city level

Guangzhou, and Shenzhen had become the main destination areas with higher settlement intentions of floating population, and their radiation range was nationwide. In addition, some stronger linkages in settlement intention also occurred between cities geographically close to each other.

In order to explore the differences in the settlement intention of the emigrants and immigrants and the total migration degree of the settlement intention in each city, the in-migration degree, out-migration degree, total migration degree and net migration degree of each city node in the settlement intention network of the floating population were demonstrated in Fig. 5.3. First, the city nodes with higher in-migration degree were concentrated in the eastern coastal area, including the three major urban agglomerations of Beijing-Tianjin-Hebei, Yangtze River Delta and Pearl River Delta. At the same time, the cities in the urban agglomeration in the west coast of the Strait also presented a higher in-migration degree. The above-mentioned eastern coastal areas were extremely attractive to the floating population due to their higher economic development level, adequate supply of social public services, and greater *hukou* values. Comparatively speaking, the cities in the central, western, and northeastern regions had lower in-migration degree, with less attractiveness to the floating population.

The spatial pattern of out-migration degree was significantly different from the pattern of in-migration degree. As shown in Fig. 5.3, cities with high out-migration degrees were mainly concentrated in the central and western regions, covering provinces such as Henan, Hebei, Shandong, Hubei, Hunan, and Sichuan. Most of the cities with high out-migration degree had a large household registered population, while the local employment opportunities, wage levels and public services were relatively poor, so their emigrants had high settlement intention in the destination cities. In contrast, the out-migration degrees were relatively lower in the eastern coastal cities with higher levels of economic development.

The results of the spatial pattern of total migration degree demonstrated that the distribution of cities with higher total migration degree showed some consistency with the distribution of cities with higher in-migration degree, i.e., the total migration degree was higher in the developed eastern coastal regions such as Beijing-Tianjin-Hebei, Yangtze River Delta, and Pearl River Delta. This was mainly due to the fact that, although the out-migration degrees of these cities were not high, their extremely high in-migration degrees caused the high values of their total migration degrees. This result indicated that the advantage of attracting immigrants to settle down in the developed urban areas had outweighed the disadvantage of population outflows in the relatively underdeveloped urban areas.

Finally, the spatial pattern of the net migration degrees were revealed. The attractiveness of the eastern coastal urban agglomerations (including Beijing-Tianjin-Hebei, Yangtze River Delta, Pearl River Delta, West Coast of the Strait, and Circum-Bohai-Sea) to the floating population made them become the main destination areas of floating population; while most cities in the central, western, and northeastern regions were less attractive to the floating population, thus becoming the main origin areas of floating population.

5.2.3.2 The "Small-World" Feature of the Intercity Settlement Intention Network

Referring to the existing literature [64], a curve fitting analysis was conducted on the cumulative probability distribution of the weighted total degree of the intercity settlement intention network (Fig. 5.4). The goodness of fit of the power function ($R^2 = 0.847$) was better than that of the exponential function ($R^2 = 0.845$). This indicated that the intercity settlement intention network in China presented complex network characteristics as a whole. Since the goodness of fit of the power function was only slightly higher than that of the exponential function, it can be argued that the intercity settlement intention network was between a completely random network and a complex network, and had "small-world" characteristics [64]. In other words, in the intercity settlement intention network in China, a few city nodes had high total migration degrees and high positions in the intercity settlement intention network, while the total migration degrees of most other cities and their positions in the network were relatively low.

5.2.3.3 City Hierarchical Structure of Settlement Intention Network

The total migration degree of city nodes was stratified into five tiers using the natural breaks grading method. Among them, the Class I city nodes only included three cities,

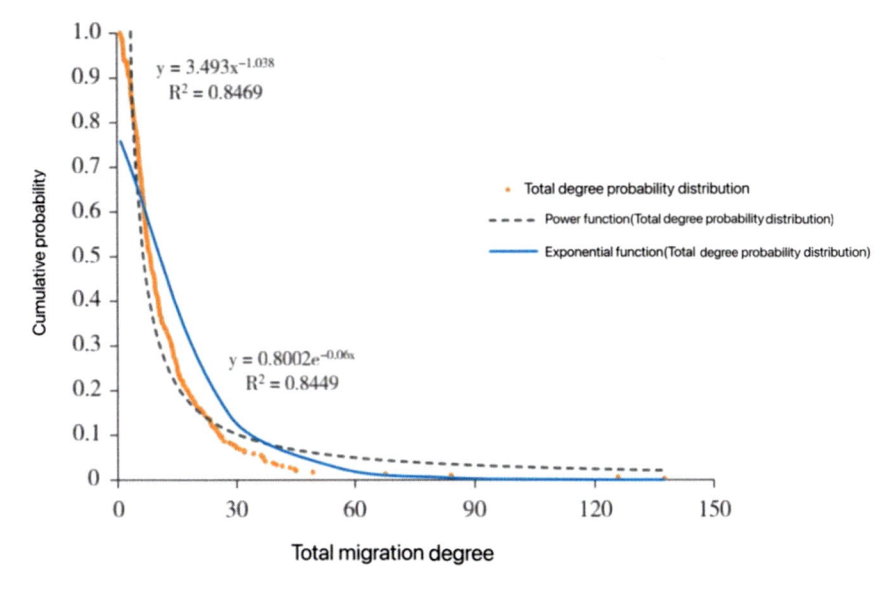

Fig. 5.4 Degree distribution of intercity settlement intention network

namely Shanghai, Beijing, and Tianjin. The floating population in these cities had very high settlement intentions, and those who had *hukou* of these cities and migrated to other cities also had certain settlement intentions in their destinations, so these three cities ranked the highest in the network. The Class II city nodes accounted for 6.92% of the total city nodes. Cities of this class can be divided into two categories, one was cities with high in-migration attractiveness and relatively low out-migration degree, such as Shenzhen, Hangzhou and Guangzhou; the other was main labor export cities in the central region, such as Zhoukou and Fuyang, whose emigrants had high settlement intentions in the destination cities, but its attractiveness to immigrants were relatively weak. The Class III city nodes consisted of ordinary provincial capital cities or second- and third-tier cities with relatively higher economic development levels in Central China, East China and Northwest China, such as Qingdao, Chengdu and Xiamen. These cities still had relatively higher positions in the network, with certain attractiveness to immigrants, while their emigrants also had higher settlement intentions in the destination cities. The Class IV city contained the largest number of cities, accounting for 48.79%, mainly ordinary prefecture-level cities in provinces in East China, North China, Central China and South China. The Class V city nodes accounted for 20.42%, on one hand, these cities were less attractive to immigrants due to their relatively lower levels of socio-economic development; on the one hand, their emigrants also had low settlement intentions at the destination cities (Table 5.4).

The above results indicated that only a few city nodes had a large network influence in China's intercity settlement intention network, while most city nodes had a

Table 5.4 Hierarchy of cities in the intercity settlement intention network

Network hierarchy	City
Class I city node (1.03%)	Shanghai, Beijing, Tianjin
Class II city node (6.92%)	Chongqing, Shenzhen, Hangzhou, Ningbo, Guangzhou, Dongguan, Quanzhou, Wenzhou, Dalian, Shenyang, Suzhou, Nanjing, Wuxi, Foshan, Zhoukou, Xining, Xi'an, Fuzhou, Harbin, Fuyang
Class III city node (22.84%)	Hefei, Qingdao, Anqing, Chengdu, Nanyang, Xiamen, Urumqi, Jinhua, Yinchuan, Nanchang, Nanchong, Bozhou, Shaoyang, Lanzhou, Shangqiu, Wuhan, Zhumadian, Taiyuan, Xinyang, Changzhou, Kunming, Changchun, Taizhou, Zhengzhou, Jiaxing, Jingzhou, Wuhu, Nanning, Haikou, Dazhou, Zunyi, Jinan, Lhasa, Langfang, Shangrao, Heze, Huanggang, Suihua, Xuzhou, Mianyang, Shijiazhuang, Zhongshan, Jiujiang, Yibin, Qiqihar, Shaoxing, Lu'an, Guang'an, Hohhot, Luzhou, Xiangyang, Yulin, Bengbu, Bijie, Changsha, Liuzhou, Hengyang, Luoyang, Suzhou, Sanya, Linyi, Yichun, Guiyang, Ganzhou, Handan, Xiaogan
Class IV city node (48.79%)	Loudi, Yantai, Zhaotong, Zhuzhou, Fuzhou, Nantong, Liupanshui, Neijiang, Xianyang, Yongzhou, Chuzhou, Suining, Putian, Yulin, Tongling, Huizhou, Datong, Pingdingshan, HulunBuir, Daqing, Kaifeng, Huainan, Tangshan, Xinxiang, Yueyang, Sanming, Jining, Ordos, Tongren, Ziyang, Pingliang, Anshan, Zigong, Huzhou, Mudanjiang, Bazhong, Huaihua, Zhongwei, Ji'an, Guilin, Changde, Baotou, Weinan, Taizhou, Jilin, Dezhou, Xuancheng, Jiangmen, Yichang, Chifeng, Ma'anshan, Jinzhong, Tianshui, Yangzhou, Yichun, Baicheng, Baoding, Xinzhou, Ulanqab, Wuzhong, Yingtan, Wuwei, Heihe, Anshun, Xuchang, Jingdezhen, Lishui, Anyang, Qingyang, Lianyungang, Tai'an, Maoming, Deyang, Zhanjiang, Songyuan, Yiyang, Guigang, Hezhou, Luliang, Panzhihua, Dingxi, Zaozhuang, Shizuishan, Guyuan, Yancheng, Shiyan, Wuzhou, Shigatse, Suqian, Yingkou, Suizhou, Xingtai, Qinzhou, Guangyuan, Qinhuangdao, Chenzhou, Huai'an, Qujing, Jixi, Bayannur, Yuncheng, Shantou, Meishan, Liaocheng, Zhangjiakou, Meizhou, Zibo, Xing'an League, Puyang, Tongliao, Shuozhou, Ankang, Jieyang, Linfen, Huaibei, Zhaoqing, Baiyin, Xiangtan, Chaoyang, Changzhi, Cangzhou, Leshan, Huludao, Rizhao, Jiamusi, Heyuan, Xilin Gol League, Tieling, Binzhou, Baoji, Weihai, Ningde, Chengde, Baise, Siping, Yan'an, Yunfu, Hanzhong, Shuangyashan, Xianning, Zhuhai
Class V city node (20.42%)	Alxa League, Hebi, Wuhai, Baishan, Baoshan, Beihai, Benxi, Yuxi, Dongying, Panjin, Chaozhou, Chizhou, Chongzuo, Fangchenggang, Dandong, Jiayuguan, Ezhou, Huangshi, Fuxin, Zhoushan, Lijiang, Pu'er, Hechi, Hegang, Hengshui, Lincang, Jinzhou, Huangshan, Jiaozuo, Jinchang, Jincheng, Yangquan, Jingmen, Longnan, Jiuquan, Laibin, Laiwu, Liaoyang, Liaoyuan, Longyan, Sanmenxia, Luohe, Ya'an, Karamay, Pingxiang, Qitaihe, Qingyuan, Quzhou, Shanwei, Shangluo, Shaoguan, Zhangjiajie, Tongchuan, Weifang, Yangjiang, Xinyu, Zhangye, Zhangzhou, Zhenjiang

small network influence. Municipalities directly under the central government, sub-provincial cities, cities specifically designated in the state plan and ordinary provincial capital cities, which had higher administrative levels and larger population sizes, exerted more influence in the network. In addition, the city nodes with greater network influence were mostly economically developed cities with high *hukou* values.

5.2.3.4 City Community Division of Intercity Settlement Intention Network

The intercity settlement intention network was divided into five communities in the Gephi software (Fig. 5.5). In general, after the community division, the intercity settlement intention linkages among cities within each community were closer, while the intercity settlement intention linkages among cities between the communities were relatively weaker. At the same time, the cities within each community often formed a spatial pattern with the central city as the core radiating to the surrounding cities. Most of the cities geographically adjacent to each other were divided into the same community, which to a certain extent indicated that the settlement intentions of floating population were still influenced by geographical frictions factors. According to the core cities within each community, the communities in the network can be

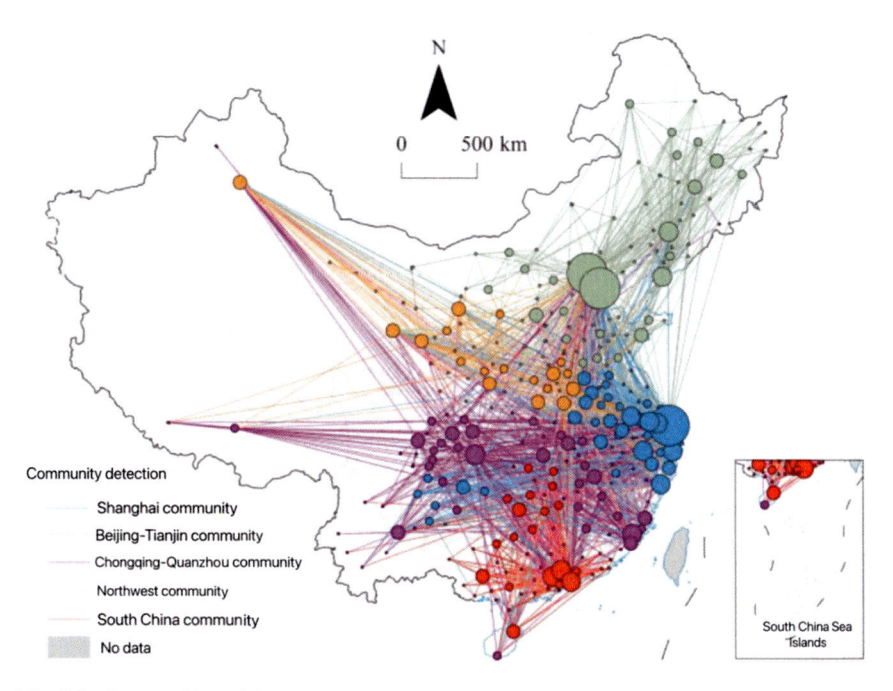

Fig. 5.5 Communities of the settlement intention network

defined as Shanghai community, Beijing-Tianjin community, Chongqing-Quanzhou community, South China community, and Northwest community.

Shanghai Community: Single-Core Structure

The Shanghai community was a typical single-core structure community, containing 55 city nodes and 382 edges of intercity settlement intentions. City nodes were mainly distributed in Jiangsu Province (e.g. Nanjing, Suzhou, Wuxi), Zhejiang Province (e.g. Hangzhou, Ningbo), Anhui Province (e.g. Hefei, Anqing, Tongling), and a few city nodes (e.g. Liupanshui, Tongren) in Guizhou Province. The hierarchical structure within this community was obvious, with Shanghai as the only core node of the community, whose total migration degree was much greater than the average total migration degree of the city nodes ranking 2nd to 10th within the community. Most city nodes within this community had network edge connections with Shanghai. Meanwhile, Nanjing, Wuxi, Suzhou, Hangzhou, Ningbo and Wenzhou, as the city nodes with the second largest influence within the community following Shanghai, had network connection edges covering almost all city nodes within the community. In contrast, cities located in Anhui and Guizhou Provinces were classified into this community as the origin areas of floating population, whose emigrants tended to stay in the Yangtze River Delta region.

The core area of the Shanghai community was mainly the Yangtze River Delta urban agglomeration, acting as the main destination area of the floating population within this community with relatively high settlement intention. This was partly due to the higher levels of socio-economic development, social inclusiveness and public service provision in the Yangtze River Delta urban agglomeration. Shanghai, as the central city of the Yangtze River Delta, had generated enormous attraction for the floating population.

Beijing-Tianjin Community: Dual-Core Structure

The coverage of the Beijing-Tianjin community included eight provinces (Beijing, Tianjin, Shandong, Hebei, Liaoning, Inner Mongolia, Jilin and Heilongjiang), and contained a total of 88 city nodes and 457 weighted directed edges. The two cores of the Beijing-Tianjin community were Beijing and Tianjin, whose total migration degrees in the network were much greater than the average total migration degree of the nodes ranking 3rd to 10th, and they had a greater network influence and higher position in the intercity settlement intention network. The network influence of Beijing was greater than that of Tianjin, with the weighted degree value of Beijing 51.2 higher than that of Tianjin. The weight of the settlement intention in the "Beijing-Tianjin" network edge was only 0.47, while that of the "Tianjin-Beijing" network edge was 0.97, which indicated that most of the floating population between the two core cities preferred to stay in Beijing. Most of the cities in Northeast China and North China were classified into the Beijing-Tianjin community as the main origin areas of the floating population, and their emigrants inclined to migrate to Beijing-Tianjin region for long-term settlement. In addition, Beijing and Tianjin' network edges covered the vast majority of nodes within this community, but there were still a few city nodes (Wuhai, Ordos, Weihai, Dongying, Laiwu, Yingkou, Liaoyang) that did not have edge connections with either Beijing or Tianjin. These cities were mainly nodes with low weighted degree values and low network positions, among which Dongying and Laiwu ranked as the first and the third from bottom respectively within the community.

Chongqing-Quanzhou Community: Dual-Core Structure

The Chongqing-Quanzhou community contained 61 city nodes and 251 weighted directed edges, and the nodes were located in 11 provinces, including Xinjiang, Tibet, Sichuan, Yunnan, Hainan, Guangdong, Fujian, Jilin, Jiangxi, Hubei, and Guizhou. There were some "outliers", such as Sanya, Baishan, Karamay, Lhasa, Shigatse, Zhuhai and Guiyang. Chongqing-Quanzhou community had a dual-core structure with Chongqing and Quanzhou as the two cores, and their total migration degree were much greater than the average total migration degree of the 3rd-10th nodes. The network influence of Chongqing was greater than that of Quanzhou. Specifically, the out-migration degree was greater in Chongqing and the in-migration degree was greater in Quanzhou, i.e., the emigrants from Chongqing had higher settlement intentions at the destination areas, while the immigrants in Quanzhou had higher settlement intentions. The cities of Chengdu and Fuzhou within the community were also regional central cities in the settlement intention network, but their total migration degrees were weaker compared to Chongqing and Quanzhou. The position of Quanzhou and Fuzhou in this community highlighted the attraction for floating population in the West Strait urban agglomeration. Though cities such as Chengdu and Chongqing were relatively developed cities in the western region, their emigrants still had a strong willingness to settle down in the destination areas. This reflected the increasing attractiveness of the coastal urban agglomerations for floating population. In general, cities in Hubei, Jiangxi and Sichuan Provinces were classified into the Chongqing-Quanzhou community as the main origin areas of floating population, and emigrants from this region tended to migrate to the eastern coastal region with high settlement intentions.

South China Community: Multi-core Structure

The city nodes of South China community were distributed in four provinces (Guangdong, Guangxi, Hunan and Hainan), and the community incorporated a total of 49 city nodes and 253 weighted directed edges. There are 4 core nodes in this community, namely Guangzhou, Shenzhen, Dongguan and Foshan, which were all concentrated in the Pearl River Delta. Guangdong Province, as an important economic province in China, provided a large number of employment opportunities and living services for the floating population, so it had played an irreplaceable role in accommodating the floating population. From the perspective of network influence, the total migration degrees of the 4 core nodes (Shenzhen, Guangzhou, Dongguan and Foshan) were 49.4, 43.6, 41.5 and 34.3 respectively, much greater than the average total migration degree of the nodes ranking 5th to 10th. Among the 4 core cities within the community, Shenzhen had the largest network influence, followed by Guangzhou and Dongguan, and finally Foshan. Each of the four core cities formed a intercity settlement intention network centered on their own, and the multi-core development trend of the whole community was remarkable. The deepening industrial division and cooperation, the local cultural style with distinctive characteristics in this region had become an important reason for the multi-core structure of South China community. At the same time, there existed differences in the coverages of core cities. For example, the network links of Shenzhen basically covered all the cities in Guangdong Province and the cities in southern Hunan Province such as Chenzhou, while the network links of Guangzhou even covered the cities in northern Hunan Province including Yueyang and Changde. The major cities in Hunan and Guangxi provinces were classified into South China community as the main origin areas of floating population, and their emigrants had high settlement intentions in Pearl River Delta.

Northwest Community: No-core Structure

The Northwest community can be defined as a no-core structure. The city nodes within this community were distributed in strips in Northwest and North China regions (including Xinjiang, Gansu, Shaanxi, Henan, Ningxia, and Qinghai Provinces). This community was composed of a total of 41 city nodes and 156 weighted directed edges. The cities within the Northwest community had similar levels of economic development, forming a certain degree of settlement intention linkages, without an obvious core city. The emigrants from this community had high settlement intentions in some destination cities, while the attractiveness of the cities within Northwest community to floating population was relatively weak. Zhoukou, Xining, and Xian were the three most influential city nodes within this community, and their total migration degrees ranked the top three (31.9, 31.9, and 30.7, respectively). Among them, Xining (in-migration degree = 31.0, out-migration degree = 0.9) and Xi'an (in-migration degree = 24.1, out-migration degree = 6.6) were the cities that were more attractive to the immigrants, while Zhoukou experienced a severe problem of population outflows and its emigrants had high settlement intentions at the destination cities.

5.2.4 Conclusion and Discussion

Based on the data of the China Migrants Dynamic Survey in 2017, this study constructs an intercity network of floating population's settlement intention, and explores the network characteristics and spatial organization of floating population's settlement intention at intercity level by means of geographic visualization analysis and social network analysis. The main findings of this study are demonstrated below: ① The high-value flows of settlement intention ware mainly from cities with relatively low levels of economic development to first-tier cities with high administrative levels and large population size; the in-migration degrees of settlement intention in cities in the urban agglomerations of Beijing-Tianjin-Hebei, Yangtze River Delta and Pearl River Delta were higher than those in other regions, while the central and western regions presented two agglomeration areas of out-migration degrees of settlement intention. ② The intercity settlement intention network showed the "small world" characteristic of a complex network; the city nodes assumed the hierarchical distribution characteristics, which can be classified into Class I city nodes, Class II city nodes, Class III city nodes, Class IV city nodes, and Class V city nodes. The economically developed cities with higher values of *hukou* had higher positions in the settlement intention network. ③ City nodes can be divided into five communities: Shanghai community (single-core structure), Beijing-Tianjin community (dual-core structure), Chongqing-Quanzhou community (dual-core structure), South China community (multi-core structure) and Northwest community (no-core structure). The settlement intention flows in Shanghai community were mainly from the central and western cities (in Anhui and Guizhou Provinces) to Shanghai and its surrounding cities in the Yangtze River Delta urban agglomeration; the settlement intention flows in Beijing-Tianjin community were mainly from the cities in Northeast and North China to Beijing and Tianjin; the settlement intention flows in Chongqing-Quanzhou community were mainly from the central and western cities (in Jiangxi and Sichuan Provinces) to Quanzhou and its surrounding cities in the urban agglomeration in the west coast of the strait; the settlement intention flows in South China community were mainly from the cities in Guangxi and Hunan Provinces to Shenzhen, Guangzhou, Dongguan and Foshan; the cities in Northwest community formed a certain degree of connections between each other without an obvious core city.

The findings of this study echo the findings of extant studies on interprovincial *hukou* transfer intention networks that floating population from economically underdeveloped regions tend to settle down in the first-tier developed cities in the eastern region [15, 28, 34, 43, 66, 67]. In the future, the floating population will be concentrated in a few megacities and megalopolises, providing a continuous supply of labor forces for these cities. In contrast, small and medium-sized cities in the underdeveloped regions are experiencing dilemma of labor force outflows, and there is still a long way to go to guide the floating population to realize the in situ urbanization and nearby urbanization. At the same time, the high difficulty of obtaining local *hukou* in megacities has created a new contradiction with the high intention of the floating population to stay in these cities. The floating population are trying to become "new citizens" by acquiring local *hukou* in these areas, however, the high threshold for obtaining local *hukou* makes it difficult for most of the floating population to settle down permanently.

Based on the above conclusions, we propose place-tailored policy recommendations for different cities: for small and medium-sized cities with labor force outflows, local governments should aim to reduce labor force outflows and enhance local urbanization, fully abolish restrictions on *hukou* obtainment, improve the labor market by providing adequate employment security and public services for both local and foreign labor forces, and raising the labor compensation level of local employment. At the same time, relevant housing and employment subsidies should be provided to high-skilled migrant labors to attract foreign talents to stay and settle down. For large cities with relatively high settlement attractiveness, restrictions on obtaining local *hukou* of key populations should be removed to attract floating population to settle down. For megacities with extremely high settlement attractiveness, the difficulties of working and settling down for the floating population should be properly handled, in order to make the floating population enjoy the equal social benefits with local residents.

The spatial pattern of urbanization in China should be further optimized from the perspective of urban agglomerations. The three major urban agglomerations, Beijing-Tianjin-Hebei, Yangtze River Delta and Pearl River Delta, present great advantages in attracting floating population. In addition, the urban agglomeration in the west coast of the strait, as an urban agglomeration that emerged in recent years, also shows a high attractiveness of floating population. The Chengdu-Chongqing urban agglomeration, with a rapid economic growth in recent years, still experiences a dilemma of population outflows with a lack of attractiveness for the immigrants. It has become a major task to take advantage of urban agglomerations to enhance the attractiveness for floating population in central and western cities. The Pearl River Delta urban agglomeration has formed a relatively balanced development pattern, with several cities showing strong attractiveness for floating population. The Yangtze River Delta and Beijing-Tianjin-Hebei urban agglomerations display an obvious structure of single-core and dual-core, respectively. For these two urban agglomerations, it is also a key issue for local governments to form a more balanced pattern of floating population distribution by reinforcing complementary advantages, and avoid a vicious competition for labor forces among cities.

5.3 Spatial Patterns and Influencing Factors of Settlement Intentions

5.3.1 Introduction

The settlement and migration intentions of floating population have been a hot topic of research in China in recent years. Based on the China Migrants Dynamic Survey (CMDS) conducted by National Health Commission, the floating population with settlement intention are defined as the floating population that have lived in the destination areas for more than one month, and intended to live here for a long time (more than 5 years). The floating population that do not intend or haven't decided to live in the destination area for a long time are considered floating population without settlement intention. Settlement intention is not an indicator of the final outcome of migration, but rather an indicator of the migration psychology. It is closely related to factors such as the tolerance of the city and the socio-cultural characteristics of floating population, and the systematic study on the settlement intention has important theoretical and practical implications for the improvement of urban governance and management.

Foreign literature has accumulated a large number of achivements in the research field of population migration, and the classical theories include labour market segmentation theory, social integration theory, the new labour migration economics and push–pull theory [15, 68, 69]. With the deepening of research, the issue of settlement intention of urban floating population has begun to appear in the foreign literature. For example, Wu [70] explored the realization of the relationship between neighbourhood ties, social participation and settlement intention among migrant workers in China and concluded that neighbourhood ties, neighbourhood stability and settlement intention were not directly related, possibly due to the institutional design that excluded social participation of floating population. Fan [33] focused on settlement intention of migrant workers in urban villages in Beijing, and found that most migrant workers did not have settlement intention, and that the number of family members accompanying them had a positive effect on their income, but did not significantly affect their settlement intention. Chen and Wang [71] found that the economic motivation had a facilitating effect on migrant workers' settlement intention, which was a marginal diminishing effect. Annell and Terman [72] analyzed the influencing mechanism of the place satisfaction on the settlement intention of creative urban groups (e.g. foreign students), on the premise that place attachment and social networks affect settlement intention.

In recent years, with the gradual opening of the application for data on floating population, domestic research on settlement intention of floating population has been flourishing, mainly including the following aspects: The first category is the studies on specific groups and specific regions with the largest number, covering the floating population born after 1990s [73, 74], the floating older population [75], the rural–urban floating population [76], the floating population in Guangzhou [77], the floating population in the border area [78], the migrant workers in Beijing [79], the rural–urban floating population in Beijing [80], etc. The second category is comparative studies based on regional differences, such as differences in the settlement intentions and their influencing factors among floating population in different cities and regions, including the comparisons among Suzhou and Zhongshan patterns, Chengdu and Zhengzhou patterns and Beijing pattern [38]. The third category is comparative studies based on group differences of floating population, including age and generation differences [81, 82], employment differences [83], economic income and social status differences [74], etc. Up to now, studies on the influencing factors on settlement intention of floating population have made some achievements, and most of them have been conducted from the micro perspective of individuals and families, while the differences in macro factors (such as economic, social and cultural factors) between cities have been comparatively under-researched.

At the city level, the settlement intentions of floating population are not homogeneous but spatially heterogeneous. In addition, as the multiple forces influencing settlement intention often show spatial spillover effects in neighbouring geographical locations, and the division or aggregation of spatial units often leads to errors in the spatial data, the settlement intention at the city level usually shows strong spatial autocorrelation. Previous research models have rarely examined the influencing factors of settlement intention of floating population from a spatial perspective, mostly using multiple linear regression models based on OLS estimation. However, there exists strong spatial autocorrelation in the model residuals, leading to biased model estimates.

Based on the current situation of existing research, this study employs spatial analysis and spatial autocorrelation analysis methods to describe the regional differences in settlement intention of China's floating population, and investigates the influencing factors on settlement intention and the spatial effects based on spatial econometric models, and try to answer the following questions: What is the spatial distribution pattern of settlement intention of China's urban floating population? How do characteristics of floating population and city-level factors affect settlement intention? Do spatial linkages have an impact on settlement intention of floating population? This study is expected to enrich the empirical research on settlement intention of floating population and provide scientific evidence for the *hukou* system reform and floating population management in various cities.

5.3.2 Research Data, Variable Selection and Research Methodology

5.3.2.1 Study Area and Data Sources

This study was conducted based on the data of China Migrants Dynamic Survey (CMDS) in 2015. The principles of data acquisition were as follows: sample points were drawn from destination areas of 31 provinces (autonomous regions and municipalities) and Xinjiang Production and Construction Corps in the mainland region of China where floating population were relatively concentrated, using a stratified, multi-stage and probability proportionate to size sampling method. A total of 206,000 valid samples were included in the data of 2015. By the end of 2015, there were 295 cities at prefecture level and above in mainland China, among which Fushun, Benxi, Fuxin, Chaoyang, Yichun, Laiwu, Sansha, Danzhou, Shangluo, Changdu, Linzhi and Hami were not included in the database, and Shigatse was not included in *China City Statistical Yearbook of 2016*. The final study area consists of 282 cities at prefecture level and above, except for the cities listed above. In addition, the intra-city migration component of floating population was not included in the valid sample for this study, resulting in a final sample size of 150,870. The explained variable is the ratio of the number of floating population with settlement intention in each city to the total floating population in each city.

5.3.2.2 Variable Selection and Pre-processing

Based on extant studies, this study refers to the classical migration theories, including Todaro's micro migration theory, labour market segmentation theory, new migration economics theory, and social integration theory [15, 69], and conducts preliminary screening of variables, which are divided into internal factors of floating population (including demographic variables, migration characteristics variables, social variables, economic variables, and family variables) and external factors of cities (including economic variables, social variables, and education level variables) [15]. The variables were further screened using stepwise regression, resulting in nine variables (Table 5.5). The variables related to internal factors of floating population were obtained from the CMDS database, and the variables related to the destination areas were gathered from *China City Statistical Yearbook of 2016*.

5.3.2.3 Research Methods

Trend Surface Analysis

This study uses the trend surface analysis method to measure the differentiation trends in the spatial pattern of settlement intention of China's urban floating population, which is calculated as follows:

$$Z_i(x_i, y_i) = T_i(x_i, y_i) + \varepsilon_i \tag{5.9}$$

where $Z_i(x_i, y_i)$ is the value of settlement intention of floating population in the ith city at the prefecture level, x_i and y_i are spatial coordinates of city i; $T_i(x_i, y_i)$ is the trend function, reflecting the changing trend of the settlement intention of floating population, which is considered to be caused by large-scale systematic factors; ε_i is the the random error of autocorrelation, which reflects the characteristics of local variations in settlement intention of floating population among cities and is considered to be caused by local factors and random factors [15]. In this study, the trend value is calculated using a second-order polynomial with the following formula:

$$T_i(x_i, y_i) = \beta_0 + \beta_1 x + \beta_2 y + \beta_3 x^2 + \beta_4 y^2 + \beta_5 x y \tag{5.10}$$

where β represents the estimated value of each term of the second-order polynomials estimated from the sample data; $T_i(x_i, y_i)$ is the same as the above equation.

Table 5.5 Descriptions and expected effects

Variable type		Variable name	Descriptions	Expected effects
Internal factors of floating population	Demographic variables	X_1	Proportion of unmarried floating population (%)	–
		X_2	Average number of accompanying family members (persons)	+
		X_3	Average number of children of floating population (persons)	+
	Migration characteristics variables	X_4	Average residence duration in destination areas (years)	+
		X_5	Proportion of interprovincial migration (%)	Unknown
	Economic variables	X_6	Average income from the last employment of floating population (100 thousand RMB)	+
		X_7	Average monthly household expenditure (100 thousand RMB)	+
External factors of destination cities	Economic variables	X_8	GDP per capita of destination areas (100 thousand RMB)	+
	Social variables	X_9	Employment Figure of the primary industry (10 thousand people)	+

Spatial Autocorrelation

The spatial autocorrelation is widespread in the spatial data. The Moran's I coefficient (MC) is a common measure to detect the spatial autocorrelation in data. The Global Moran's I (GMC) statistic can measure the spatial spillover effects among all spatial units, with the formula as:

$$GMC = \frac{n}{\sum_{i=1}^{n}\sum_{j=1}^{n} w_{ij}} \frac{\sum_{i=1}^{n}\sum_{j=1}^{n} w_{ij}z_i z_j}{\sum_{i=1}^{n} z_i^2} \qquad (5.11)$$

where z_i stands for the deviation of the expected average of attributes of element i, w_{ij} denotes the element (i, j) of the spatial weight matrix W; n sinifies the number of elements. The Global Moran's I is employed to detect whether there exists significant characteristics of spatial autocorrelation in the settlement intentions among the cities.

The Local Moran's I (LMC) can examine whether one spatial unit had spatial autocorrelation with other spatial units, with the formula as:

$$LMC_i = \frac{n(x_i - \overline{x})\sum_{i \neq i} w_{ij}(x_j - \overline{x})}{\sum_i (x_i - \overline{x})^2} \qquad (5.12)$$

where $\overline{x}$ is the average of the observations, and the other parameters are the same with the above formula. The Local Moran's I is employed to analyze the spatial agglomeration pattern of settlement intentions in each spatial unit.

Spatial Econometric Models

As shown in Eq. (5.13), classical linear regression models mainly use least squares regression (OLS). For spatial data with strong spatial autocorrelation (and often positive), the results obtained from traditional OLS regressions are biased. In order to better explain spatial dependence and spatial spillover in spatial data, spatial econometrics emerge as the times require [84]. The spatial lag model (SLM) and the spatial error model (SEM) are currently the most commonly used regression models in spatial econometrics, where the spatial lag model incorporates into the spatially lagged term of the explained variable to characterize the its spatial spillover effects. In other words, the dependent variable of a spatial unit depends on the dependent variables of its surrounding spatial units, expressed as in Eq. (5.14); the spatial error model, on the other hand, deals with the spatial dependence effect by adding a spatial autocorrelation setting for the error term, and the unobservable presence of spatial autocorrelation affecting the explained variable is present in the model, expressed as in Eq. (5.15) [85, 86].

$$\mathbf{y} = \mathbf{X}\boldsymbol{\beta} + \boldsymbol{\varepsilon}, \boldsymbol{\varepsilon} \sim (\mathbf{0}, \sigma^2 \mathbf{I_n}) \qquad (5.13)$$

$$\mathbf{y} = \mathbf{pW_y} + \mathbf{X}\boldsymbol{\beta} + \boldsymbol{\varepsilon}, \boldsymbol{\varepsilon} \sim (\mathbf{0}, \sigma^2 \mathbf{I_n}) \qquad (5.14)$$

$$\mathbf{y} = \mathbf{X}\boldsymbol{\beta} + \boldsymbol{\epsilon}, \boldsymbol{\epsilon} = \lambda\mathbf{W}\boldsymbol{\varepsilon} + \boldsymbol{\mu}, \boldsymbol{\varepsilon} \sim (\mathbf{0}, \sigma^2 \mathbf{I_n}) \qquad (5.15)$$

where the dependent variable y is an n × 1 vector; the independent variable X is an n × k data matrix; the regression coefficient β is a k × 1 vector; the independently identically distributed random error term ε is an $n \times 1$ vector; W is the spatial weight matrix; λ and ρ are the spatial regression coefficients. In this study, spatial econometric models are used to analyze the influencing factors of settlement intention of floating population and explore which factors have spatial spillover effects.

5.3.3 Spatial Aucorrelation Analysis of Settlement Intentions of Floating Population

5.3.3.1 Spatial Distribution Characteristics of Settlement Intention of Floating Population

The spatial distribution characteristics of settlement intention of China's floating population are shown in Figs. 5.6 and 5.7.

Figure 5.6 reflected the spatial distribution characteristics of floating population's settlement intention in China. Figure 5.7 showed the results of the trend surface analysis. In Fig. 5.7, the black points are the sample points, and the length of the grey line indicates the intensity of floating population's settlement intention in each city; the purple points are the projection of the sample points on the XZ plane, and the red

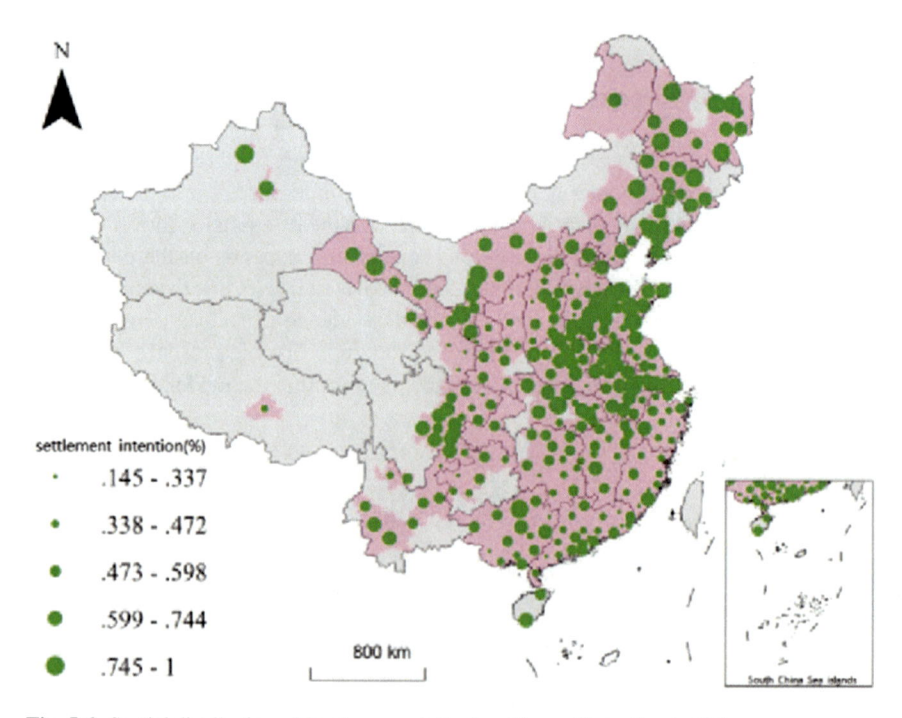

Fig. 5.6 Spatial distribution of floating population's settlement intention in China

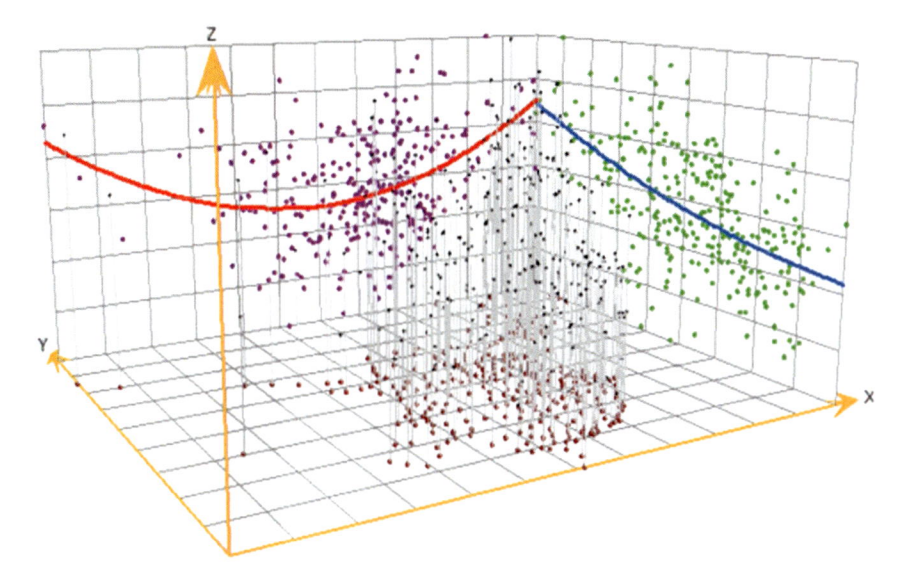

Fig. 5.7   Result of trend surface analysis

curve shows the distribution trend of the purple points in the east–west direction; the green points are the projection of the sample points on the YZ plane, and the blue curve displays the distribution trend of the green points in the north–south direction. In general, the spatial distribution of floating population's settlement intention in China generally showed a gradual increase from south to north, while the east–west direction presented a "U" shaped trend of decreasing first and increasing later from west to east. There were 104 cities with settlement intention less than 0.5, and 178 cities with settlement intention greater than or equal to 0.5. This demonstrated that there was a general trend of population migration in China, but there also existed a trend of return migration and continued migration in some cities, mainly concentrated in the south. The top ten cities in terms of settlement intention were Suihua (Heilongjiang), Rizhao (Shandong), Suzhou (Anhui), Dongying (Shandong), Tongliao (Inner Mongolia), Zhongwei (Ningxia), Panjin (Liaoning), Jiamusi (Heilongjiang), Liaocheng (Shandong) and Wuhai (Inner Mongolia), all of which are located in the northern part of China.

5.3.3.2   Spatial Autocorrelation Analysis

Floating population's settlement intention in cities at the prefecture level and above in 2015 presented significant agglomeration characteristics, with strong spatial autocorrelation and spatial dependence effects, and there existed significant spatial effects in settlement intention of each geographical unit. The GMC value of spatial autocorrelation reached 0.34 (significant at the 0.01 level), indicating that floating population's

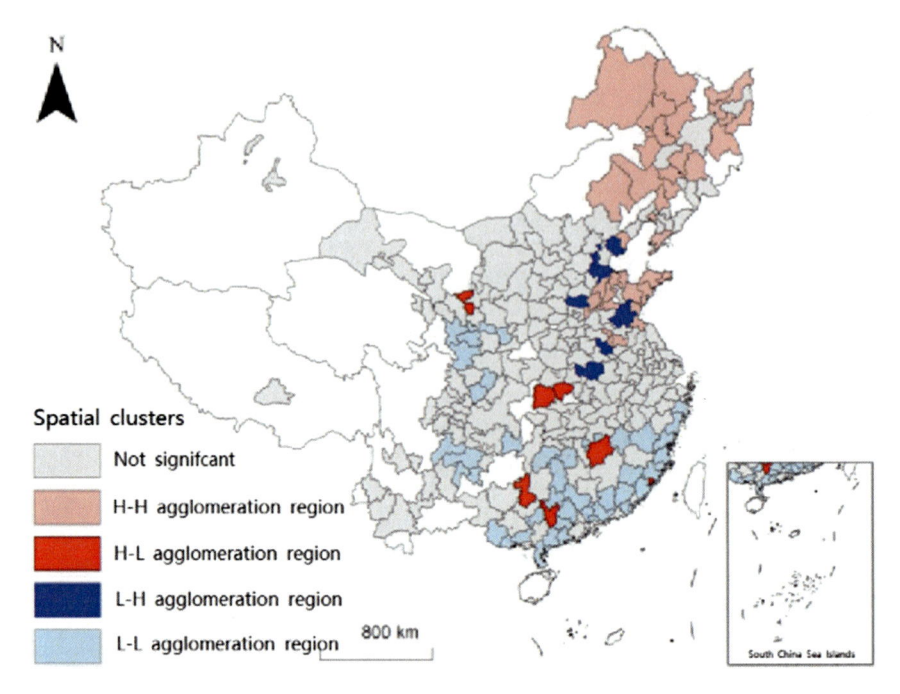

Fig. 5.8 Spatial clustering result of settlement intention of floating population in China

settlement intention among cities had the characteristics of spatial dependence, and that floating population's settlement intention in one city had a spatial spillover effect, i.e., exerting a certain influence on the surrounding cities. In addition, we further calculated the LMC of all cities, in order to analyze the clustering pattern of floating population's settlement intention among cities. As shown in Fig. 5.8 cities showed an "H-H" agglomeration pattern, mainly in the northeast region and the Shandong Peninsula, where the floating population's settlement intention in a city was high, and its counterparts in neighbouring cities were also high, thus forming a high-value agglomeration of floating population's settlement intention; seven cities assumed the "H-L" agglomeration pattern, including Zhongwei, Yichang, Jingmen, Liuzhou, Ji'an, Wuzhou and Xiamen. These cities had a high settlement intention, while their neighbouring cities had a low settlement intention, so these cities were attractive to floating population in neighbouring cities. Eight cities, including Xinyang, Zaozhuang, Linyi, Handan, Cangzhou and Langfang, showed an "L-H" agglomeration pattern, with its low settlement intention surrounded by high settlement intentions in the surrounding cities. For this type of cities, efforts should be made to increase floating population's settlement intention through improving social security and other measures, so as to prevent them from migrating to neighbouring cities. Finally, most of the southeastern coastal cities and a small number of central and western cities were located in a "L-L" agglomeration area, i.e., their low settlement intentions were surrounded by low settlement intentions in the surrounding cities. In the case of central and western cities, the reason for this phenomenon was their relatively low level of economic and social development and poor infrastructure development. For southeastern coastal cities with a larger floating population, the rising cost of living and the increasing "urban diseases" such as traffic congestion were often the causes for the relatively low settlement intention of floating population.

5.3.4 Spatial Econometric Analysis of Settlement Intentions of Floating Population

5.3.4.1 Selection and Estimation of Spatial Econometric Models

To address the issue of possible multicollinearity among variables, this study employed forward stepwise regression for variable screening, followed by establishing a classical linear regression model and a spatial econometric model, and conducting a comparison between them. The spatial econometric model faces two alternative choices: a spatial error model (SEM) and a spatial lag model (SEM), so a non-spatial econometric model is needed to identify potential spatial effects. Table 5.6 reported the tests of spatial autocorrelation: the test statistic of MC couldn't reject the null hypothesis at the 1% level, but the MC test was not decisive for model selection [87]. The Lagrange Multiplier (lag) and the Lagrange Multiplier (error) in the LM test rejected the null hypothesis at the 10% and 1% significance levels respectively. In the Robust forms of the LM test statistics, only Robust LM (error) was significant at the 1% level. The SMAMA test was then used to identify the spatially lagged dependent variable with the error dependence [88], which was significant at the 1% level. In summary, spatial lag effects coexisted with spatial error effects, and the settlement intention of floating population in a city was jointly determined by this city and its neighbouring cities. At the same time, unobservable shocks such as population policy changes had spatial transmissibility.

All the three models in Table 5.7 passed the BP test, indicating that the models followed the assumption of homoscedasticity. Among the three models of OLS, SLM and SEM, most of the test values for SEM were better compared to OLS and SLM, hence SEM was preferable for estimation, which controls for spatial variables.

Table 5.6 The spatial correlation test on the rook spatial weight matrix

TEST	VALUE	PROB
Moran's I (error)	3.812	0.000
Lagrange Multiplier (lag)	3.772	0.052
Robust LM (lag)	0.000	0.985
Lagrange Multiplier (error)	11.875	0.001
Robust LM (error)	8.104	0.004
Lagrange Multiplier (SARMA)	11.876	0.003

Table 5.7 The regression models based on the rook spatial weight matrix

	OLS	SLM	SEM
X_1	-0.198^{***}	-0.183^{***}	-0.191^{***}
X_2	0.073^{***}	0.075^{***}	0.075^{***}
X_3	0.289^{***}	0.266^{***}	0.267^{***}
X_4	0.020^{***}	0.018^{***}	0.019^{***}
X_5	0.088^{***}	0.089^{***}	0.077^{***}
X_6	-0.366^{***}	-0.337^{***}	-0.358^{***}
X_7	0.007^{***}	0.007^{***}	0.006^{***}
X_8	-1.754^{***}	1.740^{***}	-1.871^{***}
X_9	3.503^{***}	3.661^{***}	4.113^{***}
CONSTANT	0.127	0.077	0.129
ρ		0.092^{*}	
λ			0.281^{***}
R^2	0.588	0.594	0.612
Log Likelihood	252.225	254.066	257.964
AIC	-484.451	-486.132	-495.927
SC	-448.032	-446.071	-459.508
Breusch-Pagan	12.176	11.4068	14.444
Likelihood Ratio		3.681^{*}	11.476^{***}
N	282	282	282

Notes: *, **, *** indicate the 10%, 5%, 1% significance levels (two-sided),respectively.

Specifically, the AIC and SC values of SEM were smaller compared with OLS and more varied than SLM. Meanwhile, SEM passed the spatial autocorrelation coefficient test, the Log Likelihood of SEM increased from 252.225 to 257.964, and the LR test for spatial dependence was significant at the 1% level, indicating that the inclusion of spatial effects in SEM improved the model goodness of fit. Therefore, this study ended up with a spatial error model as the main model to analyse the influence mechanism of settlement intention of floating population.

5.3.4.2 Result Analysis of the Spatial Econometric Model

Internal Factors Versus External Factors

The results showed that the characteristics of floating population had a greater impact on settlement intention of floating population than the city characteristics, with the nine significant variables contributing to the settlement intention in descending order of influence degree: the proportion of interprovincial migration (X_5), the number of accompanying family members (X_2), the average number of children of floating population (X_3), the average residence duration in destination areas (X_4), GDP per capita of destination areas (X_8), the proportion of unmarried floating population (X_1), the employment Figure of the primary industry (X_9), the average income from last employment of floating population (X_6) and the average monthly household expenditure (X_7). Among these variables, only GDP per capita of destination areas (X_8) and the employment Figure of the primary industry (X_9) were city-level variables, while the rest were variables of the characteristics of floating population. This finding was contrary to the literature on the *hukou* transfer intention of urban floating population [15], due to the fundamental differences between settlement intention and *hukou* transfer intention: Firstly, in contrast to migration with *hukou* conversion, settling down in the destination area did not require giving up the advantages associated with the original *hukou* (e.g. rural homesteads, rural community share-holding, etc.) to enjoy the benefits attached to the new *hukou* (e.g. children's education, etc.), i.e. there was no need to weigh the advantages and disadvantages between the original *hukou* and the new *hukou*; secondly, migration with *hukou* transfer was longer, more difficult and more complicated in terms of procedures than settling down in the destination area, resulting in a greater opportunity cost for floating population if they left the city; thirdly, permanent migrants (with *hukou* transfer) were more inclined to make rational choices based on economic benefits and their personal prospects, and the tendency of seeking profits ran through the whole decision making process of *hukou* transfer, while the settlement intention of floating population was more a subjective initiative, concerning more about their own perceptions and experience in the city, and whether they can integrate into the destination areas economically, socially and culturally, without considering objective factors such as the city positioning. Therefore, the effects of external factors had less impact on the settlement intentions than the effects of internal factors, compared with the *hukou* transfer intentions.

The Effects of Family Factors

The family factor, as an important part of the social network factor, had a significant effect on settlement intention of floating population. The number of accompanying family members (X_2), the average number of children of floating population (X_3), the proportion of unmarried floating population (X_1) and the average monthly household expenditure (X_7) all had a significant influence on settlement intention of floating population, because family resources acted as a positive incentive to enhance the floating population's ability to survive in destination areas. This finding was consistent with the inference of New Migration Economics about the impact of family resources on population migration [69]. Firstly, families formed unique and relatively stable social networks in destination areas, and the differences in social networks among family members were small, which was conducive to families seeking their own positions in social networks and thus integrating into the local society, and the opportunity cost of reconstructing family social networks became too great if they left the destination areas. The geographical concentration of the social network of the family members led to the assimilation of local identity in destination areas and an consensus on settlement intention, and the accompanying of family members reduced the attachment of floating population to their hometowns. Secondly, the children of floating population in destination areas had become a "gravitational force" for floating population to settle down for a long time, and the destination areas had become, to a greater or lesser extent, a real "hometown" for floating population. Thirdly, marriage relationship was a special relationship. If the partner of the migrant was a local resident in the destination, the emotional experience, social network and resource incentives that the migrant recieved from his partner would strengthen his settlement intention;if the partner of the migrant was not a local resident, the positive incentives for the migrant from family resources were greater than those for the unmarried migrants, and the opportunity costs of migration were also higher. Fourthly, the household expenditure reflected, to a certain extent, the social status of floating households and their income and consumption levels in destination areas, i.e. the position of individuals in the social network and their sense of identification with the destination area. The migrants that had greater investment in destination areas would have greater dependence on the destination areas and a stronger sense of place identity.

The Effects of Migration Characteristics Variables

In terms of migration characteristics, lower proportion of inter-provincial migration (X_5) and longer average residence duration in destination areas (X_4) would lead to a stronger settlement intention of floating population. Firstly, compared with inter-provincial migrants, intraprovincial migrants would benefit more from the similarity of institutions, language and cultures between the destination area and the origin area, and bore relatively lower costs due to a smaller physical and perceived distance, which led to their stronger sense of belonging to the destination city, and accelerated the process of their economic integration and social integration. Secondly, for the floating population, living in destination areas was a process of re-socialization. The enrichment of personal urban memories brought about a greater sense of local identity, and a longer residence duration in destination areas gave rise to the localisation of the social capital and social networks of floating population, thus contributing to a higher settlement intention. In addition, the long-term settlement indicated in part a sustainable social interaction process of floating population in destination areas, including building information, knowledge linkages and emotional interactions with the local residents and other migrants, which was an irreversible process that changed the social attributes of the floating population. At the same time, the social interaction among other people in origin areas caused different changes in the society of origin areas. As the floating population stayed longer in the destination areas, there existed a greater estrangement between the floating population and the society of their origin areas, so the residence duration in destination areas obviously affected settlement intention of floating population.

The Effects of Socio-economic Development Levels of Cities

GDP per capita of destination areas (X_8) was a measure of the socio-economic development level of a city, and a higher GDP per capita would result in a higher settlement intention of floating population. The reason for this was that cities with a high socio-economic development level are characterized by more employment opportunities, diversified urban culture and quality public services, which were attractive for floating population. A larger employment size of the primary industry employment generated a stronger settlement intention of floating population, probably due to the fact that more urban villages remained in these areas during the rapid urbanization process, which reduced the cost of living for floating population. The "small society" that formed within the urban villages allowed some floating population to find a foothold in the social integration process without impacting their social networks associated with their geographical relationships. When external factors were considered alone, cities with a high socio-economic development level and a high degree of inclusiveness are more likely to retain their floating population.

The Spatial Spillover Effects

The spatial error parameter λ measured the spatial dependence effect of settlement intention of floating population in a given range. λ in the model was 0.281, significant at the 1% level, with a positive spatial dependence in the error term. This phenomenon was often caused by the presence of some unobserved independent variables with spatial autocorrelation in the model, such as the following two scenarios: ① The introduction of cross-regional policies, the construction of cross-regional public goods resources, and the emergence of cross-city services brought about by the "Internet + " initiative had impacted on the relatively segregated administrative divisions of cities, and inter-city connection had become more frequent. The cities with relative advantages in attracting floating population could influence their neighbouring cities by intercity factors flows and resource sharing between cities. ② The effects of different talent policies in each city on the settlement intention of floating population were often difficult to observe and quantify. Given that talent policies acted as an important factor for cities to attract in-migrants, favourable talent policies in one city tend to stimulate improvements in the talent policies in neighbouring cities due to competition effects, which resulted in a spatial agglomeration of favourable talent policies.

Spatial connection was an important reason for the formation of spatial dependence. In terms of the types of variables that influence the settlement intention in this study, from the perspective of spatial spillover, on the one hand, internal factors of floating population tended to be more spatially independent, because it was difficult for these characteristics to form interactions through intercity exchanges. However, from a microscopic point of view, the construction of social networks of floating population across cities and the diffusion of social networks based on geographical ties, which brought about cultural exchange and diffusion among individuals, may also lead to a convergence of internal factors characteristics, i.e. the phenomenon of "Birds of a feather flock together". On the other hand, spatial dependence caused by external factors (city characteristics) was more likely to happen, as spatial connection among cities generated spatial spillover effects from a macro perspective, such as spatial spillover caused by the sharing of policies, infrastructure, information and labour among cities due to geographical proximity. The existence of information, transport and capital flows among neighbouring cities resulted in a geospatial restructuring (the formation of "space of flows"), i.e., the spatial spillover effects of the "flows" on the administrative spatial restructuring, which was difficult to quantify in practice. Therefore, the macro carriers of the spatial spillover of settlement intention were the spatial spillover of city characteristics due to geographical proximity, and its micro carriers were the spatial spillover of social and cultural characteristics due to changes in the social networks of floating population.

5.3.5 Conclusions and Policy Recommendations

Based on the China Migrants Dynamic Survey data of 2015, this study employed GIS spatial analysis, trend surface analysis and spatial autocorrelation methods to describe regional differences in the settlement intention of China's floating population and investigated the spatial effects of settlement intention with the spatial autoregressive models, and mainly obtained the following conclusions:

Firstly, the spatial distribution of settlement intention of China's floating population showed a "north high-south low" trend and a "U" shape in the east–west direction. In general, there existed a significant agglomeration of settlement intention of floating population, i.e., characteristics of spatial autocorrelation; the "H-H" agglomeration pattern emerged in the northeast region and the Shandong Peninsula, while most of the southeastern coastal cities and a small number of central and western cities were located in the "L-L" agglomeration area. Secondly, settlement intention of China's floating population was influenced by both internal factors of floating population and external factors of city characteristics. Unlike *hukou* transfer intention, internal factors had a greater impact on settlement intention than external factors. Among the internal factors, social networks and resource incentives, as family factors, affected settlement intention of floating population, while the migration characteristics variables, which characterized social integration, also had a significant influence on settlement intention of floating population; among the external factors, destination areas with a higher socio-economic development level and higher inclusiveness were more attractive to floating population for long-term settlement. Thirdly, the spatial dependence was significantly present in the influence process of the above factors on settlement intention of floating population, among which macro carriers were the spatial spillover of city characteristics and the micro carriers were the spatial spillover of social and cultural characteristics caused by changes in the social networks of floating population.

According to the above conclusions, the following policy recommendations can be proposed for the management and services of the urban floating population: from the perspective of regional development, the spatial spillover effect of settlement intention of floating population will increase with the diffusion of new technologies. Therefore, compared to population management pattern within a spatial unit, cross-regional population management patterns should also be considered, governments need to establish overall cross-regional planning, improve regional mechanisms for land planning and social security systems. Besides, it is necessary to consider the settlement intentions of floating population from a better spatial perspective, and promote the effective allocation of inter-regional factors as well as the rational and orderly distribution of floating population. For city management, in the competition for talents, efforts should be made to improve the socio-economic development level of the city and to create an inclusive urban culture, so that floating population in 'non-hometown' geographical locations can have an emotional experience of 'hometown'. At the same time, since the family based migration is most stable, the families of floating population should be fully taken into account when attracting foreign talents; in the development of the city, diversified jobs should be created so that the family members of talents can gain a foothold and realize their values in all walks of life. The small and medium cities should be encouraged to attach themselves to large central cities, so as to share resources such as transportation and employment, and benefit from the spatial spillover benefits brought by central cities in the process of introducing talents.

Despite its contributions, there are still some shortcomings in this study: Firstly, although the spatial econometric model has identified the spatial spillover effect of settlement intention of urban floating population, the analysis of the specific spatial spillover mechanism is still mainly based on previous literature and theoretical extrapolation, and lack of model empirical evidence. Secondly, this study is limited to the cross-sectional data of one year, so its conclusions do not fully reflect the real situation of the spatial pattern and influencing factors of settlement intention of floating population. In the future, a more systematic and comprehensive empirical study on settlement intention of floating population can be conducted at the level of prefecture-level cities and above, based on multi-year data.

5.4 Influencing Factors of Settlement Intentions at the Individual Level: A Perspective of Social Integration

5.4.1 Introduction

China has been undertaking a rapid and massive urbanization with enormous trans-regional migration, since its reform and opening up policy in 1978. The migration population can be divided into permanent migration with *hukou* (household registration status) transfer and temporary migration (floating population) without *hukou* transfer. *Report on China's Floating Population Development* in 2017 issued by National Health and Family Planning Commission (NHFPC) has demonstrated that the total floating population has reached 245 million by the end of 2016 (nearly accounting for 3/4 of the population of USA and 1/3 of the population of Europe). Although floating population have worked and lived for a long time in destination cities, they cannot be granted with the local *hukou*, thus it is difficult for them to get equal rights of employment, social welfare and formal education for their children, compared with residents with local *hukou*. A considerable portion of tremendous floating population entering destination cities have a long-term plan to live here, which exert enormous influence on the urbanization process and socio-economic development in destination cities, involving social issues including population management, public service provision and coordinated development of urban and rural economy. Therefore, it is of great significance to conduct studies on settlement intentions of floating population that represent long-term residence decision. With a current trend towards long-term residence in destination cities presented by floating population, the influence factors on settlement intentions of floating population have gradually become a research focus. However, related studies seem to neglect the influence of social integration of floating population on settlement intentions.

Social integration is a multi-dimensional concept that has multiple definitions across disciplines, developed to understand and explain immigrants' behavior, adaptation, the acculturation process, and self-identity [89]. In China, social integration can be defined as a process of floating population integrating into the urban society from the aspects of residence, employment, social engagement, life style and value concept, and finally transforming into urban residents. How well the floating population integrate into the local society is intimately connected to their long-term settlement decisions. Hence, it is necessary to investigate the role of social integration in the settlement intention of floating population, which has vital practical significance for promoting the process of citizenization of floating population and improving conditions of social integration. In recent years, the new generation of migrant workers (born after 1980) have become the main force of floating population, accounting for nearly half of the total migrant workers by 2017, according to the National Bureau of Statistics. The education level, social background and life willingness of the younger generation are quite different from the former generation, leading to an assimilative tendency of migrants towards destination cities in terms of value system, social mentality and socializing way [90]. The social integration of floating population is an important social issue in current China: if the floating population cannot integrate well into the destination cities, not only will they be not able to make contributions to the economic development of destination cities, but also they will be discriminated and excluded by local society, which will affect the social harmony and stability and cause huge costs for urbanization. In the context of China's people-oriented new-type urbanization, the social integration degree of floating population in destination cities is a key variable that decides whether the new-type urbanization construction will be successful, directly related with their settlement intentions.

Therefore, this study will aim to contributing to the growing literature of settlement intentions by focusing on the influence of social integration. Drawing upon the data of the personal questionnaire about social integration and mental health from the China Migrants Dynamic Survey (CMDS) in 2014, this study examines the determinants of settlement intentions of floating population in China, especially the effects of social integration.

5.4.2 Literature Review

There exist a series of economic and social theories that can provide explanations for migration and settlement decision of migrants in destination cities. The core standpoint of push–pull theory is that the factors affecting migration decision are the pull forces of destination region and the push forces of origin region, and the tension between them will cause people to migrate [91]. The human capital theory indicates that young and highly-qualified people are more likely to migrate [92]. The social network theory holds that the support from blood relationship and geographical relationship will reduce the cost and risk of migration, thus increasing the return of moving [93]. The important viewpoint of social integration theory is that the settlement intention is highly related with integration degree, for good social integration contributes to the settlement of migrants in destination region, which includes 2 aspects: one is forming attachment and identification to destination region by learning new culture, working hard to obtain social status and establishing social connections with local people; the other one is the long process of tolerance and acceptance of migrants by local mainstream society [94]. The basic idea of the dual economy theory by Lewis is that surplus rural labor will continuously flow into urban modern industrial sector, when its wage level is higher than that of traditional agricultural sector [95]. The Todaro theory argues that rural–urban migration is driven by an expected divide of income between urban and rural areas, introducing the variable of the employment probability in urban area to improve the dual economy theory [96]. New Economics of Labour Migration (NELM) claims that labour migration is part of the household strategy instead of the decision by an individual migrant under the background of an imperfect market, with the allocation of labour force, capital, and other resources within households influences both the short-term and long-term interests of a household [24]. However, extant studies have demonstrated that the settlement intentions of migrants are determined by various factors, which cannot be explained by a single theory.

According to the above theories and China's actual situations, the determinants on settlement intention of floating population can be divided as interior influence factors and exterior influence factors. The interior factors refer to individual characteristics including gender, age, education level and marital status [17, 97] and migration features covering flow reason, flow range and residence time, as well as the household characteristics [33]. The exterior factors represent the characteristics of destination cities composed of economic development level, social welfare, living conditions, social network and geographic features [19, 20, 71, 98, 99], such as spatial location of cities and city size. With diverse data sources and various methods, plenty of scholars have conducted studies on the influence factors on settlement intention from different perspectives in different regions [14, 18, 36, 37, 40, 56, 100–102]. The social integration can be deemed as the interaction between interior factors of floating population and exterior factors of destination cities.

Regarding social integration, "integration" was first studied by Park and Burgess [103] through the concept of assimilation. They defined it as "a process of interpenetration and fusion in which persons and groups acquire the memories, sentiments, and attitude of other persons and groups and, by sharing their experience and history, are incorporated with them in a common cultural life". They systematically divided the integration process into 4 main interactions: economic competition, political conflict, social accommodation and cultural integration. Classical theories on social integration incorporate assimilation theory, pluralism theory and segmented assimilation theory. The assimilation theory is mainly used in the studies on international migration, stating that assimilation is the process of disadvantaged group discarding original cultural and behavior patterns, gradually adapting to the culture and life style of the mainstream society, and finally obtaining equal opportunities and rights with the mainstream group [104]. Contrast with the assimilation theory, the pluralism theory holds that different social groups interact and adapt with each other to form diversified cultures and socioeconomic orders, rendering all social participants to have equal rights [105, 106]. As a supplement and extension to the traditional linear integration theory, the segmented assimilation theory aims to explaining why the second/new generation migrants take a new path to integrate into the local society different from the former generation, from the aspects of the human capital of migrants and how they were treated when they first arrived at destination regions [107, 108].

As the social integration is a multi-dimensional concept, there doesn't exist a unified index system of the social integration of migrants, the measurements of which contains economic, behavioral (or social), cultural, political and psychological (or identity) dimensions, with each dimension covering various indexes represented by different measurable variables, according to the data accessibility and research focus of different scholars [109–119]. Gordon [94] firstly put forward 7 dimensions of integration: acculturation, structural assimilation, amalgamation, identification assimilation, absence of prejudice, absence of discrimination and civic assimilation, and plenty of scholars have further developed the measurement of social integration [120–123]. In China, Yang [124, 125] establishes a relatively comprehensive, systematic and scientific indicator system to measure the social integration of floating population. This system includes 4 dimensions: economic integration, social adaptation, cultural acceptance and psychological identity. First, the economic integration refers to the challenges of making a living facing floating population, i.e., the integration situations in terms of employment, economic income, working conditions, social security, living conditions and job training, reflecting their economic status. Second, the social adaptation indicates that migrants conform their behaviors to local rules, through social network, social communication with local people, participation in local social activities and organizations in destination cities, which will enhance their understanding and mastering of local culture and customs. Third, the cultural acceptance signifies the understanding and approval of local language and culture, manners and customs, life style and social ideas. Fourth, the psychological identity means the psychological distance of migrants from local people and hometown people, and the sense of identity and belonging based on this, which is an advanced stage of social integration.

Despite quite a close relationship between social integration and settlement intention, there exists an absence of studies on the influence of social integration on settlement intention of floating population [77, 126, 127]. To rectify this deficiency, this study will systematically and comprehensively measure the social integration of floating population, and then analyze the influence factors of settlement intention from the perspective of social integration.

5.4.3 Research Data and Methodology

5.4.3.1 Research Data

The special survey of "Social Integration and Mental Health of Floating Population" initiated by National Health Commission of China is based on the annual report data of floating population in 2014 as the sampling frame, targeting to the floating population aged from 15 to 59 in the destination regions of in-migration (county, district or city), who have been residing here for over 1 month without local *hukou*. Adopting multi-stage stratified random sampling method with probability-proportional-to-size (PPS), the survey was undertaken in 8 representative cities (districts) in China: Chaoyang District of Beijing, Jiaxing City of Zhejiang Province, Xiamen City of Fujian Province, Qingdao City of Shandong Province, Zhengzhou City of Henan Province, Shenzhen City and Zhongshan City of Guangdong Province, and Chengdu City of Sichuan Province. The sample size of floating population collected in each city is 2000 persons, totaling 16,000. Although these 8 cities are not selected at random, they are main destination cities covering different regions and various city sizes of China, with samples selected by the PPS sampling method, hence having certain representativeness. Due to the lack of variables, we delete 3 samples, making the final effective sample to be 15,997.

5.4.3.2 Variable Selection

In this study, we put emphasis on the effect of social integration on settlement intention. Therefore, the settlement intention of floating population is chosen as the dependent variable, derived by the question whether you want to stay in the destination region for a long time (more than 5 years). The social integration of floating population is deemed as the independent variable, which includes 4 dimensions: economic integration, social adaptation, cultural acceptance and psychological fusion [125]. Each dimension is composed of several measurable indicators according to the data accessibility (shown in Table 5.8). The social integration situations of floating population in destination cities can be regarded as exterior influence factors on settlement intention, which can represent all aspects of circumstances including economic development level, social welfare, living conditions and social network of destination cities.

Social integration is an abstract process, more focused on the inner feelings. The living habits and values of floating population will form a strong collision with urban residents. Based on extant studies, 14 indicators are selected and assigned values, and the four principal components of economic integration, cultural acceptance, social adaptation and psychological fusion are extracted based on the factor analysis method. The social integration value is calculated based on the degree of these 4 dimensions and their weights (variance contribution rates), and converted into a specific score between 1 and 100 through standardization. Finally, the scores of the four dimensions and the comprehensive score of social integration are regarded as independent variables in the logistic regression model [128, 129].

The economic integration is the prerequisite for the survival and development of the floating population in cities and the basic guarantee for their integration into the local society. The dimension of economic integration includes three indicators: monthly income, participation in social security and occupational stability. The monthly income is the income of last month or last employment, a continuous variable that can be assigned values based on different levels. The participation in social security comes from the question whether you participate in the following types of insurance, such as new rural insurance, unemployment insurance, housing provident fund, and is assigned values based on the number of insurance types. The occupational stability is measured by the employment unit type, according to the degree of occupational stability, unemployed or temporary work are assigned a value of 1, private company or self-employed are assigned a value of 2, short- and medium-term work are assigned a value of 3, fixed and long-term work are assigned a value of 4.

The cultural acceptance include four indicators: proficiency of local language, conformity to local manners and customs (the attitude towards the idea that obeying manners and customs of hometown is important), adaption to local life style (the attitude towards the idea that keeping the life style of hometown is important), acceptance of local social ideas (Whether opinions of migrants about social ideas are different from local people). The proficiency of local language is divided into 4 levels: no understanding, understanding but no speaking, understanding and speaking a little, understanding and speaking are assigned a value of 1–4 respectively. The other indicators are assigned a value of 1–5 respectively, from strongly disagree to strongly agree.

Table 5.8 Description of variables in the model

Variable type	Specific indicators	Data source	Data processing
Economic integration	Monthly income	Personal income of the last month or the last job	(0–2000) 1 (2000–4000) 2 (4000–6000) 3 (More than 6000) 4
	Participation in social security	What kind of social security have you participated in?	(Assignment based on the number of social insurance) 0—1 1 kind—2 2 kinds—3 3 kinds—4 4 or more kinds—5
	Occupational stability	What is your type of employment?	Unemployed or temporary work—1 Private company or self-employed—2 Short- and medium-term work—3 Fixed and long-term work —4
Cultural acceptance	Proficiency of local language	What is your mastering level of local language?	No understanding 1 Understanding but no speaking 2 Understanding and speaking a little 3 Understanding and speaking 4
	Conformity to local manners and customs	Do you agree or disagree with the following statement? Obeying manners and customs of hometown is important.	Strongly disagree 5 Disagree 4 Neither agree nor disagree 3 Agree 2 Strongly agree 1
	Adaption to local life style	Do you agree or disagree with the following statement? Keeping the life style of hometown is important	Strongly disagree 5 Disagree 4 Neither agree nor disagree 3 Agree 2 Strongly agree 1
	Acceptance of local social ideas	Do you agree or disagree with the following statement? Your opinions about social ideas are different from local people	Strongly disagree 5 Disagree 4 Neither agree nor disagree 3 Agree 2 Strongly agree 1

(continued)

Table 5.8 (continued)

Variable type	Specific indicators	Data source	Data processing
Social adaptation	The number of accompanying family members	The number of accompanying family members (alone/spouse/parents/children)	Alone—1 With 1 person—2 With 2 people—3 With 3 people—4 With 4 or more people—5
	Participation in social organizations	Are you currently a member of the following local organizations? A Trade union B Volunteer association C Mobile party/youth league branch D Alumni association E Hometown Chamber of Commerce F Local party/youth league branch G Townsmen association	(Assignment based on the number of organizations) 0—1 1 kind—2 2 kinds—3 3 kinds—4 4 or more kinds—5
	Participation in social activities	Which kinds of the following activities have you participated in 2013? A Community recreational activities B Social activities for public good C Election activities (village/neighbourhood committee, trade union election) D Excellence selection activities E Owners' committee activities F Management activities of neighborhood committee	(Assignment based on the number of activities) 0—1 1 kind—2 2 kinds—3 3 kinds—4 4 or more kinds—5
	Participation in free government training	Have you received any free government training in the past 3 months?	Yes—1 No—0
Psychological fusion	Getting along with local people	How do you or your family get along with local people?	Not harmonious 1 Very few contacts 2 So so 3 Harmonious 4 Very harmonious 5
	Acceptance attitude of local people	Do you agree or disagree with the following statement? The locals are willing to accept me as one of them	Strongly disagree 1 Disagree 2 Agree 3 Strongly agree 4

(continued)

Table 5.8 (continued)

Variable type	Specific indicators	Data source	Data processing
	Satisfaction with life	Do you agree or disagree with the following statement? I'm quite satisfied with my life at present	The satisfaction degree (from strongly disagree to strongly agree) is assigned 1–7
Individual characteristics	Gender	Gender	Male 1 Female 0
	Age	Date of birth	26–35, 36–45, > 45—1 15–25—0 (reference)
	Education attainment	What is your educational attainment level?	Primary school or below—0 Junior high school—1 Senior high school/ technical secondary school—2 College degree or above—3
	Marital status	Marital status	Unmarried (unmarried, cohabitation, divorce, widowhood)—0 Married (first marriage, remarriage)—1
	hukou	Household registration	Non-agricultural—0 Agricultural—1 Other—2
Migration features	Flow range (interprovincial/intercity)	The range of flow this time	Interprovincial—1 Intercity—2 Across counties within cities—0
	Residence duration	The residence duration in the destination region	1–3 years—0 4–6 years—1 7–11 years—2 12 years and more—3

(continued)

Table 5.8 (continued)

Variable type	Specific indicators	Data source	Data processing
	Flow reason	Flow reason at this time	Work/business—1 Accompanying Migration—2 (Accompanying family members, marriage, going to relatives or friends, being born, caring for the elderly, caring for children) Others—0 (Demolition and relocation, learning and training, joining the army)
	Destination region	The type of the destination region	Beijing and Shenzhen—Eastern megacities Qingdao and Xiamen— Eastern megalopolises Zhengzhou and Chengdu—Central and western megacities Jiaxing and Zhongshan— Eastern type-I large cities
Connection with the hometown	Worries about hometown	What do you worry about in your hometown?	The number of affairs
	The amount of homestead	What is the residential housing area in your hometown?	Area (square meter)

The social adaptation is an essential part of social integration, which reflects the interaction of the migrants with local residents and their participation in activities in the destination areas. It includes four indicators: the number of accompanying family members, participation in social organizations, participation in social activities, and participation in free government training. The number of accompanying family members a continuous variable, including spouses, parents, children and siblings. The participation in social organization is obtained from the question whether you participate in the following kinds of organizations, such as trade unions, volunteer associations, party/youth league branch, and is assigned values based on the number of organization types. The participation in social activities is derived by the question whether you participate in community recreational activities, social activities for public good, election activities (village/neighbourhood committee, trade union election), excellence selection activities, owners' committee activities, and is assigned values based on the number of social activity types. The particiaption in free government training is acquired by the question whether you participate in free training from the government, the answer yes is set to 1, otherwise 0.

The psychological fusion is the sense of belonging of the floating population in the destination city, and it is a process of mutual acceptance and recognition between migrants and local residents. It consists of three indicators: getting along with local people (whether the migrant gets along well with local people), acceptance attitude of local people (whether the local people are willing to accept the migrant as a member), satisfaction with life. The values of these three indicators are assigned based on the degree of the answers (from poor to good, from strongly disagree to strongly agree).

Concerning interior influence factors on settlement intention, we also select some variables of individual characteristics (age, gender, education level, marital status, *hukou* type), migration features (flow range, flow reason, residence duration, destination region) and family factors (worries about hometown, the amount of rural homestead in hometown) as control variables [130]. Due to the fact that the dependent variable is a dichotomous variable, this study will employ the binary logistic regression model to examine the influence factors of settlement intentions. The indicator selection and processing of the variables in the model can be found in Table 5.8.

5.4.3.3 Research Methods

Factor Analysis

The factor analysis method is employed to covert multiple variables into several unrelated comprehensive indicators that summarize all information to the maximum, to reduce the number of variables and the complexity of the problem.

The analysis process is as follows:

Suppose the original data matrix of N samples and P variables is

$$X = (x_{ij})_{n*p} \tag{5.16}$$

Calculate the correlation coefficient matrix of variables

$$R = (r_{ij})_{m*n} = \frac{1}{n} X' X \tag{5.17}$$

Factor load α_i was calculated, and the score of each factor was calculated through the rotated factor load matrix

$$F_i = \alpha_i x \tag{5.18}$$

Factor comprehensive score was calculated based on factor score F_i and variance contribution rate of the principal component W_i.

$$UQ = F_1 * W_1 + F_2 * W_2 + F_3 * W_3 + \cdots + F_i * W_i \tag{5.19}$$

The factor comprehensive score is obtained by using the variance contribution ratios of the four dimensions (economic integration, cultural acceptance, social adaptation and psychological fusion) as weights, and the values of the general social integration and its four dimensions are converted into the range of 1–100, based on the factor maximum-minimum conversion formula as shown below.

$$index = (factor score + B) * A \tag{5.20}$$

$$A = 99/(Maximum factor - Minimum factor) \tag{5.21}$$

$$B = [(Maximum factor - Minimum factor)/99] - Minimum factor \tag{5.22}$$

Multicollinearity Test

Multicollinearity refers to the significant linear correlation between variables, that is, the existence of one variable will affect the effect of other variables on the results, or several variables have the same information and influence each other causally. If there are multicollinearity problems, the variance analysis results of the model are inconsistent with the regression coefficients of the respective variables, and the coefficients or symbols of the independent variables are inconsistent with the actual situation, the model analysis will have no statistical significance. The test methods generally include Tolerance and Variance inflation factor (VIF), among which the VIF test is the most commonly used. Generally, the value of VIF is greater than 1 and less than 10, indicating that there exists no multicollinearity.

Logistic Regression

The dependent variable of the logistic regression is a dichotomous variable. The equation is shown as follows:

$$logit(p) = \ln\left(\frac{p}{1-p}\right) = \beta_0 + \beta_1 x_1 + \ldots + \beta_n x_n \tag{5.23}$$

β_0 is the constant term; $\beta_1, \beta_2, \ldots \beta_n$ is the regression coefficient of each variable; p is the probability of floating population having settlement intentions in 8 cities; $\frac{p}{(1-p)}$ is the ratio of the probability of floating population having settlement intentions to the probability of them without settlement intentions, leading to the odds ratio $\exp(\beta_i)$; X_i is independent variables.

Maximum Likelihood Estimation (MLE) is used to estimate the regression parameters, and the value of $-2LL$ (Log likelihood) is mainly used to test the goodness of fit of the model, with a smaller value indicating a better goodness.

In addition, other statistics, such as Likelihood Chi-square (LR Chi2) and Presdo-R^2 can all play a role in testing the quality of the model.

5.4.4 Analysis of Results

5.4.4.1 Analysis of Social Integration Level

Measurements of Social Integration Level

Based on the data from the 2014 Social Integration and Mental Health Questionnaire C of the China Migrant Dynamic Survey released by the National Health Commission (formerly the National Health and Family Planning Commission), the social integration level is measured by the factor analysis method.

First, the KMO test and Bartlett sphericity test values in the results were observed. In general, KMO value greater than 0.9 means that the data is very suitable for factor analysis; KMO value greater than 0.8 means that the data is suitable for factor analysis; KMO value greater than 0.6 means that a factor analysis can be conducted, but it should not be less than 0.5; KMO value less than 0.5 means that the data regression is meaningless. The Chi-square statistic of Bartlett's sphericity test is less than 0.05, indicating that the regression result is very significant. It can be seen from Table 5.9 that this data is suitable for factor analysis.

Secondly, the common factors of 14 social integration indicators are extracted, and the orthogonal rotation of factor load is carried out by using Kaiser's standardized orthogonal rotation method. The number of factors is determined according to the calculation results of eigenvalues in the screeplot (Fig. 5.9), and the principal component with eigenvalue greater than 1 is usually selected as the initial factor. According to the statistical results, the cumulative variance contribution rate of the five principal components reached 53.454%. However, the eigenvalue of the fifth principal component was so small that the factor naming lacks interpretation, hence the last principal component was deleted.

Naming principal components after extracting principal components is an important part of factor analysis. According to the statistical results of the rotated component load matrix, the factor load coefficient values were observed. Since there was no multicollinearity among the measurement indexes of social integration, the corresponding relationship between each factor and the research dimension was directly judged and each factor was named. As shown in Table 5.10, F1 refers to psychological fusion, F2 to social adaptation, F3 to economic integration, and F4 to cultural acceptance. It is worth noting that previous studies generally considered a factor load

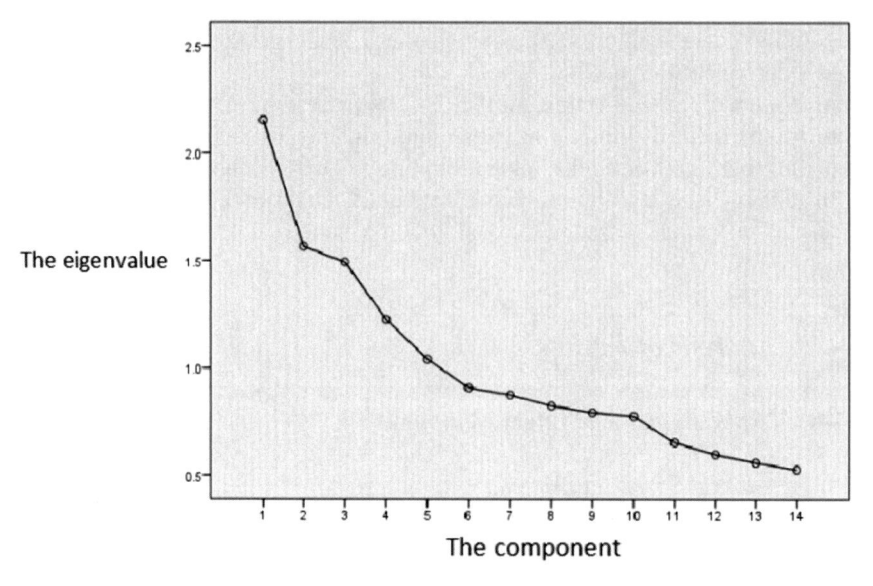

Fig. 5.9 Screeplot

Table 5.9 KMO and Bartlett tests

KMO sampling suitability quantity		0.635
Bartlett sphericity test	The approximate chi-square	19,239.538
	Degrees of freedom	91
	Significance	0.000

with an absolute value greater than 0.3 as significant, and 13 indexes in Table 5.10 were all greater than 0.3 and met the selection requirements.

We regard the variance contribution ratios of the four dimensions (economic integration, cultural acceptance, social adaptation and psychological fusion) as weights to obtain the comprehensive scores of factors, and calculate the score of each dimension based on the maximum-minimum conversion formula by converting them into a range of 1–100. The comprehensive scores of all dimensions of the 8 cities are listed in the following Table 5.11.

The above results are represented by a bar graph for clear display in Fig. 5.10.

Analysis of Measurement Results of Social Integration Level

Social integration in this study includes economic integration, cultural acceptance, social adaption and psychological fusion. The composite scores of 8 cities all are no more than 50 points, indicating a relatively low social integration level. From the perspective of economic integration, Beijing has the highest level with a score of

Table 5.10 Component load matrix after rotation

Dimensions	Measurement indexes	Extracted common factors				
		F1	F2	F3	F4	Communalities
Economic integration	Monthly income	0.076	0.244	0.678	0.017	0.527
	Participation in social security	−0.021	−0.044	0.648	0.052	0.486
	Occupational stability	0.051	0.034	0.742	−0.019	0.632
Cultural acceptance	Proficiency of local language	0.456	0.222	−0.097	0.142	0.344
	Conformity to local manners and customs	0.066	0.017	0.018	0.847	0.723
	Conformity to local manners and customs	−0.015	−0.018	0.028	0.845	0.715
	Acceptance of local social ideas	0.577	−0.001	0.059	0.113	0.350
Social adaptation	The number of accompanying family members	−0.066	−0.033	−0.099	0.036	0.671
	Participation in social organizations	−0.041	0.688	0.284	−0.042	0.558
	Participation in social activities	0.031	0.802	0.105	0.000	0.655
	Participation in free government training	0.197	0.628	−0.114	0.032	0.450
Psychological fusion	Getting along with local people	0.703	0.064	0.049	−0.070	0.538
	Acceptance attitude of local people	0.667	0.032	0.027	−0.068	0.462
	Satisfaction with life	0.303	0.017	0.056	−0.066	0.373

44.23. As the capital of China, Beijing possesses a superior geographical position, a long history and splendid culture. It is the national center of politics, culture, science and technology, information and foreign exchanges, with its economic development level among the highest. From the perspective of cultural acceptance, Zhengzhou in Henan province has the highest level of cultural acceptance, with a score of 44.40. Zhengzhou is located at the Central Plains area, the cradle of Chinese civilization. As the provincial capital of Henan province and one of the eight ancient capitals in China, Zhengzhou has a deep historical and cultural foundation. From the perspective of social adaptation, Xiamen city and Chengdu city have the highest levels

Table 5.11 Overall social integration level and scores of four dimensions of 8 cities

City	Economic integration	Cultural acceptance	Social adaptation	Psychological fusion	Social integration level
8 cities as a whole	36.99	36.96	26.13	63.78	42.81
Beijing	44.23	42.06	26.52	50.60	41.63
Shenzhen	41.88	40.47	23.75	57.36	49.59
Qingdao	37.95	40.73	23.43	59.89	48.78
Xiamen	39.10	35.97	41.18	63.36	44.75
Zhengzhou	43.06	44.40	32.38	62.82	41.03
Chengdu	38.83	43.41	41.30	66.74	43.75
Jiaxing	39.79	40.84	19.60	54.72	30.75
Zhongshan	39.82	39.58	14.94	54.03	4.76

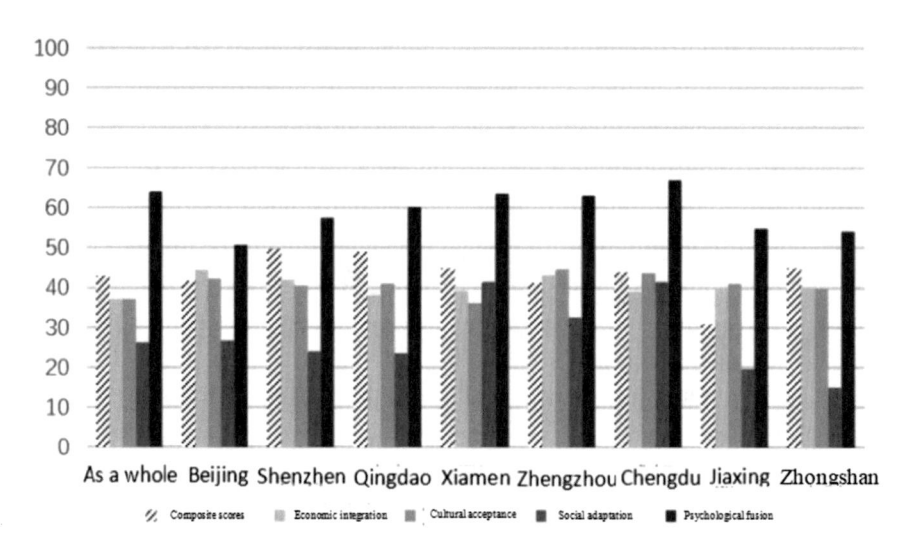

Fig. 5.10 Composite scores of social integration and scores of each dimension

(41.18 and 41.30). Xiamen and Chengdu are both among the first pilot cities to equalize basic public services and promote social integration of floating population, which have made a long-term exploration in coordinating urban and rural development and promoting *hukou* system reform. From the perspective of psychological fusion, all the eight cities score more than 50 points, among which Xiamen and Chengdu score the highest, with 63.36 and 66.74 points respectively. As demonstration cities of social integration, these two cities have great performance in terms of both social adaptation and psychological fusion.

Economic integration is the premise and basic guarantee for long-term settlement of floating population in the destination cities. According to Maslow's Needs-Hierarchy Theory, people will seek the realization of higher needs only after satisfying lower needs. Income is crucial to the survival of the floating population. If personal income and employment cannot meet the needs of floating population, it will directly restrict their development in the destination cities. The relatively higher income level and more employment opportunities in large cities and megacities have attracted the floating population, while the excessive living costs inhibit their social integration. Therefore, the cities with the highest scores of economic integration are Beijing and Shenzhen.

Social adaption represents the degree of social participation of individuals in destination cities, and the most important one is the number of accompanying family members, which involves more public service issues. Taking the initiative to participate in political organizations is an important way for the floating population to realize their political rights. Without the status of citizenship, the floating population usually do not have a strong sense of political participation, especially those whose main purpose is to earn money by working in destination cities. They do not care much about political activities in cities and believe that they cannot obtain corresponding interests even if they participate in political activities. As can be seen from the results, except Xiamen and Chengdu, which achieved demonstrable results in social integration, the overall level of social adaptation in eastern cities was extremely low, among which Jiaxing and Zhongshan even scored less than 20 points. Whether the government can take the initiative to accept floating population plays a key role in improving the social integration level of floating population. When the floating population receives the government's attention during the free training, it will enhance their sense of identity to the destination city, which will greatly promote the long-term settlement intention of the floating population [131].

Concerning the cultural acceptance, there exist significant differences in the living habits, language and cultural background between floating population and the local people, which restrict the interpersonal circle of the floating population in destination cities and result in the difficulties in the social integration of floating population from the cultural level. The promotion of local culture to floating population and the acceptance of external cultures are important to reduce the cultural gap between floating population and local residents and to enhance mutual understanding. Results show that the cultural acceptance level is generally not high and has a great influence on the overall level of social integration. Compared with the central and western city, the eastern cities have a lower cultural acceptance level. The possible reason is that the interprovincial migrants in the eastern region account for a large proportion of floating population, a longer migration distance indicates larger differences in cultural custom and living habits between floating population and local residents [130].

The psychological fusion of floating population directly reflects the evaluation of floating population on the destination city and acts as a key link of the social integration of floating population. "Getting along with local people" and "Acceptance attitude of local people" are important indicators to reveal psychological fusion. A

Table 5.12 Descriptive statistics of continuous variables

Variables	Observations	Average	Standard deviation	Minimum	Maximum
Independent variables					
Psychological fusion	15,997	63.782	14.68	1	100
Social adaptation	15,997	26.134	15.92	1	100
Economic integration	15,997	36.994	14.83	1	100
Cultural acceptance	15,997	36.963	15.25	1	100
Control variables					
Worries about hometown	15,997	1.746	1.49	0	8
The amount of homestead	15,997	146.896	92.76	0	066

large amount of floating population in the destination city will result in a competition for employment and public service resources with the local residents and the psychological resistence from the local residents. It will lead to the social exclusion and isolation of the floating population and worsen their living environment in the destination cities. Therefore, the blocking effect of local discrimination on the social integration level of floating population should not be underestimated. As can be seen from the results, the overall level of psychological integration in the eight cities only exceeds 50 points, indicating that there are still certain obstacles preventing the floating population from integrating into the local society, so there is still room for further improvement. A higher level of economic development, a more humanized management system, more employment opportunities and more perfect housing security for the floating population, will greatly enhance the floating population's sense of belonging to the city. Zhengzhou and Chengdu have such advantages, because the pace of life in these cities is relatively slow, and the floating migrants do not have to bear huge economic pressure, so their sense of identity and happiness are relatively high.

5.4.4.2   Analysis of Determinants on Settlement Intention

Descriptive Statistics of Variables

Before conducting the regression analysis, we have calculated the descriptive statistics of continuous variables and categorical variables in Tables 5.12 and 5.13:

Table 5.13 Descriptive statistics of categorical variables

Variables	Frequency	Percentage (%)	Frequency of long-term settlement intention	Percentage of long-term settlement intention (%)
Dependent variable				
Long-term settlement intention (%)				
Plan to	9,456	59.11	9456	
Don't plan to	6,541	40.89	6541	
Beijing	2000	12.50	1095	54.75
Shenzhen	2000	12.50	1129	56.45
Qingdao	2000	12.50	1409	70.45
Xiamen	2000	12.50	1323	66.15
Zhengzhou	2000	12.50	956	47.80
Chengdu	1999	12.49	1330	66.53
Jiaxing	1999	12.49	1093	54.68
Zhongshan	1999	12.49	1129	56.48
Individual characteristics				
Gender (%)				
Male	8798	55	5289	60.12
Female	7199	44	4167	57.88
Age (%)				
15–25	2924	18.28	1106	37.95
25–35	6913	43.21	4181	60.48
35–45	4425	27.66	3071	69.40
> 45	1735	10.85	1098	63.29
Education level (%)				
Primary or below	1,504	9.4	896	59.57
Junior high school	8,084	50.53	4562	56.43
Senior high school	4,051	25.32	2416	59.64
College or above	2,358	14.74	1582	67.09
Marriage (%)				
Married	11,707	73.18	7735	66.07
Unmarried	4,290	26.82	1721	40.12
Hukou (%)				
Non-agricultural	2240	14.00	1567	69.95
Agricultural	13,757	86.00	7891	57.4

(continued)

Table 5.13 (continued)

Variables	Frequency	Percentage (%)	Frequency of long-term settlement intention	Percentage of long-term settlement intention (%)
Migration features				
Flow range (%)				
Intercity	6,635	41.48	4259	64.19
Intercounty	593	3.71	406	68.47
Interprovincial	8,769	54.82	4791	54.64
Residence duration (%)				
0–3	9,164	57.29	4491	49.01
4–6	3,281	20.51	2178	66.38
7–11	2,298	14.37	1761	76.63
>=12	1,254	7.84	1026	81.82
Flow reason (%)				
Other	40	0.25	27	67.5
Accompanying migration	769	4.81	506	65.8
Work/business	15,188	94.94	8923	58.75
Type of destination region				
Midwestern megacities	3,999	25	2730	68.27
Eastern Type-I large cities	3,998	24.99	2220	55.53
Eastern megalopolises	4,000	25	2222	55.55
Eastern megacities	4,000	25	2284	57.10

The floating population's overall settlement intention is 59.11%. Among the eight cities, Qingdao, Xiamen and Chengdu have the highest settlement intention of floating population (70.45%, 66.15% and 66.53% respectively), which is consistent with the fact that the three cities are "demonstration cities of social integration".

The average scores of economic integration, social adaption, cultural acceptance and psychological fusion were 63.782, 26.134, 36.994 and 36.963, respectively. The score of psychological fusion dimension was the highest, and the score of social adaption dimension was the lowest.

In terms of personal characteristics, the males accounted for 55% of the totality. The respondents were 15–59 years old, with an average age of 32, and the proportion of long-term settlement intention over 25 years old was more than 60%. The education level of floating population is mainly concentrated in junior high school, accounting for 50.53%. The married people occupy the majority (73.18%), and have higher settlement intentions than unmarried people. Migrants with agricultural *hukou* take up 86%, and have lower settlement willingness than migrants with non-agricultural *hukou*.

Regarding the migration features, the flow range is mainly inter-provincial migration, accounting for 54.82%. However, the settlement intention of inter-provincial migrants is lower than that of the intercounty and intercity migrants. The residence duration is based on 0–3 years (57.29%), and migrants who have stayed longer in the destination city will have stronger settlement intention. The main reason of migration is work and business (94.94%), but the settlement intentions of migrant workers and business people are relatively low (58.75%). The types of destination regions are divided into eastern type-I large cities, eastern megalopolises, eastern megacities and midwestern megacities. The settlement intention of floating population in central and western megacities is the highest, occupying 68.27%.

Concerning the connection with the hometown, the average number of things to worry about in the hometown is 1.746, and the average area of homestead is 146.89 square meter, and there are no outliers in the two indexes.

Analysis of Logistic Regression Results

Before regression, it is necessary to check whether there is multicollinearity in the data. The VIF values of the 14 variables are all lower than 2, so there exists no multicollinearity. The binary logistic regression model is employed to analyze the influencing factors of settlement intentions, and the independent variables (economic integration, social adaptation, cultural acceptance and psychological fusion) are gradually incorporated into the model for analysis. Model 1 only examines the influence of independent variables on settlement intention. Model 2 to 6 stepwisely introduce into the economic, social, cultural, and psychological dimensions and the overall level of social integration, with the control variables unchanged. Thereinto, Model 5 investigate the effects of all the independent variables and control variables on the settlement intentions, with the best goodness of fit (the smallest value of -2 Log Likelihood and the highest R^2, so we will analyze the effects of social integration and other influence factors on the settlement intentions of floating population based on Model 5 (Table 5.14).

The overall level of social integration and four dimensions of social integration (economic integration, social adaption, cultural acceptance and psychological fusion) all exert significantly positive impacts on the floating population's settlement intention.

The first independent variable is the migrants' economic integration level, including their monthly income, participation in social security and occupational stability. The greater economic integration of floating population (having stable job, considerable income and being covered by local social security) will provide the floating population with more reliable living security and contribute to the settlement intentions of floating population.

Table 5.14 Binary logistic regression analysis of floating population's settlement intention

	MODEL1	MODEL2	MODEL3	MODEL4	MODEL5	MODEL6
Independent variables						
Social integration						0.378*** (−18.35)
Economic integration	0.159*** (−9.44)	0.127*** (−6.39)	0.131*** (−6.57)	0.132*** (−6.61)	0.129*** (−6.37)	
Social adaptation	0.196*** (−11.5)		0.167*** (−8.72)	0.167*** (−8.76)	0.216*** (−11.04)	
Cultural acceptance	0.0669*** (−4.03)			0.0333 (−1.87)	0.0495** (−2.74)	
Psychological fusion	0.389*** (−23.03)				0.377*** (−19.22)	
Control variables						
Individual characteristics						
Gender (Reference: Female)						
Male		0.0843* (−2.35)	0.0948** (−2.63)	0.0949** (−2.63)	0.119** (−3.25)	0.0946** (−2.63)
Age (Reference:15–25)						
25–35		0.223*** (−3.89)	0.218*** (−3.8)	0.216*** (−3.77)	0.231*** (−3.98)	0.205*** (−3.56)
35–45		0.458*** (−6.75)	0.448*** (−6.59)	0.448*** (−6.58)	0.455*** (−6.6)	0.439*** (−6.4)
> 45		0.179* (−2.22)	0.159* (−1.97)	0.163* (−2.02)	0.160* (−1.97)	0.174* (−2.15)
Education Level (Reference: Primary school or below)						
Junior high school		0.0996 (−1.56)	0.0796 (−1.24)	0.0734 (−1.15)	0.0361 (−0.56)	0.0219 (−0.34)
Senior high school		0.384*** (−5.34)	0.340*** (−4.71)	0.331*** (−4.58)	0.275*** (−3.74)	0.250*** (−3.43)
College or above		0.699*** (−8.19)	0.637*** (−7.41)	0.628*** (−7.3)	0.528*** (−6.06)	0.500*** (−5.8)
Marriage (Reference: unmarried)						

(continued)

Table 5.14 (continued)

	MODEL1	MODEL2	MODEL3	MODEL4	MODEL5	MODEL6
Married		0.951*** (18.09)	0.966*** (18.31)	0.965*** (18.30)	0.959*** (17.93)	0.967*** (18.20)
hukou (Reference: Non-agricultural)						
Agricultural		−0.213*** (−3.66)	−0.196*** (−3.66)	−0.193*** (−3.30)	−0.132* (−2.23)	−0.136* (−2.32)
The flow characteristics						
Flow range (Reference: Intercounty)						
Intercity		0.149 (−1.5)	0.149 (−1.5)	0.151 (−1.52)	0.00525 (−0.05)	0.0857 (−0.86)
Interprovincial		−0.484*** (−10.44)	−0.485*** (−10.44)	−0.483*** (−10.39)	−0.387*** (−8.19)	−0.432*** (−9.26)
Residence duration (Reference: 0–3)						
4–6		0.554*** (−12.3)	0.546*** (−12.08)	0.546*** (−12.09)	0.527*** (−11.52)	0.537*** (−11.79)
7–11		0.965*** (−17.01)	0.951*** (−16.72)	0.950*** (−16.7)	0.931*** (−16.16)	0.934*** (−16.31)
12		1.237*** (−15.36)	1.220*** (−15.12)	1.220*** (−15.11)	1.167*** (−14.32)	1.188*** (−14.62)
Flow reason (Reference: others)						
Accompanying Migration		0.289 (−0.78)	0.298 (−0.81)	0.298 (−0.8)	0.266 (−0.69)	0.304 (−0.81)
Work/business		−0.0985 (−0.27)	−0.0814 (−0.22)	−0.0799 (−0.22)	−0.153 (−0.41)	−0.14 (−0.38)
Type of destination region (Reference: Midwestern megacities)						
Eastern type-I large cities		−0.0226 (−0.37)	0.104 (−1.66)	0.109 (−1.74)	0.365*** (−5.6)	0.252*** (−4)
Eastern megalopolises		0.214*** (−4)	0.235*** (−4.37)	0.235*** (−4.38)	0.378*** (−6.88)	0.288*** (−5.4)
Eastern megacities		−0.114 (−1.90)	−0.0259 (−0.43)	−0.0272 (−0.45)	0.216*** (−3.43)	0.0781 (−1.28)

(continued)

Table 5.14 (continued)

	MODEL1	MODEL2	MODEL3	MODEL4	MODEL5	MODEL6
Connection with the hometown						
Worries about hometown		−0.146*** (−12.08)	−0.158*** (−12.96)	−0.157*** (−12.79)	−0.136*** (−10.93)	−0.140*** (−11.46)
The amount of homestead		−0.00014 (−0.74)	−0.00021 (−1.09)	−0.0002 (−1.05)	−0.00025 (−1.29)	−0.0002 (−1.22)
Constant	−2.183*** (−21.85)	0.262 −0.7	−0.0365 (−0.10)	−0.124 (−0.32)	−2.045*** (−5.03)	−0.923* (−2.36)
N	15,997	15,997	15,997	15,997	15,997	15,997
−2 Log Likelihood	20,852.11	19,229.92	19,152.46	19,148.95	18,767.37	18,920.23
Pseudo R^2	0.0365	0.1115	0.1150	0.1152	0.1328	0.1258
Chi-square	790.29	2412.47	2489.93	2493.45	2875.03	2722.17

Notes: t statistics are shown in parentheses; * signifies $p < 0.05$,** signifies $p < 0.01$, and *** signifies $p < 0.001$

The second independent variable reflects the migrants' social adaptation situations, incorporating the number of accompanying family members, participation in local social organizations, social activities and free government training. It is evident that migrants are more prone to the decision making of settlement with the augment of accompanying family members. The potential reason contributing to this tendency may be that more family members living together in destination cities facilitate the earning of urban wages and reduce worries about left-behind family members in hometown, helping migrants better adapt to local life. Whether a migrant's spouse and family members have joined him or her in the city is indicative of the transition from circular migration to permanent migration. Migrants' participation in local social organizations and activities do increase the probability of living locally for long periods, attributing to more interactions with local people and more concerns about the destination cities. Therefore, stronger social adaptation of floating population will lead to a stronger desire to live permanently.

The third independent variable is related with the acceptance of floating population towards local culture and language, covering proficiency of local language, conformity to local manners and customs, adaptation to local life style and acceptance of local social ideas. It is apparent that the migrants that can speak local language can communicate better with local residents and enjoy more convenience in life, thus are more determined to settle down in the destination areas. Besides, migrants who tend to accept local manners and customs, life styles and social ideas have higher settlement intentions, similar to the effect of supporting 'mainstream' cultural values [132]. Hence, better cultural acceptance of floating population (stronger local language ability, tending to accept local manners and customs, life style and social ideas) will greatly contribute to the long-term plan to stay.

The fourth independent variable represents the psychological fusion of floating population in destination cities, composed of getting along with local people, acceptance attitude of local people, satisfaction with life. Higher psychological fusion (getting along well with local people, positive acceptance attitude of local people, high satisfaction with life) will exert positive effects on settlement tendency.

Furthermore, we analyze the effects of control variables on settlement intentions. To begin with, the settlement intention of floating population is closely associated with their individual characteristics, with female, married, older, and more educated members of the floating population being generally more willing to reside in the destination cities, in comparison with their male, unmarried, younger, and less educated counterparts. The effects of the gender and marital status on settlement intentions are uncertain in extant studies, while the migrants with a higher education level are usually more competitive in the job market and easier to adapt to the life in the destination areas. It is noteworthy that our results about the influence of age are not consistent with some previous studies, which claim that the "post-80s" have stronger intentions to stay in the cities, due to the fact that they are more interested in non-farm jobs and city life so that they tend to establish more networks at their destination cities [17]. We divide the floating population in to 4 categories by age: 15–25, 26–35, 36–45 and above 45. As the employed data records the information of 2014, the migrants in age groups of 15–25 and 26–35 belong to the "post-80 s" new generation migrants, and those in age groups of 36–45 and above 45 are the former generation. Using the 15–25 category as a reference, the settlement intention of individuals in age groups of 26–35, 36–45 and above 45 are 1.2597 times, 1.5768 times and 1.1741 times that of the reference group, respectively. The older migrants stay longer in destination cities, accumulate more work experiences and social capital, thus are more inclined to remain, with the settlement intention reaching the peak between the age of 36 and 45. The migrants above 45 years old are more likely to return to their hometown due to more family commitments and rural attachments.

As the second group of control variables, migration features also play an important role in affecting settlement tendency. To begin with, compared to the long distance migration (flow range of inter-province), the short distance migration (flow range of intra-city and intra-province) increases the probability of floating population to settle down, resulting from the similarities in language, culture and customs due to geographical proximity. Besides, the longer residence duration corresponds to a greater willingness to live permanently in destination cities, because a long-term accumulation of social capital in the destination area acts as a positive incentive. The p values of flow reasons are not statistically significant, so its effects can be ignored here. As regards destination regions, the settlement intentions of floating population in eastern type-I large cities and eastern megalopolises are higher that of midwestern megalopolises, indicating that eastern cities have more attractiveness to migrants than central and western cities, and city sizes are usually positively related with settlement intentions. The reason derives from the fact that larger cities have more job opportunities and better social welfare. Nevertheless, the eastern megacities have currently taken strict measures to control population and impose restrictions on obtaining local *hukou*, thus reducing the likelihood of floating population to settle down permanently.

Last but not least, in terms of the family characteristics, worries about hometown is in reverse relation with the decision of settlement significantly, and the amount of homestead in hometown is also negatively related, whereas its influence is not significant.

5.4.5   Conclusions and Policy Implications

The urbanization rate of China has reached 58.52% by 2017, and there is still way to go compared with developed countries. Hence, pushing forward the urbanization process especially from the viewpoint of people is still an important mission in the next decades, with the social integration of floating population as a vital part. Under the context of China's new-type urbanization, the settlement intentions and social integration of floating population in destination cities have aroused great interest of scholars and policymakers in China. This study reports the results of a special survey of "Social Integration and Mental Health of Floating Population" initiated by NHC that focus on a range of determinants of settlement intentions comprehensively, discovering that the social integration condition is a decisive factor leading to stronger settlement intention. Most of the results of this study are consistent with previous studies, demonstrating that our research results are authentic and reliable. Individual characteristics, migration features and household factors are all nonnegligible determinants of settlement willingness.

Furthermore, the social integration condition of floating population includes various dimensions, which can be categorized into 4 types: economic integration, social adaptation, cultural acceptance and psychological fusion. In general, the social integration level of floating population is not high enough (42.81), among which the psychological fusion level is the highest (63.78) and the social adaptation level falls behind (26.13). This result reveals that migrants currently tend to integrate into local communities and become a member of destination cities, by working hard, interacting with local people and learning local language and culture. Nevertheless, it is essential to improve their participation in local social organizations and activities. We can offer 2 potential reasons contributing to this phenomenon: One reason is that the modern society progress and high-tech development have shortened the spatial distance between regions and increased cultural homogeneity, and migrants have learned and understood local culture and customs through daily life. Actually, the behaviors of migrating to destination cities can be considered as some kind of acceptance and approval of local culture and life style. The other reason is that different from subjectively controllable psychological and cultural factors, the conditions of economic integration and social adaptation exhibit strong objectivity, constrained by government policies, employment market and community environment. The floating population are usually engaged in low-paying and unstable physical work without social security in the destination areas, so they only concern their own survival rather than the development of local society, which are adverse to the social integration of floating population.

Last but not least, the social integration conditions of floating population play a crucial role in determining migrants' decisions of settlement. Greater economic integration, stronger social adaption, better cultural acceptance and higher psychological fusion are all very helpful in increasing settlement willingness of floating population. Therefore, it is urgent that measures should be taken to help floating population better integrate into destination cities from different aspects. Based on the results of this study, it is of great significance to realize the full coverage of basic public services among rural and urban residents, especially the improvement in the floating population's security system of employment, housing and social insurance in destination cities; meanwhile, it is necessary to motivate migrants to take part in social and community governance, thus increasing their sense of identity and affiliation with destination cities.

In conclusion, the social integration of floating population depends on not only the government dominance, but also the efforts of enterprises and social organizations, as well as the active participation of floating population. It is essential to develop various channels to learn about the actual difficulties and appeals of floating population, and construct an interactive platform helping floating population integrate into local society, economy, culture and people. The policy making about social integration should be aimed at endowing floating population with equal rights of employment, education, public services and social participation with local residents, which can be implemented step by step considering different situations of different cities. In addition, it is important to foster human resource of floating population, through providing free job training or opportunities of continuing education, hence improving their professional skills to face the challenges posed by the fourth industrial revolution. As the most important part of floating population's local life, the enterprises employing migrants are supposed to assume their social responsibilities towards floating population, including signing labor contracts, providing social insurance, improving working conditions and living conditions as well, helping them better integrate into the local society economically. The communities where migrants reside and related social organizations are ought to make efforts to encourage floating population to participate in all kinds of social organizations and community activities, create opportunities for them to fully communicate with local residents and learn about local culture, and also provide them with more detailed management and considerate services. The social integration of floating population in destination regions is a long and arduous process, according to the population migration rules and the historical law of economic and social development. This study of China can be further explored to contribute to a better understanding of human mobility and migration integration in the current world.

References

1. Fan CC (2005) Interprovincial migration, population redistribution, and regional development in China: 1990 and 2000 census comparisons. Prof Geogr 57(2):295–311
2. Fan CC (2005) Modeling interprovincial migration in China, 1985–2000. Eurasian Geogr Econ 46(3):165–184
3. Liu Z, Gu H (2019) Evolution characteristics of spatial concentration patterns of inter-provincial population migration in China from 1985 to 2015. Appl Spat Anal Policy 1–17
4. Chan KW (2009) The Chinese hukou system at 50. Eurasian Geogr Econ 50(2):197–221
5. Chan KW, Liu T, Yang Y (1999) Hukou and non-hukou migrations in China: comparisons and contrasts. Int J Popul Geogr 5(6):425–448
6. Fan CC (2002) The elite, the natives, and the outsiders: migration and labor market segmentation in urban China. Ann Assoc Am Geogr 92(1):103–124
7. Fan CC (2002) The elite, the natives, and the outsiders: migration and labor market segmentation in urban China. Ann Assoc Am Geogr 92(1):103–124
8. Liu Y, Xu W (2017) Destination choices of permanent and temporary migrants in China, 1985–2005. Popul Space Place 23(1):e1963
9. Gu H, Jie Y, Li Z, Shen T (2020) What drives migrants to settle in Chinese cities: a panel data analysis. Appl Spat Anal Policy 13:631–648
10. Chan KW (2019) China's hukou system at 60: continuity and reform. Handbook on urban development in China, pp 59–79
11. Wei H, Su H (2013) Research on degree of citizenization of rural-urban migrants in China. Chin J Popul Sci 2013(5):21–29 (in Chinese)
12. National Bureau of Statistics of China (2018) 2017 migrant workers monitoring survey report. http://www.stats.gov.cn/tjsj/zxfb/201704/t20170428_1489334.html
13. Gu H, Xiao F, Shen T, Liu Z (2018) Spatial difference and influencing factors of settlement intention of urban floating population in China: evidence from the 2015 national migrant population dynamic monitoring survey. Econ Geogr 38(11):22–29 (in Chinese)
14. Huang X, Liu Y, Xue D, Li Z, Shi Z (2018) The effects of social ties on rural-urban migrants' intention to settle in cities in China. Cities 83:203–212
15. Lin L, Zhu Y (2016) Spatial variation and its determinants of migrants' hukou transfer inten-tion of China's prefecture-and provincial-level cities: evidence from the 2012 national migrant population dynamic monitoring survey. Acta Geogr Sin 71(10):1696–1709 (in Chinese)
16. Tan S, Li Y, Song Y, Luo X, Zhou M, Zhang L, Kuang B (2017) Influence factors on settlement intention for floating population in urban area: a China study. Qual Quant 51(1):147–176
17. Yue Z, Li S, Feldman MW, Du H (2010) Floating choices: a generational perspective on intentions of rural-urban migrants in China. Environ Plan A 42(3):545–562
18. Zhu Y (2007) China's floating population and their settlement intention in the cities: beyond the Hukou reform. Habitat Int 31(1):65–76
19. Zhu Y, Chen W (2010) The settlement intention of China's floating population in the cities: recent changes and multifaceted individual-level determinants. Popul Space Place 16(4):253–267
20. Liu Y, Deng W, Song X (2018) Influence factor analysis of migrants' settlement intention: considering the characteristic of city. Appl Geogr 96:130–140
21. Stillwell J, Daras K, Bell M (2018) Spatial aggregation methods for investigating the MAUP effects in migration analysis. Appl Spat Anal Policy 11:693–711
22. Todaro MP (1969) A model of labor migration and urban unemployment in less developed countries. Am Econ Rev 59(1):138–148
23. Krugman PR (1991) Geography and trade. MIT Press
24. Stark O, Bloom DE (1985) The new economics of labor migration. Am Econ Rev 75(2):173–178
25. Glaeser EL, Kolko J, Saiz A (2001) Consumer city. J Econ Geogr 1(1):27–50

26. Graves PE (1976) A reexamination of migration, economic opportunity, and the quality of life. J Reg Sci 16(1):107–112
27. Tiebout CM (1956) A pure theory of local expenditures. J Polit Econ 64(5):416–424
28. Gu H, Liu Z, Shen T (2019) Spatial pattern and influencing mechanism of interprovincial migration's hukou transfer intention in China. Scientia Geographica Sinica 39(11):1702–1710 (in Chinese)
29. Liu Y, Shen J (2014) Jobs or amenities? Location choices of interprovincial skilled migrants in China, 2000–2005. Popul Space Place 20(7):592–605
30. Liu Y, Shen J (2017) Modelling skilled and less-skilled interregional migrations in China, 2000–2005. Popul Space Place 23(4):e2027
31. Xiang H, Yang J, Zhang T, Ye X (2018) Analyzing in-migrants and out-migrants in urban China. Appl Spat Anal Policy 11:81–102
32. Xu Z, Ouyang A (2018) The factors influencing China's population distribution and spatial heterogeneity: a prefectural-level analysis using geographically weighted regression. Appl Spat Anal Policy 11:465–480
33. Fan CC (2011) Settlement intention and split households: findings from a survey of migrants in Beijing's urban villages. China Rev 11–41
34. Gu H, Liu Z, Shen T, Meng X (2019) Modelling interprovincial migration in China from 1995 to 2015 based on an eigenvector spatial filtering negative binomial model. Popul Space Place 25(8):e2253
35. Huang X, He D, Liu Y, Xie S, Wang R, Shi Z (2020) The effects of health on the settlement intention of rural-urban migrants: evidence from eight Chinese cities. Appl Spat Anal Policy 1–19
36. Huang Y, Guo F, Cheng Z (2018) Market mechanisms and migrant settlement intentions in urban China. Asian Popul Stud 14(1):22–42
37. Liu Z, Wang Y, Chen S (2017) Does formal housing encourage settlement intention of rural migrants in Chinese cities? A structural equation model analysis. Urban Stud 54(8):1834–1850
38. Wei Z (2013) A region-specific comparative study of factors influencing the residing preference among migrant population in different areas: based on the dynamic monitoring & survey data on the migrant population in five cities of China. Popul Econ 4:12–20 (in Chinese)
39. Chen S, Liu Z (2016) What determines the settlement intention of rural migrants in China? Economic incentives versus sociocultural conditions. Habitat Int 58:42–50
40. Cao G, Li M, Ma Y, Tao R (2015) Self-employment and intention of permanent urban settlement: evidence from a survey of migrants in China's four major urbanising areas. Urban Stud 52(4):639–664
41. Gu H, Liu Z, Shen T (2020) Spatial pattern and determinants of migrant workers' interprovincial hukou transfer intention in China: evidence from a national migrant population dynamic monitoring survey in 2016. Popul Space Place 26(2):e2250
42. Gu H, Li Q, Shen T (2020) Spatial difference and influencing factors of floating population's settlement intention in the three provinces of Northeast China. Scientia Geographica Sinica 40(2):261–269 (in Chinese)
43. Gu H, Meng X, Shen T, Wen L (2019) China's highly educated talents in 2015: patterns, determinants and spatial spillover effects. App Spat Anal Policy 1–18
44. Zhou L, Tian L, Gao Y, Ling Y, Fan C, Hou D, Shen T, Zhou W (2019) How did industrial land supply respond to transitions in state strategy? An analysis of prefecture-level cities in China from 2007 to 2016. Land Use Policy 87:104009
45. Freeman LC (2000) Visualizing social networks. J Soc Struct 1(1):4
46. Haug S (2008) Migration networks and migration decision-making. J Ethn Migr Stud 34(4):585–605
47. Yang G, Zhou C, Jin W (2020) Integration of migrant workers: differentiation among three rural migrant enclaves in Shenzhen. Cities 96:102453
48. Dustmann C (2003) Return migration, wage differentials, and the optimal migration duration. Eur Econ Rev 47(2):353–369

49. McGranahan DA (1999) Natural amenities drive rural population change (no. 1473–2016–120765)
50. Rappaport J (2009) Moving to nice weather. In: Environmental amenities and regional economic development. Routledge, pp 25–53
51. National Health Commission (2018) Report on floating population development 2018. China Population Publishing House, Beijing (in Chinese)
52. Shen J (2002) A study of the temporary population in Chinese cities. 26(3):363–377
53. Shen J (2012) Changing patterns and determinants of interprovincial migration in China 1985–2000. Popul Space Place 18(3):384–402
54. Wang G, Pan Z, Lu Y (2012) China's inter-provincial migration patterns and influential factors: evidence from year 2000 and 2010 population census of China. Chin J Popul Sci 5:2–13 (in Chinese)
55. Gu H, Meng X, Shen T, Cui N (2020) Spatial variation of the determinants of China's urban floating population's settlement intention. Acta Geogr Sin 75(2):240–254 (in Chinese)
56. Xie S, Chen J (2018) Beyond homeownership: housing conditions, housing support and rural migrant urban settlement intentions in China. Cities 78:76–86
57. You Z, Yang H, Fu M (2018) Settlement intention characteristics and determinants in floating populations in Chinese border cities. Sustain Cities Soc 39:476–486
58. Jiang X, Wang S, Yang Y (2017) Research on China's urban population mobility network based on Baidu LBS big data. Popul Dev 23(1):13–23 (in Chinese)
59. Jiang X, Wang S (2017) Research on China's urban population mobility network: based on Baidu migration big data. Chin J Popul Sci 2:35–46+127 (in Chinese)
60. Li Y, Liu Y, Jin Y (2017) Complex network modeling spatial pattern and trend of interprovincial migration. Stat Res 09:56–64 (in Chinese)
61. Pan J, Lai J (2019) Research on spatial pattern of population mobility among cities: a case study of "Tencent migration" big data in "National day-mid-autumn festival" vacation. Geogr Res 38(7):1678–1693 (in Chinese)
62. Pan J, Lai J (2019) Spatial pattern of population flow among cities in China during the spring festival travel rush based on "Tencent migration" data. Hum Geogr 34(3):108–117 (in Chinese)
63. Liu J (2009) Lecture on whole network approach: a practical guide to UCINET. Truth & Wisdom Press, Shanghai (in Chinese)
64. Fan Y (2019) Evolution and simulation analysis of global industrial network—based on link prediction theory. Peking University, Beijing (in Chinese)
65. Blondel VD, Guillaume JL, Lambiotte R et al (2008) Fast unfolding of communities in large networks. J Stat Mech: Theory Exp (10):P10008
66. Gu H, Shen T, Liu Z, Meng X (2019) Driving mechanism of interprovincial population migration flows in China based on spatial filtering. Acta Geogr Sin 74(2):222–237 (in Chinese)
67. Gu H, Qin X, Shen T (2019e) Spatial variation of migrant population's return intention and its determinants in China's prefecture and provincial level cities. Geogr Res 38(8):1877–1890 (in Chinese)
68. Fu Y, Gabriel SA (2012) Labor migration, human capital agglomeration and regional development in China. Reg Sci Urban Econ 42(3):473–484
69. Massey DS, Arango J, Hugo G, Kouaouci A, Pellegrino A, Taylor JE (1993) Theories of international migration: a review and appraisal. Popul Dev Rev 431–466
70. Wu F (2012) Neighborhood attachment, social participation, and willingness to stay in China's low-income communities. Urban Affairs Rev 48(4):547–570
71. Chen J, Wang W (2019) Economic incentives and settlement intentions of rural migrants: evidence from China. J Urban Aff 41(3):372–389
72. Annell J, Terman F (2017) What does it take to make them stay? How place satisfaction relates to willingness to stay of the creative class. Kristianstad University, Kristianstad, pp 1–80
73. Yang D (2016) A comparative study on settlement intention of the floating population in northeast China. Popul J 38(5):34–44 (in Chinese)
74. Yu X, Chen X (2017) Research on post-90s floating youth's willingness to live in Guangdong Province. Commer Res 59(5):177 (in Chinese)

75. Hou J, Li X (2017) The analysis of the status of China's floating elderly population and It's influencing factors. Popul J 39:62–70 (in Chinese)
76. Chen Z (2016) Study on the will for long-term residence of agricultural transfer population. J Shandong Norm Univ (Soc Sci) 61(4):147–156 (in Chinese)
77. Zhang H, Cao Y, Wang M (2015) The influence of social integration on the migrants' willingness of long-term residence in Guangzhou City. Northwest Popul 36:7–11 (in Chinese)
78. Liang H (2017) Basic characteristics and settlement intention of floating population in border areas. Popul Soc 2:59–67 (in Chinese)
79. Sun J, Liu Y (2015) Group characteristics and residing preference of migrant workers in Beijing. Soc Sci Beijing 2015:76–80 (in Chinese)
80. Yang Z, Luo Y (2015) Study on the settlement intention of rural-urban floating population in Beijing. Popul Soc 1:69–80 (in Chinese)
81. Hu X (2017) A study on the differences in settlement intention between the new and old generations of floating population: cases of Beijing, Shanghai and Guangzhou. World Surv Res 7:28–32 (in Chinese)
82. Yang Q, Li P (2017) New generation of migrant workers' family development capacity and urban settlement intention—an empirical study based on the data of the China migrants dynamic survey in 2014. China Youth Study 10:50–56 (in Chinese)
83. Li S, Wang W, Yue Z (2014) A comparative study on settlement intentions between self-employed and employed migrants. Popul Econ 2:12–21 (in Chinese)
84. Shen T, Feng D, Sun T (2010) Spatial econometrics. Peking University Press, Beijing (in Chinese)
85. Xiao Z, Xu S, Liu J (2018) The assessment of social integration of urban migrant population: an investigation based on 50 cities of migration destination. Popul Res 43(5):96–112 (in Chinese)
86. Xiao F, Ren J, Wu M et al (2018) The spatiotemporal evolution and the influence mechanism of high-tech enterprise locations in China during the twenty-first century. Econ Geogr 38(2):27–35 (in Chinese)
87. Li T, Fu W (2015) Spatial processes of regional innovation in Guangdong Province, China: empirical evidence using a spatial panel data model. Asian J Technol Innov 23(3):304–320
88. Anselin L, Bera AK, Florax R, Yoon MJ (1996) Simple diagnostic tests for spatial dependence. Reg Sci Urban Econ 26(1):77–104
89. Lin Y, Zhang Q, Chen W, Li L (2017) The social income inequality, social integration and health status of internal migrants in China. Int J Equity Health 16:139
90. Zhang X, Zhou S, Yao J (2018) Settlement decision, hukou transfer intention and social integration: an empirical study on rural-urban migrants. J Humanit 4:39–48
91. Lee ES (1966) A theory of migration. Demography 3:47–57
92. Narasimhan S (1995) Labour out-migration to cities: search for an appropriate theory. Man Dev 17:78–88
93. Massey DS (1990) The social and economic origins of immigration. Ann Am Acad Pol Soc Sci 510:60–72
94. Gordon M (1964) Assimilation in American life: the role of race, religion, and national origins. Oxford University Press, New York, pp 26–52
95. Lewis WA (1972) Reflections on unlimited labor. Int Econ Dev 75–96
96. Todaro MP (1980) Internal migration in developing countries: a survey. In: Easterlin RA (ed) Population and economic change in developing countries. University of Chicago Press, Chicago, IL, pp 361–402
97. Tang S, Feng J (2015) Cohort differences in the urban settlement intentions of rural migrants: a case study in Jiangsu Province, China. Habitat Int 49:357–365
98. Tang S, Feng J (2012) Understanding the settlement intentions of the floating population in the cities of Jiangsu Province, China. Asian Pacific Migr J 21(4):509–532
99. Yang C, Xu W, Liu Y, Ning Y, Klein KK (2016) Staying in the countryside or moving to the city: the determinants of villagers' urban settlement intentions in China. China Rev 16(3):41–68

100. Hao P, Tang S (2015) Floating or settling down: the effect of rural landholdings on the settlement intention of rural migrants in urban China. Environ Plan A 47(9):1979–1999
101. Tang S, Hao P (2018) Floaters, settlers, and returnees: Settlement intention and hukou conversion of China's rural migrants. China Rev 18(1):11–34
102. Zhang B, Druijven P, Strijker D (2017) Does ethnic identity influence migrants' settlement intentions? Evidence from three cities in Gansu Province, Northwest China. Habitat Int 69:94–103
103. Park RE, Burgess EW (1921) Introduction to the Science of Society
104. Park RE (1928) Human migration and the marginal man. Am J Sociol 33:881–893
105. Glazer N (1997) We are all multiculturalists now. Harvard University Press, Cambridge
106. Kallen HM (1956) Cultural pluralism and the American idea. University of Pennsylvania Press, Philadelphia
107. Portes A (1995) Children of immigrants: segmented assimilation and its determinants. In: Portes A (ed) The economic sociology of immigration: essays on networks, ethnicity and entrepreneurship. Russell Sage Foundation, New York
108. Zhou M, Portes A (2012) The new second generation: segmented assimilation and its variants. The New Immigration, Routledge, pp 99–116
109. Threlfall M (2003) European social integration: harmonization, convergence and single social areas. J Eur Soc Policy 13:121–139
110. Braun M, Glöckner-Rist A (2012) Patterns of social integration of Western European migrants. J Int Migr Integr 13:403–422
111. Martinovic B, Van Tubergen F, Maas I (2009) Changes in immigrants' social integration during the stay in the host country: the case of non-western immigrants in the Netherlands. Soc Sci Res 38:870–882
112. Vigdor JL (2008) Measuring immigrant assimilation in the United States. Civic Report No. 53. Manhattan Institute for Policy Research
113. Yue Z, Li S, Jin X, Marcus W (2013) Feldman. The role of social networks in the integration of Chinese rural-urban migrants: a migrant-resident tie perspective. Urban Stud 50:1704–1723
114. Åslund O, Böhlmark A, Skans ON (2015) Childhood and family experiences and the social integration of young migrants. Labour Econ 35:135–144
115. Chen Y, Wang J (2015) Social integration of new-generation migrants in Shanghai China. Habitat Int 49:419–425
116. Kearns A, Whitley E (2015) Getting there? The effects of functional factors, time and place on the social integration of migrants. J Ethn Migr Stud 41:2105–2129
117. Wang Z, Zhang F, Wu F (2016) Intergroup neighbouring in urban China: implications for the social integration of migrants. Urban Stud 53:651–668
118. Hainmueller J, Hangartner D, Pietrantuono G (2017) Catalyst or crown: does naturalization promote the long-term social integration of immigrants? Am Polit Sci Rev 111:256–276
119. Wei L, Gao F (2017) Social media, social integration and subjective well-being among new urban migrants in China. Telemat Inform 34:786–796
120. Massey DS, Mullan BP (1985) Residential segregation and color stratification among Hispanics in Philadelphia—reply. Am J Sociol 91:396–399
121. Penninx R (2005) Integration of migrants: economic, social, cultural and political dimensions. The new demographic regime: population challenges and policy responses. 5:137–152
122. Snel E, Engbersen G, Leerkes A (2006) Transnational involvement and social integration. Global Netw 6:285–308
123. Ager A, Strang A (2008) Understanding integration: a conceptual framework. J Refug Stud 21:166–191
124. Yang J (2010) Index of assimilation for rural-to-urban migrants: a further analysis of the conceptual framework of assimilation theory. Popul Econ 2:64–70 (in Chinese)
125. Yang J (2015) Research on the assimilation of the floating population in China. Soc Sci China 2:61–79+203–204 (in Chinese)
126. Ette A, Heß B, Sauer L (2016) Tackling Germany's demographic skills shortage: permanent settlement intentions of the recent wave of labour migrants from non-European countries. J Int Migr Integr 17:429–448

127. Wang P (2015) The study of inter-provincial floating population's long-term residence intention in Xinjiang from the perspective of social integration theory. Popul Dev 21:66–71 (in Chinese)

128. Wei J, Zhu Y (2018) Differences and determinants of the levels of social integration of inter-and intra-provincial floating population. J Subtrop Resour Environ 13(4):69–77

129. Yu Y, Gao X, Guo Q (2012) Research on social integration for new generation of rural-urban migrants: based on the survey in Shanghai. Popul Econ 1:57–64 (in Chinese)

130. Yang J (2017) Double-dual property of Hukou system and social integration of internal migrants in the context of new-blueprint urbanizatiom in China. J Renmin Univ China 31(4):119–128 (in Chinese)

131. Zhu P (2017) Analysis on floating population's living intention and its influencing factors: a survey in Jiaxing City. J Jiaxing Univ 29(5):128–134 (in Chinese)

132. De Vroome T, Van Tubergen F (2014) Settlement intentions of recently arrived immigrants and refugees in the Netherlands. J Immigr Refug Stud 12:47–66

Chapter 6
Return Intentions of Floating Population

6.1 Return Intentions at the City Level

6.1.1 Introduction

International migration is an important force in shaping the global population patterns. According to the International Migration Report 2017, there are 253 million international migrants worldwide, increasing by 49% compared with 2000, accounting for about 3.4% of the total global population. In China, population migration also profoundly affects the levels of economic and social development in all regions. In 2016, the size of China's floating population reached 245 million, becoming an important factor influencing population change. From the perspective of the direction of the population migration, as some of the country's major cities have strict restriction on the sizes of their populations and the economy of the central and western regions continues to grow, the return migration has become a growing concern of society. From 2011 to 2016, the growth rate of China's migrant rural workers showed a decreasing trend year by year, and the proportion of migrant rural workers to the total number of rural workers also gradually decreased from 62.8% in 2011 to 60.1% in 2016. In provinces with large population outflows such as Hainan, Hubei, Anhui and Sichuan, there appears an obvious trend of return migration. For example, in 2017, the population inflow in Hubei province was 1.57 million, 80,000 more than that of the previous year, and the population outflow was 4.91 million, 60,000 fewer than the previous year. The floating population's return intention is an important indicator of the future trend of return migration in China. At the national level, there exist differences in the economic development and social culture in geographical locations or administrative units, and the floating population's return intention is often characterized by heterogeneity across regions. This study aims at addressing the following questions: what is the current situation of the floating population's return intention in China? What spatial differences do they exhibit?

T. Shen et al., *Migration Patterns and Intentions of Floating Population in Transitional China*, Spatial Demography and Population Governance, https://doi.org/10.1007/978-981-19-3375-2_6

What are the drivers of return intention? Answering these questions will be of great significance to the new urbanization construction and the *hukou* system reform in each region.

Foreign scholars have conducted early theoretical studies on the return migration. The neoclassical economic micro theory represented by the Todaro model considers return migration as the decision-making behaviour of the migrant after maximizing the difference between the expected benefits and the costs of migration [1, 2]. The New Migration Economics theory advocates that the return migration is a behaviour that maximizes the welfare of the migrant's family, and that once the migrant's economic purpose has been achieved, he or she will return to hometown, diversifying household income through remittances in order to hedge against the risks associated with the deficiencies of the credit market in the origin areas [3]. Social network theory emphasizes that social ties and social networks in the origin areas are the main motivation for return migration [1, 4]. The push-and-pull theory states that return migration is influenced by a combination of pull forces from the origin areas (e.g. ease of access to employment, familiar social networks) and push forces from the destination areas (e.g. high unemployment risks), with Gmelch [5] argue that the pull force from hometown is a more important factor.

In terms of empirical research, empirical studies on return migration in foreign literature mainly started in the 1980s. Return migration is a complex issue influenced by many factors such as economic, family, social and environmental factors [4]. Generally speaking, migrants with lower wage levels in destination areas, weaker social integration, stronger family ties with origin areas, shorter residence duration in destination areas, and lower education level tend to return [6–11]. In addition, the employment choices of returning migrants are one of the hot research topics. Piracha and Vadean [12] found that international migrants who returned to Albania were more likely to become entrepreneurs and to have a positive impact on local economic activity than those who did not migrate. In the twenty-first century, some Western scholars have begun to focus on the subjective return intention of international migrants, especially on how this intention is influenced by the integration of migrants in destination areas and by the transnational connection between the origin country and the destination country. Based on a survey of African immigrant groups in Spain and Italy, De Haas and Fokkema [13] found that for African immigrants in both countries, socio-cultural integration in the destination areas had a negative impact on their return intention, while economic integration and transnational connection had an unclear impact on their return intention. In contrast, Anniste and Tammaru [14] found that the integration in destination areas did not have a significant effect on international migrants' return intention, and that migrants were likely to have a stronger return intention even if they were well integrated in the local society. Subsequently, Carling and Pettersen [15] pointed out that the integration and the relative strength of transnational connection were key determinants of international migrants' return intention. In addition, some scholars have focused on the impact of social capital on the return intention. For example, Haug [16] found that social capital in destination areas has a significant negative effect on international migrants' return intention, while social capital in origin areas has a positive effect.

Compared to foreign studies, domestic research on the floating population's return migration is mainly at the stage of drawing on the foreign theories [4]. In recent years, with the opening of the application of statistical data in China, research on floating population's return intention has been on the rise [17–25]. Although the return intention does not fully represent the final outcome of return migration, this indicator reflects the future return migration trend of floating population to a certain extent, which has certain implications for the *hukou* system reform and the management policy formulation of the floating population. The existing studies on floating population's return intention can be divided into the following three aspects: ① Analysis of the overall influencing factors on floating population's return intention. For example, Yin and Li [21, 22] used a logistic regression model to analyze the return intention of rural migrant workers from Yunfu, Guangdong Province and its influencing factors based on the survey data of rural households in Yunfu from 2010 to 2011, and found that the return intention is higher among migrant workers who are married, older, have lower human capital and a larger number of children in the family. ② The study on the influencing factors of floating population's return intention in specific regions. For example, through field research and questionnaire interviews, Wang et al. [26] conducted a study on the return intention of migrant workers in traditional agricultural areas and its planning effects, taking Zhoukou in Henan Province as an example, discovered that the employment opportunities, education and medical level were the most important driving factors for the floating population's return intention. ③ The specific factors influencing the floating population's return intention. For example, Yu et al. [23] used data from a questionnaire survey of migrant workers in Shanghai in 2010 to focus on the influence of social security on return intention, and found that the participation of migrant workers in urban pension insurance, urban medical insurance and urban unemployment insurance had a significant impact on migrant workers' return intention. Zhang et al. [25] conducted a survey on the migrant workers working in Ningbo without the local *hukou*, focusing on the influence of family factors on their return intentions. They found that family factors can significantly influence migrant workers' return intention, and that the integrity of the family in destination areas is an important determinant in migrant workers' settlement decision.

A review of the literature reveals that little attention has been paid to the spatial variation in floating population's return intention. In addition, previous studies have mainly focused on the return migration outcomes of those migrants who have already returned and the related influencing factors, while few studies have been conducted on the return intentions of those who have not returned. Therefore, we investigated the spatial pattern of floating population's return intention in China's 279 cities using GIS spatial statistical tools (such as the Moran index and hotspot analysis), with the data of China Migrants Dynamic Survey (CMDS) in 2016, and explored the influencing mechanism of each factor on floating population's return intention.

6.1.2   Study Area and Research Methodology

6.1.2.1   Study Area Description

The study area is the prefecture-level and above units in China in 2016. Whether for analyzing the spatial pattern and influencing mechanism of floating population's return intention, or formulating corresponding management strategies for floating population, cities are a more suitable research unit. According to the *China City Statistical Yearbook 2017*, by the end of 2016, there were 297 cities at the prefecture level and above, excluding Hong Kong SAR, Macau SAR and Taiwan. Among them, 16 cities, including Changdu, Danzhou, Fushun, Fuxin, Hami, Heze, Huai'an, Linzhi, Maoming, Mudanjiang, Shigatse, Sansha, Shannan, Shangluo, Suqian and Yichun, were not included in the CMDS database, while Jiyuan was not included in the China City Statistical Yearbook. In addition, Turpan and Qujing have more missing data. Therefore, the study area consists of 279 cities.

6.1.2.2   Data

The data were obtained from the CMDS database of the National Health Commission in 2016. Data were collected by randomly drawing sample points in 31 provinces (autonomous regions and municipalities) and Xinjiang Production and Construction Corps in mainland China with a relatively high concentration of floating population, through a stratified, multi-stage and proportional to size PPS method for sampling [27]. The final number of effective samples was 153,320. The respondents of the database were the migrants over 15 years old who had lived in destination areas for more than one month without local *hukou*. Thereinto, the migrants intending to return to hometowns are defined as the migrants with the return intention. The dependent variable in this study is the proportion of the floating population with the return intention to the total floating population in each city.

6.1.2.3   Research Methods

Global Moran's I

Measuring the spatial autocorrelation of floating population's return intention at the national level [28–31] is an important aspect of understanding its spatial pattern. The Moran's I Coefficient (MC) is the most widely used method to detect spatial autocorrelation in data, based on the Pearson correlation formula. With the help of MC calculations, it is possible to analyze whether there is a spatial spillover effect in floating population's return intention among cities. The calculation formula is as follows:

$$MC = \frac{n}{\sum_i \sum_j w_{ij}} \frac{\sum_i \sum_j w_{ij}(x_i - \overline{x})(x_i - \overline{x})}{\sum_i (x_i - \overline{x})^2} \tag{6.1}$$

In the formula: n is the number of samples; w_{ij} is the (i, j) element of the spatial weight matrix W. According to the first law of geography, the principle of the inverse distance weighted method is used in the construction of W in this study; x_i and x_j are the observed values of spatial units i and j respectively; $\overline{x}$ is the mean of the observed values; positive values of MC reflect positive spatial correlation, while negative values reflect negative spatial correlation. If the spatial weight matrix is row normalised, MC can be expressed as a more concise formula:

$$MC = \frac{X'WX}{X'X} \tag{6.2}$$

In the formula: X represents the column vector of observations; W represents the spatial weight matrix. In this study, MC measures the spatial autocorrelation of floating population's return intention at the national level, and indicates whether the spatial pattern of floating population's return intentions is concentrated distribution, random distribution or discrete distribution [32].

Getis-Ord G_i^*

The Getis-Ord G_i^* statistic is used to measure the hot spots and cold spots in the spatial distribution of floating population's return intention. The Getis-Ord G_i^* statistic detects whether each geographical element belongs to a high or low value agglomeration pattern in space by calculating the interrelationship of geographical attributes between a certain location and its neighbouring locations. The formula for calculating the hotspot analysis is as follows:

$$G_i^* = \frac{\sum_{j=1}^{n} W_{i,j} - \overline{X} \sum_{j=1}^{n} W_{i,j}}{S\sqrt{\frac{n\sum_{j=1}^{n} W_{i,j} - \left(\sum_{j=1}^{n} W_{i,j}\right)^2}{n-1}}}, \quad \overline{X} = \frac{\sum_{j=1}^{n} X_j}{n}, \quad S = \sqrt{\frac{\sum_{j=1}^{n} X_j^2}{n} - (\overline{X})^2}$$

$$\tag{6.3}$$

In the formula: X_j is the attribute value of spatial element j; $W_{i,j}$ is the spatial weight between elements i and j; n is the total number of spatial elements; $\overline{X}$ is the mean value of spatial elements; S is the standard deviation of spatial elements. G_i^* statistic is the z-score, a higher z-score indicates that the spatial elements show a tighter agglomeration of high values; a lower z-score indicates that the spatial elements show a tighter agglomeration of low values [32].

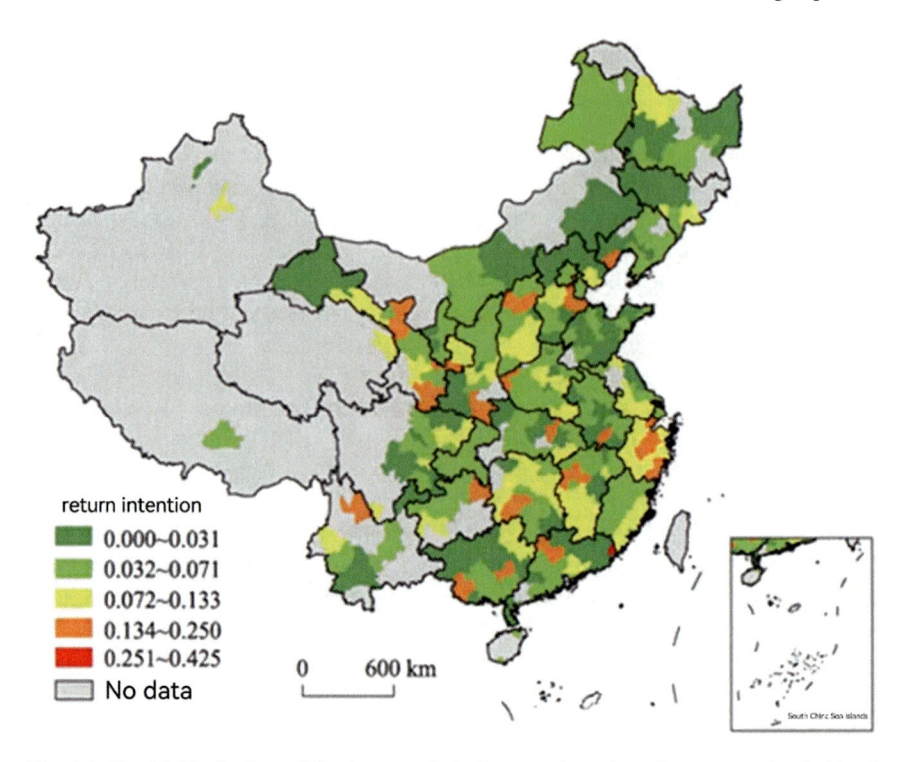

Fig. 6.1 Spatial distribution of floating population's return intention of prefecture-level cities in 2016

6.1.3   The Floating Population's Return Intention and Its Spatial Variation Characteristics

6.1.3.1   Descriptive Statistics

China's Overall Return Intention is Low, and Most of the Return Migrants Return to Their Hometowns

The proportion of the floating population with the return intentions at the prefecture level in China is 6.17%, the proportion of the floating population with the settlement intention is 61.23%, and the proportion of the floating population with the *hukou* transfer intentions is 37.86%. The distribution of floating population's return intention is shown in Fig. 6.1. Compared to the settlement intention and the *hukou* transfer intentions, the floating population's return intention is relatively low, only accounting for 10.07% and 16.30% respectively of the settlement intention and the *hukou* transfer intentions. An analysis of the destination areas of the return migration shows that the majority (74.05%) of floating population with the return intention will return to their villages, mainly migrant workers with a rural *hukou*. In addition, 10.92%

of the respondents return to the seat of the county government, while 6.52% of the respondents return to the seat of the town government. The rest of the respondents have a desire to return to their hometowns but do not determine where they want to go. This shows that family is an important factor in attracting migrants to return: the origin areas have advantages of established family and friend ties, familiar culture and living environment, thus becoming the destination areas where most migrants return to. The number of return migrants choosing the seat of the county government as the destination area is larger than those choosing the seat of the township governments as the destination area, indicating that higher-ranking destinations are preferred by the return migrants.

The Asymmetrical 'U-shaped' Pattern of City Size, City Level and Return Intention

The 279 sample cities are divided into municipalities directly under the central government, sub-provincial cities, cities specifically designated in the state plan, provincial capital cities and ordinary prefecture-level cities, and the floating population's return intention at different city levels are demonstrated in Fig. 6.2. The return intention is the highest in ordinary prefecture-level cities and municipalities directly under the central government (6.64% and 5.92% respectively), compared to 5.07, 5.17 and 5.62% for cities specifically designated in the state plan, sub-provincial cities and provincial capital cities. With the decrease of city rank, floating population's return intention shows a 'U-shaped' pattern of falling first and rising later. The return intention is higher in lower-ranked cities than in higher-ranked cities, so the pattern is asymmetrical. From the perspective of city size, the sample cities are divided into "five categories and seven grades" according to *A Notice on Adjusting the Standard of City Size Division* issued by the State Council in 2014, and the floating population's return intention is calculated for each level of city size. The results show that the return intention in megacities is 5.92%, and the return intention slightly decreases as the city size declines, followed by a rapid upward trend. Thus, the return intention in cities with different sizes also presents the asymmetrical 'U-shaped' characteristic similar to that of different city levels. The reason for this is that cities at higher levels and with larger sizes usually have higher income levels, more job opportunities, and more robust social security and public service systems due to the agglomeration of population and economy. As a result, cities of high rank and large size become the preferred place for the floating population to settle down, thus the return intention decreases. However, these cities also impose certain administrative barriers that prevent migrants from obtaining local *hukou*, thus creating obstacles for their settlement. In addition, for cities with low rank and small size, although they encourage migrants to settle down, their relatively lower level of economic development and imperfect job market discourage further inflows of migrants and increase their return intention.

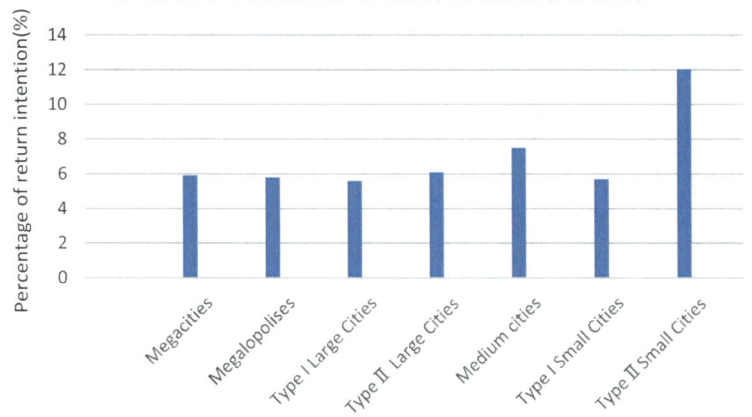

Fig. 6.2 Differentiation characteristics of floating population's return intention of cities in different sizes and hierarchies in China. *Notes:* The abbreviations in the figure are shown below: MDCG—municipalities directly under the central government, CSDSP—cities specifically designated in the state plan, SPC—sub-provincial cities, PCC—provincial capital cities, OPLC—ordinary prefecture-level cities

6.1.3.2 Spatial Variation Characteristics of Floating Population's Return Intention

Return Intention Is Highest in the Yangtze River Delta Urban Agglomeration and Lowest in the Harbin-Changchun Urban Agglomeration

According to the relevant documents promulgated by the State Council (Development Plannings of Chengdu-Chongqing Urban Agglomeration, Harbin-Changchun Urban

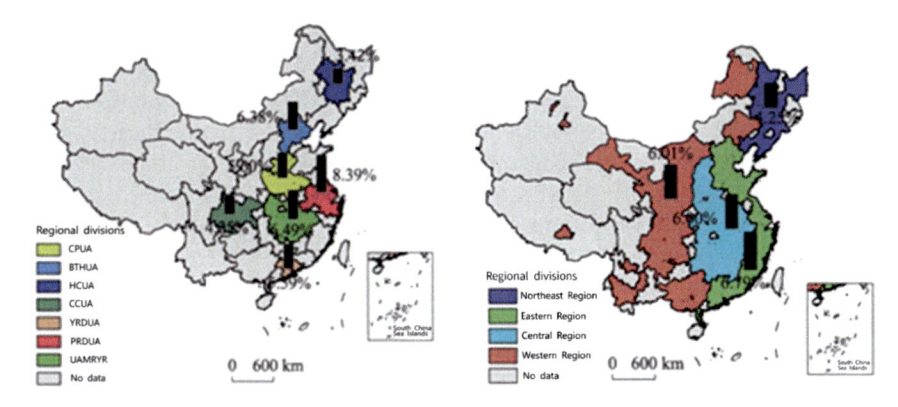

Fig. 6.3 Spatial distribution of floating population's return intention in different urban agglomerations and geographical divisions. *Notes* The abbreviations in the Figure are shown below: Central Plains urban agglomeration (CPUA), Beijing-Tianjin-Hebei urban agglomeration (BTHUA), Harbin-Changchun urban agglomeration (HCUA), Chengdu-Chongqing urban agglomeration (CCUA), Yangtze River Delta urban agglomeration (YRDUA), Pearl River Delta urban agglomeration (PRDUA), the urban agglomeration in the middle reaches of the Yangtze River (UAMRYR)

Agglomeration, the urban agglomeration in the middle reaches of the Yangtze River, Central Plains Urban Agglomeration) and the delineation of major urban agglomerations by various scholars in recent years [33, 34], we compare the differences of floating population's return intention in the Yangtze River Delta urban agglomeration, Beijing-Tianjin-Hebei urban agglomeration, Pearl River Delta urban agglomeration, Central Plains urban agglomeration, the urban agglomeration in the middle reaches of the Yangtze River, Harbin-Changchun urban agglomeration and Chengdu-Chongqing urban agglomeration. The results are shown in Fig. 6.3, with the Yangtze River Delta urban agglomeration having the highest return intention (8.39%). With the increasing of labour costs, labour supply is becoming increasingly tight. In addition, the transition and upgrading of labour-intensive industries in the Yangtze River Delta urban agglomeration in recent years has contributed to the return migration of large floating population. The return intention is lowest in the Harbin-Changchun urban agglomeration (3.42%), which is related to the fact that the floating population in this urban agglomeration mainly come from the three northeastern provinces and this urban agglomeration has a similar socio-cultural environment with their origin regions.

Eastern Region Has the Highest Return Intention, While the Northeast Region Has the Lowest Return Intention

The sample cities are divided into four major sub-regions: the eastern region, the central region, the western region and the northeast region, and the average floating population's return intention in each sub-region is calculated separately. As shown in

Fig. 6.3, the eastern region has the highest return intention (7.40%), indicating that the direction of return migration is generally from developed regions to less developed regions. The return intention is similar in the central and western regions (5.35% and 5.34% respectively). The return intention is the lowest in the northeast region (4.17%). In the context of the economic downturn and the huge population outflows in the northeast region in recent years, the floating population in the northeast region may have gained more employment opportunities in the destination cities, hence their return intention is relatively low.

The Floating Population's Return Intention Shows a Agglomeration Distribution Pattern with a Significantly Positive but Weak Spatial Autocorrelation

The spatial autocorrelation characteristics of floating population's return intention at the city level are calculated through the Geoda platform. The MC is calculated to be 0.03 (significance level $P = 0.006$, z-score $= 2.73$), which indicates that there is a agglomeration distribution pattern of return intention in China, with a significant positive spatial autocorrelation. However, the MC is relatively low, suggesting a weak spatial autocorrelation of return intention. At the city level, a city's return intention has a weak positive correlation with that of the neighbouring cities, probably due to cultural and economic exchanges.

South China and Central-Southern China Are the Hotspots of Return Intention, While Northeast China and North China Are the Coldspots of Return Intention

The Getis-Ord G_i* index is used to further identify high and low value agglomerations of floating population's return intention. As shown in Fig. 6.4, the blue part is the low-value agglomeration region, the coldspots of return intention; the red part is the high-value agglomeration region, the hotspots of return intention; the yellow part indicates that there are no obvious coldspots or hotspots. Both hotspots and coldspots of return intentions show clustering characteristics in space. The hotspots of return intentions are mainly concentrated in South China, Central-Southern China and part of East China, comprising 62 cities with the average return intention of 7.25%. Against the backdrop of economic transformation, competition in the industries and labour markets has become increasingly fierce for the above-mentioned regions with large floating population. In addition, in recent years, governments at all levels have introduced relevant policies to encourage migrants to return to their hometowns for re-employment, promoting a boom in return migration. The coldspots of return intentions are mainly concentrated in Northeast China and North China, comprising 49 cities with the average return intention of 4.94%. The reason for this is that the migrants in Northeast China mainly come from the three northeastern provinces,

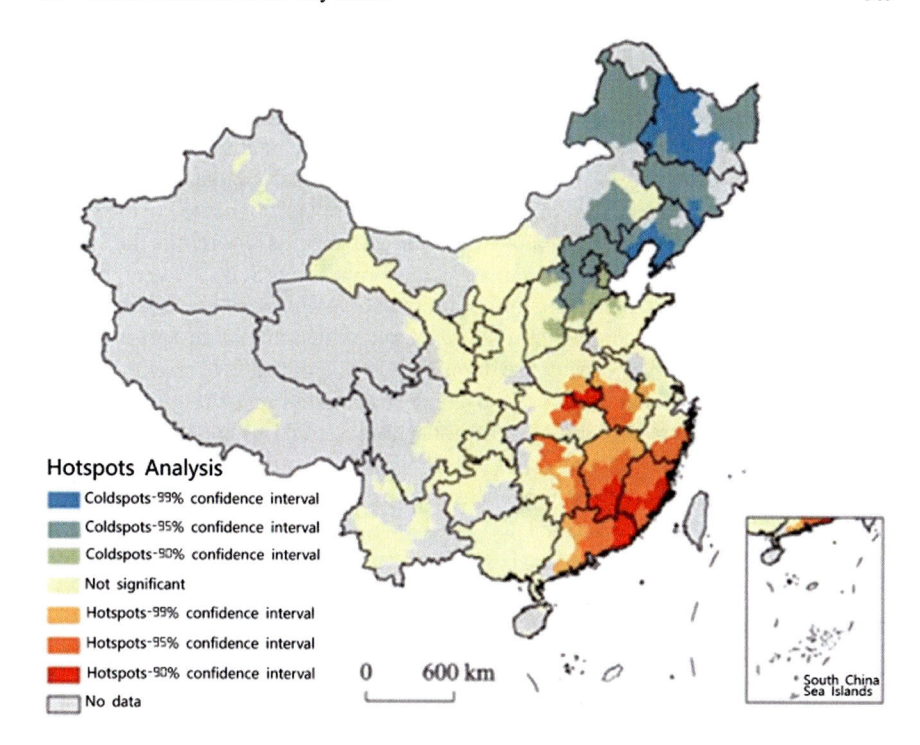

Fig. 6.4 Hotspot analysis of floating population's return intention of prefecture-level cities

so the travel distances are relatively shorter and the socio-cultural integration is relatively easier for them.

6.1.4 Influencing Factors of Floating Population's Return Intention

6.1.4.1 Variable Selection and Model Construction

The classical theories that explain the influencing factors of floating population's return intention include macro and micro theories of neoclassical economics, new migration economics, social network theory, social integration theory, and push-and-pull theory [1]. Based on the extant empirical studies, this study draws on the approach of Lin and Zhu [35] to explain floating population's return intention from two perspectives: the characteristics of floating population (internal factors) and the characteristics of destination areas (external factors). In terms of internal factors, the lower the education level of migrants is, the more costly and difficult it is for them to find job opportunities in destination areas, hence the higher the likelihood of returning to hometown is [36]. The decision of returning to hometowns is usually made on a household basis and is influenced by social network factors, housing and economic factors and employment factors in destination areas [1, 3, 4]. In general, migrants with larger family size, longer residence duration, smaller share of housing expenditure, higher income and higher employment status in destination areas tend to settle down and thus have a lower return intention. In terms of external factors, the economic development and education level of destination cities are closely related to the return migration. Based on this, 14 explanatory variables are selected. Thereinto, the factors of floating population characteristics include education level (School: average years of education), family and social network (Familyelse: family size outside destination areas; Liv: number of accompanied family members in destination areas; Times: number of movements; Stay: residence duration; Own: proportion of moving alone), the economic and housing factors (Houseown: proportion of owning property in destination areas; Payments: the ratio of household income to house expenditure; Housefund: proportion of having a housing fund), the employment factors (Insure: the participation rate of urban employee insurance; Hirer: proportion of employers). The factors of destination area characteristics consist of the economic factors (GDP: GDP per capita; Saving: year-end savings balance per capita) and the education level factors (Pschool: the number of primary schools per 10,000 people). The names, descriptions and expected effects of the variables are shown in Table 6.1.

A conventional OLS regression (Model 1) is constructed to estimate the relationship between the explained variable and the explanatory variables. Through White's test and BP test, it is found that there exists significant heteroskedasticity in the model, violating the "spherical perturbation term" assumption in OLS regression. Therefore, the "OLS + Robust standard error" approach (Model 2) is used [37]. In addition, in the VIF test, the VIF values of all variables in Model 2 are less than 4, with an average VIF value of 2.2, and there exists no multicollinearity. In regard to the goodness of fit of the model, the R^2 of Model 2 has been improved to a certain extent, indicating an enhanced ability to fit and explain the data. Therefore, the analysis below is based on the results of Model 2. The economic data, such as GDP per capita and year-end savings balance per capita, is logarithmically processed and the final regression model is constructed as follows.

$$
\begin{aligned}
Return_i = \beta_0 &+ \beta_1 School_i + \beta_2 Times_i + \beta_3 Stay_i + \beta_4 Own_i \\
&+ \beta_5 Familyelse_i + \beta_6 Liv_i + \beta_7 Houseown_i \\
&+ \beta_8 Payments_i + \beta_9 Housefund_i + \beta_{10} Insure_i \\
&+ \beta_{11} Hirer_i + \beta_{12} ln(GDP)_i + \beta_{13} ln(Saving)_i \\
&+ \beta_{14} Pschool_i + \varepsilon_i
\end{aligned}
\tag{6.4}
$$

In the formula: i represents each prefecture-level city; ε is the random disturbance term; $Return$ is the explained variable; β_0 is the constant term; $\beta_1 \cdots \beta_{14}$ are the regression coefficients of each explanatory variable.

Table 6.1 Types, descriptions and expected effects of variables

	Variable type	Variable name	Descriptions	Expected effects
Floating population characteristics	Education level	School	Average years of education (years)	–
	Family and social network	Familyelse	Family size outside destination areas (persons)	+
		Liv	Number of accompanied family members in destination areas (persons)	–
		Times	Number of movements (times)	+
		Stay	Average residence duration (years)	–
		Own	Proportion of moving alone or not (%)	+
	Economic and housing factors	Houseown	Proportion of owning property in destination areas (%)	–
		Payments	The ratio of household income to house expenditure (%)	–
		Housefund	Proportion of having a housing fund (%)	–
	Employment factors	Insure	The participation rate of urban employee insurance (%)	–
		Hirer	Proportion of employers (%)	–
Destination areas characteristics	Economic factors	GDP	GDP per capita (ten thousand RMB)	–
		Saving	Year-end savings balance per capita (ten thousand RMB)	Unknown
	Education level	Pschool	Number of primary schools per 10,000 people	+

6.1.4.2 Results and Interpretation of Coefficients

According to Eq. (6.4), a model is constructed for analysis with the support of the Stata14 platform, and the regression results are shown in Table 6.2. The mechanism of the influencing factors (including education level, family and social network, economy and housing, employment and social security) on floating population's return intention is further analyzed.

Table 6.2 Overall results of OLS models of floating population's return intention in China

Variable name	Model 1				Model 2			
	Coefficient	Standard error	t	P	Coefficient	Robust Standard errors	t	P
School	−0.0087**	0.0041	−2.1	0.037	−0.0087*	0.0045	−1.94	0.053
Familyelse	0.0331***	0.0106	3.12	0.002	0.0331***	0.0105	3.15	0.002
Liv	−0.0204**	0.0115	−1.77	0.078	−0.0204**	0.0082	−2.49	0.013
Times	0.0389***	0.0105	3.7	0	0.0389**	0.0157	2.48	0.014
Stay	0	0.0017	0.03	0.977	0	0.0018	0.03	0.979
Own	−0.0517	0.0345	−1.5	0.135	−0.0517	0.0313	−1.65	0.101
Houseown	−0.0408**	0.0186	−2.19	0.029	−0.0408**	0.0154	−2.65	0.008
Payments	0.0257**	0.0116	2.22	0.027	0.0257*	0.0134	1.92	0.056
Pindustry	0.0826	0.0568	1.45	0.147	0.0826	0.0552	1.5	0.136
Insure	−0.0532	0.0402	−1.32	0.186	−0.0532	0.0388	−1.37	0.172
Hirer	0.0179	0.0191	0.94	0.35	0.0179	0.0246	0.73	0.467
GDP	−0.0136	0.0085	−1.61	0.108	−0.0136*	0.0079	−1.73	0.086
Saving	0.0191**	0.0076	2.51	0.013	0.0191***	0.007	2.73	0.007
Pschool	0.0090**	0.004	2.29	0.023	0.0090**	0.0044	2.05	0.041
constant	0.0846	0.0664	1.27	0.204	0.0846	0.0696	1.21	0.226
Number of samples	279				279			
(Adj)R^2	0.318				0.3523			
F-statistic	10.14				12.76			
Prob > F	0				0			

Notes: ① *, ** and *** indicate the 10%, 5% and 1% significance levels respectively; ② Model 1 is the traditional OLS model and Model 2 is the "OLS + robust standard error" Model

The Education Level Variable Has a Positive and Negative Bi-directional Effect on Floating Population's Return Intention

As internal factors, the education attainment level of the urban floating population group has a negative impact on their return intention; as external factors, the education development level in destination areas has a facilitating effect on floating population's return migration.

The impact of the average years of education as an internal factor on the return migration of floating population is first examined. The longer average years of education the urban in-migrants have, the weaker their return intention is. This finding is consistent with the findings of many previous studies [9, 25]. The level of education significantly enhances the labour skills of migrants, thus increasing their competitiveness in labour market, which is transformed into higher economic returns. To a certain extent, education is a barrier between social classes, and an increase in the education attainment level is conducive to floating population entering higher social classes and gaining a higher social status. Educational attainment can also reflect the adaptation and identification of migrants with urban culture, the higher the level of education, the easier it is for migrants to integrate into urban life.

Furthermore, we examine the impact of the education level in destination areas, as an external factor, on floating population's return intention. The larger is the number of primary schools per 10,000 people in destination areas, the stronger is floating population's return intention. This is because the number of primary schools per 10,000 people reflects the level of basic education in a city, directly relate to whether the children of migrant workers can receive a quality education in destination areas. However, only 49.2% of urban floating population have children accompanying with them in destination cities in the sample used in this study, and nearly half of the floating population's children do not move with them. Relatively speaking, this segment of floating population is not so concerned about the availability of good basic education in their destination areas. On the other hand, although cities provide better-quality basic education resources, the floating population have difficulties in accessing quality education services due to objective conditions such as household registration and financial capacity. The higher costs of education and living in cities with advanced levels of basic education also add to this problem. Consequently, the level of education in destination areas becomes a "push force" for urban floating population's return migration, leading to an increase in their return intention.

Family Ties and Social Networks Are Important Drivers of Floating Population's Return Intention

Migrants with smaller family sizes in destination areas and larger family sizes outside destination areas have a stronger return intention, and migrants who move more often are more inclined to return for reasons such as the greater cost of reconstructing social networks.

Family ties are an important influencing factor on floating population's return intention. The results of the model show that the family sizes of destination areas have a dampening effect on return migration, while the family sizes of non-destination areas have a facilitating effect. This is due to the fact that a larger family size of migrants in the destination city helps expand the local family network, reducing the costs of integration and settlement of migrants. Besides, an increase in the family size in the destination city is beneficial to floating population avoiding the risks of living and residing there, reflecting the positive effect of family size on the settlement of floating population, which is consistent with the findings of extant studies [23, 24]. On the other hand, a larger family size outside the destination city increases the cost of integration of floating population in destination areas, thus prompting them to choose to continue to migrate or return.

The higher is the average number of movements of urban floating population, the stronger is their return intention. An increase in the number of movements of migrants leads to not only an increase in the migration cost, but also an increase in the cost of integrating into the local society and reconstructing the social network in the new destination areas, thus enhancing the return intention of migrants. Another reason is that the marginal utility of migration in terms of economic returns, employment and social status decreases as the number of movements increases, while the influence of the 'hometown feeling' intensifies as the number of movements increases, ultimately contributing to floating population's return intention. Contrary to expectations, the effect of average residence duration on return intention is not significant, the reasons of which need to be further investigated. In addition, the proportion of moving alone is also not significantly related to the return migration of urban floating population.

Housing and Economic Factors Are Key Drivers of Return Migration Decisions

The migrants who own a house in destination areas have relatively lower return intention. Return migration can be seen as a reflection of being an economic 'success', with higher-income migrants tending to return to hometowns, and the level of economic development in destination areas acts as a disincentive for return migration as an external factor.

Extant research has found that housing is an important factor influencing floating population's return intention, and the higher is the proportion of migrants who own a house in destination areas, the lower is their return intention. Housing is a spiritual backing and a material guarantee for floating population in China, and living and working in peace and contentment is the goal of floating population. Therefore, once a person owns a property in destination areas, he or she will "take root" there, and in this sense, housing is a "pull force" on floating population's return intention and has a negative effect on it. Besides, the model results demonstrate that having a housing fund in destination cities did not significantly affect the return intention of floating population.

The higher is the ratio of the monthly income to the expenditure of the family, the stronger is the return intention of migrants. This finding is in line with the new migration economics' explanation of the return migration, that is, the migration of floating population is an economic decision based on family development, and once they have achieved their economic goals in destination areas, they will return to their hometowns as a "success" [3]. By diversifying household income through remittances and savings, the migrant workers overcome the risks associated with the deficiencies of the credit market in hometowns and accumulate capital for investment and consumption [4]. On the other hand, the increase in their income in destination areas will lead to a decrease in the marginal utility of wealth, as the floating population will achieve greater utility for consumption and investment in their hometowns [4]. Finally, the GDP per capita of the destination areas has a dampening effect on the floating population's return intention, i.e., the level of economic development of the city has a "pull" effect on the floating population. The higher are the per capita savings in the destination area, the stronger is floating population's return intention. On the one hand, the savings per capita reflects to a certain extent the income level of the floating population, and the positive effect of this indicator on the return intention supports the thesis of the new migration economy theory. In addition, per capita savings are more a reflection of the economic and consumption levels of the household registered population. Higher per capita savings tend to represent higher regional economic development level and income levels, as well as a fiercer competition for jobs, leading to an increase in floating population's return intention.

The Employment Status and Social Security Conditions of Floating Population in Destination Areas Do Not Show a Significant Relationship with Their Return Intention

Contrary to expectations, regarding the employment status, the share of employers among urban floating population is not related to their return intention. A possible explanation is that self-employed migrants are superior in terms of economic integration, social participation and psychological integration compared to employed migrants. At the same time, self-employed people have a higher employment status and a higher value recognition in the job market, thus having a higher settlement intention and a lower return intention. However, the self-employed migrants tend to have a greater job mobility and higher income levels, and are more likely to meet their household income expectations and return to hometowns. The combination of these two forces results in an unclear effect of employment status on the return intention. Furthermore, the results of the model do not show that social security factors have a significant impact on the floating population's return intention, and there is no significant relationship between the participation rate of urban employees' insurance among the urban floating population and their return intention, which has some implications for the government in formulating policies to manage the floating population.

6.1.5 Conclusions and Discussion

(1)   Overall, the floating population's return intention in China is low compared
       to the settlement intention and the *hukou* transfer intention, with only 6.17%
       of the floating population having the return intention, accounting for 10.07%
       and 16.30% of the settlement intention and the *hukou* transfer intention. The
       majority (74.05%) of urban floating population with return intention tend
       to return to their origin areas. There is an asymmetrical 'U-shaped' pattern
       between city size, city rank and the return intention. The return intentions in
       cities of different sizes and levels show significant heterogeneity, among which
       cities with higher ranks and larger sizes are characterized by low return inten-
       tion, and cities with lower ranks and smaller sizes are featured by high return
       intention.

(2)   Urban floating population's return intention shows significant spatial variation
       characteristics. From the perspective of urban agglomerations, the return inten-
       tion is highest in the Yangtze River Delta urban agglomeration and the Beijing-
       Tianjin-Hebei urban agglomeration, and lowest in the Chengdu-Chongqing
       urban agglomeration and the Harbin-Changchun urban agglomeration; from
       the perspective of geographical divisions, the return intention is highest in the
       eastern region and lowest in the northeastern region. The results of the spatial
       autocorrelation analysis show that the floating population's return intention in
       China presents an agglomeration distribution pattern, with significantly posi-
       tive and weak spatial autocorrelation characteristics. The Getis-Ord G_i^* index
       reveals the hotspots and coldspots of the floating population's return intention
       in China, with South China, Central-Southern China and part of East China
       being the hotspots and Northeast China and North China being the coldspots.

(3)   The return migration of urban floating population is influenced by a variety
       of forces, consisting of internal factors including education levels, family ties
       and social networks, housing and economic and employment factors, as well
       as external factors such as economic development and education levels from
       the destination areas. From the perspective of internal and external factors,
       variables such as education level and economic development have different
       directions of influence on the urban floating population's return intention: the
       floating population's own average years of education have a negative effect on
       their return intention, while the numbers of primary schools per 10,000 people
       in destination areas have a facilitating effect on the floating population's return
       intention; migrants with a higher ratio of household income to expenditure are
       more inclined to return to hometowns, while the GDP per capita in destination
       areas has a dampening effect on the local floating population's return intention.

(4)   Family ties, social networks, housing and economic factors are the main vari-
       ables that shape the spatial patterns of China's floating population. In terms of
       family ties, family sizes in destination areas have an inhibiting effect on the
       return migration, while family sizes in non-destination areas have a promo-
       tion effect; in terms of social networks, migrants who have moved more often

are more inclined to return due to the higher costs of reconstructing social networks; in terms of housing, migrants who own a house in destination areas are less inclined to return; in terms of economic factors, return migration can be seen as a manifestation of being an economic "success", and urban floating population with high incomes are more prone to returning to their hometowns. In addition, there is no significant relationship between the employment status and social security conditions of the floating population in destination areas and their return intention.

This study has certain policy implications based on the above findings: It is imperative to formulate management strategies for the floating population according to local conditions, based on the results that floating population's return intention varies in terms of city size, city level and city location. It is important to promote new-type urbanization and a reasonable and orderly distribution of the floating population among cities. For cities of lower ranks, smaller sizes and relatively stronger return intention, special attention should be paid to their future development directions, by putting more emphasis on the industrial agglomeration and population gathering, and the in-situ urbanization of floating population through improving public service facilities. For cities of higher ranks, larger sizes and relatively weaker return intention, reasonable measures should be taken to deal with the environmental degradation, traffic congestion and other "urban diseases" caused by the over-agglomeration of population and guide a reasonable return migration. For the hotspots region of return migration, it is necessary to firmly grasp the multiple forces that influence the return migration, pay attention to the improvement of the conditions of the floating population themselves, adopt lectures and other forms to promote urban culture and facilitate better integration of floating population into the local community. The following measures are also useful in the hotspots region: helping the children of the floating population to solve educational issues such as enrolling in public schools and transferring to other schools, implementing policies that migrant workers' children are allowed to take the exams of high school and college entrance in the city where their parents work and live; providing low-rent housing, affordable housing and housing purchase subsidies to address the housing needs of the floating population. At the same time, more attention should also be paid to the impact of external urban conditions on return migration, so that the economic growth in the destination city can contribute to the settlement of more floating population. For some megacities and megalopolises that are cold spots for return migration, it is important to guide a reasonable outflows of the floating population through industrial transfer, encourage the floating population to return to hometowns in family groups through subsidies and other forms, set up a social security fund for the floating population to help them go through the adaptation period of looking for jobs, and encourage floating population with successful careers to return to hometowns to start their own businesses.

The following areas for further improvement exist in this study: first, this study is conducted on the floating population as a whole and does not specifically analyze the representative segments of it (e.g. migrant workers, elderly floating population);

second, when aggregated to the city level, some of the variables in the database are missing due to the insufficient data acquisition methods. Based on this, future research needs to pay special attention to the specific groups of the floating population, and empirically model more variables that may affect the floating population's return intention through additional surveys.

6.2 Return Intentions at the Individual Level

6.2.1 Introduction

In 2014, the Chinese government formulated the New Urbanization Development Plan, which encouraged floating migrants to transfer their rural *hukou* to urban areas, especially small and medium-sized cities near their hometowns. This initiative has been successful in prompting a massive return migration among the floating population. Also in recent years, numerous industries in China have begun to shift their operations from the eastern regions, where manufacturing has historically been centred, to the middle and western regions, and from larger to smaller cities [38]. These conditions have also altered the pattern of migration from one-way, rural–urban flow to two-way, rural–urban and return urban–rural migration. Provinces that experienced massive out-migration, such as Hubei, Sichuan, and Anhui, have in recent years been witnessing the return of a large number of workers [30, 39].

The emergence of this sort of return migration in China has had significant impacts on economic development and social governance in both origin and destination cities [4]. As a consequence, the return intentions of migrant workers have attracted considerable attention from policymakers, the media, and academia. While there has been a surge in research into these issues in recent years [24, 26, 40, 41], little of this work has been conducted with national-level data.

This study represents an effort to help fill this gap in the literature. Using the China Migrant Dynamic Survey (CMDS) data from 2016, we consider the determinants of return migration by Chinese workers across the country. The CMDS contains a questionnaire on return intentions of migrant workers in destination cities. For this study, we use econometric models to estimate the return intentions of these workers. The results of this research would contribute to the formulation of effective governmental policies for managing China's floating migration.

6.2.2 Literature Review

Classical migration theories—including neoclassical migration theories [2, 42], the new migration economics [3], and the dualist labour market theory [43]—established the foundation for current research on the subject, in which international return migration has received considerable attention [6, 8, 12–16, 44]. Work done thus far has identified specific factors that influence the decisions of inter-national migrants regarding whether to remain in a host country or return to their countries of origin. Generally speaking, the intention to return is stronger among migrants who work in low-paying jobs, are only weakly integrated into the social fabric of the host country, enjoy strong connections with family back home, have resided in the host country for a relatively short period of time, and have relatively little formal education [6, 8–11]. Employment status is another key factor, thus Piracha and Vadean [12] found that international immigrants returning to Albania were more likely to become entrepreneurs than Albanians who had not migrated and that this entrepreneurship had a positive impact on local economic activity. Since the beginning of this century, some scholars have started to pay attention to the subjective return intentions of international migrants as well [13, 14, 16]. They were especially concerned with the degree to which migrants' social integration in their destinations and the cross-border linkages between origin and destination countries affected the return intentions of international migrants [13–15]. Thus, for example, a survey of African immigrant groups in Spain and Italy by De Haas and Fokkema [13] found that sociocultural integration correlated negatively with return intentions, though the impacts of degrees of economic integration and cross-border connections were not clear. Other scholars have considered the impact of social capital, which Haug [16] found to have a negative effect on the return intentions of international immigrants whose social capital is embedded in host countries, and the opposite effect for those whose social capital is located in home countries.

Given the nature and configuration of borders, there are some differences in the drivers of international as opposed to internal return migration. Linguistic and cultural barriers characterize international return migration more evidently than internal return migration in most circumstances [45]. However, despite the crossing of an international boundary as a distinguishing trait, internal and international return migrations are often driven by similar forces and are closely linked [46]. In this sense, prior studies of international return migration nevertheless offer useful points of reference for understanding internal return migration.

A burgeoning body of literature has focused on the internal return migration in western countries [47–53]. Earlier scholars have explained internal return migration using concepts of location-specific capital and information costs [48–50]. Based on a large-scale Swedish survey, Niedomysl and Amcoff [53] studied the motivations of internal return migration in Sweden. Amcoff and Niedomysl [47] also examined the internal return migration in metropolitan regions in Sweden and highlighted the differences in the characteristics between returnees to metropolitan regions and other return migrants. Supported by 19-year tracking data from rural Tanzania, Hirvonen and Lilleør [51] evidenced that the return of migrants to rural Tanzania areas was largely related to unsuccessful migration. Junge et al. [52] distinguished local return migrants from regional return migrants in a comparative study of return migration in Thailand and Vietnam in which they found differences between the two nationalities in the factors that predicted intention (e.g. employment level, education attainment, and wage level). Overall, the above studies have revealed that complex decision-making processes among return migrants took into account multiple factors, including individual characteristics, migration patterns, social reasons, education reasons, and employment factors. These studies have also enlightened subsequent research in China [54, 55].

In China, the massive circulation of migrants among regions in recent decades has prompted attention to the characteristics and determinants of their intentions [24, 30, 40, 56]. Researchers have surveyed migrant workers who have returned to their hometowns [21, 22]. The return intentions of migrant workers involve not only a change in their places of residence from urban to rural areas [57] but also an adjustment in their professional status, as the accumulation of human and social capital during migration may have enhanced their employment ability, thereby altering their return intentions [24]. It has also been reported that the main motivation for Chinese migrant workers to return home is the desire to start businesses and purchase homes [18]. Further, migrant workers who have urban pension projects, medical insurance, and unemployment insurance tend to be reluctant to return home, while those with rural pension schemes, medical insurance, and unemployment insurance have a strong willingness to return home [23]. Research deriving data from telephone interviews or questionnaire surveys has also assessed the influence of multiple drivers on migrant workers' return intentions, including economic, individual, social networks, and social capital factors [21–23]. Yu et al. [23] collected survey data on migrant workers in Shanghai and found that, after controlling for economic and individual factors, social security factors played a significant role in migrant workers' return intentions. Researchers have also distinguished between the determinants of the return intentions of distinct demographic groups, such as first-generation migrants and elderly migrants [58, 59].

Owing to the availability of place-based surveys and the national-level CMDS data, much attention has been devoted to the migration intentions of the floating population in China [60]. Several scholars have focused on the long-term settlement intentions and *hukou* transfer intentions of migrant workers in destination cities [29, 60–66]. Related literature suggests an association between settlement (or *hukou* transfer) intentions and such personal characteristics as employment status, social integration, income level, and the specific characteristics of destination cities [60]. In 2016, the CMDS began to incorporate questions relating to the return intentions of floating migrants, thereby making possible several follow-up studies on those returning from Nanjing, Suzhou, or Shenzhen [40, 41]. Other researchers reported spatial differentiation in the return intentions of floating migrants at the city level [30].

As informative as this work is, most of these studies have examined the determinants of migrant workers' return intentions in particular regions of China [24, 26, 40, 41, 67, 68], so their findings may be less relevant to the return propensities of migrant workers in broader contexts. In other words, prior to this study, there has been little scholarly attention on factors that determine migrant workers' return intentions at the national level.

6.2.3   Data and Methodology

6.2.3.1   Data

As mentioned, the data for this study are derived from the 2016 CMDS. Since 2009, the National Health Commission of China's annual, large-scale sample survey of the floating population nationwide has produced the CMDS data. Compared with other surveys of the floating population, the CMDS includes more participants, contains a larger sample size, and includes a larger number (31 of 34) of the provincial-level divisions across the country; thus, it extends well beyond any particular regions. The survey employs stratified, multi-stage, scale-based (PPS) criteria for sampling and uses community questionnaires and individual questionnaires [62, 63, 69]. The respondents of the survey are non-native floating migrants (without local *hukou*) aged 15 years or more who had lived in the research areas (i.e. respondents' destination cities) for more than a month. The total sample size for this survey in 2016 is 169,000. Since our research focuses on migrant workers, we exclude respondents with urban *hukou*; we also eliminate samples from which information is missing. The final effective sample size of our dataset is 78,484. It includes the respondents' individual characteristics regarding family background, employment status, and income level. This information is sufficient for quantitative analysis.

6.2.3.2   Description of the Variables

The dependent variable in this study is the return intentions of migrant workers, which are elicited through the survey question, 'Do you intend to live in the local area for a long time (i.e. more than 5 years)?'. The possible responses to this question are 'preparing to migrate', 'settling down', 'returning home', and 'undetermined'. We construct a binomial variable, rendering 'preparing to migrate', 'settling down', and 'undetermined' as 'being unwilling to return to hometown', and 'returning home' as 'being willing to return to hometown'. In 2016, the proportion of migrant workers with return intentions was 6.4%. For the explanatory variables, drawing on previous studies of population migration and migrants' returning behaviours [64, 70–74], we summarize the factors influencing migrant workers' return intentions into five aspects: individual, economic, housing, family, and social and spatial factors (see Table 6.3). In the selection of variables, we try to include all of those used in previous relevant studies, thereby largely solving the problem of endogeneity caused by missing variables. The following discussion considers each of the five factors in turn.

(a)   Individual factors. We select the variables of gender, ethnicity, education, and age to measure the individual characteristics of migrant workers. The decision to return home can be influenced by the conditions that individual migrant workers experience. Those who are older and less educated in particular face high costs and limited opportunities for employment in cities with large

Table 6.3 Descriptions of variables

Variable	Variable name	Description
Dependent variable	Return intention	Dummy variable: willing to return = 1; unwilling = 0
Independent variables		
Individual	Gender	Dummy variable: male = 1; female = 0
Variables	Ethnicity	Dummy variable: minority = 1; Han = 0
	Age	Categorical variable: young aged (15–19 years old) = 1; young to middle aged (20–29 years old) = 2; middle aged (30–39 years old) = 3; old aged (40–49 years old) = 4; seniors (equal or over 50 years old) = 5
	Education	Categorical variable: young aged (15–19 years old) = 1; young to middle aged (20–29 years old) = 2; middle aged (30–39 years old) = 3; old aged (40–49 years old) = 4; seniors (equal or over 50 years old) = 5
Economic factors	Income-expenditure ratio	Continuous variables:family monthly income/family monthly expenditure (%)
Housing factors	Housing expenditure	Continuous variables: family monthly expenditure on housing/family monthly income (%)
	Housing tenure	Dummy variable: others = 1; self-purchase or/and self-build house = 0
	Local property	Dummy variable: whether to own a property in destination city or not, yes = 1; no = 0
	County property	Dummy variable: whether to own a property in where county government of household registration place located, yes = 1; no = 0
	Township property	Dummy variable: whether to own a property in where township government of household registration place located, yes = 1; no = 0
	Village property	Dummy variable: whether to own a property in where village government of household registration place located, yes = 1; no = 0
	Group living	Dummy variable: living separately = 1; living collectively = 0
Family factors	Spouse	Dummy variable: whether to migrate with spouse or not, yes = 1; no = 0

(continued)

Table 6.3 (continued)

Variable	Variable name	Description
	Parents	Dummy variable: whether to migrate with parents or not, yes = 1; no = 0
	Children	Dummy variable: whether to migrate with children or not, yes = 1; no = 0
	Siblings	Dummy variable: whether to migrate with a brother or/and sister or not, yes = 1; no = 0
	Family members	Continuous variables:number of family members living together/the scale of family (%)
Social and spatial factors	Type of industry	Categorical variable: primary industry = 1; secondary industry = 2; tertiary industry = 3
	Employment status	Categorical variable: others = 1; employer = 2; employee = 3
	Rural insurance	Dummy variable: whether to purchase new-type rural cooperative medical insurance (*xin nong he bao*), yes = 1; no = 0
	Resident insurance	Dummy variable:: whether to purchase urban resident medical insurance (*cheng ju bao*), yes = 1; no = 0
	Employee insurance	Dummy variable: whether to purchase urban employee medical insurance (*cheng zhi bao*), yes = 1; no = 0
	Location	Categorical variable: other locations = 1; Yangtze River Delta = 2; Pearl River Delta = 3; Beijing-Tianjin-Hebei Region = 4
	Distance	Dummy variable: interprovincial = 1; provincial = 0
	Duration	Continuous variable: the time interval that the target stays in the place of migration (year)

numbers of migrants and so are predisposed to return home [72]. Gender—the division of work in both the labour market and family—and ethnicity—which relates to ways of life—may also affect return intentions.

(b)   Economic factors. Economic theories of migration have pointed to economic factors as important drivers of migration [75]. The ratio of family monthly income to expenditures can serve as a measure of economic capacity in this regard. Simply put, the greater the income of migrant workers in their destination cities, the less likely they were to return home [76]. Conversely, the high cost of living in destination cities encourages migrant workers to return home.

However, high incomes and a high cost of living always correlate in these cities. [77] found that, without considering expenditure, income had no significant effect on long-term residence intentions, so the income-to-expenditure ratio is a good measurement of the impact of economic factors on return intentions.

(c)   Housing factors. To reflect the effects of housing factors, we choose the variables of the family-monthly-housing-expenditure-to-income ratio, housing tenure (i.e. owner or renter), ownership of local property or not, ownership of property in *hukou* places or not, and group living or not. In contemporary China, urban housing costs have been rising steadily, especially in economically developed areas, a situation that makes it increasingly difficult for migrant workers to settle down [29–31]. Urban housing is, then, a key variable in terms of restricting migration, with a negative effect on migrant workers [37, 73], and thus may affect their return intentions. At the same time, housing also has considerable social significance. For migrant workers, owning property in destination cities represents major progress in social integration and therefore weakens return intentions, while, conversely, owning a house in the hometown reduces the psychological cost of returning home and therefore acts as a positive incentive for doing so [73, 78]. Housing factors include comprehensive economic implications and social values, both of which have a large impact on the willingness of migrant workers to return home [78].

(d)   Family factors. Family connections are the core of family factors. To represent them, we choose the variables of whether to migrate with a spouse, whether to migrate with parents, whether to migrate with children, whether to migrate with brothers or sisters, and the proportion of local households. The economics of migration theory holds that migrants make immigration decisions that maximize family utility. With the emergence of household-based mobility trends, the network of family connections has become an important influence on migrant workers' return intentions [9]. Moreover, social network theory emphasizes the connections between migrant workers and their relatives or friends in places of origin in explaining the desire to return home [71].

(e)   Social and spatial factors. Several studies have shown that social and spatial factors play a role in return migration [11, 41, 64]. Here we measure the social and spatial factors with respect to the type of industry, employment status, social insurance coverage, migration distance, duration of stay, and the location of the destination city. Industrial classification, career identities, and social insurance reflect migrant workers' social status in destination cities to a certain extent, while migration distance and the location of destination cities reflect differences in the social environment at the origin and destination.

6.2.3.3   Method

We use descriptive and regression analysis to explore the characteristics of migrant workers' return intentions. The descriptive analysis focuses on the relationships between the dependent variable and the independent variables. In the regression analysis, since the dependent variable is binary, we carry out the analysis using a binary logistic model for which calculation formula is

$$\log \frac{p}{1-p} = a + b_1 x_1 + b_2 x_2 + b_3 x_3 + \cdots + b_n x_n \qquad (6.5)$$

where p is the probability of return intention, x_1, x_2, x_3, ... x_n are independent variables, α is a constant. β_1, β_2, β_3, ... β_n represent the estimated coefficients of corresponding independent variables; and $\exp(\beta)$ is the odds ratio of migrant workers' return intentions and the probability that they will not return home. If the odds ratio is greater than 1, the corresponding categorical group has a stronger return intention than the base categorical group absent any change in the other conditions.

A probit model is conducted to test the robustness of the results from the logistic model. Also, we deal with possible endogeneity of some variables in our model by introducing suitable instrumental variables (IVs) for them along with the IV method.

6.2.4 Results

6.2.4.1 Characteristics of Return Intention

According to Table 6.4, the return intentions of migrant workers vary depending on their personal characteristics. Thus, to begin with, minority migrant workers have stronger return intentions than non-minorities. Further, the proportion of migrant workers with strong return intentions at first declines with age but then increases, with relatively young and old migrants showing stronger return intentions than middle-aged ones. Education also negatively correlates with return intentions. We find no gender difference in migrants' return intentions, however.

These results suggest a close relationship between housing factors and the willingness of migrant workers to return home. Those who have purchased or constructed housing in destination cities are less willing to return, as are those who live separately. Conversely, migrant workers who own property in their local townships or government seats back home are more willing to return than those who do not.

Regarding family factors, workers who migrate with spouses, parents, children, or siblings have less strong intentions to return, while other social and spatial factors also play a role [41]. Migrant workers are more willing to return home when they are employed in secondary than in primary industries. Further, those who have purchased urban residential medical insurance (cheng ju bao) and urban employee medical insurance (cheng zhi bao) have weaker return intentions than those who have not, while those who have insured under the new-type rural cooperative medical insurance (xin nong he bao) have stronger return intentions than those who have not.

Migrant workers' return intentions also show spatial heterogeneity. Thus, a comparison of return intentions across economic regions shows that migrant workers

Table 6.4 Descriptive analysis of migrant workers' return intention

		Sample size	Unwilling to return (%)	Willing to return (%)			Sample size	Unwilling to return (%)	Willing to return (%)
Gender	Female	32,990	93.6	6.4	Spouse***	No	23,318	91.8	8.2
	Male	45,494	93.5	6.5	Parents***	Yes	3316	96.7	3.3
Ethnicity**	Han	72,895	93.6	6.4		No	75,168	93.4	6.6
	Minority	5589	93	7.0	Children***	Yes	31,517	96	4.0
Age***	15–19	134	90.3	9.7		No	46,967	91.9	8.1
	20–29	19,417	94.1	5.9	Siblings**	Yes	1488	95.2	4.8
	30–39	29,314	95.1	4.9		No	76,996	93.5	6.5
	40–49	22,900	92.7	7.3	Industry***	Primary	2214	93.8	6.2
	Over 50	6719	88.5	11.5		Secondary	21,272	90.5	9.5
Education***	Junior college and above	6577	97.1	2.9		Tertiary	54,998	94.7	5.3
	Junior high school, senior high school and technical secondary school	58,484	93.7	6.3	Employment***	Others	1249	94.9	5.1
	Primary school and illiteracy	13,423	91.2	8.8		Employer	14,290	95.3	4.7
Housing tenure***	Self-purchasing house or self-built	18,857	99	1		Employee	62,945	93.1	6.9

(continued)

Table 6.4 (continued)

		Sample size	Unwilling to return (%)	Willing to return (%)
	Others	59,897	91.9	8.1
Local property***	Yes	20,520	99.1	0.9
	No	57,964	91.6	8.4
County property***	Yes	4046	90.4	9.6
	No	74,438	93.7	6.3
Township Property***	Yes	3410	90.1	9.9
	No	75,174	93.7	6.3
Village Property***	Yes	12,887	90.8	9.2
	No	65,597	94.1	5.9
Group living***	Separately	72,271	94.4	5.6
	Collectively	6213	84.3	15.7
Spouse***	Yes	55,166	94.3	5.7

		Sample size	Unwilling to return (%)	Willing to return (%)
Rural insurance***	Insured	58,356	92.9	7.1
	Not insured	20,128	95.6	4.4
Resident insurance***	Insured	2103	97.7	2.3
	not insured	76,381	93.4	6.6
Employee Insurance***	Insured	10,537	95.9	4.1
	Not insured	67,947	93.2	6.8
Location***	Others	48,721	94.3	5.7
	Yangtze river Delta	12,258	89.8	10.2
	Pearl River Delta	4267	94.5	5.5
	Beijing-Tianjin-Hebei region	13,238	94.1	5.9
Distance***	Provincial	39,593	95.6	4.4
	Interprovincial	38,891	91.5	8.5

Notes: The value of p is the result of fisher's exact test; ***, **, and * represent $p < 0.01$, 0.05, and 0.1; Continuous variables are not included in the Yangtze River Delta have stronger return intentions than those in the Beijing-Tianjin-Hebei, Pearl River Delta, and other regions, and intra-provincial migrant workers have lower return intentions than those who migrate within provinces.

6.2.4.2 Drivers of Return Intention

We employ a binary logistic regression model to examine the drivers of migrant workers' return intentions. To deal with the problem of heteroscedasticity, we use a robust standard error. Also, we test the collinearity of our variables and construct a correlation matrix. We find that all the correlation coefficients between pairs of variables are less than 0.5. We then add the variables of individual characteristics, economic and housing factors, family connections, and social and spatial factors into the model and create Model 1 (Table 6.5).

Individual Factors

The results indicate that gender, ethnicity, age, and education level are closely related to the return intention of migrant workers. Male migrant workers have a lower propensity to return home than female migrants, and minority migrant workers are more willing to return home than Han migrant workers. We also observe that migrants over 50 have a higher return intention than those below 19, which reveals the differences in competitiveness of migrant workers of different ages in the urban employment market. Besides, these results suggest that, compared with the other two groups, the return intentions of migrant workers with college or higher levels of education are significantly weaker than those with lower levels of formal education. This finding is consistent with the conclusions of most previous studies of the topic (e.g. [79]). Education can significantly improve the labour skills of migrant workers and thus enhance their competitive advantage in the labour market and their economic success; in addition, educational level correlates positively with social status. Both education and social status weaken migrant workers' return intentions significantly.

Economic Factors

As for the economic factors and the housing factors, the results suggest that a 1% increase in the income ratio increases the odds of returning by 4.5%, whereas some previous studies have found a negative association between migrants' return intentions and their incomes at their destinations (e.g. [11]). A possible explanation for the discrepancy is that the migration purpose for a large percentage of migrant workers is to work and achieve their income goals [4]. Besides, the increase in migrants' income in their destination cities enhances their ability to spend or invest in their hometowns more than in their destination cities (income effect), which strengthens their intentions to return [8].

Table 6.5 The results of the regression model of migrant workers' return intention

	Model 1 (n = 78,484)		Model 2 (n = 78,484)	Model 3 (n = 78,484)
	Logistic		Probit	IV probit
	B	exp(β)	β	β
Gender (female = base)	−0.064**	0.937	−0.030**	−0.28*
Ethnicity (Han = base)	0.128**	1.137	0.066**	0.075**
Age (≤19 = base)				
20–29	−0.006	0.993	0.008	0.012
30–39	−0.048	0.953	−0.011	0.015
40–49	0.302	1.35	0.169	0.193
50 and above	0.784**	2.191	0.422	0.397*
Education (junior college and above = base)				
Junior high school, senior high school and technical secondary school	0.248***	1.282	0.114***	0.160***
Primary school and illiteracy	0.319***	1.376	0.153***	0.198***
Income-expenditure ratio	0.044***	1.045	0.025***	0.020***
Housing expenditure	−0.481***	0.618	−0.202**	−0.209***
Housing tenure (self-built house or self-purchased house = base)	0.836***	2.308	0.356***	0.322***
Local property (no = base)	−1.191***	0.304	−0.492***	−0.486***
County property (no = base)	0.301***	1.351	0.162***	0.159***
Township property (no = base)	0.341***	1.407	0.177***	0.170***
Village property (no = base)	0.294***	1.342	0.151***	0.142***
Group living (collective = base)	−0.386***	0.680	−0.218***	−0.224***
Spouse (no = base)	−0.106***	0.900	−0.053***	0.074***
Parents (no = base)	−0.161	0.851	−0.079*	−0.522**
Children (no = base)	−0.279***	0.757	−0.131***	−0.461***

(continued)

Table 6.5 (continued)

	Model 1 (n = 78,484)		Model 2 (n = 78,484)	Model 3 (n = 78,484)
	Logistic		Probit	IV probit
	B	exp(β)	β	β
Siblings (no = base)	−0.155	0.856	−0.072	−0.071
Family members	−0.752***	0.471	−0.387***	−0.178***
Type of industry (the second = base)				
The primary	0.325***	1.383	0.131***	0.179***
The tertiary	−0.160***	0.853	−0.083***	−0.087***
Employment status (others = base)				
Employer	0.059	1.061	0.037	0.040
Employee	0.318***	1.375	0.160**	0.161**
Rural insurance (no = base)	0.137***	1.147	0.073***	071***
Resident insurance (no = base)	−0.377***	0.686	−0.176**	−0.071***
Employee insurance (no = base)	−0.296***	0.744	−0.149***	−0.163***
Location (others = base)				
Yangtze river Delta	0.184***	1.202	0.099***	0.079***
Pearl River Delta	−0.318***	0.727	−0.157***	−0.171***
Beijing-Tianjin-Hebei region	−0.065	0.937	−0.037*	−0.052**
Distance (provincial = base)	0.316***	1.371	0.163***	0.146***
Duration	−0.047***	0.954	−0.023***	−0.026***
Constant	−2.903***	0.055	−1.261***	−1.979***
Prob > chi^2	0.000		0.000	0.000
Pseudo-R^2	0.113		0.1139	–
Wald test of exogeneity	–		–	0.000

Notes: *** represent represents significant at the 1% level, ** represents significant at the 5% level, and * represents significant at the 10% level

Housing Factors

Our model shows that housing factors play a key role in migrant workers' return intentions. Thus, those with large housing expenditures are less willing to return to their hometowns, with the cost of housing representing the primary economic threshold that migrant workers need to cross to integrate into their destinations; owning a house is also an important symbol of integration into the local society. Larger housing expenditures, then, reflect the greater housing demand of migrant workers and their social integration [29–31]. The implication is that migrant workers' willingness to invest in housing correlates with their willingness to spend more in order to adapt to and integrate into destination cities. Likewise, large housing expenditures, especially the purchase of a house, may increase the intention of migrant workers to stay in their destination cities and weaken their return intentions [78]. Housing tenure similarly impacts migrant workers' return intentions, Compared to migrant workers with self-built or self-purchased properties, those possessing other types of properties in destination cities are more willing to return to their hometowns.

The results also show that migrant workers who own housing properties in destination cities have weaker return intentions. Yet, migrant workers possessing housing properties in their household registration places, whether in villages, townships, or county government seats, have higher return intentions. Housing means a lot in traditional Chinese culture, and people regard houses as their spiritual supports and as material security [78]. On account of the soaring prices of urban housing and the fact that the housing policies, guarantees, and subsidies that benefit local citizens are not applicable to them, migrants often cannot afford houses in their destination cities [78]. The relatively low price of houses in their hometowns, on the other hand, may entice them to return.

Whether to live collectively also correlate with return intentions. Migrants who live collectively are more likely than those who live separately to return home. A possible reason is that the collective living environments are less conducive to happiness than living separately; in addition, migrant workers who live collectively are more likely to be identified as migrants in host society, increasing the psychological pressure on them and hampering their integration into the social fabric [80].

Family Factors

Considering the family factors, we discover that migrant workers' family members and whether to migrate with children have a significant impact on their return intentions. Generally speaking, the proportion of family members living together in destination cities correlates negatively with return intentions. This proportion reflects the tightness of migrant workers' family connections in destination cities; and these connections can ameliorate their costs of social integration and settlement, thus weakening return intentions. In addition, our results reveal that migrating with children or spouses significantly weakens the return intentions of migrant workers. When considering the problems of children's education and the long-term development of the family, migrant workers prefer to stay in destination cities where their children may receive better education and their family may enjoy better social conditions in the long run [81, 82]. However, migrating with parents or siblings has no significant relationship with return intentions.

Social and Spatial Factors

When looking at the results of social and spatial variables, we find that type of industry, employment, insurance, and migration distance and duration have significant effects on return intentions. Migrant workers engaged in primary industries have stronger return intentions than those working in secondary industries, whose return intentions are in turn stronger than those engaged in tertiary industries. This is partly because migrant workers engaged in tertiary industries can receive a more stable employment environment than those working in manufacturing [21, 22]. Also, migrant workers engaged in tertiary industries often enjoy higher social identity and social status than those engaged in primary and secondary industries [83]. Moreover, migrant workers' employment status also correlates with their return intentions [84]. Our results show that, compared to those with other employment statuses, employees are more willing to return home. However, the relationship between employers and their return intentions is not significant.

Social insurance coverage is another important social factor. Our results suggest that migrant workers with the new type of rural cooperative medical insurance (xin nong he bao) have relatively stronger return intentions while those with urban resident medical insurance (cheng ju bao) or urban employee medical insurance (cheng zhi bao) have relatively weaker intentions. This shows a differential impact of social insurance for urban and rural residents on the return intentions of migrant workers. Because the coverage offered by the social security system in destination cities significantly decreases migrant workers' return intentions, those with either form of urban insurance are less inclined to return to their hometowns [85].

In addition, our model confirms the significant impact of migration distance and duration on return intentions. Closer migration distances and longer durations of stay in destination cities weaken migrant workers' willingness to return home. This result corroborates some previous findings [11, 40, 64]. Closer migration distances and longer durations of stay may imply a higher degree of social integration in destination cities weakening return intentions.

Lastly, we explore the impact of geographical location on migrant workers' return intentions. We assign the destination cities to either the Yangtze River Delta region, the Pearl River Delta region, the Beijing-Tianjin-Hebei region, or a catch-all category including all other regions in China. We observe that migrant workers in the Yangtze River Delta region are more willing to return home while those in the Pearl River Delta have weaker return intentions, a finding consistent with previous research [29–31]. The upgrading of labour-intensive industries in the Yangtze River Delta in recent years has promoted the return of a large number of floating migrants from this region. Overall, our results show the effect of geographical location on return intentions.

To explore this effect further, we aggregate the micro-level data of return intentions to the city-level data by dividing the number of migrant worker respondents who have an intention to return by the total number of migrant worker respondents in cities [62, 63, 69]. As is shown in Fig. 6.5, the return intentions of those residing in cities are categorized into seven groups by natural breaks criteria. It is found that migrants in cities along the Yangtze River Delta show relatively strong return intentions, as

Fig. 6.5 Return intentions
of migrant workers in cities

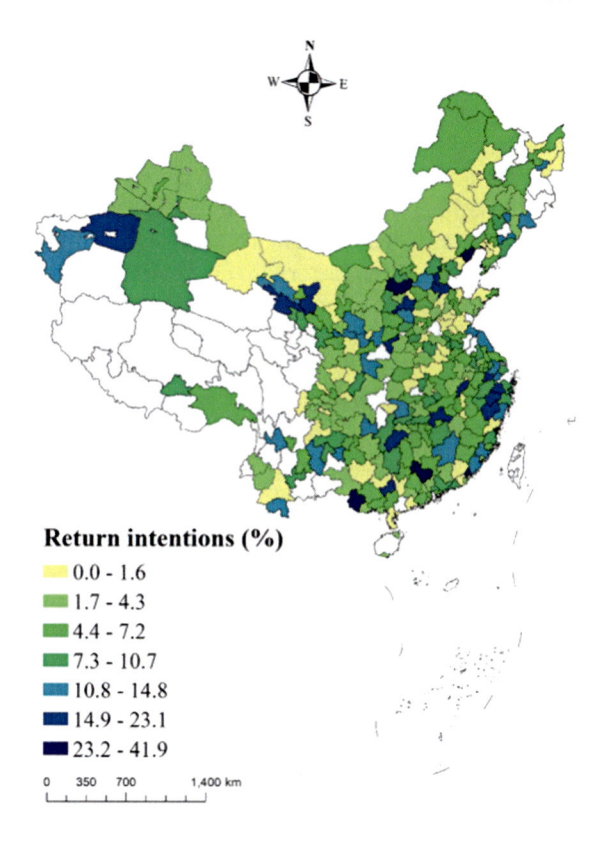

Return intentions (%)

- 0.0 - 1.6
- 1.7 - 4.3
- 4.4 - 7.2
- 7.3 - 10.7
- 10.8 - 14.8
- 14.9 - 23.1
- 23.2 - 41.9

is the case in the cities surrounding Beijing and several interior cities in China's western and central regions. In general, the results show spatial heterogeneity in the distribution of return intentions, further demonstrating the effect of geographical location.

Robustness and Endogeneity

We test the robustness of the previous results by applying a probit model and regressing the return intention on the same set of independent variables. The probit model differs from the logistic model in its assumption regarding data distribution (i.e. a normal distribution). Compared with the logistic model (Model 1), the results of the probit models (Model 2) show slight differences in the coefficients of the variables but almost no change in their significance and thus display robustness. Exceptions are: influence of age above 50 becomes insignificant, while that of migrating parents and the Beijing-Tianjin-Hebei region shows significance. Overall, results from the probit model provide evidence for the effects of individual, housing, economic, family, social and spatial factors on return intentions.

We also note possible endogeneity in our models that could lead to inconsistencies in the estimates. Specifically, some family variables may raise the issue of reverse causality, including whether to migrate with a spouse, parents, or children. That is, family members are likely to migrate with workers who intend to stay in destination cities. We accordingly employ IVs to address the underlying reverse causality issue (Model 3). Guided by the availability of the data, we select the variables 'Whether the parents have ever been migrant workers', 'marital status', and 'number of children' as exogenous IVs. These factors are not determined by the current migration decisions of migrants' parents, spouses, and children, but they correlate strongly with the current migration decisions of the latter groups. Notably, the results from the weak instrumental robustness test show that, based on the Wald test, the null hypothesis 'beta = 0' is rejected, and the F joint statistics in the first-step regression are far greater than 10. Both of these results are considered useful criteria for judging the validity of IVs and indicate that our IVs are valid. Although we observe minor differences in the estimate of the variable of whether to migrate with spouses, the key findings implied by the two-step IV probit model (Model 3) echo those of the model without the IVs (Models 1 and 2).

6.2.5 Conclusions and Discussion

The return migration of migrant workers in China has had a significant impact on regional development and the urbanization of small and medium-sized cities in the country's interior. Understanding the return intentions of migrant workers residing in destination cities helps local governments to formulate effective population manage- ment policies. Previous studies of return migration have focused primarily on the intentions of migrant workers in particular regions within China, with few having been conducted at the national level. The present research uses the CMDS data to examine the determinants of the return intentions of migrant workers residing in Chinese cities. The sample employed in the econometric data analysis makes it possible to consider Chinese migrant workers generally, to arrive at accurate conclusions, and to suggest promising policy recommendations.

The results reveal the effects of individual and economic factors (gender, ethnicity, education level, and income-expenditure ratio) on return intentions. It also highlights the influence of family connections and housing factors on the return intentions of migrant workers. It reveals that living with more family members in destination cities and migrating with children have a positive effect on the return intentions. Further, housing expenditures, housing tenure, housing ownership, and group living have significant impacts on return intentions. Migrant workers who own housing in their destination cities and spend a relatively large amount on housing and who live separately have relatively weak return intentions because satisfactory housing provides a basis for long-term stability.

The results also point to social and spatial factors that influence the return inten- tions of migrant workers. It is found that employment status and type of industry are significantly associated with return intentions. Social insurance coverage also influences return intentions, as does the migration distance and duration of stay. It also reveals that geographical location factors into the return intentions of migrant workers. Those residing in the Yangtze River Delta have relatively strong return intentions and those residing in the Pearl River Delta relatively weak intentions. We find a spatially differentiated pattern across cities with respect to return intentions.

In many respects, our findings corroborate those of previous researchers. To begin with, we find that, generally speaking, the return intentions of migrant workers are shaped by multiple factors [40, 67, 86]. Not surprisingly, several individual characteristics such as gender, ethnicity, and education level are significantly associated with return intentions [86, 87]. Income is naturally the primary motivation for migrant workers' decisions about where to reside, so the type of industry, employment status, and income level have especially strong influences on those decisions [21, 22]. Engagement in a tertiary industry in destination cities increases migrant workers' intentions to settle and thus weakens their intention to return [12]. Also, social insurance coverage lessens the risks that migrant workers face in destination cities and therefore weakens their return intentions [23]. Our findings of a positive association between income ratio and return intentions are likewise consistent with the results of some previous studies. In many cases, the total family income of migrant workers working in destination cities can be enhanced through remittances, with migrant workers returning to their hometowns once they reach their revenue goals [4]. Lastly, our findings indicate that homeownership is a significant factor in return intentions, representing a sense of belonging to the destination city [40, 78].

Unlike some previous studies, however, we find evidence that family connections in destination cities influence return decisions. Tang and Hao [40] suggested that family obligations in migrant workers' hometowns can influence their return intentions, but our results indicate that such obligations in destination cities are equally important. This study also goes beyond previous research in highlighting the effect of geographical location on migrant workers' return intentions.

The findings presented here have important implications for local governments seeking to formulate policies for managing China's floating population. First, measures should be taken to ensure that the children of migrant workers can receive education in cities so that migrant workers with children can feel a greater sense of belonging to the destination city. Second, governments should enact policies to provide affordable housing, low-rent housing, or housing subsidies to migrant workers in destination cities. Third, governments should work to provide migrant workers with social insurance, to connect and integrate rural and urban insurance systems, and to make more equitable access to social security. Fourth, policies should be adopted to promote the integration of migrant workers into the local society of destination cities. Lastly, more attention should be given to spatial variation in the return intentions of migrant workers; especially in areas in which migrant workers' intentions to return are strong (e.g. the Yangtze River Delta), governments need to give attention to the actual needs of migrant workers and promote their social integration in cities. Meanwhile, it is necessary to offer guidance to migrant workers who are willing to return to their hometowns so that the shift in population does not cause social problems.

References

1. Massey DS, Arango J, Hugo G et al (1993) Theories of international migration: a review and appraisal. Popul Dev Rev 431–466
2. Todaro MP (1969) A model of labor migration and urban unemployment in less developed countries. Am Econ Rev 59(1):138–148
3. Stark O, Bloom DE (1985) The new economics of labor migration. Am Econ Rev 75(2):173–178
4. Yin J (2015) Advances in research on driving factors of return migration and employment behavior of migrants. Prog Geogr 34(9):1084–1095 (in Chinese)
5. Gmelch G (1980) Return migration. Annu Rev Anthropol 9(1):135–159
6. Bastia T (2011) Should I stay or should I go? Return migration in times of crises. J Int Dev 23(4):583–595
7. Dustmann C (1996) Return migration: the European experience. Econ Policy 11(22):213–250
8. Dustmann C (2003) Return migration, wage differentials, and the optimal migration duration. Eur Econ Rev 47(2):353–369
9. Dustmann C, Kirchkamp O (2002) The optimal migration duration and activity choice after remigration. J Dev Econ 67(2):351–372
10. Lindstrom DP, Massey DS (1994) Selective emigration, cohort quality, and models of immigrant assimilation. Soc Sci Res 23(4):315–349
11. Reagan PB, Olsen RJ (2000) You can go home again: evidence from longitudinal data. Demography 37(3):339–350
12. Piracha M, Vadean F (2010) Return migration and occupational choice: evidence from Albania. World Dev 38(8):1141–1155
13. De Haas H, Fokkema T (2011a) The effects of integration and transnational ties on international return migration intentions. Demogr Res 25(24):755–782
14. Anniste K, Tammaru T (2014) Ethnic differences in integration levels and return migration intentions: a study of Estonian migrants in Finland. Demogr Res 30:377–412
15. Carling J, Pettersen SV (2014) Return migration intentions in the integration-transnationalism matrix. Int Migr 52(6):13–30
16. Haug S (2008) Migration networks and migration decision-making. J Ethn Migr Stud 34(4):585–605
17. Gao G, Zeng W, Mingyue L (2017) Backflow location and influence factors of inter-provincial migrant workers: a case study for 12 villages in Henan province. Econ Geogr 37(6):151–155 (in Chinese)
18. Liu Y, Yan T (2013) Types of the return migrations from mega-cities to local cities in China: a case study of Zhumadian's return migrants. Geogr Res 32(7):1280–1290 (in Chinese)
19. Ming J, Zhang J (2011) The homebound intention, migration costs and the remittance to home: an analysis of interval regression model. South China Popul 26(1):48–56 (in Chinese)
20. Tian Z, Yu Z, Liyue L (2017) The residential location choices of returned migrant workers in the context of local urbanization—a case study of Yongcheng city in Henan province. Econ Geogr 37(4):84–91 (in Chinese)
21. Yin J, Li X (2012) Analysis of influencing factors of rural return labor: a study for Yunfu city, Guangdong Province. Top Geogr 32(2):64–69 (in Chinese)
22. Yin J, Li X (2012) Influencing factors of return choice for rural migrant workers: a case study of Yunfu city. Guangdong Province. Trop Geogr 32(2):128–133, 140
23. Yu Y, Sun B, Sun X (2014) Can social security influence migrant workers' return intention?: an analysis based on Shanghai survey data. Popul Econ 2014(6):102–108 (in Chinese)

24. Zhang X, Bao J (2009) Tourism development and return migration of rural labor force—case study on Xidi village. Scientia Geographica Sinica 29(3):360–367 (in Chinese)
25. Zhang L, Zhu Y, Lin L (2012) Analysis of influencing factors of rural return labor: a study for Yunfu city, Guangdong Province. Top Geogr 32(2):64–69 (in Chinese)
26. Wang L, Feng C, Xu S (2014) Return intention of migrant workers in a traditional agricultural area and planning response: based on a questionnaire survey in Zhoukou, Henan Province. Prog Geogr 33(7):990–999 (in Chinese)
27. Gu H, Xiao F, Shen T, Liu Z et al (2018) Spatial difference and influencing factors of settlement intention of urban floating population in China: evidence from the 2015 national migrant population dynamic monitoring survey. Econ Geogr 38(11):22–29 (in Chinese)
28. Chen J, Zhang Y, Yu Y (2011) Effect of MAUP in spatial autocorrelation. Acta Geogr Sin 66(12):1597–1606 (in Chinese)
29. Gu H, Shen T, Liu Z, Meng X et al (2019) Driving mechanism of interprovincial population migration flows in China based on spatial filtering. Acta Geogr Sin 74(2):222–237 (in Chinese)
30. Gu H, Liu Z, Shen T (2019) Modelling interprovincial migration in China from 1995 to 2015 based on an eigenvector spatial filtering negative binomial model. Popul Space Place 25(8):e2253
31. Gu H, Qin X, Shen T (2019) Spatial variation of migrant population's return intention and its determinants in China's prefecture and provincial level cities. Geogr Res 38(8):1877–1890
32. Cui N, Feng C, Yu S (2017) Spatial pattern of residential land parcels and determinants of residential land price in Beijing. Acta Geogr Sin 72(6):1049–1062 (in Chinese)
33. Hao C, Lin L, Zheng S (2011) The tourism spatial pattern evolution of the Pearl River Delta. Acta Geogr Sin 66(10):1427–1437 (in Chinese)
34. Li D (2015) Function orientation and coordinating development of subregions within the Jing-Jin-Ji Urban Agglomeration. Prog Geogr 34(3):265–270 (in Chinese)
35. Lin L, Zhu Y (2016) Spatial variation and its determinants of migrants' hukou transfer intention of China's prefecture-and provincial-level cities: evidence from the 2012 national migrant population dynamic monitoring survey. Acta Geogr Sin 71(10):1696–1709 (in Chinese)
36. Yue Z, Li S, Feldman MW et al (2010) Floating choices: a generational perspective on intentions of rural-urban migrants in China. Environ Plan A 42(3):545–562
37. Li B (2008) Structured urban housing: a mechanism of selection for migrants. Chin J Popul Sci 4:53–60 (in Chinese)
38. Zheng W, Wang X, Tian D et al (2013) Water pollutant fingerprinting tracks recent industrial transfer from coastal to inland China: a case study. Sci Rep 3(1):1031
39. Lao X, Gu H (2020) Unveiling various spatial patterns of determinants of hukou transfer intentions in China: a multi-scale geographically weighted regression approach. Growth and change
40. Tang S, Hao P (2019) The return intentions of China's rural migrants: a study of Nanjing and Suzhou. J Urban Aff 41(3):354–371
41. Yang G, Zhou C, Jin W (2020) Integration of migrant workers: differentiation among three rural migrant enclaves in Shenzhen. Cities 96:102453
42. Lewis WA (1954) Economic development with unlimited supplies of labour. Manch Sch 22(2):139–191
43. Berger S, Piore MJ, Suzanne B (1980) Dualism and discontinuity in industrial societies. Cambridge University Press
44. Waldorf B (1995) Determinants of international return migration intentions. Prof Geogr 47(2):125–136
45. Skeldon R (2006) Interlinkages between internal and international migration and development in the Asian region. Popul Space Place 12(1):15–30
46. King R, Skeldon R (2010) 'Mind the gap!' Integrating approaches to internal and international migration. J Ethn Migr Stud 36(10):1619–1646
47. Amcoff J, Niedomysl T (2013) Back to the city: internal return migration to metropolitan regions in Sweden. Environ Plan A: Econ Space 45(10):2477–2494

48. DaVanzo J (1981) Repeat migration, information costs, and location-specific capital. Popul Environ 4(1):45–73
49. DaVanzo J (1983) Repeat migration in the United States: who moves back and who moves on? Rev Econ Stat 65:552–559
50. DaVanzo JS, Morrison PA (1981) Return and other sequences of migration in the United States. Demography 18(1):85–101
51. Hirvonen K, Lilleør HB (2015) Going back home: internal return migration in rural Tanzania. World Dev 70:186–202
52. Junge V, Diez JR, Schätzl L (2015) Determinants and consequences of internal return migration in Thailand and Vietnam. World Dev 71:94–106
53. Niedomysl T, Amcoff J (2011) Why return migrants return: survey evidence on motives for internal return migration in Sweden. Popul Space Place 17(5):656–673
54. Chen M, Lloyd CJ, Yip PS (2020) Growing rich without growing old: the impact of internal migration in China. Asian Popul Stud 16(2):183–200
55. Zhu Y (2018) Advancing research on internal migration in Asia: the mobility transition hypothesis revisited. Asian Popul Stud 14(1):1–4
56. Bernard A, Bell M, Zhu Y (2019) Migration in China: a cohort approach to understanding past and future trends. Popul Space Place 25(6):e2234
57. Zhang T, Zhu Y, Lin L (2017) The residential location choices of returned migrant workers in the context of local urbanization—a case study of Yongcheng city in Henan province. Econ Geogr 37(04):84–91 (in Chinese)
58. Liu R, Chen R (2018) The comparative analysis of the intergenerational differences among back flow migrant workers. Zhejiang Soc Sci 2018(10):87–94 (in Chinese)
59. Zhang R (2018) Evaluating the government subsidy on rural workers' self-employment decision making—Based on a DBDC approach. J Agrotech Econ 018(2):88–103 (in Chinese)
60. Zhu Y (2007) China's floating population and their settlement intention in the cities: beyond the hukou reform. Habitat Int 31(1):65–76
61. Chen S, Liu Z (2016) What determines the settlement intention of rural migrants in China? Economic incentives versus sociocultural conditions. Habitat Int 58:42–50
62. Gu H, Liu Z, Shen T (2020) Spatial pattern and determinants of migrant workers' interprovincial hukou transfer intention in China: evidence from a national migrant population dynamic monitoring survey in 2016. Popul Space Place 26(2):e2250
63. Gu H, Jie Y, Li Z, Shen T (2020) What drives migrants to settle in Chinese cities: a panel data analysis. Appl Spat Anal Policy 1–18
64. Huang X, Liu Y, Xue D, Li Z, Shi Z (2018) The effects of social ties on rural-urban migrants' intention to settle in cities in China. Cities 83:203–212
65. Huang X, He D, Liu Y, Xie S, Wang R, Shi Z (2020) The effects of health on the settlement intention of rural–urban migrants: evidence from eight Chinese cities. Appl Spat Anal Policy 1–19
66. Zhu Y, Chen W (2010) The settlement intention of China's floating population in the cities: recent changes and multifaceted individual-level determinants. Popul Space Place 16(4):253–267
67. Mohabir N, Jiang Y, Ma R (2017) Chinese floating migrants: rural-urban migrant labourers' intentions to stay or return. Habitat Int 60:101–110
68. Wei X, Zhu H (2020) Return migrants' entrepreneurial decisions in rural China. Asian Popul Stud 16(1):61–81
69. Gu H, Meng X, Shen T, Cui N (2020) Spatial variation of the determinants of China's urban floating population's settlement intention. Acta Geogr Sin 75(2):240–254
70. Chen J, Wang W (2019) Economic incentives and settlement intentions of rural migrants: evidence from China. J Urban Aff 41(3):372–389
71. Fan CC (2011) Settlement intention and split households: findings from a survey of migrants in Beijing's urban villages. China Rev 11–41
72. Wang Z, Zhao Z (2013) The dynamic choice of migration mode of migrant workers: going out, reflow or remigration. Manag World 2013(1):78–88 (in Chinese)

73. Xie S, Chen J (2018) Beyond homeownership: housing conditions, housing support and rural migrant urban settlement intentions in China. Cities 78:76–86
74. Yang X, Wei H (2017) New features and influencing mechanisms of migrant long-term residence tendency. Popul Res 41(05):63–73 (in Chinese)
75. Massey DS (1993) Latinos, poverty, and the underclass: a new agenda for research. Hisp J Behav Sci 15(4):449–475
76. Ritchey PN (1976) Explanations of migration. Ann Rev Sociol 2(1):363–404
77. Yang D (2016) A comparative study on settlement intention of the floating population in Northeast China. Popul J 38(05):34–44 (in Chinese)
78. Liu Z, Wang Y, Chen S (2017) Does formal housing encourage settlement intention of rural migrants in Chinese cities? A structural equation model analysis. Urban Stud 54(8):1834–1850
79. Jing X, Ma F (2012) The study of migrant workers' preference of staying in cities or returning home under the perspective of life course theory: based on the survey of Chongqing and the Pearl River Delta. Popul Econ 2012(3):57–64 (in Chinese)
80. Li P (2016) Social attitudes, behaviors, and the significance of social governance among new-generation migrant workers. In Great changes and social governance in contemporary China, pp 91–112
81. Chen Y, Feng S (2013) Access to public schools and the education of migrant children in China. China Econ Rev 26:75–88
82. Fan CC, Sun M, Zheng S (2011) Migration and split households: a comparison of sole, couple, and family migrants in Beijing, China. Environ Plan A: Econ Space 43(9):2164–2185
83. Afridi F, Li SX, Ren Y (2015) Social identity and inequality: the impact of China's hukou system. J Public Econ 123:17–29
84. Cao G, Li M, Ma Y, Tao R (2015) Self-employment and intention of permanent urban settlement: evidence from a survey of migrants in China's four major urbanising areas. Urban Stud 52(4):639–664
85. Tang S, Hao P, Huang X (2016) Land conversion and urban settlement intentions of the rural population in China: a case study of suburban Nanjing. Habitat Int 51:149–158
86. Piotrowski M, Tong Y (2013) Straddling two geographic regions: the impact of place of origin and destination on return migration intentions in China. Popul Space Place 19(3):329–349
87. Fan CC (2002) The elite, the natives, and the outsiders: migration and labor market segmentation in urban China. Ann Assoc Am Geogr 92(1):103–124

Part III
The Urban Governance on Floating Population

Chapter 7
Hukou System Reform and Floating Population

7.1 The Development Trend of Floating Population Under the *Hukou* System

The *hukou* system originating from the late 1950s is China's unique population management system, and an important issue in the economic system reform process since reform and opening-up. Since *hukou* has been endowed with multiple functions (including citizenship certification and public welfare attachment), the *hukou* system reform has exerted widespread and far-reaching impacts, not only on China's urbanization and migration pattern at the macro level, but also on the employment, education and social integration of people. Therefore, the *hukou* system reform is still one of the most important reform themes in China. It is strongly related with the migration patterns and migration intentions of floating population, becoming a major institutional barrier to the road for urban dream chasers.

The process of China's *hukou* system reform and its corresponding population migration development process since the reform and opening-up can be divided into the following stages [1, 2]:

(1) **The stage of dual urban and rural *hukou* system loosening under the context of planned economy (1978–1991)**

Before reform and opening-up, to control the population outflows from the rural areas and control the population sizes of large cities, and guarantee the provision of basic necessities and minimum social welfare in the urban areas, the central government adopted a strict dual *hukou* management system to prevent peasants from entering cities. Since reform and opening-up, the rural household contract responsibility system resulted in a substantial growth in the grain output, thus leading to a large number of surplus rural labor forces; meanwhile, the development of market economy, especially the industrial development, generated a great demand for labor forces. The combined action of these two forces began to change the attitude of

T. Shen et al., *Migration Patterns and Intentions of Floating Population in Transitional China*, Spatial Demography and Population Governance, https://doi.org/10.1007/978-981-19-3375-2_7

governments towards migration from "blocking up" to "channelling". The governments began to gradually finitely loosen the *hukou* system restrictions on the migration of rural labor forces, by allowing some professional and technical staff to change from "agricultural to non-agricultural" status, and allowing some peasants to bring their own grain ration to work in the cities. Under the context of local adjustment and loosening of *hukou* system reform, the urban–rural migration trend occurred with a relatively small number of floating population. The dawn of a road to chase urban dreams for migrants emerged, whereas the first migrants had a difficult time struggling to survive in the stringent policy restrictions.

(2)   **The stage of dual urban and rural *hukou* system limited breakthrough in the transition to market economy (1992–2001)**

At this stage, as the transition speed from the planned economic system to the market economic system increased obviously, the rapid development of labor-intensive industries in the southeastern coastal region began to attract a large number of labor forces from the rural areas and the central and western regions, resulting in an interregional peasant worker flood. Corresponding to this trend of labor market enlargement and interregional large population flows, there appeared significant breakthroughs and progress in the *hukou* system reform, with a series of systems that hinder the labor migration being adjusted, especially the *hukou* management system reform in small towns in full wing. The *hukou* system reform of this period has two main breakthroughs: on one hand, the peasants can settle down in the small towns, and enjoy the equal social benefits with the local residents; on the other hand, the social benefits attached to the *hukou* system has been gradually stripped, such as the institutional arrangement of the articulation between the *hukou* and grain ration, which is an important step towards the market economic system. Due to the worries of the impacts of large rural–urban population flows on the employment of urban residents, the relaxing of *hukou* restrictions were mainly limited to small cities and small towns, while the thresholds of obtaining *hukou* in medium and large cities were still very high. In general, the urban–rural dual welfare system had not been broken, and there still existed obvious differences in the social benefits between the urban and rural residents. During this period, the scale of floating population increased sharply, and a large number of labor forces from rural areas and undeveloped areas migrated to economically developed areas. The coastal developed areas and large cities had become the destinations of floating population where they chased urban dreams.

(3)   **The stage of basic public service equalization system establishment (2002–2011)**

With the gradual improvement of socialist market economy system, the institutional barriers for rural labor forces entering urban areas to work has been basically broken, and the periodical policy goals of realizing large-scale employment transfer and establishing a unified market of urban and rural labor forces have been basically realized. Meanwhile, the increasingly strong appeals of migrant workers for improving their social welfare and reducing the gap of social welfare between the migrants and urban residents have aroused wide attention. Under this circumstances, the policy focus of the *hukou* system reform has transitioned from promoting the free migration of rural labor forces and establishing an urban–rural uniform labor market, to establishing a system of basic public service equalization. In general, the *hukou* system reform of this stage began to focus on the equalization of urban and rural basic public services and the gradual detachment of social welfare functions from *hukou*, and the *hukou* system reform had reached the critical stage of eliminating the benefit differences between urban and rural *hukous*. However, this progress was relatively slow, and the social benefit functions attached to the urban *hukou* still existed, making it difficult for migrant workers to actually receive the same treatment with the urban residents. During this period, the increasingly favorable policy environment had further driven the interregional population migration, so the floating population size had hit a record high, with an enlarged employment range, a longer residence duration and a more diversified structure of migrant groups in the destination areas.

(4) **The stage of accelerating *hukou* system reform under the context of new-type urbanization (from 2012 to now)**

The main focus of the *hukou* system reform in the new era is actively promoting the people-centered new-type urbanization development. With the issue of *National New-type Urbanization Planning (2014–2020)*, the *hukou* system reform has achieved great breakthroughs. The *hukou* system reform adheres to the people-centered development idea, aims at accelerating the equalization of public services, and adopts the promoting path of relaxing the conditions for obtaining local *hukou*. A series of reform measures has achieved significant progress in many cities: setting a goal of promoting 100 million rural–urban floating population and other permanent population to obtain *hukou* in urban areas by 2020; comprehensively implementing the residence certification system and promoting the full coverage of urban basic public services among the permanent population; comprehensively relaxing the conditions of obtaining local *hukou* for rural–urban floating population; further relaxing the quota restrictions on the point-based *hukou* tor tloatıng population in megalopolises. However, the differences of social benefits associated with *hukou* are still significant in some megalopolises and megacities, especially in terms of employment permission and children education. The policies of controlling population sizes in magacities are still very stringent. Though the urban dreams of floating population have been realized step by step with the progress of *hukou* system reform, with the increasing subjective well-beings of floating population in the destination cities, the welfare systems closely associated with *hukou* is still an important factor preventing floating population from completely realizing their urban dreams.

In general, China's *hukou* system reform mainly focuses on the population migration and the adjustment of benefits associated with *hukou*, gradually breaks the institutional barriers to restricting the free population flows, in order to promote the population spatial horizontal mobility across regions and population social vertical mobility across social stratification (Fig. 7.1). With the development of market economic system and urban and rural labor markets, the *hukou* system reform has enabled the labor forces to migrate freely among regions, while the benefits associated with

evolution path of population spatial mobility

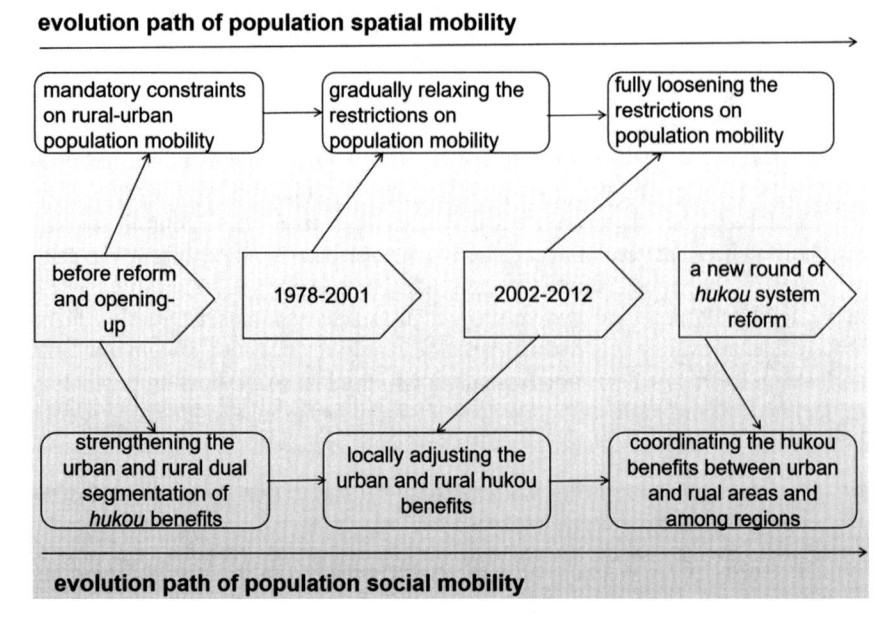

Fig. 7.1 Effect of the evolution path of *hukou* system reform on the population mobility

hukou between urban and rural areas and among regions will be the focus of the new round of *hukou* system reform.

7.2   The Existing Problems in the Current *Hukou* System Reform

Despite its great progress in the past decades, the *hukou* system reform is doomed to be a long and arduous process obstructed by multiple stakeholders, which is a process of gradual adjustment and improvement. With the deepening of reform and opening-up and the urbanization development process, there emerge several new problems in the *hukou* system reform practice.

(1)   **The dualistic contradiction between urban and rural areas caused by the**
       ***hukou* system has transformed into the contradiction among regions**

Since reform and opening up, with the establishment and gradual improvement of market economic system, the *hukou* system barriers impeding the rural–urban labor migration has been gradually broken, and the rural labor forces can migrate freely between rural and urban areas following the market law. The welfare differences between urban and rural resident within a region has been gradually adjusted and balanced, and the urban and rural dual division system dominated by the *hukou* system tends to weaken. However, the large-scale population migration has broken the original interest patterns among regions, resulting in a new contradiction that the public service pressures of the origin areas will decrease with the huge population outflows, while those of the destination areas will increase with the huge population inflows, due to the fact that the related resource allocation is still based on the household registered population size in each region.

(2) **The public service provision of cities have obvious regional character, so city governments are reluctant to abolish the *hukou* restrictions**

At present, the fiscal revenue system, land index ration system and administrative management system of cities basically serve the household registered population within the jurisdiction. This resource supply and allocation methods lead to the institutional restrictions on the intercity factor flows and a decrease in the opening degree of cities. It is difficult to break through the *hukou* system reform, mainly because the public services provided by the city governments have strong closedness. The increase of immigrants will exert certain financial pressures on the public service provisions of city governments and related management pressures, hence the city governments are reluctant to relax the *hukou* system management.

(3) **The local peasants can enjoy the double benefits from urban and rural areas, thus unwilling to transfer their *hukou* to the urban areas**

The *hukou* system reform has removed the barriers for peasants in the suburban area to enter cities or towns. The local peasants face the choice of whether to give up the rural *hukou* for the urban *hukou*, by comparing the advantages of rural and urban *hukou* (rural land upvaluation and welfare of collective economic organizations vs. the urban public services). Most peasants are not willing to transfer their *hukou* to the urban areas, especially the peasants in the suburban area with a high expectation of rural land appreciation. They can enjoy the benefits form both the urban areas and the rural areas: on one hand, they can earn higher income through the non-agricultural employment in the urban areas, and enjoy the equal social benefits with urban residents through the urban–rural integration of public services; on the other hand, they can have their own rural homesteads and contracted land in the rural areas, and benefit from the land appreciation and rural collective economic welfare. Though the central government clearly stipulated that it is not permissible to make peasants obtain urban *hukou* on condition that they have to quit the land contract rights in the rural areas, many rural areas still regard the local *hukou* as a requirement to enjoy the rural collective land rights. Therefore, the rural land system reform is an important part in the current *hukou* system reform.

(4) **The threshold of obtaining local *hukou* is high in megalopolises and megacities, and their *hukou* system reform relatively lags behind**

A series of measures of *hukou* system reform has solved the problems of migrant workers obtaining *hukou* in the small and medium cities, whereas the thresholds of obtaining local *hukou* are still high in megalopolises and megacities with a large number of floating population. If the *hukou* sytem reform in megalopolises and megacities cannot make breakthroughs, it is difficult for the enormous floating population to share the dividends of *hukou* system reform. The governments of these cities usually set thresholds of education attainment, investment or skills to select the higher-educated, skilled and wealthier groups to promote the local economic development, which actually exclude the ordinary migrant workers from the range of obtaining local *hukou*. In fact, there are very few floating population who can obtain local *hukou* through the current point-based *hukou* system in megalopolises and megacities in recent years. Under the context of market economy, the *hukou* restrictions cannot change the fact that people can freely migrate and work in different cities, but only prevent the floating population from enjoying the equal social security and public welfare with the local urban residents.

7.3   The Policy Suggestions on the *Hukou* System Reform

The policy design of the new round of *hukou* system reform should focus more on the differences in benefits attached to *hukou*, and establish a unitary *hukou* system to realize the equalization and universalness of public services in the destination areas.

(1)   **Comprehensively relaxing the restrictions on obtaining *hukou* in cities, and adjusting the *hukou* policies of megacities**

Based on the consideration of the overall carrying capacity of cities and towns, the socio-economic development need and public interest appeals, it is urgent to further relax the restrictions on obtaining urban *hukou* and set clear and specific standards, in order to make the floating population and their accompanying members enjoy the equal social security and public services with the residents with local *hukou*. Except for a few megacities, the restrictions on obtaining *hukou* in different cities for different groups should be abolished to settle the *hukou* issues of existing permanent population without local *hukou*, and further attract newly-increased population to settle down in the cities. For megacities (such as Beijing, Shanghai, Guangzhou and Shenzhen), it is feasible to implement differentiated *hukou* policies in different regions, for example, the *hukou* restrictions in the suburbs and the new districts of the cities can be further relaxed. Meanwhile, the thresholds for obtaining *hukou* should be further lowered, and the access to one type or part of basic public service rights and benefits should be opened to some permanent population that haven't met the requirements of obtaining *hukou*.

(2)   **Comprehensively implementing the residence permit system, and realizing the equalization and universalness of basic public services based on the residence permit**

The implementation of residence permit system should be accelerated to make sure that the permanent population without local *hukou* can enjoy the equal basic public services and social security with the local household registered population, including employment permission, the education of accompanying children, basic social insurance (endowment, medical, employment injury and maternity insurance), family planning services, public cultural services, temporary assistance and basic medical care, etc. The coverage of public benefits will gradually expand from the basic public services to all the public services, thus creating conditions for finally abolishing the *hukou* system.

(3) **Establishing a financial distribution system among governments at different levels based on the permanent population**

It is important to further improve the cost sharing system of pubic services in the *hukou* system reform, focusing on the finance transfer payment system of governments at different levels based on the permanent population. On one hand, the responsibilities of governments of different levels (central, provincial, prefectural (district/county) governments) should be clearly specified: the central government should formulate an instructional, leading and unified *hukou* system, including the standard requirements of national basic public services, and the central finance should mainly support the provinces with a larger number of interprovincial floating population; the provincial government should formulate the standards and requirements of public services within this province, and the provincial-level finance should not only bear the the public service costs at the provincial level, but also support the cities with a larger number of intercity floating population; the prefectural (district/county) governments mainly bear the primary public service costs, the costs of urban infrastructure construction, operation and maintenance at the city level. On the other hand, the finance transfer payment should favour the cities with more interprovincial and intercity floating population. In the mean time, it is necessary to deepen the financial management system reform according to the principle of matching the financial power and administrative power, and enable the basic-level governments to provide public services and regulate the population distribution.

(4) **Improving the *hukou* system related supporting reforms**

The first measure is to promote the financial distribution system reform of governments at different levels. Centered on the system of tax distribution, the basis of the financial distribution system should transform from the government administrative levels to the actual urban permanent population. Specifically, the placed-tailored policy measures should be taken, such as establishing the system of tax distribution at the town level in the economically developed regions. The second measure is to further reform and optimize the administrative organization and personnel allocation of local governments, based on the actual permanent population sizes of cities. The pilot exploration of the "provinces directly administrate counties" pattern can be considered in the small towns that attract enormous floating population in the economically developed regions. In addition, the standards of the establishment of cities and towns as well as the standards of government administrative organization and personnel allocation should be determined by the permanent population change and economic development power of cities. The third measure is to establish a bidirectional flow mechanism of urban and rural factors on the premise of guaranteeing the property rights of peasants. At the present stage, it is forbidden to regard the coercive exit of rural property rights as the conditions for peasants to obtain urban *hukou*, while the peasants should be paid to transfer and exit the contractual right of land, homesteads and collective asset shares under the conditions that their wishes have been fully respected. For example, it is feasible to build a market trading platform of collective profit-making assets to enhance the rural–urban factor flows, and solve the exit problems of rural idle resources through the redeeming of governments and further land reclamation, and then establish a benefit sharing system of reclamation land indicators reuse to make the regions that exit the collective construction land can also share the appreciation profits of land reuse.

References

1. Zhao J, Fan Y (2019) Historical investigation and realistic observation of household registration system reform since reform and opening-up. Economist 3:71–80 (in Chinese)
2. Zhao J, Zhang X (2021) China's *hukou* system reform: history review, reform valuation and trend judgement. Macroeconomics 9:125–132+160 (in Chinese)

Chapter 8
The Social Integration of Floating Population

8.1 The Social Integration Evaluation Results of Floating Population

Based on the extant literature, the floating population service center of National Health Commission constructed a social integration assessment index system of floating population from four dimensions (politics, economy, public service, and psychological culture), and evaluated the social integration level of floating population in 50 major destination cities in 2017 [1, 2]. This social integration assessment index system consisted of 4 dimensions, 15 first-level indicators and 34 second-level indicators (Table 8.1). The political integration dimension included citizenship, system guarantee and political participation; the economic integration dimension covered employment rights, income and expenditure, and housing conditions; the public service integration dimension incorporated health and family planning, basic education and social insurance; the psychocultural integration dimension contained sense of identity, sense of belonging, subjective well-being, community participation, living customs and social network.

The main conclusions of this study were shown as below:

(1) **The overall social integration level**

Though the work on social integration of floating population had achieved positive progress, the overall integration level of floating population was not very high (only 51.62 out of 100), and there existed significant differences among different dimensions of social integration and different cities. Among the four dimensions, the public service integration had the highest score (57.29), followed by the political integration (52.55), economic integration and psychocultural integration had the lowest scores (47.13 and 44.57, respectively).

The top ten cities in the social integration assessment in 2017 were Xiamen, Erdos, Chengdu, Changsha, Hefei, Huizhou, Qingdao, Suzhou, Jiangmen and Tangshan. As the first pilot cities of basic public service equalization, Xiamen and Erdos had

T. Shen et al., *Migration Patterns and Intentions of Floating Population in Transitional China*, Spatial Demography and Population Governance, https://doi.org/10.1007/978-981-19-3375-2_8

Table 8.1 The social integration assessment index system of floating population

Dimension	First-level index	Second-level index	Dimension	First-level index	Second-level index
Political integration	Citizenship	*Hukou* opening degree	Economic integration	Employment rights	Employment rate
		Proportion of migrants obtaining local *hukou*			Employment duration
	System guarantee	Housing security policy			Occupational structure
		Public health policy			Proportion of labor contract signing
		Policy for seeking treatment in other places		Income and expenditure	Income level
		Policy for taking senior high school entrance examination in other places			Consumption level
	Political participation	Participation in election		Housing conditions	Ratio of rent to income
		Participation in democratic management			Proportion of having housing fund
Public service integration	Health and family planning	Planned immunization of children	Psychocultural integration	Sense of identity	Proportion of willing to be local residents
		Services for pregnant and lying-in women		Sense of belonging	Proportion of actively integrating into local society
		Free pre-pregnancy checkups		Subjective well-being	Personal subjective well-being
		Birth control technical services		Community participation	Community participation degree

(continued)

Table 8.1 (continued)

Dimension	First-level index	Second-level index	Dimension	First-level index	Second-level index
	Basic education	Proportion of accompanying children at school in preschool education stage		Living customs	Leisure activities
		Proportion of accompanying children at school in compulsory education stage		Social network	Interpersonal circle
		Proportion of accompanying children at school in senior secondary education stage			
		Proportion of accompanying children at public schools in compulsory education stage			
	Social insurance	Unemployment insurance			
		Endowment insurance			
		Medical insurance			
		Employment injury insurance			

Sources: Database of social integration evaluation of urban floating population in China in 2018

undergone an insistent exploration in terms of promoting the floating population's enjoyment of basic public services. As the central city in the western region, Chengdu was listed as the National comprehensive reform pilot area for integrated urban–rural development by State Council in 2009, and had taken many reform measures in promoting the *hukou* system reform and balancing urban and rural development. Changsha, Hefei, Qingdao and Suzhou were listed as demonstration pilot cities of social integration of floating population by National Health Commission. The bottom ten cities in the social integration assessment in 2017 included 5 cities in Zhejiang Province, 2 resource-based cities in the western region, and 3 tourism cities with scarce climatic resources.

Among the four dimensions of social integration, the political integration reflected the realization degree of citizenship of floating population centered on *hukou*, social rights and political participation situations. The public service integration represented the situations of provisions for floating population with basic public services, resources and opportunities, focusing on the equalization of basic public services. The evaluation results showed that the political integration and public service integration, mainly driven by the state force, had achieved remarkable success. The economic integration reflected the two-way selection between the floating population and the destination cities under the context of market economy, and its core was that floating population can have stable jobs and housing and proper income levels. The economic integration was the foundation of gaining a foothold for floating population in the destination cities, without economic integration, it was difficult for floating population to survive in the destination cities, not to mention the integration in other dimensions. The score of economic integration was very low, indicating that floating population were standing on shaky ground from the economic perspective in the destination cities. The psychocultural integration, as the advanced part of social integration, was established on the political and economic dimensions and a changing process of personal subjective perception of floating population. The results demonstrated that the psychocultural integration and economic integration had become the main obstacles to improving the overall social integration level, because the former was a long process of running in and the latter was a two-way selection process.

(2)   **The political integration level**

The political integration level was both affected by the government system of destination cities and policy factors and the personal subjective initiative of floating population. It was relatively difficult for floating population to realize the political integration in eastern megalopolises. The possible reason was that as main destination cities, eastern megalopolises bore huge pressures caused by the relatively large population flows, so these city governments imposed strict restrictions on obtaining citizenship, equal social rights and political participation for floating population. Compared with other regions, the political integration level was relatively low in the eastern megalopolises, which became an important factor limiting the promotion of new-type urbanization.

(3)   **The economic integration level**

There exists remarkable disparity in the economic integration among different regions, among which the central cities had the highest economic integration level (51.40), followed by the western cities and eastern cities (47.31 and 47.14 respectively), and the northeastern cities had the lowest economic integration level (41.50). The higher housing price, lower consumption levels and inadequate labor security all contributed to the relatively low level of economic integration.

(4)   **The public service integration level**

In recent years, Chinese governments attached great importance to the basic public service system construction for floating population, embodied in the fact that the National Health Commission initiated the pilot work of basic public service equalization for floating population in 40 cities in 2013. The equalization of basic public service had achieve positive progress, driven by the national and city governments. The public service integration level was relatively high. Among the 50 cities, Xiamen had the highest score (70.75) and Taizhou had the lowest score (45.97). Regarding the city size, the public service integration levels in megalopolises were higher than those of the large and medium cities. In terms of different indicators of the public service integration, more attention should be devoted to the preschool education and senior secondary education of accompanying children of floating population, the free pre-pregnancy checkups and social insurance participation of employed population.

(5)   **The psychocultural integration level**

Concerning the city size, larger cities tended to have higher psychocultural integration level, reflecting the stronger cultural diversification and inclusiveness of large cities. At the regional level, the northeast region had the highest psychocultural level (51.17), followed by the central region and western region (45.50 and 44.47, respectively), and the eastern region came in the last place (43.19). As the main destination region of floating population, the eastern region had more interprovincial floating population, which caused cultural discrepancies and conflicts among regions that would result in a lower psychocultural integration level. In terms of different indicators of the psychocultural integration, the sense of belonging, the sense of identity and the subjective well-being of floating population were relatively low in the destination cities.

In general, there still existed many problems in the social integration of floating population, including institutional barriers, low-level employment, low social insurance participation, and a deviation between the settlement intentions of floating population and the national strategic orientation.

8.2   The Policy Suggestions on the Social Integration of Floating Population

Based on the above conclusions, the following policy suggestions have been proposed:

(1)   **Accelerating the *hukou* system reform and breaking down the institutional barriers to the social integration of floating population**

With the gradual completion of urban and rural household register system reform, the explicit *hukou* barrier has decreased restriction on the rural–urban floating population, while the implicit *hukou* barrier has become the main barrier to the social integration of floating population. Therefore, the focus of the future *hukou* system reform is not *hukou* per se, but the adjustment of interest relationship, especially gradually stripping the social benefits and resource allocation functions attached to *hukou* and making *hukou* system return to its due functions of register and statistics.

The current *hukou* system reform is a process of local governments implementing specific policies according to their own actual situations, based on the central policies. However, regarding the actual effects, local governments will decide the opening degree of *hukou* based on their own balance of interest in the *hukou* system reform process, resulting in significant differences of *hukou* reform scheme among different cities.

The *hukou* opening degree is relatively higher in cities with low *hukou* transfer intentions of floating population, and the *hukou* opening degree is relatively lower in cities with high *hukou* transfer intentions of floating population, thus affecting the effect of *hukou* system reform. Since the *hukou* system is a national basic system, all the citizens should be treated equally without discrimination, and the future reform should be dominated by the central government in system designing and whole advancement, in order to make the *hukou* system become a selection system for floating population to "vote with feet".

Since the restrictions on obtaining local *hukou* have been completely abolished in small and medium cities, the future *hukou* reform should focus on large cities, megalopolises and megacities. The floating population are mainly concentrated in the large cities in the eastern coastal area, especially the urban agglomerations of Beijing-Tianjin-Hebei, Yangtze River Delta and Pearl River Delta. Except for several megacities such as Beijing and Shanghai, the *hukou* restrictions in other cities should be gradually relaxed, and the eligible floating population (with stable employment and housing) should be incorporated into the local household registered population.

(2) **Enhancing the education and employment training for floating population to improve their ability to integrate into the destination cities**

The integration degree of floating population into the local society is influenced by not only the external systems, but also the education level and technical skills of floating population. The education, training and work experience are important ways for floating population to accumulate human capitals, and stronger human capital will contribute to the social integration. The migrant workers have accounted for over 80% of the floating population, and the education level of migrant workers are relatively low. Without professional vocational skills training, most migrant workers can only undertake simple physical work. Meanwhile, due to their low education level, it is difficult for migrant workers to change their original life styles, thus increasing difficulty of integrating into the urban society.

Corresponding to the demands of floating population integrating into the city, the governments should increase not only the compensatory social policies for floating population, but also the developmental social policies related with cultural education and vocational skills training for floating population. It is necessary to develop the vocational education in large scale, and incorporate the vocational education and skill training for floating population into the national educational system. The population of the right age that cannot enter senior high schools after 9 years of compulsory education, should be enrolled in vocational schools instead of directly entering the labor market. For the floating population that have entered the labor market, it is feasible to encourage the enterprises, society and individuals to provide them with professional vocational training through purchasing services or offering subsides by governments, in order to improve the employment and social adaptation abilities of floating population.

(3)   **Providing the floating population with basic social security and public services to reduce their dependence on the rural land and traditional social relationships**

The floating population are detached from the social security provide by the original rural society in the migration process. After entering the modern urban society, they have to face various modern risks different from the traditional society. Generally speaking, the basic social security is an important protection system for floating population to avoid social risks, which is an important experience in the industrialization and urbanization process of western countries. The social insurance coverage is not enough for the floating population, which results from the system design of urban-rural segmentation and region segmentation of social security. The main reason for the regional segmentation of welfare system is the decentralization of welfare financing.

To help the floating population gain a foothold in the destination cities, it is imperative to implement a low-standard, equalized and portable "national basic social security package" funded by the central government. A national unified social security can be established based on this, with the unified basic endowment insurance for each Chinese citizen regardless of regional differences and urban-rural differences. The transfer and the continuance of various social insurances among regions should be accelerated to meet the actual needs of floating population.

It is important to address the basic life issues of floating population in the destination cities, focusing on the basic public service including education, housing and medical care. The emphasis of current educational services should be put on preschool education, senior high school education and college entrance examination of floating children in the destination cities. Since the nine-year compulsory education has been basically universal, it is time for the governments to incorporate the preschool education and senior high school education into the range of compulsory education. Considering the connection issue of the education system, it is possible to link the quota allocation of college entrance examination and the number of floating children receiving senior high school education in the destination cities, to solve the issue of taking college entrance examination in other places for floating children. The focus of medical care issue should be on expediting the medical insurance reimbursement in other places by simplifying the procedures to settle the problem of difficulty in reimbursement for floating population. Besides, as housing is the key determinant on the social integration of floating population, governments of destination cities should incorporate the eligible floating population into the coverage of housing security, focusing on providing affordable public rental housing for floating population.

(4)   **Adjusting the urbanization strategies according to the migration patterns and intentions of floating population**

In China, there exist different strictness of obtaining local *hukou* in different levels of cities, and the population control measures are stricter in the larger cities. This urbanization strategy is challenged in the practice: on one hand, the trend of floating population migrating to large cities is very significant; on the other hand, the *hukou* transfer intentions of floating population in small and medium cities are relatively low.

The development law of urbanization in the world demonstrates that the population tends to agglomerate in the largest cities, thus forming the metropolitan areas. The urbanization development is a long-term complex process, driven by the internal causes and the external causes. Whether the floating population migrate and which cities they migrate to is the outcome of their rational choices. The governments need to create an equitable institutional environment to make sure that everyone can enjoy the equal public services and development opportunities. It is suggested that the governments adjust the new-type urbanization strategies based on the migration patterns and migration intentions of floating population.

(5)   **Constructing a social support network of floating population based on the communities**

The migration process is actually a process of re-socialization of floating population. As the floating population migrate from the rural areas to the urban areas, their original social relationship network based on blood relationship and geographical relationship have been broken, and the lack of social support system will decrease their abilities to counteract the social risks. The carriers where the floating population live in the destination cities are communities. It is of great significance to establish an acquaintance society similar to the villages through communities, to form a social network of interpersonal communication in the destination cities for floating population through communities, thus contributing to the social integration of floating population. In recent years, studies on the social integration in western countries focus more and more on the function of communities.

Consequently, the governments should establish a system of community participation for floating population: gradually relaxing the restrictions on the community electorate qualification, and expanding political participation of floating population; actively organizing community activities and encouraging the co-participation of local residents and floating population; making full use of the function of governmental agencies, neighbourhood communities, social organizations, economic organizations of communities and residents and establishing a network of floating population participating in the community affairs; establishing the mutual assistance and coordinating mechanism for disadvantaged floating population groups. Through the platform of communities, the floating population can participate in the social activities and community management, enjoy the public services provided by the communities, establish social relationships, form the consciousness of community, thus realizing the harmonious coexistence of different groups in the community.

(6) **Establishing a social system to enhance the social integration of floating population drawing on the experience of developed countries**

The social integration issue has been an important issue in social policies and social work in developed countries. Many countries regard social integration as a leading indicator of living quality of people, and a higher social integration level has become one of the goals of social development of human beings. There are a few experience from developed countries worth learning from: establishing a law system based on the rights of equality and a policy system based on the law, which favour the social integration of floating population; regarding the floating population as an important resource, enhancing the social integration capacities and cultural integration of floating population by providing various training and courses; establishing a supervision and evaluation system of social integration of floating population, which is dominated by governments and participated by academic institutions, and then conducting the assessment and publishing the evaluation results based on this system in each year.

References

1. Xiao Z, Xu S, Liu J (2018) The report on urban migrant population's social integration in China No. 1. Social Science Academic Press, Beijing (in Chinese)
2. Xiao Z, Xu S, Liu J (2019) The assessment of social integration of urban migrant population: an investigation based on 50 cities of migration destination. Popul Res 43(05):96–112 (in Chinese)